JENNY
PITMAN
THE AUTOBIOGRAPHY

D0412250

BANTAM BOOKS
LONDON · NEW YORK · TORONTO · SYDNEY · AUCKLAND

JENNY PITMAN: The Autobiography
A BANTAM BOOK : 0553 50491 6

Originally published in Great Britain by Partridge Press,
a division of Transworld Publishers Ltd

PRINTING HISTORY
Partridge Press edition published 1998
Bantam Books edition published 1999

Set in Times New Roman by
Phoenix Typesetting, Ilkley, West Yorkshire

Bantam Books are published by Transworld Publishers,
61–63 Uxbridge Road, London W5 5SA,
a division of The Random House Group Ltd,
in Australia by Random House Australia (Pty) Ltd,
20 Alfred Street, Milsons Point, Sydney, NSW 2061, Australia,
in New Zealand by Random House New Zealand Ltd,
18 Poland Road, Glenfield, Auckland 10, New Zealand
and in South Africa by Random House (Pty) Ltd,
Endulini, 5a Jubilee Road, Parktown 2193, South Africa.

Reproduced, printed and bound in Great Britain by
Cox & Wyman Ltd, Reading, Berks.

CONTENTS

ACKNOWLEDGEMENTS

Throughout my life and during my career, I have received invaluable love and support from my family. Although they have shared in the pleasure of our success, I realize that they have also suffered pain, particularly from some of the more upsetting newspaper headlines that have appeared over the years. There have been times when I've wondered whether I should have put them through so much anguish. Without their support and that of my owners, staff, vets, financial advisers, and friends, I would simply not have survived.

Yet again I had to call on my family to help me with this book. My nephews Danny and Mark Harvey stepped in to do the typing and my sister Jacquie and her daughter Vanessa helped with a lot of proofreading. They also had a crash course in how to understand a form book.

I would also like to pay tribute to the medical teams who have, quite literally, helped me to survive. No-one knows what the future holds, but what I do know is that I have been very fortunate. I have received superb care and much kindness from many dedicated practitioners. I would particularly like to thank Charlie Schreiber and Alan Walker for their sound and very timely advice, Professor Newman-Taylor for his skill and judgement, and all the doctors and nurses at the Royal Brompton Hospital, the Royal Marsden Hospital and the Ridgeway Hospital. Their care and compassion, together with all the letters and cards I have received from the general public, helped me to get through some very dark days.

Finally, the love and support of David and my sons Mark and Paul are vital. During all our trials and tribulations David has never ceased to make me laugh when I have least felt like laughing.

They are all very special people.

PREFACE

I clearly remember the day, nearly thirty years ago, when I was travelling on a plane with the trainer, Fred Winter. It was well before I took out my trainer's licence, but maybe the guv'nor could see which way the wind was blowing because he looked me straight in the eye and suddenly said, 'Whatever happens, you don't want to start training.'

'Why?' I asked, surprised.

'Because it's such a hard life.'

'Coming from you, guv'nor, that's some statement,' I said.

He looked puzzled. 'What do you mean?'

'Well, to have had all those champion horses that you've trained – any one of them would have done most people in a lifetime.'

I often look back and remember our conversation and realize that the same is now true for me. I've been blessed – fortunate, call it what you like – to have had the horses I've had in the past twenty-five years. Horses like Corbiere, Burrough Hill Lad, Toby Tobias, Garrison Savannah, Royal Athlete, Willsford, Mudahim, Master Tribe and Princeful. Any one of them would have been enough to make being a trainer worthwhile.

And I've been lucky too to have lived the life I have – outdoors, and surrounded by countryside that takes your breath away. I remember driving back from the races with my son Mark one day. We'd been to Uttoxeter and he'd been moaning about having a bad day because we hadn't had a winner. We had been driving down the M6 and were at Spaghetti Junction so I pointed to the tower blocks and the concrete landscape that surrounds them. 'Listen,' I said, 'that's what I call a bad day – waking up to this view every morning.'

Working in a male-dominated profession hasn't all been plain sailing, by any stretch of the imagination. Things are easier now than they were, and there are more women trainers today, but the influence of the old school tie in this profession is very strong. I think some trainers, stewards and media people have found it difficult to relate to me – and not just because I've been trying to succeed in a man's world. Perhaps it's because I'm not the sort of woman they are used to. Or maybe it's because I don't wear the right 'uniform', and I speak with a northern accent. It's as if they've never known quite what to make of me. But in my experience, grown men can sometimes behave like naughty little boys towards the opposite sex. They close ranks. They like to pull your pigtails and torment you, so you have to give as good as you get.

I recall being the only woman at a function one day when one of my colleagues came up to me and said, 'You're looking bloody good, Jenny. Tell me, has your sex life improved?'

I was taken aback by his rudeness, but I wasn't going to let him see it. 'Yes, it certainly has,' I said. 'But I can see yours hasn't.'

He'd obviously wanted to embarrass me, but he was the one who slunk off with his tail between his legs. I usually find that the best way to deal with men like that is to have a few stock phrases to hand. It's a bit like snowballing one another as kids. If you have a few snowballs already made, when the first one comes you can rapidly return the fire, which is inclined to make them retreat! My policy is: you throw it at me and I'll throw it right back.

I freely admit that I have a better understanding of horses than I do of people – probably because horses are less likely to move the goalposts and then pretend they haven't! There are things you learn in this job that you don't find in textbooks. When I walk into a horse's box I know if something is wrong as surely as if a fluorescent light were flashing outside the door.

When I'm called a perfectionist, rather than a compliment it seems it's intended as a criticism, as though it is a character fault to want to do your job properly. A million people can do a job, but it is the person who does it consistently well who I'm looking to promote. I would sooner have somebody with less experience who wants to learn and is diligent than someone with more knowledge who is less caring.

The whole point of training horses is to win races and if I can't persuade my horses to like what they're doing, they're not going to perform their best. Sometimes persuading them to perform can stretch your patience to the limit, but you just have to work with them hour after hour, day after day, month after month, until the penny drops. You can't bully it out of them or you will not have a horse with any character left by the end.

A classic example of this was Egypt Mill Prince. When he arrived from Doncaster sales he was downright dangerous – a right so and so. At first he was so bad tempered he would go down on his knees and bite the ground. At other times he would try to walk up the road on his hind legs. He was virtually unrideable. I spent ages trying to gain his trust and sometimes when I talked to him and stroked him he looked as though butter wouldn't melt in his mouth. When we took him to Windsor, where the track runs beside the river Thames, the other jockeys warned Mark to be sure to wear his swimming trunks under his riding breeches. That day Egypt Mill Prince finished second despite whipping round at the start and giving away a lot of ground. Eventually we discovered that if you gave Egypt Mill Prince one day off he would start World War Three the next morning. So for three months he was ridden out every day without a break, and all our patient hard work was finally rewarded when he began to win races. He was just like a wayward teenage kid who suddenly grew up. One morning he seemed to say to me, 'All right, we'll be friends now.' And I replied, 'Okay mate.' Thank God for that, I thought.

Each autumn, when I've looked at young horses being ridden round at home, my mind has travelled on a year or two and I've visualized them running down the hill at Cheltenham or jumping the last at Aintree. To me, they've all been potential champions. Along with my family, horses are my life. I'll always love 'em and I'll always need 'em.

JENNY
PITMAN
THE AUTOBIOGRAPHY

CHAPTER ONE

THE HARVEYS OF LODGE FARM

Not long ago I was having a ding-dong argument about some new-fangled theory of racehorse training with the Irish trainer Ted Walsh. It was something I felt quite strongly about and I was getting really fired up when all of a sudden Ted grinned. 'God, Jenny,' he said. 'You're so passionate it drives me mad.' We burst out laughing. I knew what he meant, and I couldn't argue. A passion for horses is in my blood. With a childhood like mine I didn't have a lot of say in the matter.

I was born at home on 11 June 1946, the middle child of seven. Before me came Jacquie, Judy and Peter (known as Joe). Afterwards came David, Richard and Mandy. Home was Lodge Farm, a small rented farm near the village of Hoby, halfway between Melton Mowbray and Leicester. It was an old-fashioned farm even in those days, with no electricity, gas or mains water supply. Like most of his neighbours Dad didn't specialize, but kept a few of everything. Our hundred acres was home to dairy cows, bullocks, sheep and pigs, as well as an assortment of chickens, bantams, geese, ducks and guinea fowl. It meant that I grew up surrounded by animals, not just outside but often in the house too. It was nothing to find a sick piglet or lamb

1

wrapped in a piece of blanket lying in the bottom oven of our old kitchen range.

My dad, George Harvey, was the most hardworking man I have ever known. He was also a wonderful stockman, quiet and kind with his animals, and with endless patience. As a small child I worshipped him, and from the time I could toddle I used to follow him around the farm like a baby goose: holding the tilley lamp in the evenings while he fed the pigs; helping weigh the cows' feed on the big metal spring scales, and shutting the hatch of the chickens' hut so the fox didn't get an easy meal. For both of us, the moment when we arrived in the stable was the highlight of the day. I could tell from the way he talked to old Nelly that, to Dad, a horse was more than just another farm animal.

In the early fifties horses did everything on farms like ours, and Nelly, Dad's big bay cartmare, was a Jill-of-all-trades. Her jobs varied, depending on the season. In winter she'd pull cartloads of mangolds out to the fields to feed the sheep and bullocks. In spring she'd harrow the growing crops. In summer and autumn she was the power behind the implements and carts we used at haymaking and harvest.

One of my earliest memories is of sitting on Nelly's broad back, holding tight to the hames of her collar as Dad walked behind us, guiding the harrow up and down the furrows between the rows of mangolds. The gentle sway of Nelly's back, the creak of the harness and the smell and feel of warm horse always produced the same effect as being rocked in my pram. When he saw I was dropping off to sleep, Dad would lift me down and lay me in the grass under the hedge for my afternoon nap.

For a few years after the war, when money was really short, even horsedrawn implements were few and far between, and it was nothing for Jacquie, Judy, Joe and me to be sent out with pitchforks to turn five acres of hay by hand. When Dad finally bought a proper horsedrawn swathe turner it seemed as wonderful to us as the invention of the wheel. I was eight or nine at the time, and I begged him to let me drive it. Dad wouldn't let me do the turning by myself, but, after the haycocks had been made, he let me clamber onto the iron seat of the turner and drive Nelly round the field, raking up stray wisps of loose hay. Unfortunately the warm sun, the musical clinking of the harness and old Nelly's steady hoofbeats again acted like a lullaby, and, half-asleep, I let her get too close to one of the haycocks, which tipped the rake. The sudden jolt unsettled Nelly, who set off galloping across the field with the rake rattling and clanking behind her. Heaven knows where we'd have ended up if Dad hadn't been keeping an eye on us. He raced across the field, grabbed the reins and brought Nelly to a halt. After that I was only allowed to rake by hand!

One of the advantages of horses was that they produced their own replacements; nearly every spring Nelly gave birth to a foal, and ten days after foaling she would be mated again. The day the stallion visited was always memorable, not so much for the covering itself – which, in spite of Mum's efforts, we usually managed to spy on – but for the ceremony beforehand. The horse chosen to be Nelly's mate had to pass a stricter inspection than the breed champion at the Leicestershire County Show. Never mind how well-bred the horse was, or how many cups it had won – Dad would make the travelling groom trot him up and down our drive half a dozen times and stand him up for inspection from every angle while he considered whether this fine thorough-bred was good enough to cover his old cartmare. It was years before I understood why the stallion man always looked so grumpy. But Dad's choosiness paid off. The horses he bred from Nelly and her daughters always fetched good money, and lots of them won prizes in the showring.

It was probably Dad's stallion inspections that first helped me develop an eye for a good horse. Through them I learned to recognize an athletic mover and to spot faults of conformation. I drank the knowledge in. To me it was much

3

more important than schoolwork. I was never much good at foreign languages, but the language of horsemen was a different matter. Terms like 'back at the knee', 'straight in front' and 'sickle-hocked' have been part of my vocabulary for as long as I can remember.

Nelly and her mates weren't the only horses around the farm. Dad used to keep a couple of ponies for me and my brothers and sisters, and we all learned to ride so young that being on horseback seemed as natural to us as walking. Not surprisingly, our favourite game was cowboys and Indians. Joe and I would harness a pony to the trap, load it up with a couple of small children, and act out covered-wagon ambushes. David, Richard and, later, baby Mandy learned to cling on like limpets as the trap bounced and skidded across cart ruts. According to David, the experience scarred him for life, and he certainly has no real love of horses to this day!

My older sisters, Jacquie and Judy, disapproved of our rough games, and stuck to more 'pony club-approved' activities, but I was always a tomboy and was happy to join in the boys' play. In the school holidays, as soon as it was light, a boy called Geoffrey Dodd and I would be off with our ponies – we didn't care if we'd had breakfast or not – and spend all morning chasing each other up and down the fields and through the woods around the farm. To add a bit of excitement we'd jump across the farm lane – if you jumped the hedge in, there was room for just two strides before you jumped out again. Riding bareback and hatless, with bridles and reins made from plaited baler twine, taught us more than riding school lessons could ever have done.

Most weekends, Geoffrey, whose father was a friend of Dad's, came to stay with us, and we'd usually find him a pony to ride too. In our games I was a cavalry officer, while Geoffrey was my flag-bearer and had to do as I said. This was useful, since he was the only one of us who ever had any money. If we felt peckish we would simply ride into Hoby and I would order poor Geoffrey into the village shop to buy a tube of Refreshers to tide us over till lunch-time. Often it would be dark by the time we reached home and we'd still be playing cowboys and Indians, dismounting to put our ears to the ground to listen for the 'enemy's' hoofbeats when we couldn't see them any more. We didn't have the computer games and videos that kids have nowadays, so we had no choice but to use our imagination, and to us our pretend world was very real.

Our ponies weren't just for play. Like us, they had to help out around the farm. Every summer Dad rented extra fields outside Leicester to graze his cattle. He would never think of hiring a cattle wagon to take the bullocks or heifers out to these fields, because that was our job. Joe, Geoffrey and I, riding bareback, would drive the cattle through Thrussington, along the Fosse Way and all through the outskirts of Leicester, before hacking home late in the evening, tired and sunburned, our jeans soaked with the ponies' sweat. The traffic wasn't too bad in those days, and cars would always slow down when they saw you, so riding down the main roads never used to bother us.

Driving bullocks to and from their summer grazing was a twice-a-year job, but most weekends in summer, especially if it was dry and grass was getting scarce, we also went 'tenting'. This meant letting the cattle graze for a few hours on the verges of the local lanes. When Dad finished milking at half past nine on Saturday mornings we'd have to be ready and waiting on our ponies outside the cowshed. He'd hand Joe a lemonade bottle full of water from the cowshed in case we got thirsty, open the gate, and the cows would walk out of the shed and onto the road, taking a mouthful here and a mouthful there, while we stood guard. Traffic was never a problem, as hardly one car a day passed down our road. We were much more worried about Mr Tinsley's hedge. Mr Tinsley was a local gentleman farmer whose immaculately trimmed privet hedge bordered the lane. Passing it was a

5

nightmare, because if you relaxed for a minute the cows would come to a halt, put their heads in the privet and help themselves. All our cows had horns, so what they didn't eat they wrecked. If he caught them in the act Mr Tinsley would rush out and give us a right old rollocking. Not content with that, he'd also ring Dad, which always led to more trouble when we got home. The solution we found was to drive the cows past the hedge as fast as we could without actually stampeding them. We quite enjoyed this, and every Saturday the lane used to echo with cries of 'Head 'em up! Move 'em out!' After they'd grazed the verges for two or three miles we'd turn them round and mosey on back nice and steady in time for dinner. Thankfully, on their way back with their bellies full the cows never found the hedge such a temptation.

Sometimes we'd have 'pretend' cattle drives with Dad's bullocks on the farm, though they soon got wise to this and when they saw us coming they waded into the river Wreake, which ran through our fields. As far as Joe and Geoffrey were concerned, this just added to the fun. They would urge the ponies on until they were chest-deep in water, then herd the unfortunate bullocks out. These were the only occasions when my nerve deserted me. Although I'd never had the slightest fear of horses, I was terrified of water. Apart from my weekly bath, my only contact with it came on our annual seaside trips to Mablethorpe. Even then I never dared go into the sea beyond my ankles. The boys kindly overlooked this weakness, which was my one and only sign of 'girliness', and put me on sentry duty while they splashed around. Sometimes, in winter, our round-up skills would be called on for real, when the river rose suddenly and marooned the cattle or sheep on little islands of high ground. Then we'd be sent out on rescue missions to bring the animals back to the farm, which stood above the flood level.

Our mounts for these horseback adventures could change from week to week. On a small farm there wasn't much room for mouths that didn't earn their keep so we were allowed only two ponies of our own. Timmy, my first, was a quiet, well-behaved little soul, while Rocket, who was a shaggy, Thelwell-type character, was more high-spirited. Two ponies didn't go very far among seven children, but Dad managed to keep us all mounted by taking in ponies to reschool. He had quite a reputation locally as a horseman and any pony that got a bit out of hand would be sent to Lodge Farm to be sorted out. Rearers, bolters and nappers – we saw them all, and since I was judged to have better 'hands' than the boys I was usually the one chosen to be the new pony's first jockey. Dad would stand in the middle of a ploughed field while I trotted around him – sometimes on the end of a makeshift lunge-line but more often loose – as he instructed me how to behave when the pony tried to get rid of me. Not surprisingly, I quickly developed a secure seat and nerves of steel.

Dad was the first person to teach me the value of patience when dealing with horses. He would never allow a horse or pony to beat him. If it took until milking time to persuade it to do something then that was fine by him, he would stay there until milking time. He had learned his skills from his own father, who had ridden point-to-pointers and taken in problem racehorses to straighten out. I, in turn, became Dad's apprentice. Nobody could have had a better tutor. It was Dad who helped me to understand the difference between a pony or horse that is genuinely frightened and one that's trying it on. He showed me when a smack is needed and when to pat and reassure. He also taught me the most important lesson of all – that in the long run you get a lot further with kindness than you do with violence.

Once the ponies were behaving themselves, I was allowed to take them to a show or two before they went back to their rightful owners. Most kids at these shows wore immaculate black jackets with red lining and smart velvet caps. My riding clothes were a combination of hand-me-downs and carefully adjusted adult garments, and I felt I stood out like a sore thumb. However, once I realized that the clothes didn't stop me winning it didn't bother me. I won ribbons for everything from gymkhana events to showjumping. In those days nearly every village had its own little show, so by the end of the summer my dressing-table mirror would be festooned with rosettes. I never enjoyed them for long, though. The bedroom I shared with Jacquie and Judy was so damp that every winter the ribbons peeled away from their cardboard backing and flopped to the floor, so the next summer I would have to start my collection all over again.

Before central heating came along, damp and cold were part of day-to-day life. On winter mornings Jacquie, Judy and I used to draw pictures with our fingernails on the ice inside the bedroom window. If the contents of the jerry under the bed had frozen over, we knew it had been a really hard frost! What little heat there was in the house came from a coal fire in the living room, which Mum laid and lit every day. All our hot water and cooking depended on this fire, which burned in a grate in the middle of the big, blackleaded kitchen range. On one side of the fire was an oven, whose temperature depended on how long the fire had been lit and how much cooking it had already been asked to do. With this ancient contraption Mum somehow managed to conjure up daily hot meals for eight or nine people. Sometimes it had to provide for even more, because if anyone called when we were about to eat Mum would always ask, 'Do you want a bit of dinner?' Nobody ever said no, and it was nothing out of the ordinary to find two or three Harvey cousins, our weekend visitor, Geoffrey Dodd, the blacksmith and the vet crammed with the rest of us around the kitchen table, all tucking into a rabbit stew intended for eight people. Mum never found it a problem. She would just go to the pantry and put another loaf of bread on the table to make it all stretch a bit further. To her, hospitality was as natural as breathing.

It was years before I appreciated how hard Mum worked. As far as I'm concerned, to have brought up seven kids with no electricity, running water, bathroom, washing machine or fridge is some kind of miracle. She was a wonderful cook. Farm work was hard in those days, and she believed in feeding her menfolk properly. The day always started with a cooked breakfast of bacon and egg, or porridge. At midday she'd serve up a hot dinner with Yorkshire puddings (sometimes she'd add plums or blackcurrant vinegar to the cooked pudding batter, and turn it into a sweet). Finally, an hour before evening milking, she'd put a tea of cooked ham, bread, homemade pickles and jams on the table.

Our meals were always formal – there was none of the snacking and TV dinners you get today. The whole family had to wash their hands at the kitchen sink and come and sit around the table. When everyone was ready, and Dad had checked that there were no elbows on the table (you'd get a whack from the bone handle of the carving knife if you were caught), he would serve the food and we would all tuck in.

Most of what we ate, including the meat, was homegrown. If we sent a pig to be killed, some of it would come back to be salted and hung in the larder. If we ran out of pork or ham Joe would be sent out to neck a cockerel or shoot a rabbit or a guineafowl, and Mum would pluck or skin and gut it. Eggs came from our own chickens, milk, butter, cream and cheese from our own cows. The milk was unpasteurized and often still warm, but we thrived on it. There was also free food in the countryside. Every autumn we'd go out to glean blackberries, sloes or crabapples from the hedgerows, and mushrooms from the fields. The only things we didn't produce ourselves were vegetables. Farmers are famous for being bad gardeners, and Dad was no exception. Mum tried her best, but it was an uphill struggle with us kids running around leaving the garden gate open all the time. Hens used to scratch up the beans and peas and make dustbaths in the seed-rows. In the end she gave up, the garden became a pony paddock, and we traded spare milk and eggs for fruit and vegetables from neighbours.

During the winter, food was less plentiful, so the summer surplus had to be preserved, just as it was for the animals. We'd never heard of a deep-freeze; Mum used to bottle fruit and vegetables, and preserve eggs in water-glass. From midsummer to late autumn, Mum's preserving pan would be simmering on the range non-stop, turning summer fruits into jams and pickles. First there'd be strawberry, gooseberry and then blackberry jams, and then she'd start on the chutneys and piccalilli. No-one could make piccalilli like my mum. The stuff they sell in the shops isn't in the same league. But if people ever asked her for the recipe she was stumped. 'Well, I don't know, me duck,' she'd say. 'I just sort of throw it all in together . . .' By the end of October the shelves in the pantry would be overflowing with jars. Even then she wasn't content, and after Christmas, when the Seville oranges for marmalade arrived in the local market, she would start again.

Not all of Mum's preserves were for us. When the annual village fête came round she'd give dozens of jars to the bring-and-buy stall. Although we lived a mile outside Hoby, Mum was very involved in village life. She belonged to the Mothers' Union and the Women's Institute, and helped with anything to do with the school or the church. On Coronation Day, in 1953, the village held a big pageant, and Mum made fancy-dress outfits for the entire family. I was a fairy, which I absolutely hated. I was dressed in layers of horrible pink net and had to parade with the others through Hoby before we all sat down to tea at trestle tables in the village hall. Mum always helped make the tea on occasions like that. Nowadays if people make twelve little cakes for a jumble sale they think they've done well, but there was a real community spirit then and everybody made a big effort. On the day of the fête my brothers and sisters and I would take our ponies to give rides, Dad would give three gallons of milk for the teas, and Mum would spend the whole day before baking cakes and scones. Just in case that wasn't enough, on the morning of the fête she would get up extra early to make piles of sandwiches.

I always reckoned Mum could have made sandwiches in her sleep. They were her speciality. During haymaking and harvest she would appear in the fields at lunchtime carrying a great big wicker basket full of sandwiches stuffed with ham, cheese, pickle and sliced hardboiled egg. To wash it down there'd be homemade ginger beer or tea. We kids would stand around like praying mantises until the men had eaten their fill, waiting for the nod from Mum which meant we could dive on what was left.

As well as being a cook, Mum was an expert laundress. The washing was done in a huge black copper set into a brick wall in the corner of the kitchen. Every Monday, she would lay and light a coal fire underneath it, then fill up the copper with water (which had to be pumped from the well and carried indoors in buckets and jugs). When the water started to simmer Mum would drop in batches of dirty washing one at a time and boil them until they were clean. When a load was ready she would lift it from the steaming water with a pair of wooden tongs, dump it in an enamel bowl, carry it to the mangle and wring it out, before pegging it outside on the washing line. On rainy days the washing would be strung up instead on the wooden clothes-airer in the kitchen, which was hauled up to the ceiling by a rope and pulley. Then, for a day or two, the whole kitchen would sweat and steam until the clothes were dry enough to iron.

Even after a hard day's washing Mum's work wasn't over. Next, rather than waste the still hot water in the copper, she would bath us in it. Some of the water would be drawn into a tin bath in front of the fire for the younger ones, but the older children would be stripped off and dunked straight into the copper. If the fire underneath hadn't quite gone out we'd be hopping up and down like missionaries in a cannibals' cauldron, trying to keep our feet off the bottom. Afterwards the copper was emptied through a tap at the bottom and the dark grey water carried outside in buckets to be thrown away. Next day, Mum would do the ironing, using a heavy flatiron heated on a trivet over the hot coals of the fire, carefully wiping off the soot before she applied the iron to the clothes. There were no drip-dry fabrics then, so it used to take her most of the day.

In order to get everything done, Mum used to divide up the smaller household jobs among the kids. Our duties included riddling through the slack coal to find missed lumps, chopping sticks and cutting newspapers into squares which we threaded on string to hang in the outside toilet. My favourite chore was riding Rocket to the village shop when we ran out of groceries, but the job had its drawbacks. Rocket was a bit of a Houdini. If I took too long to emerge from the shop he would abandon me and I would be greeted by the sight of his empty bridle tied to the rail outside. At such times, when I had to lug the shopping the mile home on foot, I must say our friendship wore a bit thin.

And then of course we were expected to help Dad around the farm. We had no paid farm help except for casual workers at harvest-time, and, until mains electricity arrived, all twenty cows had to be milked by hand twice a day. Although Dad usually did the morning milking on his own, Joe had to help in the evenings. The routine never varied. At six o'clock Mum would put tea on the table. At a quarter to seven, while she cleared the dishes, Dad would switch on our brown bakelite wireless and listen to *The Archers*. The next fifteen minutes were his only relaxation of the day. The moment the first notes of the closing theme-tune sounded, he'd say, 'Right then, Joe,' and the pair of them would be up and out to the cowshed. I usually tagged along too. My hands were too small to fit around the teats of the Friesians and Shorthorns, so I was given the house cow, a little black Dexter, to milk. I never really got the knack of it, and by the time I'd finished I only ever had half a bucket of milk and my wrists ached like mad, so I was always relieved when Dad appeared to strip her out for me. One day my little cow put her foot in the bucket and knocked me flying off the stool into a pile of muck, and I gave up being a milkmaid for good. However, I always made sure I was in the kitchen as Dad came in after milking, when he'd take two bowls, one for him, one for me, fill them with chopped-up bread, sprinkle sugar over them and cover the lot with fresh boiled milk. What a nightcap!

Once a week was another night-time ritual that I wasn't quite so fond of. Dad would line us all up in the kitchen, each of us with a teaspoon in our hands, and bring out a big jar of codliver oil and malt. He'd dip everybody's spoon in (if you looked a bit 'poor' the spoon would get an extra wind) and watch to make sure we swallowed it. 'That'll put a bit of bloom on your coat,' he'd say. I suppose it must have done some good, because we were a healthy bunch and hardly ever went down with coughs or colds.

As the fifties passed, life on the farm became easier for both Mum and Dad. The first big change in our way of life came when Dad bought a van. Until then we'd had to rely on pony and trap, or the twice-daily village bus, if we wanted to go anywhere, so the arrival of the old Commer van was a great moment. Getting it going was a two-man job, with Dad cranking the starting handle and someone else pressing the accelerator when the engine fired. I was the only one who could get the timing right and often I'd get home from school to find Dad waiting impatiently for me to arrive so that he could drive to Syston or Leicester for some supplies. The van was a dual-purpose vehicle. During the week the back would be screened off, bedded down with straw and used to take sheep, calves or pigs to market, but on Friday night the straw and manure would be swilled out so that the next day we could all pile into it and drive off to a point-to-point or a show. In the winter we used it to go to church as well. If we ever smelt a little strong after our trip in the livestock-transporter, nobody commented on it. Nearly all the congregation came from farming families, including our Harvey cousins from Hoby (between us we filled two whole pews). To us all, the smells of the farmyard were part of life, like eating and sleeping. Forty years later, when we have an open day at Weathercock House and I see town children wrinkling up their noses at a stable door when they smell real live horse for the first time, I wonder what 'progress' has done for these kids. We may not have been as sophisticated as today's youngsters are, but we were a lot closer to nature and real life.

For better or worse, progress continued at Lodge Farm. I remember very clearly the day that electricity was installed. I must have been about six or seven when some men erected a big space-age thing, with poles and glass discs, at the bottom of the drive. It hummed day and night and scared me to death. In fact I begged Dad to make the men take it away again. I didn't want electricity. I thought we managed fine without it. But Mum loved it. It meant she could have a washing machine, a fridge, an electric cooker and, best of all, electric lighting. Before electricity the farmhouse had been lit by paraffin lamps whose wicks had to be trimmed and bases filled with oil every day. In the living room there'd been one really big oil lamp with a tall glass chimney and a round glass globe. Every night, moths would fall into this chimney, which used to drive Mum mad. Between sizzling moths and the smell of paraffin she wasn't the least bit sorry when the lamps were replaced by the flick of a light switch.

Electricity also made a big difference to Dad, who was able to buy a milking machine, which halved the time it took him to milk Kicker, Peggy, Bluey and the rest of the herd. And soon afterwards, Nelly's life was made easier by the arrival of a tractor. Until then, the only tractors we'd seen belonged to the contractors who came at harvest-time.

When Dad bought a little green three-wheeled John Deere we learned for the first time that tractors weren't only used for cutting hay and corn. They could pull ploughs and harrows, too, and what's more they did it a lot quicker than horses. Soon, Nelly's work was reduced to light jobs, like carting muck and shifting mangolds to feed the cattle in outlying fields.

There were other changes. A combine harvester replaced the threshing machine's once-a-year visit. A mechanical baler put an end to the hand-built haycocks of loose hay. Arnold the bull was sold and replaced by the AI man. Soon afterwards, the arrival of a cattle-wagon meant the end of our cattle-droving days. As children, we welcomed these 'improvements' with open arms. We had no idea that we were living through the end of an era, or that our old way of life would one day seem as remote to our own children as ancient history.

It was a hard life in those post-war years, and there wasn't a lot of luxury, but we didn't feel badly done by because we didn't know any different. Looking back, I wouldn't have swapped my childhood with anybody. It taught me valuable lessons, not just about horses and stockmanship, but about duty, and the importance of hard graft. Most of all, the hardships we shared turned us into a close and caring family. I didn't know it then, but there were going to be times, later in my life, when that would be worth more than anything.

CHAPTER TWO

'IT'S ANNIE OAKLEY . . .'

At the age of eleven I left our little village school in Hoby and went to the Sarson Secondary Modern Girls' School in Melton Mowbray. Our family was a bit of a mixed bag where brains were concerned. Mum was the intelligent one. She used to rattle off the answers to general knowledge questions on *Top of the Form* and *Round Britain Quiz* like an encyclopaedia. Jacquie and David both took after her. They went to grammar school and shone in their exams. Unfortunately, Mum's genius passed me by. I not only failed the eleven-plus, but I never saw the point of school. In fact, when people used to tell me that schooldays were the happiest days of your life, I was horrified. If these are the *best* days, I thought, what the heck's going to come next? What on earth could be worse than school?

Apart from sport the only school subject I was any good at was biology. I could see the point of that, because it explained about the world I lived in. But French, history and maths just didn't seem to relate to my own life. What did I want to do history for? I was only interested in what I was going to do in the future, so who cared what happened in 1066? And geography meant nothing to me. The furthest I'd ever travelled was to the beach at Mablethorpe. It was fatal to put me by a window at school because I'd find myself gazing out of it, daydreaming about all the useful things I could be doing instead of being imprisoned in the classroom. Towards the end of my schooldays I found ways of getting out of lessons altogether. I started arriving later and later at the school bus stop. After stopping in Hoby, the bus did a big loop round several other villages before heading back to Melton Mowbray. If you missed it at the first stop you had to run half a mile with your satchel banging on your back to catch it on its way back. If you didn't want to catch it, you just ran a bit slower. By the time my final year at school came round, the only days I ran fast were Thursdays, when we had three PT lessons and played rounders or hockey. I really enjoyed sport, and in my final year I was appointed games captain at school. Winning matches, I must confess, was my only scholastic achievement.

Mum and Dad were never too bothered when I walked in after missing the bus, because it meant there was an extra pair of hands to help on the farm. On market days an unspoken understanding grew up that I *would* miss the bus, so that I could go on the cattle-wagon to make sure Dad got a good price for his animals. Joe felt pretty much like I did about school, and at harvest-time we'd both be out in the fields rather than in class. In winter, on at least two days each week, we'd go hunting.

I was introduced to hunting when I was very young. For my first meet or two, Joe had kept me and my pony anchored on the end of a lead rein. But as soon as I could sit straight and stay on at the canter, I was let loose. From the very first day, I absolutely loved it. In all the years I hunted I only once saw a fox killed, so I certainly didn't have any bloodlust. It just gave me a fantastic thrill to ride hell-for-leather across country, not knowing what I was going to have to jump next.

Our local hunt was the Quorn, which was one of the poshest in the country. Its subscribers included most of the local landed gentry. Looking back, I suppose they must

17

have cringed in horror when the Harvey kids arrived. Our ponies lived out all winter and would have been dragged in from the field that morning all shaggy and muddy. There was only ever time for a quick brush-down before we saddled them up, because we didn't possess a trailer and had to hack to the meet, which might be five miles away. Just as for the local horse-shows, we'd be kitted out in an odd assortment of clothes. Joe would be wearing ancient lace-up leather boots that had belonged to our granddad, and I'd have on a faded black jacket three sizes too big. But however old they were, our clothes were always clean and tidy. Dad and Mum both insisted on that. Our boots were well worn but they were brightly polished. The velvet was missing from the button on my riding hat, but underneath it my hair was always tucked into a net or tied neatly in bunches.

. If people looked down their noses at us we weren't aware of it. Certainly the Master, Colonel Murray-Smith, never made us feel we shouldn't be there. When he appeared at a gateway, or a hunt jump, people would yell, 'Make way for the Master!' but he would always wave Joe and me ahead. 'Oh, let these young jockeys go first,' he'd smile. He was a real gentleman. Once, at the end of a day's hunting, he invited Joe and me into his house at Gaddesby for a cup of tea. It was my first glimpse of a way of life different from my own. I was struck dumb as I sat in a kitchen the size of our school assembly hall and drank Earl Grey tea out of a large china breakfast cup. Colonel Murray-Smith's kindness to ordinary kids like Joe and me made a great impression. I often remember him when I meet the sort of people who think they are too good to talk to you.

At the end of a day's hunting, when we arrived home, no Harvey child would dream of just unsaddling their pony and chucking it out in the field. Dad would have skinned us alive. You might want to listen to a radio programme or get your wet clothes off, you might be tired or be hurting somewhere from taking a fall, but these things didn't matter. First you

18

had to wash your pony's legs off and check them for thorns. After that, you'd dry them and rub the pony down with a straw wisp to get his circulation going. Dad's philosophy was simple. The ponies had served us well. In return, we must deal with their needs before our own.

In the summer, when there was no hunting, we attended the regular local shows. It was while competing in a gymkhana at Syston that I had the most serious accident of my childhood. I was riding a neighbour's pony in a showjumping class when it suddenly slammed on its brakes. I shot through the air and landed in a heap in the middle of the fence. We had no chinstraps in those days, so my hat flew off just as a falling pole crashed down on my head. I didn't remember the next few minutes, but apparently my hat was replaced, I was hoisted back into the saddle, and I completed the round. Everything seemed fine until that night. As I was drifting off to sleep in the double bed I shared with Judy, I suddenly heard her start to scream. Mum came rushing in, took one look at me and shouted for Dad to phone for the doctor. I couldn't understand what on earth was the matter. It was as if all the excitement was happening a long way away and had nothing to do with me. The most frightening thing was that amid all the noise of people talking and Judy crying, I kept trying to ask, 'What's going on?' but nobody seemed to understand me or even hear me. In fact, I was having a convulsion.

Once or twice over the next few weeks the same thing happened again. In addition, every time I rode my pony, especially when we trotted, I suffered the most dreadful headaches. I was sent for tests to the Leicester Royal Infirmary. Nobody could discover any reason for my fits, but, to be on the safe side, riding was banned. I was devastated. As far as I was concerned, the world had ended. I still sneaked out to ride Timmy when I could, but I wasn't allowed to go to any more shows that summer.

For many months nobody connected the fits with my

19

showjumping accident, because nobody in my family had seen the pole fall on my head and I didn't think to mention it! It was only after a fruitless investigation using electrodes and flashing lights that a specialist at Nottingham Infirmary ran his hands over my head and discovered a strange ridge at the back (which I have to this day).

'How long have you had this bump, Jenny?' he asked.

'Since the pole fell on my head at Syston Gymkhana,' I answered, in all innocence.

The surgeon stared at me in disbelief. Then he turned to my mother with a wry smile. 'I rather think we may find that your Jenny has a fractured skull, Mrs Harvey.'

His diagnosis turned out to be correct. While a fractured skull wasn't exactly good news, it was better than a brain tumour, which was the other possibility being considered. I was put on phenobarbitone tablets three times a day and told to rest. Two weeks later, when I returned for a further check-up, Mum put the question I hadn't dared ask.

'Will she be able to ride again?'

My face must have told the specialist how much it meant to me. He smiled. 'I don't see why not. Life's full of risks. You might as well let her do what she wants to do and enjoy it.' I could have kissed him.

When the next show season started Mum kept a closer eye on me than before, especially when I entered a jumping class. Although I still won rosettes with other people's ponies, most of my successes at that time came with my own pony, Rocket. Unlike Timmy, who was a placid, good-natured character, Rocket could be a little swine, but I loved him to death. His name came from the fact that Dad had bought him on 5 November from some gypsies who'd camped near the farm. Dad and I had broken him in together, and when I was nine or ten years old I'd been allowed to ride him to primary school. During lessons he would be turned out in one of my Uncle Percy's fields and at night I'd catch him again to ride home.

It was a relief not to have to walk the mile to school, especially in winter when the farm drive got muddy. To walk down it then, you had to wear wellingtons and carry your shoes. At the end of the drive you'd have to change your footwear and leave your wellies under the milkstand, where the churns were picked up each day. When school finished, at three thirty, you'd have to reverse the performance. The trouble was that after seven hours under the milkstand your wellies had often become home to spiders, voles or, worse still, frogs. Riding to school was a much better option. Not that the horseback journeys were always plainsailing. Rocket had a mind of his own, and we often had disagreements. His most annoying habit was lying down whenever he thought he'd done enough. He played this trick for years – even when I was in my teens, and quite a strong rider – and there was nothing in the world I could do about it. He was especially fond of doing it in the hunting field, which was extremely embarrassing.

As I moved through secondary school the local attendance officer became a regular visitor to Lodge Farm. I thought he was one of our relatives until I realized why he was always enquiring after my health. Mum never nagged me too much about playing truant. She could see where my interests lay and she knew that I would never be academic, however long I was made to sit in class. She didn't try to force any of us into a mould that didn't fit. She was also brave enough to allow me to be a tomboy. I say brave because in the fifties there was none of today's unisex upbringing. Girls were supposed to play indoors with dolls, while boys ran around outside with guns. Girls helped with the housework and kept themselves clean and neat. Boys did outside jobs and got their hands dirty. I'm afraid I never matched the pattern and, luckily for me, Mum recognized that.

I think Mum sometimes dreamed that I might become more like my sisters. Even when I was grown up she'd look at me occasionally and sigh, 'Oh, Jen, why don't you put a dab of lipstick on, me duck?' but on the whole she accepted me as I was. It was thanks to her that I grew up to be an 'outdoor' person. From the age of five or six I thought of the house simply as somewhere you ate and slept. My brothers and our friend Geoffrey felt the same way, so I didn't see anything strange in it. David, Richard, Joe and Geoffrey always treated me like an honorary boy. Geoffrey and I once became blood brothers in a secret ceremony involving a rusty penknife. It was Geoffrey, too, who introduced me to smoking. He used to nick cigarettes from his father and always arrived for his weekend stays with two or three untipped Player's and a couple of matches in his pocket. After walking home from Brooksby railway station, Geoffrey, Joe and I would stop at the end of our drive and sit under the milkstand. Geoffrey would fish out these broken, fluff-covered fags from his pocket and we'd sit there puffing on them till we felt sick. Sometimes, if he'd brought a cigar from his father as a present for our Dad, we'd try that too.

Our mischief didn't stop there. Often, in the autumn, after Joe and I had met Geoffrey at the station, we'd stop off at Brooksby Hall Farm Institute and scrump apples from their orchard. It was risky, because the students used to look out for us, but the only time we ran into trouble was one night when we'd bullied Judy into joining us. She couldn't run as fast as we could and was caught and given a cuff round the ear.

When they were in their teens my brothers were given air-guns, and I got them to teach me to shoot. When I'd got the hang of it we'd go out on patrol, using trees and fence-posts for target-practice. One day I was walking with Geoffrey and Joe down by the riverbank on our farm, taking pot-shots at bulrushes, when we came across three lads fishing. There were a lot of roach and chubb in the river Wreake that you needed a licence to fish for. There was even a water bailiff, Charlie Wyard, who used to patrol the bank looking for poachers. Nobody had asked Dad's permission to fish that day so we felt quite excited at catching trespassers in the act.

'What do you think you're doing here?' Joe asked.

The lads, who were sixteen or seventeen and quite cocky, started giving Joe a load of lip. The one doing most of the talking was a tall, good-looking lad who seemed to find Joe quite amusing, which got my back up.

'If you don't shut up and get out,' I said suddenly, 'I'll shoot your float out of the water.'

The lad threw back his head and laughed. 'You wouldn't dare and you couldn't do it anyway,' he said.

I didn't stop to think. I cocked up the air-rifle, took aim and fired.

'Bloody hell,' said the boy.

I had shot the top of his float clean off. All that was left was the small round base bobbing in the water. I was as shocked as everybody else. The lad looked absolutely horrified and for a moment I thought he was going to hit me. Joe stepped between us.

'If she can do that to the float, think what she could do to you,' he said. 'Now get going before I call my dad.'

There was no arguing. They shoved their fishing gear into their bags and they were off. I was quite proud of myself. I knew it had been a bit of a fluke, but there was no way I was going to admit that to Joe and Geoffrey. I felt I'd earned my stripe that day.

It was one of the few occasions when Joe tried to protect me from a fight. Usually he didn't need to. Not that I got into many fights, but when I did I could give as good as I got. The most memorable occasion was on the school bus. Like all school buses, the popular seats were the back ones, where you could share cigarettes and get up to mischief. The Harveys had claimed them long before. One day, I climbed on board after school to find a lad sitting in my seat.

23

'That's mine,' I told him.

He folded his arms and grinned. 'Make me move, then.'

As I stepped towards him he stood up and squared up to me. 'Touch me and I'll thump you!' he said.

He was older than me, and bigger, and I decided not to wait for him to hit me. I swung my fist and punched him on the nose. To my horror, blood spurted out like a fountain all down his shirt and he fell back onto his seat holding his nose. It was only a nosebleed, nothing was broken, but my reputation was made. From that day on his mother met him off the bus.

Mum probably wondered sometimes whether her policy of letting me be a tomboy was wise. There'd been plenty of other occasions when I'd caused her grief. Once, she'd bought me a beautiful doll for Christmas, which she must have saved for months to buy. As I pulled it out of its wrapping paper my heart sank, and I didn't even bother to pretend. 'I don't like dolls,' I told Mum. Within minutes I had all its legs and arms off.

She never made the same mistake again. The following year my Christmas parcel contained a brand-new pair of jodhpurs. They were my first-ever proper ones, with big wings at the sides, bought from Parr's in Leicester. World War Three broke out about those jodhpurs.

'How much did *they* cost?' Dad asked, as I danced around the kitchen in them.

'Not much,' said Mum, but I could tell something was wrong. Mum and Dad rarely had rows in front of us but that night Jacquie, Judy and I heard heated words coming through our bedroom wall, and I knew they were about my jodhpurs. It was the first time it had ever occurred to me that money might be a problem. In spite of all our hand-me-down clothes we had never felt poor. We had everything we wanted. We were loved, well fed, and, because there were no TV advertisements or better-off neighbours, we never felt discontented. It was many years before I realized how hard up we must have been. It wasn't because she loved sewing that Mum sat down every night with a darning mushroom to mend our socks and patch our jeans. She didn't shop at rummage sales and second-hand clothes shops for fun. Life on a small farm with a big family must have been a constant struggle. The amazing thing about Mum was that somehow, every year, she managed to put away enough pennies to buy presents, like my jodhpurs, or the bike Jacquie was given when she started work. There were smaller treats too. Most Tuesday nights, when Stan Rowley, the mobile grocer, came round, we'd be allowed to choose sixpennyworth of sweets out of his Bedford van. If there was a film Mum thought would interest one of us there'd be an outing to the pictures at Syston. To her, we were all individuals, and she tried to give each of us the treat that would give us the most pleasure.

Of course, it wasn't all perfect. Like every mother and daughter we had rows. Mum's patience did wear thin and, sometimes, after a long day, some small misdeed was all that was needed to make her boil over. I remember her once, when I'd said something to annoy her, chasing me round the table waving a hairbrush and threatening to hit me with it. I was so furious with her that I shouted, 'You're a maniac, you are!' It didn't seem a bad enough insult, so I added, 'In fact, you're a sex maniac!' I hadn't a clue what it meant. It was a headline I'd seen in a newspaper and I just thought it must be worse than an ordinary maniac. The effect on Mum was amazing. I thought she was going to kill me. Jacquie whipped between us, shouting, 'She doesn't know what she's saying! She doesn't know what she's talking about!' As a result, Jacquie ended up getting smacked instead of me, because while that was going on I'd bolted!

On the whole, though, Mum and I had a good relationship. It was Dad who gave me my passion for horses, but Mum recognized it and encouraged it. She actually knew more about horses than I realized at the time. Like Dad, she came from a country background. Her grandfather had been a gamekeeper on an estate at The Brand, near Woodhouse Eaves in Leicestershire, where she'd grown up and learned to ride. Once, looking through a box of old photos, I found a picture of her looking very handsome on a big hunter. As a teenager, she'd gone to work on Granddad Harvey's farm, where she'd fallen in love with Dad, and after her own family came along she never sat on a horse again. Maybe it was because she'd enjoyed riding herself that she encouraged me. I remember her taking me to the pictures at Syston to see films like *The Red Pony* and *The Rainbow Jacket* with Mickey Rooney. Best of all I remember *National Velvet*, with Elizabeth Taylor, a film about a young girl who dresses as a boy so that she can ride her horse in the Grand National. It was the first time I'd heard of the Grand National and I thought the film was wonderful (I still do, and watch it at least once a year!).

It was Mum who took me to the local horse shows, and most Saturdays in the summer she'd be up at the crack of dawn helping me get ready. She always wanted me to look as well turned out as possible. My tack had to be saddle-soaped, my boots polished and, last of all, my hair, which was fine, straight and difficult, had to be curled. Hair-curling was quite an ordeal, because Mum's curling tongs were heated by putting them in the fire. The only way of checking if they were the right temperature was to test them on a piece of newspaper. If the newspaper curled without catching fire she considered them safe to use (occasionally the distinct smell of singed hair followed me round all day). When the pony and I both passed inspection, Mum would climb on her bicycle and ride alongside for five or six miles as I trotted off to a show or gymkhana.

When I was ten, as a birthday treat, Mum took me on the train to see Pat Smythe competing at the White City on Prince Hal. Like lots of girls, I hero-worshipped Pat Smythe. She was a brilliant horsewoman and showjumper. In fact she was the first woman to take on the best men in the world and beat them at their own game. I was so inspired by seeing her ride that I came home with a new ambition. Until then, when I went to shows, I'd entered any class that came along, whether it was gymkhana, working hunter, handy pony or jumping. Now, suddenly, I was focused. I wanted to be a great showjumper.

I was encouraged in my ambition by someone closer to home. Ted Williams was just as famous as Pat Smythe, and Mum and Dad knew him quite well. He lived only a few miles away from us, and had a lovely grey horse called Pegasus, who was a real crowd-puller, though at our small local shows he would often ride young horses to introduce them to the idea of competing. On these occasions he would always stop to have a word with Mum and Dad, and ask after my progress. I never spoke up for myself – I was too much in awe of him. Ted was quite an imposing figure in his trademark red coat. He had a weathered look about him, as if he'd been hung out in the sun to dry for a long time. Because of that, I always thought he must be extremely old, though actually I don't suppose he can have been more than forty. I still think he was one of the best horsemen I've ever met or seen.

I always loved watching Ted school his young horses outside the ring before they went in to compete. I'd hide myself behind a tent flap or horsebox and watch him nagging them around in the collecting ring, trotting circles and figures-of-eight, as a final touch to get them disciplined and attentive before they went in to jump. He had a natural affinity with horses. Without ever raising his voice, or roughing them up, he could make them obey him. They respected him, the way kids respect a good schoolteacher, and that inspired me. I knew that I wanted to have the same relationship with horses myself one day. Mum thought Ted could help me to get started in professional showjumping, and had already asked him if I could work for him as a

27

groom after I left school, and then fate stepped in. I was just fourteen when my ambition went veering off in another direction altogether.

Like most teenagers I wanted more pocket money, and it seemed a good idea to look for a weekend job. But there was no chance of any work in Hoby, and if I got a job in Leicester it would mean spending most of my pay on bus fares. It was Mum who thought of asking Tom Venn if he wanted a weekend girl at his stables.

Tom Venn was a wealthy businessman who owned a small racing yard at Brooksby Grange, near Rearsby, a few miles down the road from our farm. I'd sometimes seen his horses out exercising when I was riding with Joe or Geoffrey, but we tended to keep well away from them. The sight of our hairy little ponies seemed to have an explosive effect on Mr Venn's sleek thoroughbreds.

One day Mum told me that she'd arranged an interview for me with Mr Venn. The following Saturday morning I dressed up in best slacks and jacket, Mum put the curling tongs through my hair, and I set off down the road to Brooksby. Mr Venn turned out to be a big gruff man of few words. Standing next to him in his office as he interviewed me was a wrinkled, grumpy little man who Mr Venn said was his private trainer. The trainer's expression told me that he had doubts about the whole idea of employing a girl. However, the interview must have gone all right because at the end of it Mr Venn nodded. 'You can start next Saturday at seven. You'll be paid ten shillings for the weekend.'

To say I was overjoyed is an understatement. I was ecstatic. I was going to look after horses, the thing I liked doing best in the world, and be paid for it. As he showed me out Mr Venn said, 'You can look around the stables if you like. The tack room is over there.' He waved towards the yard and walked back into his house, leaving me to wander round. In the tack room, which was hung with well-polished saddles and bridles, I found three lads sitting on wooden benches drinking mugs of tea. Something about the faces staring back at me seemed familiar. Then I realized why. The last time I'd met these lads they'd had fishing rods in their hands and I'd had an air-gun. Recognition dawned on them at the same moment it did on me.

'Bloody hell,' said the tall dark-haired boy whose float I'd shot. 'It's Annie Oakley . . .'

I stared at him in dismay, convinced that my job was over before it had begun. Then he grinned, and the other boys burst out laughing, so I knew it was going to be all right. But the nickname was to stick with me for years . . .

CHAPTER THREE

BROOKSBY GRANGE

From the day of my interview until leaving school a year later I spent every weekend and school holiday at Tom Venn's yard. It was my introduction to the world of racing, and from my very first morning there I loved it. I'd arrive at seven o'clock on a Saturday morning, muck out two horses, then ride out with the other lads round the lanes and up Mr Venn's private grass gallop. Afterwards we'd have a quick break for a cup of tea in the tack room before the second lot. Riding racehorses was a new experience, but I soon found that it wasn't very different from riding the ponies. You were a bit higher off the ground and you pulled your leathers up shorter, that was all. All the nappy little sods Dad had put me up on had been a good education for riding thorough-breds.

In fact, I never rode anything at Tom Venn's yard that was half as tricky as some of the ponies. There were one or two characters at Brooksby Grange, though. One horse I was never allowed to ride out was a very powerful chaser called Timber who was renowned for running away. Nearly every morning he'd flash past the rest of us on the gallops with his lad sawing vigorously at his mouth. It happened so often that eventually they tried a different tactic. When he'd been hacked up to the gallop with the other horses his rider would get off him, put the reins behind the saddle and simply turn him loose. Amazingly, it worked a treat. Timber would calmly follow the other galloping horses up the grass, and stop at the end when they stopped. As long as he hadn't got anyone on his back he was as good as gold. It taught me a valuable lesson: you don't always have to follow the rule book to get the best out of racehorses!

Luckily for me, until I learned the basics of bridging my reins, cantering upsides another horse and riding with short stirrups, I was given quieter mounts than Timber. The three lads who worked at Brooksby Grange were Peter Sutton (known as Sooty), the boy whose float I'd used for target practice, his mate, Victor Perfect, a pleasant, rather quiet lad, and Peter Brightwell, who was quite a lot older. There was also another girl, Betty, who according to Sooty – who used to tease her something rotten – had been there for 'centuries'. A few months after I started work there Bill Cox, Tom Venn's smartly dressed claiming jockey, joined the team. We all got on well, and none of the others seemed to mind having to teach me the ropes.

After the second lot came back in on Saturday mornings we'd sweep the yard and clean tack until we knocked off at one o'clock. Evening stables started again at four and we were all supposed to go home for those three hours. This was no problem for the others. Victor and Sooty had push-bikes, Pete Brightwell a motorbike and Betty a bubble-car. But I just had my own two legs. Luckily, I was fit as a grey-hound from all the sports I'd done at school, and for the first few weekends I used to run home across the fields and back again. But even as the crow flies it was three miles, and when the fields were planted with corn, and I had to go the long way round, it was four. I soon decided it wasn't worth it, and instead hung around the stables all afternoon. There were always odd jobs to do and I'd offer to white-wash empty boxes, strip the paint off doors, or cut chaff.

You needed strong muscles for the chaff-cutting. First you'd have to feed the hay into the chaff machine, then heave the handle round and round to drive the huge blades, cutting the hay into small pieces, ready to be mixed in the feeds. It was really hard work, but I didn't mind. I didn't mind the long hours, either. I just loved anything to do with horses and looking after them. I took a real pride in 'doing my two'. Dad had taught me how to strap a horse properly, and I'd wisp and body-brush until my whole body ached and their coats gleamed like silk. I was determined that nobody's horse would look better than mine.

Not that I got much credit for it. Tom Venn's private trainer at that time – the little man who had glared at me during my interview – turned out to be a hard taskmaster. Nothing pleased him. We called him Whistling Willy because he used to walk around whistling and hissing through his teeth. He was extremely miserable – I never once saw him laugh or smile. He obviously didn't like women in the yard, and he really seemed to have it in for me. The only way I could tell he was satisfied with my work was if he didn't shout at me. I used to joke to the others that I was going to buy him a dog so that he might treat me a bit better. I was the smallest 'lad' on the yard but he seemed to think it was amusing to give me Timber, who was the biggest horse, to do. He gave me a box to stand on, so I could brush his back and the top of his rump, and if he ever caught me brushing him without standing on this box he would go absolutely crackers. If I hadn't been as mad about horses as I was I don't think I'd have stood it. But I wouldn't let myself be put off. In the Harvey family you gave things your best shot, and once you'd started something you stuck at it. During every rollocking I bit my lip, kept my head down and made up my mind to try even harder, so he wouldn't have anything to pick on next time.

Looking back, I think perhaps I ought to be grateful to Whistling Willy, because it was actually from him that I learned to have high standards in the yard and be thorough. The yard at Brooksby Grange was kept as spick and span as an army barracks. Every window gleamed, the horses' feet were always picked out before they were allowed out of their boxes, and all our tack (the buckles, as well as the leather) was polished till it shone. To be fair, I think Willy's grumpiness had a lot to do with Tom Venn, who was a difficult employer and probably gave him a lot of grief. Over the years Mr Venn had employed a number of private trainers. You could always tell when he was due to inspect the yard because everyone would be on their toes, as nervous as if they were expecting royalty.

Tom Venn had about sixteen horses in training, mostly jumpers, and not long after I began working there we started to have runners at some of the Midland meetings. Riding out had been exciting enough, but helping to prepare a horse for a race was even better. Race days really got my adrenaline going. As a part-timer, I wasn't allowed to go to the meetings, but that didn't matter. Just seeing Timber or my other horse – a good sprinter called Star Princess – off to the races in the old wooden horsebox was magic to me. Welcoming them home after a race, making them comfortable and soothing any cuts and bruises was even better. Horseracing was the most exciting thing I'd ever been involved with. Being paid for this life of bliss was like having my cake and eating it too.

Earning money, even if it was only ten bob a week, made me feel grown up and independent. It meant I could afford the one and sixpence entry fee to play badminton at the village hall and didn't have to ask Mum for it. It also meant I could save up to buy any special clothes I wanted. (I was growing so fast I was always needing new jeans, or boots or riding gloves.) Last, but not least, it meant I got a bigger ration of sweets when the grocery van called on Tuesday evenings.

From Mum's point of view I started to earn my own

money at just the right time, as there was an extra mouth to feed at home. I'd vaguely noticed that Mum was putting on weight. A few months after I started working at weekends, she told us she had to go to hospital, and when she arrived home again she was carrying a new baby. I found out later that Mum had been quite ill with toxaemia but had recovered once Mandy was born. I thought having a new little sister was great, and from the time Mum brought her home from the hospital I made it my mission in life to turn Mandy into a rider. Each day Mum would park her outside in a big old-fashioned pram to get some fresh air. As soon as she could sit up I would ride up on Rocket, pluck her out of the pram by the scruff of her coat and sit her in front of me on the saddle. With her little hands round the reins I'd trot off and Mandy would scream with laughter as I lifted her up and down in front of me, teaching her to bump the saddle. When she'd had enough of that, I'd kick Rocket into a canter. It's a wonder I didn't kill her, but I didn't think I was doing anything dangerous. I just felt I was giving her a head start on other kids. Thinking about it now, I'm surprised Mum never banned my 'lessons', but I suppose she probably didn't know about most of them. Since those days, Mandy has ridden several point-to-point winners and also won races on the Flat for Paul Mellon and Ian Balding. Recently she took out a licence to train, so maybe my scheme paid off!

Since I'd been spending my weekends at Brooksby Grange, my whole life had revolved around the horses I looked after. Timber and Star Princess took up a lot of my thoughts, even when I was at school, but there was another horse in my life that year too. While I was learning to ride racehorses I had also been riding a young hunter of Dad's every night at home. Since tractors had taken over on the farm, Dad's interest in horses had centred on breeding them. In fact, his interest had got a bit out of hand. Every filly Nelly produced was kept and bred from herself. Not content with that, Dad would occasionally come home from the market with a new broodmare he hadn't been able to resist. One of these mares was a thoroughbred who'd been mated with the local premium stallion, and she produced a useful-looking colt. It became a bit of a family joke that every time Dad looked over the fence at this colt he'd say, 'That'll make a point-to-pointer one day.'

Point-to-point racing was a big local interest. All the hunts staged their own meetings and some of our neighbours used to enter their horses in the members' races. Until this colt came along we'd never had anything well bred enough to run, but the idea that he might win a race for us took root, and by the time he was five years old Mum and I were as keen as Dad for him to have a go. I was given the job of getting him fit. The colt, long-since gelded, was known at home as Danny, but Mum decided that our first racehorse should be called something more dignified. What more suitable name than a character from our favourite radio programme, *The Archers*? Mum was never one to do things unofficially, so she wrote to Harry Oakes, the actor who played Dan Archer. In reply she received a wonderful letter, which she carried round in her handbag for years, saying that he would be *honoured* to have a horse named after him, and even more honoured if the horse ran in the colours of his club. So Danny became Dan Archer, and Mum knitted a light blue jumper with black crossbelts for his jockey to wear.

The attendance officer had made it clear that I was expected to spend at least some weekdays at school, so, somehow, I had to fit Dan Archer's training schedule around my school day. This wasn't easy. Since we had no spare stable at home he had to be kept a mile away, at Albert Riley's farm in the village. This meant that I had to get up early and walk to Hoby in time to muck out and feed him before the school bus left at ten past eight. On the way home I'd jump off the bus in the village, then ride Danny back to the farm in my school uniform. I'd tie him to the fence outside the house while I ran upstairs to change into jodh-purs to ride him out. We had no gallop, and in winter my Dad's riverside fields were too wet to work a horse on, so I used to canter round any local field that was available. Usually I'd ask permission from the owners first, but, to be honest, only if I thought they'd say yes . . .

Dad was the trainer, so I was supposed to do exactly as he told me. 'Canter him eight times round Miss James's stubble field,' he'd say. The snag was that Dad had no trainer's hack or Land Rover, so he couldn't follow and see what I got up to. I would ride back and say I'd done it, but it wasn't always the strict truth. I loved the horse too much, so I was soft on him. If he started blowing a lot I used to pull him up and let him have a walk, not realizing what a stupid thing it was to do with a horse that was going to have to gallop three miles across country. I had a lot to learn. Once or twice a week (three times in the school holidays) I'd take him hunting, and discovered that Dan Archer was a natural jumper.

At the start of the point-to-point season, when he was probably only half-fit, Dad ran him in a couple of races with a local jockey on board. He didn't come anywhere but he managed to stay on his feet and learned a little more with each race. In May, Dad entered him in the Quorn point-to-point at Garthorpe, which was one of the last meetings of the season. His regular rider wasn't available, and, with only a few weeks to go, a jockey had still to be decided on.

Soon afterwards, I was discussing the possibilities with my Uncle Percy, who was also a keen point-to-point fan. Dad was considering several young local jockeys and I was asking Uncle Percy for his opinion of them, when he gave me a side-ways look.

'I don't know what you're talking about other jockeys for. Why don't you ride him yourself? Are you frit or summat?'

I stared at him. The thought hadn't entered my head till then. Although I rode Dan Archer in his work I didn't feel that that qualified me to ride him in a race, any more than riding the horses at home entitled me to ride them on the racetrack. In my mind they were two different jobs.

'I reckon you're frit!' Uncle Percy repeated. I glared at him. I could truthfully say I had never been frightened of riding anything in my life.

'I am *not* frit,' I said.

'I bet you are,' he teased. 'I bet you any money you wouldn't ride him.'

'How much?'

'A pound! There you are. I bet you a pound you won't do it!'

By the time I'd walked home from the village the idea Uncle Percy had planted had become a burning ambition. When I got in I told Mum and Dad about the bet and announced that I wanted to ride Dan Archer in the point-to-point myself.

Dad wasn't at all keen on the idea and pointed out that I was still only fourteen. Although I was officially allowed to ride at that age, in his opinion I was far from ready. To my surprise, it was Mum who took my side and persuaded Dad to let me have a go. She seemed to have every confidence in me.

Dan Archer was duly entered in the ladies' race, and I informed my disbelieving workmates at Tom Venn's yard that I was about to become a jockey. They announced that they would all turn out to watch my debut. I wasn't at all nervous. To me, riding in a point-to-point didn't seem any more frightening than riding across country behind hounds. I'd jumped bigger fences on Dan Archer out hunting than the ones on the Garthorpe point-to-point course. Not only that, I'd jumped them with other horses all around me. So why should I be worried about a race? Little did I know. I had no idea that ladies' races tend to be run at a hell-for-leather pace which makes hunting look like a gentle hack.

I was as thin as a navvy's dog in those days, and on the day itself I weighed in at less than 8st. Since I had to carry

11st 3lb, my saddle had to be packed with so much lead it was almost too heavy for me to lift, so Dad helped me saddle Dan Archer, while giving me a constant stream of advice. He seemed much more nervous than I was. I was so confident that I hadn't even bothered to walk the course, but Dad had. As he did up the girth he said quietly, 'Whatever you do, Jenny, jump them fences in the middle. They're on such a slope they're nigh on impossible to jump on the inside.'

There were more runners in the race than I'd expected. One of the other jockeys was the country's leading lady rider and wise to all the tricks. When the starter told us to line up, she got a flyer and Dan Archer instinctively leapt after her. To my delight, as we headed for the first fence I found myself in third place. When a man in front of us started waving a red flag and shouting, 'False start!' I could have wept. Second time round Dan didn't jump off so quickly, but we were still up with the field and going so fast to the first I couldn't believe it. I had never galloped at a fence at this pace in my life. I suddenly realized these women meant business. They weren't here for a jolly ride in the countryside. All Dad's instructions flew out of my head and I just sat there and left it to Dan Archer. One fence after another passed under us in a blur until, as we approached the fifth, I knew with a sickening feeling that not only were we on a wrong stride, but we were exactly where Dad had told me *not* to be – on the inside. Like me, Dan Archer was inexperienced, and instead of standing back he put in an extra stride and got right underneath the fence. The next thing I knew I was cartwheeling through the air with the ground rushing up to meet me. Nothing was badly hurt except my pride, but I was winded, so I had to lie still for a few seconds, catching my breath, as the field disappeared into the distance. Dan Archer clambered to his feet unharmed and galloped off after the other runners.

I shut my eyes for a moment. When I opened them I saw a man in a black uniform, holding a little black bag, trotting towards me. I stared at him in horror. An ambulanceman! I had visions of him undoing my clothes and giving me artificial respiration in full view of the watching public and the lads from Brooksby Grange. 'He ain't touching me,' I thought. A moment later I was up and running like a jack-rabbit towards the horseboxes.

Back home that night the main emotion I felt was disappointment. It had all happened so quickly. I hadn't really minded falling off, but I wished I'd gone further to have really got the feel of it. I'd only been in the race for about a minute, but it was enough to know that I wanted to do it again. Alas, it wasn't to be. There were no more point-to-points that season, and by the time the next season came round the powers-that-be had decided to raise the minimum age for point-to-point riders to sixteen. By the time I reached that age I was working full time in racing, and as a 'professional' wasn't allowed to ride between the flags, so my career as a point-to-point rider was short, if not sweet.

Dan Archer, however, continued racing, and though he was no superstar he gave us a lot of pleasure. Sadly, two years later he was poisoned when he gorged himself on fallen willow leaves down by the riverside. He was the first horse I'd ever lost and because I'd looked after him since the day he was born it nearly broke my heart. His death was a taste of things to come. For me, horses were friends, and losing them was never going to be easy to deal with.

Soon after the race at Garthorpe, and two weeks before my fifteenth birthday, I left school for good and went to work full time at Brooksby Grange. My weekly wages were £3 4s 5d. From the day I'd first set foot in Tom Venn's yard I'd never had the slightest doubt where my future lay. Looking after racehorses was bliss to me, and I had no ambition to be anything other than a stable girl.

As a full-time 'lad' I was given more responsibility. As soon as I was sixteen I was allowed to accompany horses to the races, which was exciting but not the most comfortable job in the world. Tom Venn's transport was a little wooden two-horse box, and the lads were expected to travel with the horses in the cramped luggage compartment between the stalls. There were no seats, so we sat on a luggage hamper or the upturned water buckets. Because there was no connection with the cab and its heater it was absolutely freezing in the back and we had to wrap the horses' rugs around us to keep warm. There were no motorways in those days and it took ages to get anywhere. Most trips involved an overnight stop. My first experience of staying away from home was at Manchester, where my filly, Star Princess, was running. Sooty was travelling with his horse too, and he and I shivered together in the back while Betty, who'd come along to show me the ropes, travelled with the box-driver in the comfort of the cab.

Once we'd settled the horses down at the racecourse stables, we went to our digs and met up with some other lads. They decided to go down the town for something to eat, so I tagged along. I was still quite shy, so I didn't really want to go into a bar with them – I'd never been into a bar in my life before – but I hadn't got any choice if I didn't want to be left on my own. I found myself in a dimly lit, crowded room, thick with cigarette smoke.

'What'll you have, Jenny?' Sooty asked me.

'An orange juice,' I replied, which they found highly amusing. I felt like a fish out of water, and I decided to duck out by going to the loo. On my way down the passage I bumped into a man coming out of the gents' opposite, who paused and muttered something.

'I beg your pardon?' I said politely.

'Are you in the business?' he repeated.

'I'm sorry, I don't know what you mean,' I said.

He looked a bit embarrassed and walked off. I thought maybe he'd mistaken me for someone else, and when I went back to the bar I told Betty what had happened. I thought she was going to choke on her drink.

'*That's* what he's talking about.' She pointed to a bench on the far wall where three women sat, made up to the eyebrows, with skirts halfway up their thighs, making eyes at every man that walked past. Even I could see they weren't there for the beer. I decided that in future I would bring sandwiches and eat them in my digs rather than risk the fleshpots of Manchester.

The next afternoon Star Princess made up for my embarrassment by winning the Diomedes Handicap on the final day of the 1962 Flat season. I felt as proud as punch leading her in. A newspaper photographer took a picture of me holding her. In those days it was quite unusual for girls to be looking after horses at the races, so as the girl who did a big winner I was quite a novelty. Betty and I had already found ourselves the centre of attention in the racecourse stables. All day lads had been peeping round corners and nudging each other as we walked by. I thought it was quite funny. I didn't mind at all being a girl in a man's world.

I was beginning to develop an interest in boys (though it came a pretty poor second to my interest in horses), and one or two of them were beginning to show an interest in me too. Sometimes, if I'd managed to borrow Jacquie's bike, Victor Perfect would cycle home with me from work. Often we used to get off our bikes at the end of our lane and stand there chatting. On one of these occasions Victor plucked up his courage and kissed me. I didn't like it very much, and I must have made my feelings clear because it was a while before he tried it again! The trouble was, the boy I fancied wasn't Victor at all, but Peter Sutton, the lad whose fishing float I'd shot to bits. Peter was a real Jack the Lad, always playing practical jokes, and for a while I had quite a crush on him, though I never let on. The others would have taken the mickey something rotten if they'd known! Eventually my crush faded and I started to realize what a nice person Victor was. For several months afterwards, until he left to take a new job, we became an 'item'.

41

I had been working full time at Tom Venn's for just over a year when Whistling Willy moved on. He was replaced by a new trainer, Chris Taylor, a tall, thin man who was much nicer to work for. Unlike Willy, he was married, and his wife, Sarah, was very involved with the horses too. Everyone got on well with them and the whole atmosphere in the yard changed, although our standards stayed as high as ever. Chris expected the same degree of care and attention as Willy. He just had a pleasanter way of asking for it.

He also differed from Willy in his riding style. Because he was so tall, he used to ride very long, with his toes stuck out at right angles, so we used to call him 'Toes' Taylor. Nor was it just his seat that was different. Chris also had some peculiar ideas about how to control horses. One morning we were riding to the gallops when he started to give us a demonstration of how to stop a runaway horse.

'When a horse starts to get strong with you,' he said, 'what you should do is lean forward down its neck like this, and get hold of the bit rings. That'll stop it.'

We looked sideways at each other, smirking. We'd all been carted at some time and using Chris's remedy on a bolting thoroughbred, with its neck stuck straight out in front of you, struck us as being impossible. Little did we know we were about to be given a demonstration.

Tom Venn's gallop went round the edge of a small square field and the bends were terribly sharp. We always cantered round it clockwise, but that morning, for some unknown reason, Chris decided to work anti-clockwise. Peter Brightwell set off in the lead, I was second on a new horse, followed by Sooty, Vic Perfect and Betty, with Chris Taylor trundling along behind so that he could watch what was going on in front. All at once there was a thundering of hooves and Chris came roaring past us like a dose of salts. As we struggled to stop our horses taking off after him we saw him go round the first bend like the wall of death. He took the second at the same rate, and I could see him leaning out to the side trying to get hold of the bit rings. I didn't have time to laugh because by this time Vic Perfect had lost control and as he shot past me my horse bolted too. The pair of us hurtled round the first two bends. By the time we got to the third bend Victor was in front, but I was hot on his tail. Suddenly, I realized we were approaching the schooling hurdles. Not only that, but we were approaching them the wrong way on, with the backs of the hurdles facing us. Somehow, Victor managed to jump them, but I pulled out to the stubble on the inside of the gallop to miss them. The sudden swerve unbalanced my horse, and on the fourth bend I felt him slip from under me. The last thing I saw, as we crashed to the ground, was Chris Taylor going round in ever-decreasing circles in the stubble, still vainly trying to get hold of the bit-rings . . .

The fall broke my collarbone. It was my first racing injury and it put me out of action for the next month. Chris was very apologetic, but at least one good thing came of it. He never mentioned the 'bit-ring technique' again.

Chris and Sarah stayed at Tom Venn's for about a year. Chris had never made a secret of the fact that he wanted to train on his own account, so it was no surprise when Sarah called me into the kitchen one day and told me they had found themselves a yard at Bishop's Cleeve near Cheltenham. They planned to leave at the end of the month. 'If you want to come with us you're very welcome,' she said. 'I know Chris thinks a lot of you.'

I didn't know what to say. I was flattered, but the thought of leaving home frightened me a bit. My horizons had widened since I had begun travelling with the horses to the races, but I still thought of 'the South' as a foreign country. Dad used to call me his 'baby goose', and like all baby geese I was in no hurry to leave the safety of my family and get out into the big wide world. I was quite happy where I was, living at home and working just down the road. On the other hand, I knew I would have to stand on my own two feet one day. To go now, with people I liked and trusted, was an opportunity that might not come again.

I was encouraged by Mum, who had ambitions of her own. She'd recently amazed us all by announcing that when Mandy started school she was going to train as a nurse. Life didn't stand still, much as I wanted it to. Jacquie had recently got married, while at work Vic Perfect had left and taken a job with Peter Walwyn in Lambourn. I was seventeen now. Maybe it was time for me to move on too.

When the new trainer who replaced Chris at Tom Venn's turned out to be a difficult man to work for, it was the final push I needed. I gave in my notice. Two weeks later, after Mum and Dad had paid a visit to Gloucestershire to approve my new workplace, I packed my case, climbed on board a Black and White coach at Leicester bus station, and set off for the great unknown.

CHAPTER FOUR

THE GREAT UNKNOWN

By the time I arrived at Bishop's Cleeve my sense of adventure had deserted me – in fact I was feeling downright scared. During the five hours I'd been sitting in the coach, the view out of the window had changed dramatically. The brick houses with slate roofs had been left behind, and now I could see stone cottages, some of them thatched. Even the sheep and cattle looked different from the ones I was used to. With every mile that passed I felt everything I knew slipping further and further away. When the coach stopped by the memorial in the main street of Bishop's Cleeve I'd have been more than happy to stay on board while it turned round and took me back home.

However, that wasn't an option. As the coach drew to a halt and I peered down the steps I saw a dark-haired woman in her twenties looking up at me.

'Excuse me, are you Jenny Harvey?' she asked.

I gave a faint nod.

'I've been sent to meet you. My name's Josie Hooley. You'll be sharing a flat with me.'

Clutching my suitcase, I followed Josie up the village street to a big wooden gate which led into a gravelled yard. An old stone farmhouse stood at the side. Attached to the farmhouse was what looked like a converted granary with concrete steps leading to the first floor. Josie led me up these steps into the room which was to be my home for the next year. It was quite a shock after my familiar, cluttered bedroom at Lodge Farm. There were two single beds, a sink, a rug spread on a chipboard floor and a small chest of drawers. That was it. It was all spotlessly clean, but it was drastically short of fixtures and fittings. 'You have to go into the main house if you want a bath or the loo,' Josie informed me.

I looked around for some sort of heating but couldn't see any. 'Doesn't it get cold in winter?' I asked.

Josie nodded. 'Just a bit. The boilerhouse is underneath, so when there's a mash on for the horses it gets quite warm. Otherwise you just have to wear a lot of clothes.'

I was beginning to feel certain I'd made a mistake, and the next few weeks didn't do much to change my mind. The worst part about the flat were the little furry things that scampered about underneath the floor at night, feasting on the spilled mash and barley in the boilerhouse. I'd always been terrified of rats and mice even though I grew up on a farm, and Josie shared my phobia. It probably went back to the days on the farm when the cornstack was put through the threshing machine, and rats and mice would run out from the bottom of the stack in all directions. The labourers would kill them with sticks and pitchforks and then throw them at us girls, thinking it was a huge joke.

For the first month at Bishop's Cleeve I was terribly homesick, and Mum's weekly parcels containing warm vests, knickers and socks just made me feel worse. I wanted to be looked after again. I wanted to come home from work into a warm kitchen and the smell of food (there was no hotplate in the flat, so we had to eat in the local pub, or with Chris and Sarah Taylor in the house). Mum seemed to be missing me too. She wrote at least twice a week, telling me to be sure to get my winter vest on and not to go out with wet hair. I wrote back, trying to be brave and pretending I was enjoying it. I never sent so many letters in my life as I did in those first weeks at Bishop's Cleeve. I wrote to my sisters, to my schoolfriends, even to Victor Perfect at Lambourn. I felt very lonely away from all the people I knew.

By today's standards the work was hard, and we had only one Sunday off in every three. However, I didn't think of it as hard, because we'd always worked seven days a week at home. I'd been born to it, and something's only tough if you've had it easy beforehand. It wasn't the work but the homesickness, the cold and the rats that I found hard to bear.

It was only thanks to Josie that I got through those early weeks. Although she could be a bit bossy – if Josie told you to do something there was no messing, you did it – she knew her job and she made sure that I knew mine too. She was an utter perfectionist. Josie's horses didn't just have their feet picked out like everybody else's. They were washed out and spotless. When Josie had clipped a horse you could spot it a mile off because there was never a tramline or nick to show where the clippers had been. She was quite crafty, though. When she clipped horses in the afternoons she'd get you to hold them for her, but somehow it always worked out that she got paid and I didn't, as I was the apprentice, but I didn't mind. I wanted to learn and it paid off. By the time I eventually left Bishop's Cleeve I could clip almost as well as Josie and my plaiting was as good as anybody's.

It was Josie who introduced me to the local social life. There were several other racing stables near by, including the big yard of 'Frenchie' Nicholson. We'd pass their string sometimes when we were riding out, and after work, if we went up to our 'local', the Apple Tree pub, for a bite to eat we'd often meet some of the Nicholson lads there. Paul Cook was an apprentice at the Nicholson stable then, and was just starting to make a name for himself as a claiming

47

jockey. Frenchie Nicholson made sure the lads didn't get above themselves, though. 'Cookie' was always grumbling because the guv'nor made the apprentices go stone-picking on the gallops every afternoon.

Sometimes Josie and I and the other three lads from our yard would go off with the Nicholson lads to Guiting Power for a game of skittles. We'd all have a good laugh, and after a while I began to feel I was among friends. By the time I paid my first visit home, after six weeks at Bishop's Cleeve, I was actually looking forward to returning to work. It's just as well I didn't go back home any earlier, as I am sure it would have been a one-way trip.

Chris Taylor paid me £4 a week, plus my keep. It was a bit more than my wages at Brooksby Grange, so I felt quite well off. I always tried to save a bit each week. Some of the lads used to go off and have a bet when their stable had a fancied horse running, but I was far too careful. As far as I knew, nobody in my family had ever had a bet, and it was a very strange custom to me. Since the lads I knew were always skint, despite their 'inside' knowledge, it didn't seem a very sensible one, either.

In the March after I started at Bishop's Cleeve, as a special treat Chris gave Josie and me a half-day off to go to the Cheltenham Festival to watch the Gold Cup. We conned our way into the Silver Ring for free by mentioning Chris Taylor's name and giving them a bit of blarney. It was my first ever visit to the Cheltenham Festival and I was as excited as any kid because my hero, Mill House, was running. I'd followed his career for years. I read everything I could about him and watched all his races on TV. The main reason I loved him so much was that he was a great big horse, the sort Dad had always liked. Actually seeing him in the flesh at Cheltenham made me go weak inside. He had a real majesty about him. I noticed that Arkle, his challenger, also had an aura about him as he led the parade with his head held high.

That Cheltenham meeting was also special because Mum was there. She'd started to 'do her own thing' now that the kids were growing up, and she told me that coming to the Festival meeting had been a lifelong dream of hers. She travelled down by coach from Leicester and we met her in the Silver Ring. It was the most wonderful day. To me, Cheltenham seemed like a huge fair rather than an ordinary race meeting. Mum, Josie and I watched the Gold Cup from the Silver Ring, and it was the first time in my life that watching a race broke my heart. I burst into floods of tears as Arkle overtook my hero, Mill House, and stormed into the lead to win the race. Arkle was on his way to becoming a legend. He was such a great racehorse that he went on to win two more Gold Cups – three in a row.

Since Chris Taylor had started to train on his own account, he had been quite successful. He had a mixed yard of about fifteen horses, and, though they weren't running in top company, they were winning a lot of races. Sarah and Chris both worked hard. They often mucked out, and rode out every morning with us. Having them so involved meant that there was a good atmosphere in the yard, and when we had a winner we felt it had been a real team effort.

There were two other lads in the yard along with Josie and me. Harry was about my age, and Scotty was a tough old cookie from over the border, who'd been doing horses for years. He always used to sing while he worked and though he wasn't very tuneful it did make you smile to hear him warbling away. While I was there, Scotty was involved in a nasty incident that made me realize you should never get too blasé about horses, even ones you think you know well. It happened one evening when I was dressing my own horse over. I could hear Scotty singing in the next box, where he was brushing a colt called Snakestone, who was always a bad-tempered horse. While he was being groomed he used to open his mouth and snap like an alligator, and it was quite obvious he didn't think much of human beings. All of a sudden the noise from the next box got louder. A lot louder. That ain't Scotty singing, I thought. I dropped my grooming kit on the floor and rushed to see what was going on. When I looked round the box door my heart nearly stopped. Scotty was lying on the ground in front of Snakestone, holding his chest and groaning. Snakestone's mouth was open and although he was chained up he was doing his best to kneel on top of Scotty. I'd never seen anyone being savaged by a horse before and I was panic-stricken. There was a pitchfork leaning against the wall outside the box. Quickly I grabbed it, ran in and whacked the horse as hard as I could over its backside with the shaft of the fork. Snakestone leapt up in surprise and Scotty managed to scramble out of the way and throw himself out of the door. He looked an awful mess. His shirt was ripped open down the front, and blood was pouring from his chest. It was obvious he was badly mauled so I took him into the house, where Sarah Taylor took one look at him and carted him off to hospital to be patched up.

It was quite a few days before Scotty was fit enough to return to work. When he did, Snakestone had been fitted with a muzzle, which he had to wear whenever anyone handled him. It was years before I saw anything like it happen again. Savage horses aren't very common but when you find one you have to give him as much respect as you would a bull.

Of my own two horses my favourite was a two-year-old filly called Clouded Lamp, a very good racehorse who went on to become a successful broodmare. (A few years ago, in November 1994, her great-grandson, Barathea, won the Breeders' Cup Mile in America.) While Clouded Lamp was in training she was very temperamental and always needed handling with kid gloves. I'd helped Josie break her in soon after I'd arrived at Chris Taylor's, and she'd been extremely difficult, bucking and kicking non-stop. In fact she once kicked herself so badly down her shin that she had three big lumps on that leg the whole time she was in training. On a really bad day she'd think nothing of lying down and biting the ground in temper. Gradually, however, she came round. She was always a bit of a fireball, but she and I seemed to hit it off. Thanks to my dad's training, I had endless patience with difficult horses. If we had any horse in the yard that was aggressive or stubborn or nervous I'd usually be the one to get the job of exercising it, which I always found a challenge.

Clouded Lamp was a filly who responded to kindness rather than to being bullied. You had to be very sensitive and tactful with her. The trouble was that this meant riding her week in, week out, and this was quite tiring. If ever I felt a bit under the weather and I told Chris I wouldn't mind a break from her I regretted it because he'd put another lad up who didn't get on with her at all. This lad often ended up smacking her, which meant all the work I'd done settling her down would be out the window. It used to distress me to see the filly get cross and upset. On top of that she would be really bad to ride for a couple of days afterwards, so I soon decided that taking a break from her just wasn't worth it.

One morning, when we'd been working up on the gallops at Cleeve Hill, Clouded Lamp and I were leading the string back to the stables and a bike came flying round the bend in front of me on the wrong side of the road. The cyclist was travelling much too fast to stop, and he had to swerve to avoid us. He missed my filly by a knife's edge. Clouded Lamp wasn't good in traffic at the best of times, so, not surprisingly, she spooked and 'whipped round'. Once I was back in control I looked over my shoulder to see that the bike rider had done a u-turn and was heading back towards us. I couldn't believe his nerve. I waited for someone to tell him off, but all Harry did was start laughing and joking with this madman who had nearly caused me to be thrown off.

It was obvious that Harry, Scotty and Josie knew the young man on the bike quite well. From what I could hear of their conversation I gathered he was a rider himself. That didn't make me feel any warmer towards him. In my opinion it gave him even less excuse for his behaviour. After a while he cycled up alongside Clouded Lamp and, ignoring the fact that my filly's eyes were popping out of her head, asked me my name. I ignored him and refused to answer. It was only that night that curiosity overcame me. 'Who *was* that idiot on the bike this morning?' I asked Josie as I got ready for bed.

'Oh, him!' Josie laughed. 'He's all right, really. He's one of John Roberts's claimers. His name's Richard Pitman . . .'

When you look back in the cold light of day and try to remember how a romance began, it's hard to recapture exactly how you felt at the time, especially thirty-odd years later. I do remember that for quite some time after he scared my precious filly I strongly disliked Richard Pitman and ignored him whenever I bumped into him in the Apple Tree. I wasn't looking for a boyfriend. I liked going out in a gang, and as far as I was concerned there was quite enough love interest in my life already. Victor was still writing to me, and he sometimes came over to Bishop's Cleeve to see me. To my surprise Paul Cook had started writing to me too. I liked Paul. He was a nice lad, a right scallywag, but he seemed to have a different idea from mine of the way our relationship was heading. I didn't ever reply to his letters. The truth was, I wasn't really attracted to him.

Richard Pitman has never been short of 'flannel' – a Northern term for 'charm'. Mind you, the charm took quite a while to appear. Our second meeting didn't produce any more evidence of it than the first. It happened one night after Josie and I had been to the pictures in Cheltenham. We reached the bus stop, and who should be waiting for the last bus home but Richard. He started chatting to Josie and complimented her on her sheepskin coat. Then he carried on at length about how he always preferred *real* sheepskin. There and then I decided he was the rudest person I'd ever met. I just happened to be wearing a brown imitation suede jacket with a pale yellow fake fur fluffy lining. I'd bought it out of a mail-order catalogue, and it was the most expensive garment I'd ever owned. Until then I'd thought it was terribly smart. I was cut to the quick, and again refused to answer when Richard tried to speak to me.

He wasn't put off. Perhaps he regarded me as a challenge. Whatever the reason, a few days later he came over to our table in the Apple Tree and asked if I'd like to go to the pictures with him. I was taken aback by his cheek but eventually I agreed. However, I wasn't exactly swept off my feet by that experience either. We saw an awful film called *Tom Thumb*, and afterwards Richard blotted his copybook even more. Instead of seeing me home he got off the bus two stops before me and let me walk home alone. *Not* very gallant, I thought. Even so, there was no denying that Richard had charm. If he'd wanted to he could have sold fridges to eskimos. When I first met him I'd walk into the Apple Tree not giving a damn whether he was there or not. Now, if he hadn't appeared by the end of the evening I'd be disappointed. Over the next few weeks Richard and I went out a few more times. Sometimes we'd go as a couple, but more often we'd just be part of the gang. Josie had bought herself an old car, and two or three times a week we'd all pile into it and go to the skittle alley or to Cheltenham Town Hall for an evening out.

I thought Richard saw our relationship as a casual friendship. The first clue that he viewed it as more than that came when he called round at our yard to see me one day. As usual he put his arm around my waist and patted my bottom by way of greeting. 'What's this?' he said, pulling an envelope out of the back pocket of my jeans. I felt myself blush. It was one of Paul Cook's romantic letters. I struggled to get it back but Richard insisted on holding the letter out of my reach and reading the whole thing through. Unfortunately, although I'd never even been out with Paul, his imagination ran away with him when he put pen to paper. I thought

Richard would laugh, but instead he went absolutely crackers and stormed off.

Later I found out from people who'd witnessed the episode that Richard had gone round to the Nicholson yard, waited for Cookie to finish work, then told him in no uncertain terms that it wasn't a good idea to write to me. I was amazed. It was the first indication I'd had that he cared about us as an 'item'. I had to admit I was rather taken with the idea. I even wrote to Victor Perfect telling him I didn't think we should see each other again.

After that episode, though Cookie still wrote me the occasional cheeky letter, none of the other lads made passes at me any more. It seemed accepted that Richard and I were 'going steady'. Richard lived with his parents in Bishop's Cleeve and when he took me home to meet them our relationship moved forward another step. It wasn't an easy meeting. Richard had three older sisters and, being the only boy, he was obviously the apple of his mother's eye. I found it disconcerting to see her jumping up and down, fetching his food and cups of tea and taking away his dirty crockery while he sat back in his chair like a sultan. Frankly, I don't think she would have welcomed any new girlfriend with open arms, but I got the distinct impression she thought Richard could do a lot better for himself than a lowly stable-girl like me. Her attitude was extremely intimidating.

Richard's dad, on the other hand, was a real gem and was always lovely to me. He was an engineer with Smith's Industries in Cheltenham but he loved racing and rode as a hobby. It was he who'd got Richard interested in horses. When Pam, one of Richard's sisters, had married the jump jockey Paddy Cowley, Richard had decided to try the life for himself.

When I met him Richard was a claiming apprentice at John Roberts's yard in Prestbury, a few miles from Bishop's Cleeve. It may have sounded impressive, but in reality it wasn't a very glamorous position. If he had a ride Richard had to take the horse to the races himself, get it ready and saddle it up. Then he'd have to give someone ten bob to lead it up while he changed into his riding kit. After the race he'd change back into his work clothes, go down to the stables to wash it off and brush it over before travelling home in the horsebox. I can't imagine any claimer doing that today!

I think Richard would agree that, while he was a pretty good rider, he wasn't a real horseman at that stage. Unlike me, he hadn't grown up handling and looking after horses every day, so he still had a lot to learn about horse behaviour. I remember him moaning once about a mare he used to ride for John Roberts. She always seemed to be in season when he rode her. In Richard's words, she was 'a real cow'. I sympathized, because I knew some fillies could be very difficult when they were in season. In passing, I mentioned that when my dad had a mare who was to be covered by the stallion he'd sometimes put stinging nettles under her tail to make her lift it. It was an old countryman's trick that was used on quiet cartmares. Even then there'd be a couple of people hanging onto the mare's head to prevent accidents. I certainly wasn't suggesting it as a solution for highly strung thoroughbreds.

Two days later Richard took the same mare to Wincanton to run in a selling hurdle. The racecourse stables were full that day so she had to stand on the back of the horsebox. It wasn't long before Richard realized that she was in season again – and might be unco-operative and not run well – and on the spur of the moment he rather foolishly decided to galvanize her using Dad's treatment. Pulling up a bunch of nettles from the hedgerow, he walked up the ramp behind the mare, lifted up her tail and shoved the nettles underneath. The reaction was dramatic. Two hooves went whistling past his ears so close he felt the draught.

'She nearly took my head off,' he told me later, his voice still quivering. Stifling my laughter, I said that I was amazed he'd done such a stupid thing, and even more amazed that he'd survived it! But that wasn't the end of the story. Richard had gone off to change for the race and had come back to find the mare walking round the parade ring in a muck sweat. Of course, the more she sweated the more the nettle-stings hurt. By the time they got to the starting gate she was ready to explode, and when the tapes went up she bolted, completely out of control. John Roberts was watching and must have wondered what had suddenly transformed his selling hurdler into a five-furlong sprinter. Little did he know that her bum was almost literally on fire!

While Richard's ideas on horse management could be a bit bizarre, his race-riding skills were improving all the time. Whenever I could get the afternoon off I'd go and watch him. I'd started taking driving lessons and if Richard didn't have to drive the horsebox, he'd borrow his dad's car, put L-plates on and let me drive it to the races while he fell asleep beside me. If we'd been stopped by the police we'd have had a bit of explaining to do, but fortunately we never were.

Richard hadn't ridden a winner yet, but he was knocking on the door. I felt sure that if he could ride some better horses he would be successful, but it was a vicious circle. Until he'd ridden winners no-one was going to risk putting him up on a good horse, but by riding bad horses he was more likely to fall than to win. There didn't seem an easy way out of the situation.

After my shaky start I was by now perfectly happy with my life at Bishop's Cleeve. I was looking after two nice horses, I had a great gang of friends, and a boyfriend who was a good laugh. What more could I want? I had no am-bition at all beyond doing my two and earning enough money to get home to see Mum and Dad every few months. My lifestyle might have carried on like that indefinitely had Fred Winter not decided to hang up his boots.

At the time, Winter was the most successful jump jockey of his generation. He had been champion jockey four times. In 1964 he bought a stable yard called Uplands, in

Lambourn, and announced his retirement from race-riding. At the news that Fred Winter was going to become a trainer Richard instantly pricked up his ears. Because of his reputation, Fred Winter was bound to have some good horses sent to him, and an up-and-coming yard like that would offer many more opportunities than a small trainer like John Roberts. Richard wrote to Fred Winter and was invited down to Lambourn for an interview. A few weeks later a letter arrived offering him a job as an apprentice. Richard was over the moon. I was really pleased for him, but sad, too. Lambourn was fifty miles from Bishop's Cleeve, and though by now Richard had a car of his own it seemed likely that we'd see much less of each other.

It was Richard's idea that I should move to Lambourn to join him. When he suggested it, a few weeks after he started his new job, I was quite taken aback. I'd imagined that like most stable lads who moved to pastures new he would soon find a new girlfriend and forget me. I didn't relish that idea but I was only eighteen and our relationship so far had been light-hearted. It had not occurred to me that Richard had thought differently. Moving to Lambourn to be with him would put it on a different level. It meant commitment, and I wasn't sure I was ready for that. On the other hand, I had been feeling rather unsettled at Chris's recently, not only because Richard had left, but because Josie had also moved on. She'd landed a plum job as head girl to the showjumper Peter Robeson, travelling his horses all over the world. It was great for her, but not so nice for me. Being in the flat alone at night was horrible. I didn't like going to the pub on my own, so I'd gone to the local dogs' home and got myself a small long-legged terrier called Rip to keep me company. One day, when I went down to see Richard in Lambourn, he had news for me. 'There's a trainer up the road that I used to work for,' he said. 'I told him about you, and he said if you want a job you can go and see him today for an interview.' The trainer was Major Champneys, an elderly gentleman of the old school, a real ex-army type. His yard was immaculate and he was obviously a perfectionist, which appealed to me. There was also a kindly twinkle in his eye, and when he offered me the job I had no hesitation in saying yes. Two years earlier I'd felt that I *had* to come down and work at Bishop's Cleeve. Now, again I had the feeling that it was out of my hands, that fate intended me to move to Lambourn. In some ways it was a logical decision. I'd been at Chris's for eighteen months and had learned as much there as I was going to. If I wanted to progress I would have to move. But, to be honest, that wasn't what was really pushing me. The fact was that in the three weeks since Richard had moved to Lambourn I'd missed him more than I'd ever imagined I could. I wasn't sure whether what I felt was love, because I had nothing to compare it with. I just knew I didn't want to be a long way away from him. If that's what love was, then maybe that's what it had grown to be.

I was sad to say goodbye to the Taylors, who had been good to me. They seemed sorry to lose me too. Sarah, especially, didn't like the idea of my following Richard. 'You're very young, Jenny,' she said. 'Don't get yourself tied down yet. See a bit of life first.'

But like the young everywhere I thought I knew better, and in the summer of 1964 I moved from Bishop's Cleeve to Church Farm Stables, Upper Lambourn, Berkshire.

CHAPTER FIVE

FAMILY LIFE

Just before I left Chris and Sarah's yard I passed my driving test and went with Richard to a car auction where I bought an ancient Ford Popular for the princely sum of £22 10s. It proved to be a costly 'bargain'. After my final day at Bishop's Cleeve I loaded the Ford's back seat with all my worldly goods, put Rip on the front seat and set off for Lambourn. During the eighteen months I'd been living in the flat I'd accumulated quite a lot of baggage, and unfortunately the car didn't take kindly to being used as a furniture van. On the first steep hill out of Cheltenham it started to splutter, and the next minute steam came pouring out from under the bonnet. I pulled up onto a garage forecourt, where I was told that the radiator had boiled dry and I would have to wait for it to cool down before refilling it. It was not a new experience to me as I had seen my dad's van do it many times, but as a result it was quite late when I arrived at Church Farm Stables. Luckily Major Champneys was understanding and asked me into his kitchen for a cup of tea. I was surprised by his kindness, as I'd been told he was quite brusque, but in the months that followed I came to realize that his abrupt manner hid a heart of solid gold.

My new home was a small caravan parked in a field behind the stables. It was pretty basic. Inside was one small bench seat, a small built-in wardrobe and a single bed, which was actually a mattress on a piece of wood. The facilities consisted of a tiny gas cooker and a cold water tap. I didn't at all mind the lack of comforts, though I wasn't too keen on the earwigs that used to come out at night and walk along the ceiling. When I switched the light off I would hear them plopping down on the lino floor. I had visions of earwigs crawling over my face and into my ears, so I quickly learned to sleep with my head under the blankets.

Living at Church Farm Stables was like stepping back fifty years. The Taylors' place had been well run and tidy, but Major Champneys' was in a different league. There was never a stray piece of straw in his impeccable yard, the mangers and water pots were all spotless and, at the doorway of each stable, the straw was turned in, using a fork-handle, so it looked like a twisted plait.

The Major had about twenty horses in training and while none of them was what you'd call top-class they were all nice sorts, and he managed to win a lot of races with them. I'm sure much of his success was down to his sheer diligence. The first thing you'd hear at half past five every morning was the sound of the Major going round feeding the horses. Last thing at night he'd be walking round the yard again, checking everything was ship-shape. His horses were his life and he left no stone unturned in trying to produce winners. His training methods differed quite a lot from today's. For one thing, he hardly ever galloped his horses flat out. He preferred to condition them through long, steady work. There couldn't have been much wrong with his system because the horses looked magnificent and they won good races. In fact, these days, I often use the Major's regime myself, particularly when I'm training horses that have had tendon or back injuries.

He expected very high standards from his lads. Every

morning and evening we'd have to rake the yard, then 'stand our horses up' in their stables while the Major went along the line to inspect his 'troops'. It wasn't just the horses he'd be looking at, either. If he thought a lad's hair was too long he'd say quietly, 'It's about time you got your hair cut, Curly.' He never had to mention it twice; by the next inspection it would be done. He had a thing about clean boots, and nobody in his yard would dream of riding out without polishing them. Some things stick with you. Even today I can't bear to see someone wearing dirty or half-polished shoes.

If something wasn't quite up to scratch the Major would never shout at you, but his approach was just as effective. If you were cleaning tack, for example, he'd walk along the wall of bridles, checking them. Every now and then he'd say, 'This one's not very clean.' He'd then unhook it and let it fall to the floor, so you'd have to pick it up and do it all over again.

One day, his four-year-old grandson Mark came into the tack room with him and soon got the hang of what was called for.

'This one's not very clean, Gang-gang, is it?' he piped up, as he came to one of my bridles.

'No it's not, Mark,' the Major agreed. He unhooked it and dropped it on the floor with the others.

You little squirt, I thought. I could have killed him. It wasn't until twenty years later, when that same 'little squirt' rode Smith's Man for me to win the Topham Trophy, that I totally forgave Mark Perrett!

Personally, I never found the Major too demanding. The higher the standards the better I liked it, because it gave me something to aim for. I might never reach perfection, but at least I could give it my best shot. One of the things I really appreciated about Major Champneys was that he allowed me to school his horses over hurdles and fences. As a girl, I wasn't ever going to get a chance to race-ride, so schooling

61

was the next best thing. At that time the rules of racing forbade girls to ride as professionals, but because I had worked and been paid as a stable girl I was considered to be a professional. I loved riding out on the rolling open Downs at Lambourn. The scenery was so glorious it took your breath away. Schooling over jumps added a pinch of excitement that made it even better. All the showjumping I'd done as a child now paid off. Going round a course of coloured poles in an arena is very different from schooling over fences at speed, but it had taught me to see a stride and to recover when a horse jumped awkwardly, as young horses often do.

One morning there was great excitement when Terry Biddlecombe, who had stepped into Fred Winter's boots as champion jockey, arrived at Church Farm to school a horse called Riversdale, which he was booked to ride in a steeplechase. I was riding a gelding called Domaru that morning and was chosen to accompany him.

'Jenny, you go ahead with Terry,' the Major instructed me, 'and whatever he does make sure you stay upsides.' I felt terribly honoured. Little Jenny Harvey schooling with the champion jockey. Wait till Mum and Dad hear about this!

We cantered down to the flights of hurdles, circled and turned towards them, gathering speed. Beside me Riversdale was going like the wind – a lot faster than I would have thought wise – but this was the great Terry Biddlecombe and the Major had told me to stay upsides him. Who was I to argue? The faster Terry went the faster Domaru and I went. By the time we jumped the last flight we were both going like five-furlong sprinters. As I brought Domaru back to a walk I could see Terry and Riversdale disappearing into the distance. It seemed to be taking him an awfully long time to pull up. When he finally succeeded and made his way back to where I was waiting Terry was so angry that he was almost spitting rust.

'What the hell did you keep chasing me for?' he yelled at me.

'I was told to keep up with you,' I stammered.

'Not if I was getting f—ing run off with!' he bawled.

I stared at him in dismay. If I'd known I'd have held back. The last thing a runaway horse needs is another horse encouraging it to keep going. But it hadn't occurred to me that the famous champion jockey could possibly be getting carted!

As we made our way back to meet up with the Major I noticed a little figure on the schooling ground. He was laughing so hard we could hear him from fifty yards away, and I realized that it was Richard's new guv'nor Fred Winter. He winked at me as we passed. 'I've got a runner in the lads' race at Wincanton next week. I was going to let your boyfriend ride it but I think maybe I'd better give you the ride instead.'

I felt rather embarrassed. I was also a bit surprised. I'd never met Fred Winter before and had no idea he knew of my existence. But I was to learn that very little escaped 'the guv'nor's' notice.

Richard was enjoying working at Uplands, where he had acquired the nickname Pip. He shared a caravan with another lad called Brian Delaney. Fred Winter wasn't one to rush his apprentices, and the race he had lined up at Wincanton was to be Richard's first for his new stable. He was looking forward to it. He saw this as his big chance to show his guv'nor what he could do. On the day, however, his mount, a horse called One Seven Seven, rather spoiled this plan by unseating him at the first fence. Afterwards, I thought it wiser not to tell Richard about Mr Winter's joking offer, or to suggest that I might have done better myself, though, I have to admit, I did wonder!

Things soon improved for Richard. On 30 December 1964 he rode his first winner – a horse called Indian Spice – at Fontwell. It was only a small race, but fifteen months later, towards the end of the next season, he made a much bigger splash when he won the Imperial Cup at Sandown on

Royal Sanction. This led to his being offered some outside rides, and his future as a jump jockey started to look more promising.

I still had no ambition for myself, except to help the Major to have as many winners as possible. Probably his best horse at that time was Riversdale, the chaser who had run away with Terry Biddlecombe. Riversdale won several good races after that little episode, but a few months later he made headline news in a way none of us would have expected. He was entered in a novice chase at Lingfield in which he was to be ridden by Michael Scudamore, father of the record-breaking champion jockey Peter Scudamore. Riversdale had previously finished second to Stalbridge Colonist and had an outstanding chance at Lingfield, which was reflected by his starting price of 2–1.

The Major had been re-roofing some boxes that week, and a load of new tin sheets had been laid on the concrete outside the stables. At about three o'clock on the morning of the race at Lingfield I was woken by Rip, who was barking madly. As I lay there half asleep I suddenly heard a terrific clattering. It sounded like someone running over the sheets of tin outside the boxes. I lay in bed too terrified to move. My heart was beating so hard I could actually hear it. I hadn't got a telephone in the caravan, so unless I confronted the intruders on my own there was absolutely nothing I could do. I lay awake for the rest of the night. At half past six I went into the Major's kitchen for my usual cup of tea and told him what I'd heard. There was no sign of breaking and entering in the yard, so I'm sure he thought my imagination had been playing tricks on me. But it hadn't.

When Riversdale reached the races and Michael Scudamore was legged up on him he was unhappy straight away. He said the horse just didn't feel right. The Major tried to withdraw him, but the stewards insisted he ran. He was in such a sorry state that Michael pulled him up after four fences and said it was as if he was 'drunk'. The stewards ordered a dope test, which came up positive. The Major was punished further by a heavy fine, which seemed very unfair as he had wanted to withdraw Riversdale from the race. All hell then broke loose, with the press having an absolute field day speculating who was responsible.

A lot of punters lost a lot of money, but for me the saddest part of the story was that Riversdale was never the same horse after that. No-one was ever convicted for the doping. To this day I have no idea who was outside my caravan that night, but I'm glad I didn't venture out. My caravan was so isolated that had I met the dopers it might have been me who made the headlines instead of Riversdale.

From one point of view the siting of my caravan was an advantage, since it meant Richard could visit me 'out of hours' without anyone noticing. Or so I thought. He'd only stayed overnight twice when the Major confronted me one morning over our early-morning cuppa. From his seat at the far end of the long kitchen table he shot me a thoughtful look.

'When are you and Pip getting married, then?'

Taken aback, I stuttered, 'Well . . . well . . . I don't know.'

The Major cleared his throat. 'Well, you might just as well,' he said. 'After what I saw this morning.'

It seemed that at five thirty that morning the Major had walked round the corner with a bucket of oats to feed the horses and had seen Richard slinking across the paddock like a fox. No more was said about the matter but the Major's message was clear. This was not the way to carry on. If you wanted to sleep with someone you should marry them first. Now, with hindsight, I think it's one of the few things I would disagree with the Major about, especially when the people concerned are only eighteen and twenty. However, I had a great deal of respect for the Major, so I stopped Richard's overnight visits at once.

Soon afterwards, Richard called round one afternoon and told me he was going into Newbury.

'I'll come with you,' I said.

'No, I don't want you to,' he replied. I felt hurt. By now I'd become very close to Richard and we spent nearly all our free time together. I wondered if he was hinting it was all getting too serious for him. But it wasn't that at all. He had a private bit of shopping he wanted to do. That night he fished in his pocket and brought out a small box. Inside was an engagement ring.

'I rang your dad last night to get permission,' he said sheepishly.

I didn't have to think twice about it. We were in love, and getting married seemed the right thing to do. The fact that we were so young didn't worry me at all. Jacquie and Judy, my two older sisters, had married young. So had my mum and dad. In any case, Richard and I seemed ideally suited. We were both passionate about horses and racing. Richard was ambitious. I was equally ambitious *for* him, and I wanted to spend as much time as I could in his company. I couldn't imagine that I would ever feel any different. So why wait?

There was just one complication. Richard was a Roman Catholic and I had been brought up as a member of the Church of England. I wasn't too bothered myself, but I was worried about how my parents would react to the idea of my marrying into a different faith. They'd been regular church-goers all their lives, and their feelings were very important to me. It was my dad who put my mind at rest. 'Well, if there is a god I'm sure he's not a god just for England, Jenny,' he said.

That was enough for me. I would convert to Catholicism. It was what I wanted and where I needed to be. Although I found some of the Catholic Church's teaching hard to swallow, I was prepared to accept it. It seems stupid now, but the one thing that preyed on my mind was that if I didn't convert, one day Richard and I would be buried in separate graves. To my romantic teenage mind that fate seemed too

66

terrible to contemplate. The downside of converting – being forbidden to use birth control – was something I pushed to the back of my mind. In the first flush of love's young dream it seemed unimportant. In the summer of 1965, after instruction from the local priest, I was received into the Catholic Church.

The next problem we were faced with was where to live. My caravan was hardly big enough for me, let alone two of us. Fulke Walwyn came to the rescue. He owned a little two-bedroomed terraced cottage in Lambourn, which he let us have rent free. All we needed to do was rake around for bits and pieces to furnish it.

Even that wasn't easy, because we had barely two pennies to rub together. I was earning £9 10s a week at Major Champneys' and Richard was on about £14, but after running Richard's car (mine had now conked out for good), feeding ourselves and spending the odd night out at the pub or ten-pin bowling, neither of us had managed to put much in the bank.

I didn't feel I could ask my parents to help, since they were going through really hard times themselves. The government had recently made tuberculin testing compulsory for dairy farmers. To his dismay, most of Dad's herd had shown up positive, which meant they'd had to be slaughtered. He was paid a little financial compensation, but not enough to replace the whole herd. Anyway, he'd bred those cows himself and had milked their mothers and grandmothers. He didn't have the heart to start again. After a lot of soul-searching Mum and Dad sold everything apart from a few horses and some cattle, gave up the farm and bought a house in Enderby, a village on the far side of Leicester. Since then Dad had got his HGV licence and found himself a job long-distance lorry driving, and Mum had started her training as a psychiatric nurse in a local hospital. It was a huge change in their way of life, but they'd adjusted to it without a fuss. They'd always made the best of whatever life threw at them, and when I looked at their example it seemed ridiculous to complain about my own shortage of money. Anyway, I would have lived in a cardboard box if it meant I could be with Richard.

On 2 October 1965, Richard Pitman and I were married at Blessed Sacrament Church in Leicester. I'd always dreamed of getting married in the village church at Hoby, where I'd spent every Sunday of my childhood, but my new religion made that out of the question. It was a big family wedding, but not posh. I wasn't happy at the idea of Dad and my brothers in top hat and tails – I thought that'd be false for a farming family – so I asked everyone to wear ordinary suits. One of Richard's sisters took a pretty dim view of this and refused to come if it wasn't morning dress, but I stood firm. To me it was a matter of principle. I was proud of my family and I didn't want them pretending to be something they weren't.

Unbeknown to me, Richard hadn't considered my 'principles' when it came to the car that would take me to the ceremony, and, I have to admit, when the white Rolls-Royce arrived without warning at Mum and Dad's front door I was completely overwhelmed. It belonged, I learned later, to one of Fred Winter's owners, Bill Shand Kydd, who always travelled in it to Uplands to see his horses. Plucking up courage one day, Richard had asked him if we might borrow it for our wedding. Bill Shand Kydd had said yes at once, and also offered some sound advice. 'Don't ever be afraid to ask people for a favour, Pip,' he said. 'The worst they can say is no.'

It wasn't Richard's fault that Bill Shand Kydd's car was responsible for one of the worst traumas of my sister Mandy's life. Everyone was so overcome when the glamorous white Rolls turned up at the front door of Mum and Dad's house that we completely forgot about Mandy, now five years old, who was to be my bridesmaid. It was only when Dad and I stepped out of the car outside the church that we realized we'd left Mandy sitting on a chair in the corner of the living room where she'd been told to 'sit still and keep clean' half an hour before. We had to get back in the Rolls and drive round in circles while one of my brothers drove back to get her. He found poor Mandy running down the street in all her finery crying her eyes out. I'm not sure that she's forgiven me to this day!

The ceremony over, we went to the Catholic Club in Leicester for the reception. Late in the afternoon someone fetched Richard's car to the door and we set off on our mystery honeymoon – at least it was a mystery to me. I was slightly taken aback when Steve Midgely, another of Fred Winter's lads, got in the back of the car with us, but I just assumed we were dropping him off at the railway or coach station to go back to Lambourn. It was an hour or so before it dawned on me that Steve was coming on honeymoon with us. It turned out we were going to his parents' pub on the North Yorkshire moors, and he'd kindly offered to come along to show us the area.

I didn't feel it was the right time to protest. There seemed little point since it was all arranged. As it happened, Steve's presence didn't interfere with our newly wed bliss; Richard's liver did that all by itself. He hadn't been feeling very well during the few days before the wedding and his stag night seemed to have been the final straw. On the first morning of our honeymoon I woke up to hear him being sick in the bathroom. From then on things went rapidly downhill. Every day followed the same pattern. Richard would be violently ill all morning and would take till midday to recover. When he felt well enough we'd have a gentle stroll before going for a drive with Mr and Mrs Midgely to Robin Hood's Bay or another local beauty spot. The sea air would make him hungry and when we got back he would tuck into supper and a good helping of Mrs Midgely's delicious Yorkshire pudding. Within minutes his hand would go over his mouth and he'd have to rush outside. After three days of this routine Richard had turned an alarming shade of yellow.

The local doctor diagnosed jaundice and shook his finger at him. 'Don't you go riding any horses until you've fully recovered, young man. It could be extremely dangerous for your liver.'

Richard was booked to ride several horses the following week, so he decided to visit our own doctor in Lambourn the minute we returned home. Dr Osmond was more philosophical. 'Your job's dangerous enough anyway.' He shrugged. 'You might as well ride.'

Richard took him at his word and his liver seemed none the worse for it, because gradually his complexion lost its yellow pallor and his energy returned.

Once the honeymoon was over I took to my new life as Mrs Pitman like a duck to water. It didn't matter to me that the loo in our first home was in a shed down the garden, or that our furniture consisted of a second-hand double bed, a cooker which gave you electric shocks and a rickety gateleg table. I didn't mind that we had to take it in turns to sit on an old car seat to watch our flickering TV. We were as happy as sandboys. Our days were spent working at what we loved doing and all our free time was spent with each other. What more could we want out of life? I kept the house smart and tidy, ironed Richard's shirts and did my best to serve meals my mother would have been proud of. Admittedly, I didn't really know how to cook properly, but there was a nice old lady living next door and if I wanted to know what to do with the pieces of meat I got from the butcher I only had to ask her.

We'd been married just six weeks when I developed very similar symptoms to the ones Richard had had during our honeymoon. I was violently sick every morning, and desperately tired by the end of morning stables. I searched anxiously in the mirror for a tinge of yellow in my eyes. I wasn't too stupid to realize that my symptoms might have been caused by something other than jaundice, but

Richard's own sickness had almost put paid to normal honeymoon activities so I told myself it *had* to be jaundice. Dr Osmond wasn't so convinced. As I got dressed I heard him talking to Richard through the door. 'I don't think it's jaundice your Jenny's got, Pip,' he said. 'I think she's pregnant.'

I felt totally shocked. What, *me*? *Pregnant?* It wasn't that I didn't know how it happened. It was just one of those things that happened to other people. I couldn't imagine it happening to me. But Dr Osmond was right. For the next three months I threw up every single morning and often during the day. I was desperate to hide my condition from Major Champneys because I felt sure he'd make me leave if he found out, and I really needed to keep my job. There was no such thing as maternity pay in 1966; if you weren't working all you got was a grant of £15. However, if you kept paying your national insurance stamps while you were pregnant, you got around £95 when the baby arrived. Without that money we couldn't afford to buy a pram and all the other things we needed. I *had* to keep working.

But when you're being sick every half-hour you can't hide it for long. Major Champneys' son-in-law – whom we called Diver – was mucking out a box one morning when I passed on the way to the dung heap and had to drop my mucksack to chuck up yet again.

'You ought to stop work,' Diver told me sternly. 'It's not good for you.'

'I can't do that!' I wailed.

'I'm going to tell the Major.'

'No, don't do that! Please don't do that. I need my maternity grant.' I started crying.

Diver never admitted to telling tales, but I think he must have. Why else would the Major suddenly decide I didn't have to ride out any more but could just muck out and clean tack instead? And why else would his Christmas card contain several pound notes when he had already given us a wedding present?

Money stayed tight the whole time I was pregnant. Our combined income was less than £24 a week, and although I was very happy living at the cottage, cooking for Richard, looking after him and keeping house, I had to budget very carefully. Instead of going to the supermarket and just picking things off the shelves, I always worked out what I needed first and added it up as I went round the shop, to be sure of having enough money to pay at the checkout. Once I started browsing in baby shops I realized that even £95 wouldn't go far towards buying baby equipment. However, I struck lucky. Looking through the *Newbury Weekly News*, I spotted an ad for some second-hand baby equipment. I rang the number, and the woman who'd advertised invited me round. She'd had a baby late in life and wasn't planning to have any more, so she was selling a coach-built pram, a pushchair, some beautiful baby clothes, a bath – the works. She was lovely to me. I think she saw how scared I was at the situation I had found myself in. She must have guessed how hard up we were too, because she let me have everything for £25.

That winter was cold, and the cottage was damp, with no central heating. We were so strapped for cash that it seemed ridiculous to think of moving house, but it was obvious, to both Richard and me, that this was no place to bring up a new baby. Some new bungalow 'starter homes' were being built in Lambourn for £2,950 each and we decided to try and get a mortgage to buy one. Luckily, the manager of the Ramsbury Building Society was a racing man. He was also a fan of Fred Winter's, and when he found out that Richard was working at Uplands it seemed to clinch it for us. It felt as if it would take us the rest of our lives to pay that much money back, but we didn't have much choice.

In June 1966, eight weeks before the baby was due, I gave up work and we moved in to 29 Tubbs Farm Close. It was

72

the end bungalow in a block of three and had the tiniest rooms I'd ever seen. However, it did have two bedrooms, central heating and an indoor toilet. Best of all, it was ours. We decorated one bedroom as a nursery and waited, a little apprehensively, to become parents.

On the evening of the World Cup final when England beat West Germany, I was in on my own watching the match on the television. With all the excitement, Mark decided that it was time to arrive and join in the celebrations. During that night I felt decidedly uncomfortable and on Monday, 1 August 1966 at 10.25 p.m., after an exhausting, thirty-six-hour labour, Mark Pitman made his way into the world. Richard was away racing during the day, so I was on my own. He arrived back from Newton Abbot to find me drugged up to the eyeballs and being prepared for a forceps delivery. Don't talk to me about the joy of childbirth. The whole thing was a nightmare of injections, drips and indignities. I had been told it was quite an experience, but I decided it was one I could well do without. At the end of it all there wasn't even the consolation of cuddling my new baby because Mark had been whisked away to the nursery and was kept in an incubator for forty-eight hours before I was allowed to see him, during which time I stayed in bed feeling rather the worse for wear. There was none of the bonding time they're so keen on nowadays. Probably that was why it took a while for me to feel the 'instant' maternal love I'd been told so much about. I was expecting the band to be playing and the cymbals to be crashing, when in fact I felt like the band had marched all over me.

I'm afraid I found Mark a bit boring at first, because all he did was eat and sleep. But then slowly, as the shock of labour wore off, I became fascinated by him and my love started to grow. Soon I was taking photographs of him all the time. You know the ones! By the time I took him home after ten days in hospital I knew I would die for him.

Though motherhood was turning into a joy, I found being

a full-time housewife and mother so soon after being married a shock to my system. Because maternity leave didn't exist then, once you had a child to bring up that was it. You stopped work. I knew I didn't have natural domestic instincts. After living half my life outdoors I'd have found it easier to live with a herd of horses than become a domestic animal. It wasn't that I wasn't houseproud – I kept the place as clean and tidy as anybody – but I felt trapped and claustrophobic living in the house all day. All of a sudden I'd gone from a wild, free existence to living in a little box. I felt like a sparrow in a budgie's cage.

I missed horses terribly. They'd been a part of my life for so long and now they'd gone. The nearest I could get to them was at the races, and I went there as often as I could. At least there were plenty of opportunities. Richard had been offered a retainer by another trainer, Major Verly Bewick, and on Fred Winter's advice had taken it. Mr Winter had always taken a fatherly interest in our welfare, and knew all about our new arrival. In fact he had helped educate me in babycare. The first time I'd wheeled Mark out in his pram around Lambourn he'd stopped me to take a look at him. To my horror, when I proudly pulled back the blankets, Mark was drenched in sweat. He looked like a blob of melted jelly. It was Mr Winter who gently pointed out that perhaps a knitted woollen pram-suit, complete with bonnet, was not the ideal clothing for a newborn baby on a sweltering August day! The guv'nor knew that after Mark's arrival it was going to be hard for us to cope on just one pay-packet, which was why he'd recommended Richard to accept Verly Bewick's retaining fee. Because of it, Richard had quite a few more rides, and though Bewick's horses weren't always the best of jumpers (in fact one horse cost him four teeth in four separate falls!), he rode more winners too.

After Mark's birth I'd vowed that nothing on earth would ever make me go through that experience again. Richard had agreed. The night he'd come into Swindon Hospital and seen me drugged up, patched up and exhausted he'd been deeply shocked. He promised then that I would never, ever have to repeat the ordeal. Human memories are short. Five months later I was shocked to find myself pregnant again.

After Paul was born, on 14 October 1967, my feeling of being trapped grew even worse. I discovered that it was almost impossible to take two babies racing and I needed so much baby equipment that it took half a day to arrange. All day every day was now spent within the cramped walls of 29 Tubbs Farm Close. I was dependent on my neighbours for company, but I didn't have a lot in common with many of them. I was used to spending my time talking about horses. Their conversation was all about nappies, playgroups and kitchen gadgets. On top of that, southern ways were so different. I was used to knocking on someone's door and going straight in. I soon learned that in Berkshire it was considered polite to wait on the doorstep until they answered. If you walked in when people were about to have a meal, nobody ever said, 'Would you like a bit?' like Mum did. Instead they'd put it to keep warm until you'd gone, or sit you down in another room while they ate. I really missed our big friendly family. Mum came down for a few days and took Mark and Paul out for long walks in the pushchair and spent hours playing with them to give me a break. But she was too busy with her training to stay for long, and Mandy, who was only six years older than Mark, needed looking after. I tried not to show it, but after Mum went back home I felt really grey inside. My mood wasn't helped when, soon afterwards, my little terrier Rip became jealous of Mark and bit him on the face. We couldn't risk him doing it again, so very sadly we had to have him put to sleep.

A few months after Paul's birth the doctor put me on tranquillizers for what he called 'postnatal depression'. But I knew it wasn't having a baby that had caused the problem. It was being caged indoors. If I'd been a sparrow I'd have been pulling out my feathers by now! I couldn't go back to work for Major Champneys because there was nobody to look after Mark and Paul. Paying a childminder was out of the question on a stable girl's pay, and anyway, I didn't want to let someone else look after them. I loved my babies.

Then out of the blue, one Saturday morning, the answer to my problems dropped through the letterbox. Although in later years my relations with the gentlemen of the press haven't always been what you might call cordial, I have to admit that I owe an eternal debt of gratitude to the *Sporting Life*.

CHAPTER SIX

BETWEEN THE FLAGS

There had been a hard overnight frost, which meant that racing was called off and riding out was impossible, so for once Richard could have a lie-in. Mark and Paul were still asleep, so we stayed in bed, browsing through the morning papers and drinking our morning cuppas. It was Richard who spotted the advertisement in the *Sporting Life*. He read it aloud.

'For sale: six acres of land with stables and indoor school. Caravan on site. Planning permission for agricultural dwelling.'

He raised an eyebrow. 'What do you think? Shall we take a run out and have a look?'

'Where is it?' I asked.

'Hinton Parva.' Hinton was a small village about eight miles away. Close enough for Richard to commute to Fred Winter's yard.

'How much do they want for it?'

'It says here offers around fifteen thousand quid.'

I burst out laughing. 'What's the point of going to see somewhere like that? We can't possibly afford it.'

Richard shook his head. 'I'm not saying let's *buy* it, I'm

saying let's go and have a look. Just for the crack. I'd like to see where it is.'

And so we went, neither of us really knowing why, except we had a morning to kill and we were feeling a bit nosy.

It wasn't easy to find. Snow had been falling for most of the night and we had to drive very slowly, peering at the half-obliterated road signs. We passed a spired church and a thatched farmhouse. Then on the edge of the village we spotted a FOR SALE sign and pulled to a halt. We had no intention of going inside. We hadn't rung the agent or made an appointment to view. In fact, we'd probably have driven on to the nearest pub for lunch if fate hadn't stepped in. As we peered through the open gate at the entrance to the stable yard an elderly gentleman walked out and came towards us.

'Are you looking for someone?' he asked.

'Not really. We just saw the place advertised,' said Richard.

'Well, since you've got this far would you like to come in and have a look around?' The man held out his hand. 'I'm Peter Tozer. Pleased to meet you.'

Richard parked the car and with Mark toddling alongside us and me carrying Paul we followed him into an oblong stable yard. It consisted of six traditional rendered stables and eight smart new wooden ones. Half a dozen dished Arabian heads stared inquisitively over the box doors as we walked in. At the far end of the yard, over a tack room, was a little clock-tower, half covered in snow. As we stood there admiring it the sun came out, as if on cue, and made the snow glisten on the roof. It was a scene straight off a Christmas card. I fell in love with the place instantly.

Years later, in an interview, my sister Mandy captured my feelings exactly when I saw the yard that day. 'It was so pretty it made your eyes sparkle,' she said. As I looked along the row of boxes the urge to be back in this world of horsy sounds and smells and to see the horses looking over the stable doors was so strong I felt my eyes fill up. One look at Richard told me he was as taken with it as I was. We followed Peter Tozer around, and the more we saw the better we liked it. As well as the boxes there was a massive barn with a lovely soft sandy floor which had been used as an indoor school, and a couple of well-maintained post-and-railed paddocks.

'Why are you selling the place?' Richard asked.

'I've been breeding Arab horses for years, but I'm retiring,' Mr Tozer told us. 'It's too much hard work at my age.'

'Can we see the caravan?' I said. The caravan was the only accommodation on the site. Mr Tozer lived in a big house over the road, which wasn't included in the sale.

'Yes, but it's not very big. My groom uses it at the moment.' Mr Tozer led us behind the stables to an ancient caravan not a bit like today's mobile homes. He was right: it wasn't very big. There were just two rooms – a small one at the back, containing two child-sized single beds, and a larger living room with a wider bed that had to be stowed up against the wall in the daytime. The seats were simply two wooden benches with a bit of padding stuck on. Near the door was the kitchen area, which consisted of a baby gas cooker with two rings, a tiny sink (no bigger than a washing-up bowl) and a draining board just about big enough to stand one dinnerplate on. It was almost as basic as the caravan I'd lived in at Major Champneys', but at least there was the benefit of an unheated bathroom in the stable yard complete with bath, flush toilet and sink.

I climbed down the caravan steps and stared at the sunshine glittering on the roof of the stable block. I thought how much I would like to be greeted by that sight every morning when I got up, instead of the neat lawn and flowerbed of 29 Tubbs Farm Close. Thanking Peter Tozer, we fastened the boys back into the car and drove thoughtfully home.

Richard spoke first. 'What do you think? Would you like to live there?'

Like wasn't the word. I was *desperate* to live there, but I wasn't sure how serious he was.

'Well,' I said cautiously, 'it would mean we could have some horses.'

'What sort of horses? They'd have to pay their way.'

Since the moment I'd first seen that yard I'd been busy hatching a plan.

'What if I took injured horses for trainers and got them sound again?' I suggested. 'You're always saying Fred Winter's stuck for boxes when his horses need nursing or resting. It could be his overflow yard. And I could break horses in for people. Not all trainers want the bother of doing it themselves. I could use the indoor school. It'd be ideal.' My mind was like a video racing in forward play.

Richard nodded thoughtfully. 'It might work. What would you do with the boys, though? Who'd look after them while you were seeing to the horses?'

'Well, I used to follow my dad round the farm when I was small and it didn't do me any harm,' I said. 'I can put Paul's pram and playpen in the tack room until he's a bit older and Mark can just come round with me. He'll be safe playing in the yard. There are gates all round it, so he won't be able to get out.'

'They can't come with you if you're riding out.'

'But horses with bad legs won't need exercising,' I argued. 'They'll just need box rest and maybe turning out in the paddocks.'

Richard looked even more thoughtful. 'You know, it's not a bad idea. I think it might work. We ought to have a go for it.'

My jaw dropped. I hadn't really expected him to support my pipe-dream. Perhaps, though, he saw a livery yard the same way as I did. Something that would serve two purposes – to help us earn extra money and stop me pining for horses.

'There's only one problem as I see it,' Richard said.

He didn't have to spell it out. I knew the problem as well as he did. We needed the money to buy the place in the first instance.

Actually there were two problems. We not only had to find a way of raising £15,000. If we bought the stables Richard and I, plus two small children, would have to move from a warm centrally heated bungalow into a very small, cold, old caravan. The second point didn't really worry me. I'd lived in a cold damp house myself as a child and survived. If I had to live in a tent or a hole in the ground in order to move to those stables, I knew I would do it. But would it be right to ask the boys to make the same sacrifice?

Our lack of money, though, was a real stumbling block. If we sold the bungalow we would have about £1,000 of our own money, which was nowhere near enough for a down payment on a mortgage of £15,000 even if we could get one for a caravan and a stable block. It was Richard who remembered Bill Shand Kydd's advice when he'd lent us his Rolls-Royce. 'Don't ever be afraid to ask people for a favour,' he'd told Richard. 'The worst they can say is no.'

Since he'd been riding for Verly Bewick, Richard had met his employer's main owner, Lord Cadogan, several times and had got on well with him. He decided to approach him and put our idea to him. He also asked him if he would advance us a loan to help start our business. The first I knew of it was when Richard came bursting in one day after racing with the news that Lord Cadogan had agree to lend us £10,000. It was to be repaid as slowly or as quickly as we could manage.

The next day I left Mark and Paul with our next-door neighbour and went round to Peter Tozer's house to offer him £10,000 for his stables.

'I'm sorry,' Mr Tozer said firmly. 'I definitely don't want to sell it for that.'

I decided to put my cards on the table. 'Mr Tozer, the most

we can possibly afford is eleven thousand pounds. I know you want more, but it really is all the money we've got in the world. Every penny. So either you take it or we won't be having it. That's all there is to it.'

Mr Tozer looked a bit taken aback. 'I'll ring and let you know when I've had time to think about it,' he said.

I went away thinking there wasn't a cat in hell's chance he was going to say yes. When he didn't ring the next day, or the next, I felt sure we had lost it. Then, on the third day, when I had given up all hope, he telephoned. 'I've considered your offer carefully,' he said. 'I've decided to accept.'

I couldn't believe my ears. It was like having all my birthdays at once! We put 29 Tubbs Farm Close on the market straight away, and once again good fortune smiled upon us. The day after we'd first visited Hinton Parva I'd been hanging out the washing in the garden when Mrs Harris, the plumber's wife from next door, who was performing the same task, came over. Mrs Harris was always chatty, and I was so full of our visit to Hinton that I hadn't been able to keep it to myself. I'd told her we'd seen a place and were thinking of moving. The day after Peter Tozer had accepted our offer she came round to see me. 'We're looking for a place for my mother. Do you think I could have first option on your bungalow if you decide to sell?' The pieces of the jigsaw were falling into place.

It was as if it was all meant to happen. By the end of March all the paperwork was completed and on 31 March 1968 we moved into the property we named the Parva Stud. Richard was working, so, with the two boys in the back, I ferried furniture all day in our Morris Minor pick-up. Because of the shortage of space in the caravan I had to park most of it, including the fridge and washing machine, in the feed-room. Nevertheless the feeling of being freed from my cage was exhilarating. It was the right move, I just knew it.

The winter of 1967–8 was a really hard one and our first night in the caravan at Hinton Parva was probably the coldest of the year. I wrapped the boys in extra layers of clothes, and went to bed wearing my overcoat over my pyjamas. Timmy, Paul's new terrier, crept onto the bed and snuggled up to us for warmth. He must have thought we were mad to leave our centrally heated 'kennel' in Lambourn. Just for an hour or so, that first night, I too wondered if we were sane. The next morning, though, as I looked out at the view from the caravan door, I had no doubts. We would be happy here. I had so many hopes and dreams for us to share.

In spite of the cold, racing was still on and Richard was riding that day at Nottingham. I gave the boys their breakfast, dressed them warmly and, carrying Paul and leading Mark by the hand, wandered around the empty stable yard, daydreaming of things to come. The greyness inside me had gone. I was about to start living a new life – the life I'd been born and bred to lead. All I needed to complete my happiness was a horse.

I didn't have long to wait. A few days later a horsebox arrived from Fred Winter's stables and disgorged a big brown gelding. He had a leg injury which needed treatment. No animal in the world would ever get more attention than that horse, I decided. Organizing the stable work around the children wasn't too difficult. The weather stayed cold all through April, but the tack room had thick, panelled walls and a bit of carpet on the floor. Once I'd put a heater in it was cosy enough for Paul to sleep there in his pram, and later in the year I installed a playpen in which Paul would sit quite content while Mark toddled round from box to box with me, carrying empty buckets and body-brushes.

Whenever Richard rode for other trainers he made a point of mentioning my 'horse hospital' and during the next few months I was sent horses by Fulke Walwyn and Barry Hills, as well as Fred Winter. By the end of the year, eight of my fourteen boxes were occupied. Mucking out, feeding and nursing eight horses every day all by myself was hard work.

During the summer holidays I had some welcome help from two young village lads. I'd caught them peeping around the gatepost one day as I was bandaging a horse's leg. 'If you've nothing better to do,' I said, 'you can come in and give me a hand.' They were in like a shot. Neither of them had worked with horses before, but they were keen to learn and were soon filling hay-nets and carrying water buckets for me. Their names were Paul Price and Paul Bentley, which caused some confusion later on when my own Paul started to toddle round the yard. Whenever I called 'Paul!' three heads would spin round to see what I wanted.

From the start, I made it my aim to give my ailing horses as much attention as a human hospital patient received. I was sure that observation was the key to good nursing. Men often say that women spoil horses to death. But I wasn't spoiling them. In my book spoiling – whether you're talking about children or horses – doesn't mean giving too much love and attention. It means not giving enough discipline. I gave my horses both. When I was walking round the yard last thing at night I always had a chat with each horse and gave him a Polo mint or a carrot, and while I chatted, I watched and observed. I didn't like missing things. Dad and Major Champneys had both taught me that stockmanship was about looking at the whole animal. Not just at whether it was lame or sound, but how it was eating and drinking. Whether it was behaving differently from normal. Whether it looked content. I found the responsibility a real challenge. I'd always been conscientious, but now the buck stopped with me. I couldn't afford to miss anything. Running Parva Stud was a great learning curve, and it has stood me in good stead ever since.

I was on good terms with our local vet, Barry Park, who spent a lot of time at the stables. What I learned from him was better than anything any book could have taught me. I had an enquiring mind, and when a vet was treating a horse in my care I would always ask them to explain exactly what they were doing. If they started blinding me with science I'd say, 'Could you explain that to me in English?' It surprised them to find that the most technical details could usually be explained in simple language, and Barry took the time to make everything clear (I've since found the same approach pays off with solicitors and accountants!). By asking questions I learned the scientific principles behind things like antibiotics, vaccinations, blisters, firing, and hot- and cold-water treatments. I kept – and still keep – a card index on all the horses, which enabled the vets and myself to see instantly what treatments each horse had been given over the years – what had worked and what hadn't. We were a very successful team. Our patients got better. Horses that came to me left ready to go back into full training and win races.

As Parva Stud's reputation grew, business increased. By the end of my first year I had a waiting-list of patients, and we were able to start paying back our loan. The only cloud in the sky was our accommodation. Living in the caravan was becoming a bit of an endurance test. In summer it was baking hot, and in winter it was freezing cold. The cold was the hardest to cope with, and in the spring of 1969 Richard and I agreed we couldn't possibly endure another winter there. Before he sold the stud, Mr Tozer had been given planning permission to build a bungalow on the site, and we decided to find out what it would cost. The answer was frightening: £3,500. I didn't see how we could possibly afford that, when we'd spent every penny we had on buying the property. Borrowing money made me nervous. I felt we should pay back Lord Cadogan's loan in full before we considered taking on another.

When Richard rode Steel Bridge into second place in the 1969 Grand National it couldn't have been more timely. His percentage of the prize money, plus a mortgage from the Ramsbury Building Society, meant that we were able to give the go-ahead to Bobby and George Baker, our local builders, and six months later we moved into our new bungalow.

After eighteen months in the caravan it felt like living in Buckingham Palace. However, with three bedrooms, a sitting room and dining room to keep clean, there was a lot more housework to do. I didn't grumble. I prided myself on keeping the bungalow clean and welcoming. I always had dinner ready and a fire going in the grate when Richard came home, and it wasn't unusual for me to be doing the ironing at nine o'clock at night. I was determined not to let home life suffer just because I was working, although I have to admit housework has never been my favourite task.

Luckily, fate stepped in once more. Paul Price's mother, Joan, came round one day to see where her son was spending all his time and offered to help me in the house for a couple of hours two mornings a week. Joan was an absolute godsend. With Mark and Paul in her safekeeping I could start riding out around the lanes and getting the horses even fitter before returning them to their trainers.

As my life became busier I was less and less able to go racing with Richard. In fact, because Richard got up early to ride out at Fred Winter's, and then went straight to the races, it wasn't unusual for me not to see him all day. He was being given better rides all the time, but race-riding wasn't a secure way of earning a living and we would have found it impossible to survive financially without the yard. Our income always dipped dramatically in the summer when the National Hunt season finished, and even during the season injuries could mean that he earned no riding fees for weeks on end. Over the years he'd taken some pretty bad falls. Since he'd started race-riding he'd lost most of his front teeth, dislocated his shoulder and broken an ankle, some vertebrae and his collarbone, and had also had concussion several times. Compared with some jockeys, though, Richard was lucky because he had a very loyal supporter in Fred Winter.

One bonus of moving into the bungalow was that the caravan became free for staff accommodation. I was still looking after all the horses on my own, my only helpers being the two Pauls, who came after school and in the holidays. I didn't mind the hard work, but eight horses were the maximum I could cope with on this basis. If I wanted to fill the remaining six boxes, and especially if I wanted to break more horses in, I needed some full-time adult help. I put an advert in a local paper and took on a young lad called Melvyn Saddler, who over the next few years was to become my right-hand man.

Although at that time Paul Bentley and Paul Price were still at school, they too were to become important members of the team. When Mandy got a new pony, I brought Rocket down from Leicestershire and used him to teach them to ride in the indoor school. Rocket could be as naughty as any thoroughbred, so after mastering him they were well prepared to move on to bigger horses. Soon both Pauls were riding out with me. When Fred Winter heard I'd been giving riding lessons he sent his youngest daughter Philippa and her pony for sessions in our indoor school. Not to be left out, my own two boys joined in, taking turns riding Rocket. They were as keen on riding as I'd been at their age. By the time he was five Mark was telling everybody that he wanted to be a showjumper when he grew up. His ambition was probably inspired by Fred Winter's new apprentice, a sixteen-year-old lad called John Francome, who had recently won the Junior European showjumping championships. John's gold-medal-winning horse, Red Paul, was stabled with us for a few months, and he used to come down regularly after work to ride it out. Mark wasn't the only person to be impressed. Mandy had started paying regular visits to Hinton Parva during her school holidays and she competed at our local shows. She developed quite a crush on Mr Winter's new apprentice and even named her new pony 'Johnny Boy' in his honour.

Usually when Mandy came to stay Mum would come too. She'd spend her 'break' moving furniture round, making pickles and generally helping out. She was a brilliant grand-mother. When Paul and Mark were very small I had a big double pushchair. Manoeuvring it was like driving a lorry – if you weren't careful you'd sweep people off the pavements with it – but Mum used to push it around the lanes for hours to give me time to get things done in the stables. When the boys were a little older she took them for long walks and even camping, showing them how to light a proper camp fire and to replace the turf afterwards, but she was never too happy about them running round near the horses. She was especially nervous about the way they pedalled their bikes and trikes on the concrete apron in front of the boxes. At the time we had a horse of Lord Cadogan's called Fashion House, who was a bit of a character, and whenever the boys whistled their bikes under his nose he used to make a grab for them. It terrified Mum – I'm sure she expected one of the kids to come from underneath his nose with his head missing – but some horses are serious and some are not, and Fashion House was only playing.

By the time Mark and Paul started school in the early seventies, our standard of living had improved quite a lot. At the end of the 1971–72 season Richard had ridden well over 200 winners and was first jockey for Fred Winter at Uplands. He was now sure of getting rides in most of the big races and when he won, or was placed, his percentage of the prize money could be quite substantial. I was still working long hours, but the combined earnings from Richard's riding and the stud made us much more secure. Richard bought a Ford Corsair, which could get him to race meet-ings faster than his old Mini. We could also afford to take a holiday at the end of the National Hunt season, usually with a group of other jockeys and their partners.

In 1973 Richard had rides in the two biggest National Hunt races of the year. Both of his mounts were strongly fancied. Sadly, however, all the dreams came to nothing. He had the greatest disappointment of his riding life at

Cheltenham in March when Pendil, who was unbeaten in eleven chases, was caught on the line by The Dikler in the Gold Cup. I was at Cheltenham that day and was really upset. Three weeks later Richard was booked to ride Australia's top chaser, Crisp, in the Grand National. Crisp was being spoken of as another Arkle. After the Cheltenham disappointment I was determined to be there and, with Melvyn's help, organized another day off. It was to prove an even more disastrous day than Cheltenham. Crisp ran his heart out but was collared right on the line by Red Rum. I was devastated.

For a long time afterwards I couldn't bring myself to watch recordings of the 1973 National. To see Crisp come over the last looking every inch the winner, then to see Red Rum gradually wear him down on the run-in and sweep past him just before the winning post was just unbearable. In fact, even months later someone would only have to mention 'Crisp's Grand National' and I would start trembling. To my surprise, Richard showed very little emotion about it. You would never have known it was his second big defeat in three weeks. The press called him 'philosophical', but I always felt he masked his true feelings.

In 1972 the BBC had made a film for their *Man Alive* series, called *Riding for a Fall*, about the dangers faced by jump jockeys. Richard was one of the stars. We were both interviewed for the film, and talking about it in cold blood really brought home to me how risky Richard's career was. Not long before, one particularly bad fall had made me start to look forward to his retirement. Richard had come home that day with grass and mud still packed up his nose after being catapulted onto the ground. He insisted he was all right and went out to the hall to make a phone call. When he didn't come back into the sitting-room I went looking for him and found him slumped on the chair semi-conscious, with the receiver dangling from his hand. It gave me a real jolt. Risk was part and parcel of a jockey's existence, but when Richard felt he'd had enough I didn't want him to carry on a minute longer than he had to, and when he was hurt I felt his pain. I decided I needed to make Parva Stud so successful that he'd be able to stop riding without worrying about money. The obvious way to increase the income from the stud was to put up more boxes to take in more horses, so that's what we did. By the time Paul started school we were equipped to accommodate a total of eighteen horses.

The trouble was that expanding the business trapped me in a vicious circle. Until Richard retired, I would need more help. Since a business our size couldn't afford another skilled man I decided to take on a trainee. In Newbury all the likely lads were quickly snapped up, so I put an advert in *Horse and Hound*: 'Wanted: lad with interest in racing to help in livery yard. Training given.'

A week later a young lad from Barnsley arrived for an interview. His dad, who was a coalminer, came with him. He didn't seem at all pleased that his son was breaking the family tradition of going down the pits. He moaned on in the background the whole time. 'Bryan's granddad wouldn't have allowed this, you know. He'd turn in his grave.' I didn't know what to say. Personally, I couldn't see the contest between going down a dark, damp pit every day and working with horses. Fortunately, Bryan Smart decided to ignore his dad and try his luck with me. Thirty years later, when Bryan trained Sil Sila to win the French Oaks, I hoped his dad finally accepted that Bryan had made the right decision.

Although Bryan had done a bit of riding at his local riding school, he still had a lot to learn. I gave him dozens of lessons on Rocket in the school before I dared put him up on a thoroughbred. But he had the right attitude and he was a good worker. Six months after he arrived he was helping Melvyn and me to break in horses. Bryan was ambitious to become a jockey, but I explained that, not being a trainer, I couldn't offer him rides. 'Why don't you train them, then?' he asked me. It had never crossed my mind. I was perfectly happy with what I was doing. We had fifteen horses in the stables, five for each of us to do. This was two or three more than lads nowadays would ever be asked to take on, but with part-time help from Paul Price and Paul Bentley we managed all right. Now that my boys were at school I was able to do a lot more riding. Recently, as well as taking on sick horses, I'd started looking after horses that were tired of racing and needed a break. I found an ideal way of sweetening them up was to introduce them to the local hunt. A day's hunting – with the noise of hounds and the hunting horn, and all the stopping and starting – was such a change from the routine of a racing yard that it gave horses a new interest in life. We'd bought an old wooden horsebox which I drove to the meets. Sometimes Richard would come out for a day too but he was rather flamboyant and would gallop our horses across ploughed fields. This, I must say, went 'against the grain'.

While we were following the Old Berkshire hounds I got to know people involved in the local point-to-point scene. I'd never forgotten the thrill of point-to-pointing Dan Archer, and now and then I'd look at my string of invalids and villains and think, 'My horse looks better than yours.' I began to wonder if it might just be possible for one of them to race in point-to-points.

My chance came late in 1973. Through all the years we'd been at Hinton Parva, Lord Cadogan had been a loyal supporter. Any horse of his that needed rest or recuperation found its way to Parva Stud. Among them that year was a horse called Road Race, a great big rangy animal who reminded me of a daddy-long-legs. He'd never won a race and had various leg problems, mainly because of his very long, straight front legs, but his worst problem was his attitude. He was a miserable old goat who was really fed up with racing. As I started to get him fit again, I would turn him loose into the indoor school after exercise to try to cheer him up. I found most horses loved the freedom of being able to buck and kick up their heels after an hour and a half of behaving themselves. Road Race was no exception. He used to go absolutely crackers in there, bucking, squealing and having a roll. In fact it was a job to catch him afterwards. When I added hunting to this programme he was transformed from being a cross old sod into a really happy horse.

Eventually the day came for Richard to ring Lord Cadogan and tell him that Road Race was mentally and physically ready to go back to his trainer, Jimmy James. He came back from the phone with an unexpected message. 'Lord Cadogan says Captain James isn't too enthusiastic about having Road Race back. He wants to know if you'd be interested in training him to point-to-point. What do you think?'

I didn't need to think about it. 'Tell him I'd love to have him,' I said.

For the rest of the season I continued to hunt Road Race and also started to do more serious training with him. I was a great believer in roadwork, and with so many hills around us Hinton Parva was the ideal base for it. I had two other 'pointers' in the yard for treatment at that time, so for roadwork Melvyn, Bryan and I would take them out together, trotting from Hinton to Wanborough village, up the big hill to the Shepherd's Rest pub and then back to Hinton. When they were three-parts fit we started to canter. People talk about interval training as being a newfangled method, but I was doing it unwittingly because, with no gallops of our own, we had to work where we could. One local farmer used to let us canter round the edge of his field, but it wasn't really big enough, so whenever we were doing roadwork and spied some stubble or rough grazing we'd 'borrow' it for five minutes. Though it built up the horses' stamina, after a while I needed somewhere to give them a decent, long bit of work. We started going to what we thought was a disused aerodrome five miles away at Watchfield. We'd arrive very early in the morning, park the horsebox out of sight in the hangar and work round the edge of the airfield. We were very well behaved and always kept to the boundary, but someone must have reported us because one day I got a phone call from the Ministry of Defence warning me off. The point-to-point season had now started, and I was desperate, so I decided to 'pinch another gallop'. A few days later we'd just come off the airfield and were leading the horses back to the box when we heard a noise like thunder. We turned to see three huge tanks roaring up to the wire fence. They stopped about twenty yards away with their guns pointing straight at us. A moment later some men in uniform poked their heads out of the top of the tanks and stared fiercely at us. They didn't say anything. They didn't have to. We never went back.

I chose the open race at Tweseldown on 9 February 1974 for Road Race's introduction to point-to-pointing. I told Bryan he could ride him for me. His riding had come on in leaps and bounds, he knew the old horse, and anyway I felt he deserved a reward for the hard work and loyalty he'd shown. The night before the race I could hardly sleep for nerves. At breakfast I tried to talk to Richard about my worries, but his mind was somewhere else. 'I'm riding Pendil at Newbury today. How can you expect me to think about your poxy old point-to-pointer?' he said.

I was mortified, cut to the quick, but there was a lot to do so I couldn't afford the time to brood on his hurtful comment. I rang Lord Cadogan to arrange to meet him and was profoundly grateful and relieved when he said, 'No, Jenny, I won't come today. You'll have enough on your mind with your first runner without having to worry about me.'

It rained all morning, and by the time we arrived at Tweseldown the course was a sea of mud. I squelched round it with Bryan, pointing out the higher ground which might have slightly better going. But by the time we'd saddled up and entered the parade ring for the open race I was quivering with excitement and anticipation. The red-hot favourite was a horse called Sir Kay. Not surprisingly, Road Race didn't figure in the betting at all – a has-been racehorse with a first-time trainer and a first-time jockey were hardly likely to attract much support.

As the flag came down and the field set off all I wanted was for them both to come back safe and sound. I'd grown very fond of the old horse by now. Bryan, too, was a friend as well as an employee. If they enjoyed themselves and didn't come to grief I would be satisfied. They certainly seemed to be enjoying themselves. I stood on the hill at the centre of the course and watched Road Race fly the fences, ears pricked, as if hounds were in full cry ahead of him. If ever there was a happy horse then I was watching him now. But as they started the second circuit something else dawned on me. Road Race wasn't just enjoying himself. He was going as well as anything. All that roadwork around Hinton Parva had paid off. He was so full of running he looked as if he'd be happy to do two more circuits, let alone one.

With two fences to go, Road Race was lying third, four lengths behind Sir Kay and Johns Joy. An enormous jump at the second last made up two of those lengths. Then, at the last, he jumped up to Sir Kay's shoulder. I watched with my mouth open as Bryan urged him on to sweep past the favourite on the run-in and win by a neck.

It was still raining but suddenly it felt like a bright summer's day. I was so happy inside. I genuinely had not been expecting it. I'd had no idea as we'd slogged round those lanes each morning that I'd be able to compete on equal terms with people who'd been in the point-to-point game for years. Just a place today would have been more than I'd dared hope for. But a win was a dream come true, sheer unadulterated magic. Even to this day that triumph is a most treasured memory.

As I ran to the unsaddling enclosure I spotted a familiar

figure on the opposite side of the course running and whooping with joy. I wondered who it could be. I looked again and did a double-take. It couldn't be Richard – he was supposed to be at Newbury. But it was. He ran across the course towards me, grinning from ear to ear.

'Racing was off,' he explained. 'I dashed back just in time to see the race.'

In the winners' enclosure the press crowded round. 'Well done, Richard. Tell us about the horse.'

Richard was used to reporters, and took over. I stood back, and as questions and answers flew a little of my elation left me as I remembered our conversation earlier that day. I was used to being in Richard's shadow but this moment was mine and Bryan's and I didn't want reflected glory. I felt a bit hurt that Richard didn't sense what I was feeling and seemed happy to take all the credit himself. He'd never even sat on the horse, let alone spent hours training it – in fact the only time he'd mentioned Roady was that morning to call him a 'poxy old point-to-pointer'!

Bryan was over the moon, and, sensing my feelings and to help me get over my disappointment, he chatted incessantly. As I listened to him talking about the wonderful ride Road Race had given him I cheered up again. Driving home in the horsebox that night I was certain of one thing: I wanted to train another winner. And I wanted to do it soon. If training racehorses was a bug, then I had been well and truly bitten.

CHAPTER SEVEN

A LICENCE TO TRAIN

Road Race's first point-to-point win marked the start of an amazing few months. I'd been hunting two other horses that season, and, in the hope that the Tweseldown race hadn't just been beginner's luck, I decided to enter them in some local point-to-points as well. Both of these horses belonged to Richard and me. One, High Tide, had been given to us by one of Fred Winter's owners, who had given up hope of getting him sound again. The other, Red Biddy, had been sold cheaply to us by another despairing owner after she'd disgraced herself in a local show by trying to buck off the judge. Neither horse was a world-beater but the plan to run them paid off. Between them, in the spring of 1974, my team of three horses ran in thirteen point-to-points, won seven of them and came second in three others.

Road Race was responsible for five of those wins. Lord Cadogan, his owner, had had a number of horses in training for quite a few years, so I imagined he'd find point-to-pointing a bit tame by comparison. Not a bit of it. He loved to see his horses run 'between the flags' and seemed genuinely thrilled that Road Race had found a new lease of life. Lord Cadogan was very proud of having been educated at Eton (his colours were Eton Blue) and it had always been his ambition to win the Eton and Harrow race at the Heythrop point-to-point meeting. We decided to enter Road Race in this famous event, and we asked another old Etonian, Nicky Henderson, to ride him.

It was nearly four months since Road Race's first run, and Lord Cadogan felt that I now had enough experience to cope with an anxious owner. We watched the race together from the hill that adjoined the course. It was a close-run contest, and in the end Road Race and another horse, Persian Yellow, crossed the finish line together, neck-and-neck. From where we were standing it was impossible to tell who had won. I felt sick with nerves as we waited for the result to be announced. I was really desperate to win it as a 'thank-you' to Lord Cadogan for all he'd done for me over the years. He was on tenterhooks too. 'All we can do now, Jenny, is pray,' he said. Our combined prayers must have done the trick, because the judge eventually declared Road Race the winner. Lord Cadogan was as thrilled as if he'd won the Cheltenham Gold Cup and I have to admit I was bursting with joy, pride and relief.

By the end of that season I'd started to believe that my success wasn't a fluke, and that maybe, just maybe, I had a knack for training point-to-pointers. But if I'd stumbled on a secret it was hard to know what that secret was. As far as I knew, I wasn't doing anything that other trainers didn't do. I gave my horses plenty of work, but then so did most people. I fed them good quality feed, but, again, so did most people. The only possible difference about my training methods was that whatever the horses' problems I always did everything I could humanly do to make them happy. When I took them hunting I always gave them a full day, unlike some trainers who just turned up at the meet to qualify and then went home again. In addition, I always tried to end their day on a playful note by letting them have a bit of a buck in the indoor school or turning them out in the field. My philosophy was simple. I couldn't bear to see miserable faces in the yard. I wanted my horses to look out of their boxes and take an interest in life. If they didn't, I fiddled about with their routine until they did. Maybe, I thought, *that* was the secret. Maybe a happy horse could overcome dodgy legs and bad conformation and win races. If I please them, I reasoned, they may please me. If I reward them they will do their best for me and, I must say, in most cases I have found that to be true. But point-to-pointing is a small pond, and I'd suddenly become quite a big fish in it. At the start of the next hunting season several owners came knocking on my door. I was only too pleased to take their horses. Apart from the excitement, I could charge more for training point-to-pointers than for giving box rest to invalids, so it helped balance the books. By Christmas 1974 nearly half of my eighteen boxes were occupied by point-to-pointers.

When the next point-to-point season came round, my new inmates were an assorted lot. A bit like the dirty dozen, most of them had problems, but by building a reputation for curing dodgy legs and bad temperaments I'd made a bit of a rod for my own back. At times that season we had so many bandaged limbs it was like *Emergency Ward Ten*. If people were coming to look round, Bryan and I would joke that we'd better hide the crutches. Despite Road Race's successes, he was still one of our patients – in fact he wasn't able to race in 1975 because of a strained tendon – but I had seven other runners that year. Bryan Smart rode most of them, and his riding was starting to impress people. Sale and Mackenzie's *Hunter-Chasers and Point-to-Pointers* 1975 edition called him 'stylish', and added 'should make the grade if turning professional'. It was rare for them to pay compliments, so Bryan felt quite encouraged. He was very receptive to praise.

A couple of my new owners, Chris Tregonning and Patrick Chichester (later Lord Belfast), wanted to ride their own horses, and they would come regularly to Hinton Parva to help exercise Sheer Courage and King Gussie. Having owner-riders was a lot of fun but I have to admit that training for Chris and Patrick did have its frustrations. I was trying to be professional about the job, but the jockey-owners weren't always as fit as they might have been, and sometimes they let me and themselves down. They'd usually ride really well for the first mile and a half, but then they'd start to get a bit loose and by the end of the race they'd look seriously shabby (that's if they hadn't plopped off with exhaustion by then). I felt that both horse and rider were my 'shop window', so drastic action had to be taken. As they'd both been in the army I'd tell them to go back to their sergeant and let him chase them round their assault-course a few times. They assured me they would 'next week', but I was never sure which 'next week' they were talking about! For them, a point-to-point meant a good day out with their parents and mates cheering them on, so I just had to accept it.

I'd learned in my first season that part of the skill of point-to-pointing lay in choosing your races wisely and not taking on competition that was out of your league. The trouble was, you didn't always know what the competition was going to be until it was too late, because the runners didn't have to be declared until three-quarters of an hour before the time of the race. When 'Smarty' and I got to know the ropes we'd go into the declaration tent where one of us would distract the bloke at the desk so that the other could sneak a look down at his book. Once we'd seen who else was declared we'd decide whether or not to run in that particular race.

One horse this policy paid off with was The Rabbi. He was an ungainly creature who had come to me as his last chance, after showing zero ability under National Hunt Rules. When he arrived I'd given him one of my little lectures: 'Here, mate, it's the bottom of the line. You know you've had your chips if you don't get on with it now.' I didn't suppose for one minute that my words would get through to him, but at least talking to him made him look a bit more cheerful.

Richard shook his head as I led The Rabbi into the horsebox on the day of his first point-to-point. 'If you win a race with that I'll eat my hat,' he said (as a matter of fact that's a cleaned-up version – what he really promised to do is unprintable!). As a result, I was feeling a bit downhearted as we set off for Kingston Blount. It wasn't a great race, which was why I'd chosen it, and when we got there Bryan discovered that none of the best horses entered had been declared, so we decided to go for it. Even so, I wasn't hopeful of our chances. The Rabbi was owned by two Welshmen, who came up to me when we arrived at the course and announced that they were going to put five hundred quid on him to win. I was horrified. 'Don't be silly,' I said. 'The horse wouldn't *cost* five hundred quid. Here, give me your money and I'll keep it safe for you.' I talked them into handing over £350, which I put in my handbag.

Going into the last circuit The Rabbi was at the back of the field and Richard's words about him were ringing in my ears. Then, to my amazement, on the far side of the course he suddenly began making up ground. By the time they reached the bottom bend he was up among the leaders and when they came off the bend he took off like a rocket.

Bloody hell, what have you done? I thought as The Rabbi flashed past the post four lengths and a distance ahead of his nearest rivals.

The Welshmen came charging up to me in the winners' enclosure looking all set to squeeze out my liver and lights. I couldn't help myself, I had to laugh. 'What's the matter with you two?' I said. 'You've won anyway and you got your £150 quid on.'

I must admit they gave me some awful stick about it, but it was all in fun. They probably wouldn't have got all the money on anyway, because the small on-course bookies wouldn't have taken it.

I couldn't wait to get home. I parked the box, unloaded The Rabbi and ran down the road to the bungalow as fast as my legs could carry me. As I burst in through the door Richard looked up from his seat in front of the telly. 'All right,' he said, 'there's no need to tell me. I know. He's won.'

All the wind was taken out of my sails. 'How on earth do you know?' I said.

''Cos you wouldn't be running in like that if he hadn't, would you?'

Richard never mentioned his forfeit, so neither did I!

Without doubt, the high-point of the 1975 season was a race won for me on 26 May by a big grey gelding called Biretta. In a way it was Biretta who changed the whole game for me. He was owned by Tony Stratton-Smith, who was the managing director of Charisma Records. Biretta was probably the best-bred horse I've ever trained. He was by St Paddy, who won the Derby in 1960, out of Sun Cap, winner of the 1954 Oaks. He was bred to catch pigeons, but so far hadn't lived up to his pedigree. He had awful warts and bad joints and, probably because they hurt him, he'd turned sour. Tony thought that some tender loving care and a spell of hunting might freshen him up. It worked a treat and after a few months he looked a lot happier. He even started doing circus tricks. I used to go into his box and tell him, 'Say please,' and he'd hold his leg up for me. I soon realized that Biretta was a cut above the class of horse I'd been used to hunting, and I asked Tony if I could enter him in some hunter-chases. These races are a halfway-house between the amateur point-to-points and professional National Hunt races. Basically, they are intended for point-to-pointers who might one day be good enough to race under Rules. I felt Biretta fitted the bill and he proved me right. In his first race at Worcester he came a good third. Unfortunately in his next race he fell, causing Bryan to break his wrist, and putting his own shoulder out. We patched them both up, and by May they were ready to run again, at Fakenham.

I'd never been to Fakenham before. When you live in Berkshire, Fakenham is about as far as you can go in a north-easterly direction without falling into the sea. Bryan, Biretta and I set off at an unearthly hour of the morning in our big wooden horsebox. There was no power steering: just a big steering wheel which you had to pull round about six times in order to get round a roundabout, then you'd have to let it go and heave it back round the other way. There were no motorways at that time but there were an awful lot of roundabouts. When you drove the horsebox any distance you really knew you'd been to the races. After that drive to Norfolk and back I couldn't move my neck for three days.

We finished second in the race, but the winner crossed Biretta badly at the last fence – in fact the jockey Joey Newton apologized to Bryan as they came in – and the stewards immediately announced an inquiry. The upshot was that we were awarded the race – my first win under National Hunt Rules. The racecourse management persuaded me that the occasion called for a celebration and they invited me to join them for a drink. 'Well done, Mrs Pitman,' an elderly gentlemen beamed, handing me an orange juice. Just at that moment Joey Newton's mother, Mrs 'Urki' Newton, walked in and stood next to me. She was a leading light in the hunter-chasing world and an extremely formidable woman who ran a lot of her horses at Fakenham. The change in the elderly steward's manner had to be seen to be believed. He started swallowing his words, saying, 'Eh, eh, oh well, er, not well done, oh this is very embarrassing,' and all but fell at Mrs Newton's feet. I felt as if I had suddenly become invisible. It was crystal clear that the steward thought I was a mere stable person while Urki Newton was someone who mattered. I was both embarrassed and furious. It certainly took the shine off my victory, and I finished my drink and left. Biretta soon put the smile back on my face by performing his party trick of begging by holding up first one front leg and then the other for a lot of enthusiastic kids, who rewarded him with Polo mints and toffee apples.

The fact that we had won wasn't going to be changed by one man's rudeness. Winning, in the end, was what mattered. Tony Stratton-Smith was naturally delighted with the result – so delighted that on the Sunday after the race, when he came round to Parva Stud for a few drinks to celebrate, he came up with an idea. 'Why don't you take out a licence and have a go at training Biretta under Rules, Jenny?' he suggested.

I thought Tony'd had one too many vodkas and laughed it off. But three weeks later he phoned. 'Have you thought any more about taking out a licence to train professionally?' he asked.

'No, I didn't think you meant it,' I replied.

'Well, I did,' he said. 'You've got another three weeks to think about it.' Plonk, down went the phone.

It had never crossed my mind to take out a professional licence but now, for the first time, I would have to consider it seriously. I had to admit the idea was tempting. For a start, if I could make a go of it I would make more money, and although we were doing okay, by now we had quite demanding financial commitments. The prize money for point-to-points hardly paid for the diesel the horsebox used to get to the races. The rewards in National Hunt racing were much better. Just as important, the season was much longer, so I would have an income from training fees for ten months of the year rather than five or six.

A couple of months earlier, without warning, Richard had told me that he was going to retire from race-riding at the end of the season. He had been offered a job as a commentator for the BBC during the next National Hunt season and had accepted. Financially, his decision could hardly have come at a worse time, as both Paul and Mark had recently started at prep school. We hadn't moved them there for snobbish reasons – village schools had been good enough for both Richard and me – but Mark had been having severe hearing difficulties caused by ear infections, and we wanted a school that was better equipped to deal with his problems. Since we didn't feel we should educate the boys differently, Paul had joined him at Pinewood. It was a lovely school, and Mark's reading had improved by leaps and bounds since moving there. However, finding enough money to pay two sets of school fees was a real worry, and would continue to be so until Richard was safely established in his new role, which again would cover only the National Hunt season.

The extra money I could earn from training professionally would be very useful indeed, but I knew that I was by no means sure of making a success of it. For a start, while I was now quite well known in point-to-point circles, not many people in National Hunt racing would have heard of me, so who, apart from Tony Stratton-Smith, would send me horses to train? Even if I did manage to find owners, being good at training point-to-pointers didn't guarantee that I'd do as well if I moved up a grade. I had seen it before with horses meeting mediocre opponents at small tracks only to get seven bells knocked out of them when they ran at the bigger courses. But I needed to earn more money.

When Tony Stratton-Smith rang me three weeks later I agreed to apply for my National Hunt trainer's licence. He reassured me about my lack of owners. 'Don't worry, Jenny, I've another horse I can send you as well as Biretta, and I've friends I'll talk into sending you other horses too,' he said.

So it turned out that in the summer of 1975 I found myself walking with Richard through the main entrance to Jockey Club headquarters in Portman Square. We waited nervously before I was ushered into the interview room and asked to sit down at a table as long as a cricket pitch. At one end, looking a bit like God and his guardian angels, sat Colonel Piers Bengough with a steward on either side of him. I waited nervously for the barrage of questions.

I don't remember the interview too clearly, though I do know they asked me various questions about management and training. They also wanted to know who had promised to send me horses. The whole time I was in there the stewards scribbled notes and passed them to each other, which struck me as rather rude, a bit like whispering in company. Mum wouldn't think much of that sort of behaviour, I thought. One question that I found strange was 'Has your husband made a will?'

'Yes, I think so,' I replied.

'And has he left everything to you?'

I stifled a laugh. 'He had the last time I read it, but he might have changed his mind by now.' (This was intended as a joke. Little did I dream that my words would later come back to haunt me.)

Eventually they asked me to wait outside while they discussed my application, and I rejoined Richard in the waiting area.

'How did you get on?' he asked.

I shook my head. 'I don't know.' I really had no idea. Their expressions hadn't given me the slightest indication. Although Fred Winter and Lord Cadogan had given me good references about my capabilities and care of their horses, I feared the worst. The Jockey Club wasn't exactly famous for its support of equal opportunities. It was only thirty years since Miss Norah Wilmot's application for a trainer's licence had been turned down with the words 'Women are not persons within the meaning of the Rules'. And although women had been permitted to hold training licences since 1966, very few had been granted. I wasn't sure how much the Jockey Club's attitude towards women had really changed, if at all. Had I done well? Had I done badly? I just didn't know.

Ten minutes later, the interview room door opened and I was called back in.

'Mrs Pitman,' Colonel Bengough said solemnly. I prepared myself for the worst. 'We are very pleased to inform you that you have been granted a licence to train racehorses under Jockey Club Rules . . .'

I left my first meeting with the Stewards of the Jockey Club with a mixture of feelings: excitement at the task ahead and the challenge of being a fully fledged licensed trainer, and apprehension at the austere manner of the officials I would now be facing, particularly if I fell foul of any of the many complicated regulations contained in their rule book. But most of all I felt afraid of failure. I couldn't afford to flunk it; we needed the extra money that only success can bring. Little did I know on that drive back from London that things would get a lot worse before they got better. But I took comfort from the fact that Fred Winter and Lord Cadogan were obviously confident enough in my ability to write letters of support, and I had no intention of letting them down.

If I was to attract owners I needed to make a mark early in the season, which meant running horses who didn't mind firm ground. Accordingly, a few days later we went to Ascot sales looking for a light-framed type of horse with fast-ground form. Our budget was £300.

The horse I took a liking to was a seven-year-old brown gelding by Tacitus, small but with good legs, who strode out well round the salesring. His name was Bonidon, and before the sale the auctioneer declared him to be a box-walker – a condition where a horse won't rest quietly in his box but parades round and round so that he loses weight and is difficult to train – and this gave me hope that we might be able to afford him. Obviously it's not exactly desirable behaviour in a racehorse, but beggars can't be choosers. At that stage of my career I was prepared to put up with box-walking if a horse had sound legs, which Bonidon had.

Unfortunately the bidding went way up beyond our limit, but when the auctioneer put down his hammer and announced 'Not sold' we realized that the vendor had put a £500 reserve on him. Shortly afterwards Richard and I paid a visit to the owner, a trainer who lived in the Cotswolds, and offered him £300 for the horse. It was promptly accepted.

When I brought him home it was clear that Bonidon didn't just walk his box. He ran round it so fast he kept bumping his head on the wall. The morning after he arrived, his face was covered in bumps and scrapes. 'This ain't no good,' I thought. 'You're not going to train this one like that.' So I decided to buy him a goat as a companion. It's an old remedy for box-walkers, though not one I'd tried before. I telephoned a lady I knew who had a goat farm in Leicestershire, and a few days later a small dark brown kid arrived at Parva Stud. I put him in Bonidon's stable and watched anxiously for a reaction. I knew that some horses could be spiteful to their companions, and I didn't want the goat to be hurt. But there was never any chance of that. Bonidon's eyes stood out of his head like golfballs, he put his head down and sniffed at it, and sniffed again. Half an hour later he'd not only taken to the goat, but, miraculously, he had stopped box-walking. What's more, the goat took to the horse (Bonidon was so small that the goat probably thought he was its father), and the two were soon inseparable.

Although this love affair was a blessing at the time, it caused problems I hadn't foreseen. The first time Bonidon ran for me was at Worcester. Naturally we took along Nicky, the goat, as his travelling companion. The trouble was that the boxes at Worcester were a bit run-down, and there were no bottom bolts on the doors. When we took Bonidon out for his race Nicky decided he wanted to follow his friend. He pushed at the door until he was able to squeeze out through the gap at the bottom. Two security guards tried to stop him escaping from the yard, but small goats can duck and dive like All Black rugby players. Nicky shot past them and ran across the middle of the course. There, he attached himself to the first brown horse he saw and tagged along behind it, elephant-style.

The first I knew of all this was when I heard a call over the tannoy that made my blood run cold. 'There is a dog loose on the course which we believe belongs to Mrs Jenny Pitman. Would she please report to the weighing room.'

Dog? I thought. I haven't brought a dog with me. A moment later I heard the most unbelievable noise and saw a large gateman heading towards me with Nicky clasped firmly in his arms. If you want to know what the term 'screaming blue murder' really means, try listening to a young goat that's being carried away from its best friend!

It was all very embarrassing. I hadn't even had a runner yet, and already I'd been called to the weighing room. However, the stewards didn't hold it against me, and Bonidon obviously didn't miss Nicky as much as Nicky missed him, because he came second that day at odds of 33–1!

A week later, with Nicky safely bolted out of the way, I ran Bonidon again at Southwell, in a selling race – a race in which the winner has to be offered for auction – which he won. I was very relieved that no-one bid for him. It was my first win as a professional trainer, and his first win ever. Soon afterwards, in September, he won for a second time. That race was also a seller, and this time someone was determined to buy him. When the bidding reached £760 I had to let him go and another trainer took him home. Still, I had the prize money from a second place and two wins, as well as a good percentage of the selling price, which wasn't a bad return for a £300 investment. Nicky, the kid, came back with me and served as a companion for many other nervous horses of mine in the years that followed. I hoped Bonidon's new owner had followed my advice and found him another goat friend to help him settle in his new home.

There could hardly have been a better start to my first training season than two consecutive wins. It was exactly what I needed to attract new owners. As a result, by the time the National Hunt season was properly under way in November I had ten horses in training plus some other boarders. With so many to ride out I needed more help than previously; fortunately Paul Price had by now left school, and he came to work for me full time. He'd grown into a good rider since his early lessons on Rocket, and was enthusiastic and hard-working. In 1975 my sister Mandy also left school and came down to join my team. At first she lived with us in the bungalow, but later, after Bryan and Melvyn found lodgings, she moved into the caravan. There were now five of us to ride out, so we could usually get through all the exercising in two lots. We would then spend the rest of the day breaking in the younger horses and dealing with the repairs on the others.

When I'd been solely looking after invalids and breaking in young horses I hadn't usually seen much of their owners, but the owners of the horses in training were much more involved. Among the first to send me a horse was Ken Dale, a lovely man who owned a large fruit and vegetable business in Swindon. He had a big Mercedes, which he always insisted I drove when we went to the races. After my old Morris Minor I found it terrifying, but I didn't argue. Mr Dale's horse, Stan's Boy, was the next winner I had after Bonidon. We had also purchased him at Ascot sales, but his victory came at Cheltenham, which was quite a step up from a seller at Southwell. I was thrilled enough, but Mr Dale was over the moon. I've never forgotten the joy on his face that day. That win, and Road Race's Eton and Harrow success, were the two races that made me realize that training racehorses isn't just about the horse's winning, or about the satisfaction of training a winner – it's the all-round pleasure it gives.

Sadly, sometimes that pleasure goes hand in hand with pain. A month after his Cheltenham win Stan's Boy dislocated a fetlock in a race at Ascot and a few days later had to be put down. It was the first horse I'd lost as a trainer and I was heartbroken. Stan's Boy was not only very handsome, he was a nice chap. However much you try to lessen the odds, racing carries risks and losing a horse is a very bitter pill to swallow; to me they're not just horses – they become friends.

Arthur Smith, of the Smith Mansfield Meat Company, was introduced to me by my brother Joe, who was by now in the meat business himself. Arthur has stayed with me as an owner to this day, and still likes to joke: 'The first time I met you, Jenny, you were stood on a bucket, plaiting up that Gylippus. All I could see was your backside. I couldn't see the horse.'

Arthur bought Red Biddy from us, and although she didn't win for him she did later breed a foal that won a race, Derbyshire Fillet. Fortunately Arthur didn't continue to name his horses after cuts of meat, but instead started to use the prefix Smith. In later years horses such as Smith's Cracker, Smith's Band, Smith's Man and Smith's Too gave us many memorable days at the races, particularly Smith's Man, who won the Whitbread Trophy at Aintree on 28 March 1985.

Another new owner was the singer Dorothy Squires. She rang me without warning one day and said she would like to send me three horses. Dorothy was an amazing person, almost two personalities. If she was at our home she'd be quite ordinary and as interesting as anybody, but at the races she was pure showbiz: loud, and frankly a bit embarrassing. In her favour, she did love her horses, and they loved her. She talked to them all the time and they responded. She had a colt once who she only talked to in Welsh, which made him go absolutely crackers.

The best horse she sent to me that first season was probably Esban, a nice old grey gelding who, at twelve, was in the twilight of his career. Even so, we managed to win the

Crudwell Cup, a famous race at Warwick, in March 1976. Dorothy always used to like her horses to make the running, but on that day I felt that wasn't the way to play it, so I told the jockey Aly Branford to ignore any instructions Dot gave him in the paddock and to settle the horse in third or fourth place. Aly wasn't in a very pleasant position. Whatever he did was going to upset either Dot or me. The only way he would keep us both happy was to win. Fortunately, his determination paid off and Esban won the race easily. The victory produced a truly dramatic performance from Dot, who hurtled down to the track to greet her horse as he came in with her arms outstretched, like an actress in one of those slow-motion film embraces. Esban and Aly were duly covered in kisses, as was anyone else within a fifty-yard radius. Dot, I thought, you are quite a case.

Of all my horses that season one stood head and shoulders above the others: Gylippus. He was the 'other horse' that Tony Stratton-Smith had promised to send to join Biretta if I took out a trainer's licence. When Gylippus first arrived at Parva Stud it came as no surprise to discover that he too had worn old legs. To try to take the heat and filling out of them we used to take him to a stream that ran through our field and stand him in it for an hour at a time. He'd been in training with Gaye Kindersley who, I was told, hadn't thought much of him. The moment I saw him, though, I knew he was my type of horse. He was powerful, not too tall, and with a tremendous character. In the beginning his character made more impact on us than his racing ability. Paul Price used to ride him out and Gylippus would be trotting along without a care in the world when suddenly he'd spin round and drop 'Pricey' on the floor. It was such a regular occurrence that eventually Paul learned to vault back on again so quickly that neither we nor Gylippus would know he'd been off! Gylippus had another trick: he used to let himself out of his stable, and he did this so often that I had a special clasp made for the bolt to stop him escaping.

My old farrier Frank would take five minutes to get into his box when this clasp was on. After he'd shod him and had left the box, refastening the clasp on his way out, it would take Gylippus just seconds to undo it again. No-one ever worked out how he managed it. I remember one night I was awoken by the sound of hoofbeats. At first I thought I was dreaming, and then I realized. I looked out of the window to see a large chestnut backside. 'What are you *doing*!' I yelled. Without further ado Gylippus trotted off back to his box, and when I arrived there he stood blinking at me, every inch the innocent.

But it was on the racecourse that Gylippus proved to be a real star. In my first season he won his first race at Sandown Park easily and followed up with another impressive win at Worcester. On the strength of those efforts I plucked up the courage to enter him in the Welsh National at Chepstow, which was quite a bold move for a first-season trainer. As a 'prep' race I decided to run him at Leicester a few weeks beforehand, and on the morning of this race I rang Tony at his London office. 'If you want to back Gylippus in the Welsh National, then back him now,' I said. 'I promise you he won't be the same price after he's run at Leicester today.'

Tony immediately sent Cracky, his driver, round to a number of betting shops with a wad of notes. I never found out how much he put on, but by the time he got to the third shop the manager was waiting for him. 'Are you with this gang that's going round London backing Gylippus?' he asked Cracky. Little did he know that Cracky *was* the 'gang'!

My prediction was right. Gylippus won the Leicester race by twenty-five lengths which made his National odds shorten dramatically. The night before he was due to run in the big race, Tony rang me up. 'We're having a party at the Red Lion in Lambourn tonight,' he said. 'I've decided that, win or lose, we're having some booze, so we're not waiting for the race.' Maybe Tony had a premonition, because, sadly for him – and me – the great betting coup never came off. In the Welsh National, when he was looking every inch the winner, Gylippus met the last fence completely wrong. I knew what was going to happen three strides away, groaned and closed my eyes briefly as he stood off too far in the very heavy ground and crashed to the floor, something I nearly did myself (fortunately Tony was there to catch me). Rag Trade, who won that race, went on to win the Liverpool Grand National that year, which certainly made me think.

A month after his Chepstow fall, Gylippus became my first runner at the Cheltenham Festival, when he came second in the Kim Muir Chase, beaten by the firm ground. It was his last race of the season, but we were left hoping for great things. I felt it was on the cards that next season we might aim higher than the Welsh Grand National, and follow Rag Trade's path to Aintree.

Before that, however, I decided to try my luck at one more National in the 1976–77 season. Encouraged by Gylippus's good run at Chepstow, I entered another of my string, a horse called Watafella, in the Midlands National, which was run on 23 April 1977 at Uttoxeter. He ran a blinder and finished third, which was a pretty good result as far as the owners and I were concerned. But it was to end up even better. As a result of some chance remarks after the race I began to suspect that the winner of the Midlands National had not actually been qualified to run in it. I also remembered that at entry stage the qualifying conditions had been rather complicated. I had to read them several times before I was confident that I had interpreted them correctly. That night I went through the form books with a fine-tooth comb to find that I was right. Not only that, but, unbelievably, the second-placed horse had not met the conditions of entry either. I was in a dilemma. Should I object? I risked making myself very unpopular if I did. I guessed that the idea of any first-season trainer (let alone a *woman*) challenging the old hands might not go down too well. Then again the difference in prize money between third place and first amounted to over £3,500, which was a lot of money in those days. The rules are there to be adhered to and I felt I owed it to my owners to make a stand.

The upshot was that I lodged an objection with the Jockey Club, my objection was upheld and Watafella was awarded the race. Perhaps it wasn't the ideal way to win the Midlands National, but it was much better than being third!

My first two seasons as a licensed trainer had seen some great moments: my first winner under Rules, my first runner at the Cheltenham Festival and, best of all, my first winner of a National, albeit a little one. I could hardly believe I'd achieved so much in such a short space of time. At least it proved that my decision to take out a licence in 1975 hadn't been a mistake. Altogether, I was feeling pretty pleased with the way things were going.

My euphoria, however, was not to last long.

CHAPTER EIGHT

WEATHERCOCK HOUSE

Shortly after the end of my first season as a licensed trainer, Richard announced that he wasn't happy with the way our marriage was going. He proposed a trial separation and, early in the summer of 1976, he moved back to his mother's house in Bishop's Cleeve. Overnight, the boys and I found ourselves on our own. I was heartbroken. I wondered what on earth was I going to say to Mark and Paul, and how I was going to manage alone.

Admittedly, in the twelve months since Richard had given up riding we'd been having more arguments than usual. But I had never, ever imagined it would come to this. I'd always believed that marriage was for life. My family was the most important thing in the world to me. That was what I had been brought up to believe, and it has been proved to me many times. Since I'd walked down the aisle with Richard ten years earlier I'd always tried not to let family life suffer, however hard I was working. I made time for outings together to agricultural shows or to the pictures and often at weekends we'd visit Richard's home in Bishop's Cleeve and I would push Granddad Pitman to the pub in his wheelchair for his weekly half-pint ration of shandy, Mark and Paul toddling alongside. Nearly every Sunday, all four of us would go to church. To anybody looking on from outside we must have seemed the ideal family. To me we *were* the ideal family. But not, apparently, to Richard.

Even today I don't properly understand why our marriage fell apart. What I do know is that it was more of a shock to me than it was to our racing friends. Sadly, then as now, jockeys' marriages often broke up when they retired, so our story wasn't all that unusual in the Lambourn area. It's not easy to work out the reasons. I do think, though, that jump jockeys go through a particularly difficult time when they give up race-riding. As long as they're racing they're living an aggressive and exciting lifestyle, and when they stop there's nowhere for them to re-channel that aggression. Some of them find the humdrum routine of day-to-day life hard to adapt to. Whatever the reasons, our marriage was one of the casualties. When something like that happens to you, though, you don't think of yourself as just a statistic. I was raw with hurt. Night after night after Richard had left I sat alone in the bungalow, trying to work out where we'd gone wrong. We'd been so happy at the beginning, even though we were hard up financially. When we were newly-weds, taking turns to sit on a car seat in front of a black-and-white television in that cold, damp cottage in Lambourn, we'd been blissfully content. Ten years later our standard of living had improved out of all recognition but our happiness had gone. We had both striven to improve our circumstances and now all of a sudden we were surrounded by material things and nothing else. I wondered whether it had been worth it. What price success?

The only thing I was sure of was that the boys didn't deserve this. Mark and Paul were upset and confused by Richard's departure. However much I was hurting, I knew the most important thing was to protect them, and to keep their life as unchanged as possible. In the early days I phoned Dad and told him not to let Mum come and stay as Richard and I needed to work this out ourselves, and anyway I knew she would cook a stew – her logic stated that if you kept on eating you would survive – and I just couldn't face any food at all.

Mandy had recently left us to work for Ian Balding at Kingsclere, near Newbury, and I desperately missed having someone in my family near by. Mum did come down after a few weeks. She never passed judgement on Richard, or got on the pitch where our relationship was concerned, but she was always there, ready to listen and to offer practical help, especially with cooking. Apparently on the journey to Hinton Mum suggested to Dad that they stopped and bought me some flowers to cheer me up and Dad said, 'A bloody cauliflower would do her a lot more good.' That's a farmer's logic and typically male, but I'm sure he was right!

Good friends, like the jockey Bill Shoemark and his wife Pam, were also a great comfort. It's difficult when a couple split up for friends not to jump one way or the other, but somehow Bill and Pam managed to walk the middle line. Although they continued to see Richard socially, not a week went by without their dropping in to see me on some pretext or other, to keep an eye on how I was coping. Their visits meant a great deal to me.

I stopped going to church after Richard left, not because I stopped believing, but because I couldn't face people's curiosity when the boys and I turned up on our own. I was so very disappointed that nobody from our local Catholic church ever rang or called to ask me if there was a problem or to offer any support. I'd been a regular attender for ten years, but I got not one iota of support from them. I felt very let down. It's something that hurts me to this day. The only contact I had with a member of the clergy was from a Church of England vicar who'd read an article in a national paper hinting that our marriage was in trouble, and wanted to see if he could help us to sort out our problems. Richard and I agreed to meet him. He was a nice man, one of God's disciples rather than someone grinding an axe for his

117

particular church. Even so, the solution he suggested – for me to stop training horses – wasn't what I wanted to hear. Whatever other people might think, I knew that my love of horses had never overridden my love of my family and that it wasn't the cause of our problems. But I was equally certain that in those difficult emotional times my horses were the one thing that would keep me going both mentally and financially.

It became necessary to put Parva Stud on the market. If the worst came to the worst, selling up would be inevitable but, on the other hand, if, as I desperately hoped, Richard and I were reconciled, it would give us the chance to make a fresh start elsewhere, somewhere free of bad memories. Until this time I had been extremely happy at Parva Stud. Obviously, when it was sold I would have to find somewhere else to live, and that 'somewhere' would have to be suitable to run my business from. I had to face up to the fact that our trial separation could become permanent. Whatever happened, I wanted the boys to be able to stay at their schools, not to have to move house yet again, and not be the losers in any financial settlement Richard and I might come to. To afford all that, I would need to work. And since I didn't know how to do anything else, working with horses was the only option. It looked likely that my job, which until now had been a pleasure, was about to become my lifebelt.

During my first season as a licence-holder I'd already come to the conclusion that Hinton Parva was too far from the public gallops to be practical. Now I decided to look for a property closer to Lambourn, which was where most of the Berkshire trainers were based. The trouble was that Lambourn prices were way beyond my budget. Parva Stud had recently been valued at £40,000, which, when split between Richard and me, left me with £20,000 to invest in a new property. That summer, everything suitable that came on the market in Lambourn was way out of my range.

I'd started to give up hope of finding anywhere when Tony

Stratton-Smith came up with an idea. Like the Shoemarks, he'd remained a good friend to both Richard and to me, never taking sides. Now he suggested that he buy a vacant yard in Upper Lambourn, a hamlet one mile from Lambourn itself, where I could live rent free and become his private trainer. I was flattered that Tony had so much confidence in me, and at first sight it seemed an ideal solution. If the deal came off I would have a lovely house, a yard, and good training facilities. Everything, in fact, that I could want. But I'd always been wary of putting all my eggs in one basket. Life might be pretty bad at present, but if I did what Tony suggested, and it didn't work out, it could get even worse. What if something happened to Tony? What if I was unsuccessful? Mark, Paul and I could end up without even a roof over our heads.

Reluctantly, I decided to carry on looking for a property of my own. My search suddenly became a lot more urgent when Parva Stud was sold, only days after being put on the market (rather ironically the purchaser was Paul Cook, my one-time pen-pal, who had since become a very successful jockey). I was getting close to panic when a local estate agent rang up to inform me that a house with some disused stables in Upper Lambourn had just been put on their books. When he added that he thought it might be within my budget, I jumped in the pick-up, collected a key from the agents and drove straight over to take a look.

I have to admit that the first time I walked through a gap in the hedge and looked down the dusty track that led to Weathercock House I was not overwhelmed. It was certainly not love at first sight, the way it had been with Parva Stud. Weathercock House was a run-down, decrepit property. Its history was the only thing that was attractive about it. Built in 1530, it was the oldest house in Upper Lambourn. Over the years its fortunes had gone up and down quite a bit. At one time it had been a pub, and three hundred years earlier half of it had fallen down; the day I first set eyes on it, the other half looked as if it was about to follow suit. As I walked around the building I noticed that several of the doors were rotting at the bottom so you could see daylight through them.

But Weathercock House had one redeeming feature. It had nineteen wooden stables, and although they were extremely dilapidated with some hard work they would be usable. They had not held horses for some time. Most of the doors were hanging off their hinges, the yard was extremely overgrown, with brambles growing through the back of the stables, and the barn floor was several feet high with layers of rotting hay and straw. The prospect of moving to a place like that was frightening, but at the same time I had no option. I knew this was all I could afford.

I was a bit taken aback to find out that, in fact, I couldn't afford it – officially, at any rate. The agents told me that Simon Morant, Weathercock House's owner, was asking £30,000 for it. By now I was getting desperate. Somewhat optimistically, I decided to put in an offer of £18,000. I telephoned and the next day the agent handling the sale informed me that Mr Morant had been rushed into Swindon Hospital and was currently in the intensive care unit recovering from the shock of my offer. I decided to pay another visit to the Ramsbury Building Society, who had helped Richard and me to buy our first home. A few days later they agreed to let me have another mortgage, which meant that I was able to increase my offer to £25,000, and Simon Morant was able to come off his life-support machine and say yes!

Time was now running out before the start of the next National Hunt season, so although the sale hadn't been completed I asked Mr Morant if he would allow us access to start doing up the stable yard. This would make it possible for me to move my horses in as soon as the contracts had been exchanged. He agreed, and for several weeks Bryan Smart, Paul Price and any other able-bodied person we could find (even Paul's mum helped muck out the barn)

120

commuted between the two properties. Usually after riding out at Hinton Parva in the mornings we spent the afternoons cleaning out, weeding and repairing boxes at Weathercock House. It was back-breaking work. We had no tractor, so we had to move every last bit of rotten chaff from the barn by hand. The transformation we brought about was wonderful. It almost rebounded on us, because when Simon Morant took a look around the yard he said we'd made it look so nice that he wasn't sure he still wanted to sell it to me. My heart almost stopped, but fortunately it turned out to be his idea of a joke, although I never did see the funny side of it myself.

When the sale was completed, in September 1976, Paul, Bryan and I waited outside Weathercock House, my goods and chattels loaded up into a horsebox, waiting for Simon to vacate the property. There was not a moment to lose. We had just one day to move the horses, as well as ourselves, into our new accommodation. For a long while the horses definitely had the better deal. Inside Weathercock House was like the Hammer House of Horrors. The first thing I did on the day I took possession was to open all the doors and windows and start sweeping out the dust. In the process I discovered several metal rat-traps. Obviously I hadn't imagined the scufflings in the walls. For days I amused Mark and Paul by banging on the walls, shouting, 'Right, there's people living here now! Get out! There's nothing for you here.' I tried to put a brave face on for the boys' sake, but inside I was terrified. Some people can't stand spiders or snakes, but I'd never learned to live with rats and mice; they made me feel physically sick.

Because the house was so old I found it quite spooky sleeping there alone. One night I noticed that there was a mysterious bulge in the ceiling right over my bed. I used to lie in bed at night looking at it, worrying that it would collapse on top of me. In the end, after several sleepless nights, I decided to investigate. I took a torch and climbed the stairs leading up to the roof space, scrambling through the loft. The floorboards were rotten, so I crept carefully along the joists to the far end and shone my torch. I couldn't believe what I saw. In the roof space directly above my bedroom was a pile of bird droppings so big it had broken the timbers with the sheer weight of it. If this lot had fallen through the ceiling onto my bed it would have killed me. The next day Paul and Bryan helped to clear it out.

The bathroom left a lot to be desired, too. A pedestal toilet, a bit like a throne, was so high that when you sat on it your feet didn't touch the floor. You had to balance very carefully because of its unsafe fixing; if you shifted your weight at all once you were settled it used to 'buck' you off!

I had hardly any money to spare for improvements, so I had to choose my priorities carefully. After a lot of thought, I decided to renovate the kitchen first. It certainly needed it. There was no proper hot water system, which meant I had to hire a boiler from the gas showrooms to heat water for baths and washing. When we wanted a bath, I had to tip water from the boiler into an old tin bath, put the boys in it first, then jump in myself before it got too cold. For cooking I had rented a small, two-ring gas cooker that worked off gas bottles. The thought of living through the winter like this was horrific, so most of my remaining funds were spent on providing somewhere hygienic for us to cook, eat and wash. Making the rest of the house habitable would just have to wait.

Things were pretty ropy outside too. It rained a lot that autumn, which meant we discovered the hard way that there were no drains in the yard. A crumbling concrete valance ran all round the boxes, and once you stepped off it you were up to your knees in slurry. When it rained the slurry would rise, and when it got high enough it would flood into the boxes. Often, I'd get up in the morning to find the whole place like a lake. John Francome's dad Norman, who was a local builder as well as a friend, lent me an old pump. If it started

122

raining in the night I'd wake Mark and Paul and they'd help pump the water away from the stables: I needed them to hold the wire on the plug while I cranked the handle. I thanked God then for the apprenticeship I'd served on my dad's van.

Although Paul Price and Bryan Smart were still working for me, we were often short-handed out in the yard. I was trying to do as much of the work myself as I could, to keep my costs down. Fred Winter had heard of my changed situation and when he spotted me on the gallops one day he came over. 'If there's anything I can do to help you, Jenny, let me know,' he said. 'If you want me to lend you any lads or anything, just ring up.' I appreciated his offer, but I didn't ring. Maybe I should have done, to make life easier for myself. But I was too proud. I didn't want to have to depend on other people to make my business work.

With so much to do outside, I found it impossible to cope with the housework in a big rambling place like Weathercock House. I decided to advertise for a house-keeper, hoping that my training fees would cover her wages, and, just before Christmas, Judy Trout joined us. Soon afterwards, Bryan Smart also moved into the house and occupied the end bedroom. I was glad of their company. Filling the house up with people stopped me worrying about ghosts.

All this time, Richard and I had continued to communicate and, to my relief, some months after my move to Weathercock House we agreed to give our marriage another try. We'd had space, and a cooling-off period, and now we both wanted to make a fresh start. Mark and Paul's unhappiness at the way their mum and dad were living apart fired my determination to make it work this time. Seeing their little faces pressed against the window on Sundays as they waited for Richard to arrive and take them out for the day had made me ache inside. This time, I promised myself, our relationship would succeed.

Richard moved into Weathercock House to find the worst

of the chaos over. There was still an immense amount of work to be done, and he decided to put his share of the proceeds from Parva Stud into the 'building fund' so that further renovations could go ahead. The most urgent need was for new downstairs floors, to replace the existing ones of bricks laid directly onto soil. Norman Francome came in to replace them, and for months that winter we were literally camping, moving our belongings from room to room, as Norman's work progressed. At times we had to walk around on planks where the floors had come up. Later, while the roof was being replaced, we laid sandbags across the dining-room doorway to stop the water flooding into my new kitchen when it rained. The results were worth being uncomfortable for. Bit by bit, the house returned to its old, half-timbered glory. The wind stopped whistling through holes in the roof and doors. The damp disappeared. Best of all, our unwanted furry visitors were banished for good.

While all this building work was going on inside the house, I was doing my best to train horses outside. Bryan and Paul continued as my right-hand men, and, despite all the upheaval, we had another successful season, with twelve winners – the same as in my first season. It was a relief, because at the beginning of the season the omens hadn't been good. One of my first runners had been my old pal Road Race, who had been out of action for the whole of the previous season. On his second outing, a three-mile chase at Fontwell Park in October, he'd run his usual brave race and had won easily by twelve lengths. When Bryan pulled him up, though, it was obvious that something was wrong. To our dismay, we found that he had broken down badly on both forelegs. The injury was so severe that rather than see him suffer any more we decided to have him put to sleep. Everybody was terribly upset about it, especially Mark and Paul, who had been Road Race's biggest fans. I told them he had gone to Horse's Heaven, which seemed to comfort them.

Among my other horses that year were two new arrivals,

whose efforts to some extent helped make up for the loss of Road Race. One of them, Fettimist, a seven-year-old bay gelding, came to me through a series of chance events. It had all started a year earlier, when I'd been approached by a financier from London called Peter Deal, who had bought a weekend cottage in Bishopstone and wanted a hack to ride at weekends. I sold him The Rabbi, who by then had retired from point-to-pointing. Peter seemed a nice enough chap, though he was a typical weekend rider. He didn't know the meaning of walk or trot, and he certainly wasn't interested in gently hacking around the countryside. He used to take The Rabbi off for long gallops every Sunday and bring him back exhausted. Often I'd have to bite my lip to stop myself giving him a piece of my mind. While we were looking after The Rabbi for him he became interested in my training activities, and one day he asked me to buy him a horse to run over fences. The horse I found for him, again at Ascot sales, was Fettimist.

Fettimist was a seriously good-looking horse, but, like nearly everything in my stable at that time, he had a problem. What's more, nearly everyone in the area seemed to know about it. The jockey Graham Thorner recognized him at once. 'I don't know what you've bought that for,' he told me. 'It'll be a novice for the rest of its life.' But I thought differently. Fettimist's drawback was that he pulled too hard, even at a walk. He was the sort of horse who wanted to do everything at once, and refused to relax. To start with I schooled him in the indoor school at Parva Stud. I thought that being confined would make him calm down and listen to his rider more, and at first it seemed to do the trick. When I felt he was educated enough I started to ride him out again, but as soon as he saw the great outdoors Fettimist immediately forgot everything he'd learned in the school. He put his head down low and started to go faster and faster until I thought he was going to pull my arms out of their sockets.

One day, when he got his 'silly head' on, I decided to try

125

another approach. I pulled him up behind the rest of the string and let him put his head down to pick grass at the side of the road. Once he'd settled, and the others had gone on a bit, I let him walk on again. As soon as I trusted him to be sensible, we trotted a bit. It worked. From then on, whenever he got headstrong, I did the same thing. In the end my patience was rewarded and Fettimist learned to switch off. By the time I moved him over with the others to Weathercock House he had settled down enough to be ridden out normally in company. In the 1976–77 season my faith in him was finally rewarded. My so-called 'perpetual novice' won two novice chases and was placed second three times.

My other new star that season had also been in training with somebody else. Not long after I moved to Weathercock House I'd been surprised to get a telephone call from Holland. The caller was the composer Peter Callander, who'd written songs for many famous pop stars including Tony Christie and Cliff Richard. Peter had a horse called The Songwriter, which he said he would like to send to me to train. Naturally I accepted. The Songwriter was not a very big horse, about sixteen hands, but when it came to jumping he was as clever as a cat. The first time I saw him school I knew that he was the sort of horse who would be able to cope with really big fences – a National horse, I thought, and my mind immediately started to work overtime. The Grand National at Aintree was a race I'd dreamed of winning ever since Crisp had been beaten there. I badly wanted to square things for the Pitman family, especially for the boys. I'd never forgotten Jacquie telling me that when Paul had watched the 1973 race on television at her house and had seen his dad get beaten, he'd been so bitterly upset he'd sobbed, 'I could die!' and promptly climbed into bed and refused to come downstairs for anyone.

For me to even think of winning the biggest race of the year in only my second season was maybe a bit ambitious.

But I thought, Faint heart never won fair maid. Gylippus had nearly won the Welsh National, so at least I knew I could prepare the horse properly.

Peter Callander, though a little taken aback at my suggestion, was eventually in favour of my plan. He liked to have a bet, and was nobody's fool when it came to racing and form. If you mentioned any horse to Peter he not only knew its trainer, but where their stables were, and how many winners they'd had. Like me, he thought the Aintree distance would suit his horse perfectly, but he wasn't totally convinced about the fences. After a bit of reassurance on my part The Songwriter was duly entered in the 1977 Grand National.

Disappointingly, when the day came loose horses gave him a rough passage and Bryan Smart had to pull him up after jumping Becher's Brook the second time, but the experience gave me an appetite for the race. It was the year Red Rum won the race for the third time, and the crowd gave him the most incredible reception as he was led in. The atmosphere was electric. I'd never experienced anything like it before. My first Grand National as a trainer was more than just another horse race to me. It was a big exciting event. And like any good event, it was one I didn't want to miss next time round. As I drove The Songwriter home that night I was already planning my return to Aintree. Next time, I decided, I was going to do better. Strangely, on 6 May The Songwriter won a three-mile chase at Towcester named after the Grand National winner Well To Do. It seemed that for the moment that was to be the closest I was going to get to winning the National.

One horse who was definitely a Grand National type was Gylippus. After his near miss twelve months earlier in the Welsh National, I might have considered entering him at Aintree in 1977, but his leg problems had flared up again. I'd built some stocks in one of the stables and I used to stand him in there in a wellington-boot contraption that circulated cold water around his legs. It worked well, but even so I was afraid I might have to give him another season off.

In spite of being an invalid, Gylippus was his old self and had quickly worked out a system for unlocking his new box at Weathercock House! He'd now left a permanent record of one of his escapes. As part of my efforts to get the yard looking nice, I'd planted a rose bed opposite the boxes. It had struck me as rather a nice touch to have a colour scheme to match my racing colours, and I'd planted Crimson Glory and Blue Moon roses alternately through the bed. When Gylippus found himself free in the yard in the very early hours one morning, he decided to amuse himself by uprooting every single one of these roses. Bryan Smart and Paul Price discovered the damage at 6 a.m., and, working on the principle of 'what she doesn't know won't hurt her', they replanted the roses before I came out to the yard. Of course, they hadn't dared tell me about it, but six months later, when the roses bloomed, the flaw in their plan was revealed. My careful pattern of red and blue had become a messy jumble of colour. I wasn't best pleased, and was all set to telephone the rose nursery and tell them what I thought of them when the boys decided they had better confess their cover-up. But Gylippus's efforts the season before had put my name on the map. Luckily for him, I owed him so much I'd have forgiven him anything.

In March 1977 I entered a horse in one of the military races at Sandown Park. It was a race for amateur riders and, though I hadn't realized when I entered, it was the Queen Mother's custom to invite the trainers and jockeys of all the horses to a gathering at her home in Windsor Great Park. Richard and I had a wonderful time that evening. The Queen Mother was every bit as charming as people said she was, and moved among us chatting easily. I was talking to Richard when I saw a lady in a red dress. I felt sure I knew her. I racked my brains to remember where I'd seen her before but it was only when I saw people being lined up to

128

shake hands with her that I realized that it was the Queen! When it came to my turn to be introduced, Her Majesty smiled and told me how much she knew about Gylippus. It was obvious to me from what she said that she would have liked my job as a racehorse trainer!

This made me see my life from a new perspective. I realized that while I might have problems I had blessings, too. If the Queen would have liked to spend her life working with horses the way I did, then I had a lot to be thankful for. I promised myself I'd remember that, the next time I felt a bit down.

In fact I had to remind myself of it several times over the next few months. My reconciliation with Richard was not proving the success I'd longed for. Partly because of the strife at home, we decided that the boys should become boarders at Pinewood School. They seemed pleased by the idea, but I was devastated by it. I cried all the way home after we'd dropped them off. In my heart, though, I knew that my tears were not only because I would miss them but for me. It was far better for Mark and Paul to be elsewhere, because of the way things were going at home. Despite my best intentions, my relationship with Richard was in turmoil. I felt he'd become a different person since he'd stopped riding, and we were unable to communicate. Just before Christmas 1977, all our differences came to a head. We had a violent fight and I knew this had to be the end – otherwise the boys might have neither parent. When Richard slammed out of the house that night, I knew that this time he wouldn't be coming back. In spite of all the problems that this split would create, a small part of me felt relieved. The stress of lurching from one crisis to another had been bad for us all, especially Mark and Paul. At least now the uncertainty was over.

That night, as I struggled to sleep, I hurt everywhere. I knew I had to carry on for the boys' sake. But by morning the black cloud hanging over me had lifted, just a little. Somehow, I vowed, Richard or not, I would keep going. I had no option. If I wanted to stay at Weathercock House I was going to have to get up and work that morning and every other morning. I would have to try and put my troubles to the back of my mind and get on with training the horses. In a strange way, I found that thought quite comforting. But then the horses had always been a comfort to me.

My roots have always been planted firmly in country soil. Here are my two great-grandfathers, Edward (Teddie) Collington with his 'hoss', and John Adkin. These two men followed country traditions and customs all their lives. *Author's collection*

With my first pony, Timmy. *Author's collection*

With my sons, Mark and Paul. *Gerry Cranham*

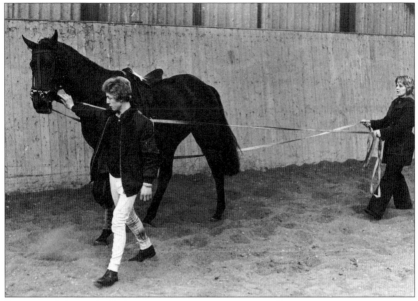

Breaking-in with Bryan Smart in the indoor school at Hinton Parva.
Gerry Cranham

Gold Cup, 1973, Cheltenham. Richard Pitman on Pendil – just pipped at
the post by The Dikler and Ron Barry. *Gerry Cranham*

Training Biretta – my first winner under Rules – at Hinton Parva,
December 1975. *Gerry Cranham*

9 February, 1974, Tweseldown. Road Race becomes my first
point-to-point winner. *Jim Meads*

Watafella,
who won the 1977
Midlands National by
default.
Fiona Vigors

Weathercock House,
looking very much like
it did when
we moved in. *Author's
collection*

Corbiere, Monty Python and Artistic Prince, my three runners in the 1983 Grand National. *B. Thomas/ News of the World*

Working on the beach at Burnham on Sea. *Left to right:* Corbiere, Macoliver, Star Of Arabia, Duesenberg and Burrough Hill Lad. *Ian Stewart/The Times*

Grand National, 1983. Corbiere and Hallo Dandy jump Valentine's Brook. *George Selwyn*

Corky comes home. Ben de Haan and I are greeted by cameras at Weathercock House. *Gerry Cranham*

CHAPTER NINE

TOUGH TIMES

During the next four or five years I went through some absolutely desperate times. My life had felt more or less under control during the previous months, but all that changed when Richard left for the second time. All of a sudden, day-to-day life at Weathercock House turned into a game of snakes and ladders, only there were more snakes than ladders, and the snakes were a hell of a lot longer.

The day after Richard departed, Mark and Paul came home from boarding school for the Christmas holidays, and I had the dreadful task of breaking the news that their daddy had left home again, and that this time he wouldn't be coming back. They were so brave I just burst into tears. Most of the time I managed to keep a brave face for their sake, but now and then it crumbled. On their first night home, when we were all snuggling up together in the armchair in front of the fire watching television, Mark suddenly said, 'Do you want a cup of tea, Mum?' and went off to the kitchen to make it. He was only eleven years old, and the sight of him being so grown up and trying to take his daddy's place was just too much for me. When he came back, I was sobbing my heart out. 'Don't cry, Mum,' he said, ''cos when you cry it makes me want to cry too. We'll just have to start at the beginning, that's all.' When you hear your kids say that sort of thing it makes you think you don't deserve them, but there's one thing I felt sure of: they didn't deserve us.

If it hadn't been for Mark and Paul, and loving them to death the way I did, I don't know how I'd have kept going through the next year. I don't even know how I'd have got through the next month. They say that it never rains without it pouring. Two days before Christmas I was to discover the truth of this for myself. It had been a horrible day, with gales blowing and rain lashing down. I was in the feed-house, mixing the horses' dinner, when I suddenly got a terrible stomachache. I waited a minute or so for it to pass, the way bellyaches usually do. When it didn't, I asked Bryan to take over the feeding, went indoors and crept up to bed. By the time Bryan finished with the horses and came upstairs to ask if I wanted some dinner, I could hardly speak for the pain. Outside, the wind had got worse and was rattling the ancient bedroom windows. All of a sudden, as I was rolling about in agony, the top section of the window blew in and crashed to the floor. As if things hadn't been bad enough already, I was now freezing cold as well. Judy Trout, who'd been cooking dinner in the kitchen, came upstairs and stood with Bryan at the end of my bed, discussing what to do about me. Bryan's first idea was to give me some Milk of Magnesia. I'm afraid I told him to put it in an orifice of his own. That suggestion made them immediately call our local GP, Dr Osmond.

A brief examination was all the doctor needed. 'Appendicitis!' he declared. An ambulance was called and three hours later I was being wheeled to the operating theatre at Princess Margaret Hospital in Swindon. I hadn't been much looking forward to spending Christmas Day at home that year, but that would have been better than the way I did spend it – in hospital recovering from an emergency operation. Fortunately, when the chips are down, your true friends show their colours. Judy Trout had been due to take Christmas off, but she volunteered to come in and help out. When my elder sister Jacquie heard the news, she dropped everything, packed her own four children and their Christmas presents in the car and came down from Leicester with her husband Peter to look after Mark and Paul. It wasn't the first time Jacquie had played Florence Nightingale. Years ago she'd been the one who'd read me books and spent hours sitting with me while I recovered from my fractured skull. I was heartbroken at not being able to spend Christmas Day with Mark and Paul, but I was so ill that I only saw them briefly with their sad, worried little faces trying to be cheerful. Throughout I felt a black cloud hanging over me, but I knew I had to be positive because my new star, Lord Gulliver, was being aimed at a novice hurdle race, the Panama Cigar Hurdle, at Newbury on New Year's Eve 1977 and I had no intention of missing it. I *had* to be well.

Lord Gulliver, like The Songwriter, was owned by Peter Callander. He was a five-year-old gelding whom I had bought in Ireland. It was quite a change for me to have raw material to work with, instead of 'second-hand' horses, and I was enjoying the challenge. Lord Gulliver was a lovely big chasing horse, so handsome and a real character, who now shared his box with Nicky the goat. He had taken brilliantly to jumping when I'd schooled him over hurdles, and although it was early days to start dreaming, I felt sure that one day he would make a chaser, and a very good chaser, too. Who knew where I might end up with him? Ever since I'd learned about the Grand National in *National Velvet*, all those years before, winning the National had been my dream. If ever I'd seen a potential Aintree horse it was Lord Gulliver, so it was quite natural for me to be desperate to see his first race.

It was probably not the wisest move in the world to virtually discharge myself from hospital and persuade Jacquie and Peter to drive me to the races. Since the operation a week before, I'd hardly eaten a thing and had only been able to keep down sips of water. I gathered, from comments people made, that I didn't look too grand either. In fact some were bold enough to tell me I looked shocking. In order to appease the hospital staff I'd agreed to use a wheelchair supplied by the racecourse, but when I got to the races I was horrified to be presented with what looked like a large child's pushchair. 'I ain't getting in that no matter what,' I told Jacquie. She was furious and did her best to persuade me, but this was my first racecourse appearance since Richard had left me, and I wanted to look dignified and in control. I had no intention of looking like I was 'licked', even though I felt dreadful.

In view of everything else that had gone wrong in the past two weeks, I suppose I shouldn't have been surprised that Paul Price had forgotten to bring Lord Gulliver's passport. A racing passport confirms a horse's identity, and without it Lord Gulliver wouldn't be allowed to run. When I heard the news, what little blood I had left drained from my face, and I felt faint and weak. Maybe it showed, because, for the first time I could remember, the stewards showed signs of humanity. Passports had to be presented forty-five minutes before the race. According to the weighing-room clock it was exactly two minutes past the deadline when Paul hurtled back in and threw the passport on the desk. That's it, I thought. They won't let him run. But, amazingly, the steward who'd been waiting for it declared, 'That's fine.' I could have kissed him. All of a sudden I felt tons better; in fact I think I could have run the race myself. In the event Lord Gulliver finished third, behind two much more experienced horses. It was an extremely promising first run, and I returned home from Newbury exhausted but very happy.

Just two days later I was back in hospital. After returning home from the races I'd had trouble getting into bed. By the next night, Sunday, I was finding moving so painful that Mark and Paul slept on a mattress on the floor in my room so that they could pull me up if I needed to go to the bathroom. It was obvious that something was badly wrong. It was our vet, Barry Park, who worked out what it was, when he visited the yard the next day to treat a horse, and afterwards came into the house to see how I was getting on. He sat on the end of the bed, grabbed my foot, which was sticking out from under the covers, and gave it a friendly waggle. I nearly hit the ceiling. It felt as though my insides were being ripped out. Barry gave me a thoughtful look. 'You've got an infection, Mother,' he said. I may have told him where to get off, but Judy took it upon herself to ring the doctor anyway. 'The vet's been in to have a look at Mrs Pitman,' she announced to the surprised receptionist. 'He says she's got an infection.'

Back in hospital they discovered an abscess deep in my abdomen, which, they explained, sometimes happened if an infected appendix touched another organ as it was being removed. Trust me to have needed an operation on Christmas Eve! The infection necessitated several weeks of treatment, including daily drainage and dressing-changing by the district nurse. Like all chronic infections, it left me feeling very run-down and tired, at a time when I needed all my strength.

The boys were due back at boarding school in the middle of January, and I decided to visit their headmaster before term started to explain the situation at home. I was apprehensive about airing my private affairs, but it was possible that Mark or Paul might appear distressed or upset and if this happened I wanted the headmaster to know why. He was very understanding, and over the next few years he and the boys' housemasters were very supportive of me. There was no question of taking the boys away from school. However difficult it might be, I was determined that a way would be found to pay the fees. Losing their father was traumatic enough for them, without having to be parted from their school where they had settled in so well.

Soon after Mark and Paul started their new term, I made an appointment to see my solicitor, Eric Smith, and my accountant Robin Platt. Richard and I had now agreed that a divorce was inevitable, so I was anxious to get it over with and reach a financial settlement. Dad had always taught us to face up to situations, and I didn't want to live for months or years in limbo, not knowing where I stood. I needed to learn the worst, so I could move forward and get on with my life. The thing I dreaded most was being told I would have to sell Weathercock House. After nearly eighteen months I looked on it as my home. I'd bought it and slaved on it. It was ideal for doing my job, and I desperately wanted to stay there. But I had the most dreadful fear I was going to lose it.

Because Richard and I had been reconciled for a year, and he'd invested his share of the proceeds from Parva Stud in renovation work, half of Weathercock House now belonged to him. If I wanted to stay, I would have to buy him out. The trouble was that our improvements, together with a buoyant housing market, had increased the house's value dramatically. Eighteen months earlier I had paid £25,000 for it. Now to my horror, independent valuers declared it to be worth £70,000. In order to buy Richard out, I would have to find £35,000.

Hearing that news from Robin Platt felt like having Henry Cooper 'sock me one'. Where was I going to find that sort of money? Most of my nineteen boxes were occupied, but even so my income from training horses barely covered our day-to-day running costs. Even if we lived off baked beans, it would take me years to pay Richard off. Since he was planning to buy a new home of his own I doubted he'd show that much patience. It looked as if my dream of carrying on at Weathercock House might be an impossibility.

I deeply regretted our brief, unhappy reconciliation. If we hadn't tried to patch our marriage up, Weathercock House would still have been uncomfortable and dilapidated, but at least it would have been mine. And most of the time we'd spent together had been a nightmare. Even so, Eric Smith and Robin Platt refused to let me despair. They recommended me to apply for a bank loan and promised that if I did they would come with me and add their professional weight to my case.

A week later I got myself ready for an interview with the manager at Lloyds Bank, High Street, Swindon. It took me nearly an hour, and several changes of clothes. I felt the look that was called for was smart but slightly threadbare. I didn't want to appear totally skint so that I wouldn't be able to repay him, but I didn't want to give the impression that I didn't need the money either. When I was satisfied with what I saw in the mirror I climbed into the car with Eric and Robin and set off for Swindon.

'What do you want me to do?' I asked them.

'Sit there and say nothing,' said Eric firmly. Robin nodded. 'That's the best contribution you can make, Jenny. Just leave the talking to us.'

By the time we were ushered in to the bank manager's office I was shaking like a leaf. He did nothing whatsoever to put me at my ease. I'd never met such a cold fish in my life. I sat in front of him, strategically parked between Robin and Eric, no doubt so that either or both could give me a dig if necessary. Robin kicked off by giving the manager all the relevant facts about my business, and its success to date. Where is he getting this from? I thought. Then Eric Smith started spouting my virtues and giving me a glowing character reference.

The bank manager listened, stony-faced. I thought he looked more like a statue than a human being. I could see he was having none of it. There weren't many women running their own businesses at that time, let alone racehorse trainers, and he obviously thought that I was a very risky venture. When Eric finished speaking, the bank manager waited for a moment before clearing his throat. 'Mrs Pitman,' he said. 'I do feel it would be better from everybody's point of view if you stayed in partnership with Mr Pitman for business purposes. That way you would avoid needing to raise so much capital to buy him out.' I hadn't expected it to be easy, but this suggestion was unacceptable.

Up to that point, I had sat like a mouse, not speaking a word, on my very best behaviour, but now I'd had enough. I turned to Eric. 'I know you told me to sit here and say nothing,' I said, 'but I'm sorry, I'm going to have my say.'

A look of horror came over Eric's and Robin's faces. I could read their thoughts and sensed their silent pleadings. *Don't, Jenny, please don't.* I looked away and ignored them. 'If you can't be married to somebody, then you can't work together in a business partnership either,' I said firmly. 'It wouldn't be any good. How can you work with someone if you don't trust them? What I need is a bank loan. If you give it to me I promise I'll work all the hours that God sends to pay it back. If I have to work all day and all night, if I have to cut the grass verges with nail-scissors, then that's what I'll do, but I *will* pay you back.' I could feel my emotions rushing to the surface and quickly regained control of them. I knew that if I were to shed just one tear all would be lost.

There was a long silence. Then the bank manager stood up and held out his hand. His face still didn't show one single glimmer of expression. Nothing, absolutely nothing. 'I'll review the situation and come back to you in a few days, Mrs Pitman,' he said.

In the car on the way back I felt a bit unwell. I wasn't sure whether it was the after effects of my abscess or of the interview. In the front the two men were chatting away about everything under the sun except my loan, trying to be jovial. By halfway home I'd had enough of their flannel and decided to confront them.

'They're not going to lend me that money, are they?' I asked. I could tell from the way Eric and Plattie looked at each other that they thought that was true. They told me

138

they'd get the money from somewhere. 'Just get on with training the horses and don't worry,' said Eric. I thought, I hope to Christ you're not going to rob a bank.

We were all wrong. Four days later a letter arrived from the bank authorizing the loan. I'd been given a reprieve. I stared at the letter in disbelief. For the time being, at least, we could stay at Weathercock House, the boys could keep their home, and I would be able to carry on training. I would *have* to carry on training. Before, there had always been the comforting thought that if the business ran into trouble, Richard's income would help bail us out. Now I was on my own.

When you find yourself man-overboard in the ocean, all of a sudden you swim an awful lot better than you ever thought you could. After twelve years of being part of a couple, living and working on my own was never going to be easy, but I adapted to it better than some people expected. Better than *I* expected, actually. The fact that my job was in the public arena probably helped, though it didn't feel like it at the time. Like most women whose marriages have failed, I didn't want to face people. Left to my own devices, I'd probably have shut myself away and lived like a hermit. But that wasn't an option. I had runners to take to the races. So, because I didn't want the world to see me as a victim, I dressed up extra smartly, put on a bit more make-up than normal and tried to look as if I hadn't a care in the world. A woman's make-up bag contains a world of different masks and I've used a lot of them over the years.

The only time my defences slipped during those early months on my own was one spring day at Brighton races. I had a runner on the Flat and as I was walking from the stables to the weighing room I passed two women. Their heads swivelled as I walked by, and I overheard one say to the other, 'There's that Jenny Pitman. Did you read about her in the newspapers?' I froze. A moment before, I'd been walking along minding my own business, getting along okay.

Not brilliantly, but okay, under control. Suddenly I felt that control threatened. Maybe I should have been prepared. My divorce had recently come through, and there had been stories in the gossip columns about Richard's involvement with a younger woman. But nothing can prepare you for having your private life turned into public property.

Eventually I learned to cope with it. From then on, before I set off for the races, I used to psych myself up and put on a mental layer of 'armour-plating'. It was a technique that was also useful in other situations, closer to home. Even in my first season as a trainer I'd never felt really accepted by the Lambourn 'establishment'. Now, my feeling of 'not belonging' got worse. It wasn't just that I was a woman. I was also divorced, from the wrong side of the tracks, and my accent didn't fit. One or two trainers used to look at me and speak to me as if I'd just crawled out from under a stone. Thank God there were others who behaved like knights in shining armour. One morning, when I was still recovering from appendicitis, I was up on the gallops in my old pick-up. It wasn't unusual at that time for me to get up there and suddenly find myself throwing up because I shouldn't have been outside the house. That particular morning I was leaning against the front of my pick-up, holding onto the bonnet because I felt just about done for. I wasn't aware that anybody could see me until suddenly a voice behind me said, 'What are you doing up here, Jenny?' I span round to see David Nugent, the owner of the Lambourn gallops and a gentleman trainer. He had driven up in his Range Rover while I was concentrating on the activities of my insides.

I tried to regain my dignity. 'I've come to see my horses work,' I said. 'You don't look at all well,' he said. 'Get into my car.' I was cold and past arguing, so I climbed inside next to him. He turned up the heater and pointed to the glove compartment. 'There's a drink in there,' he said. 'You look as though you could do with it.' Alcohol was the last thing I wanted, but to oblige him I pretended to take a sip from his hip flask. Whether it was the kindness or the smell of brandy I don't know, but I felt just a little better. I have never forgotten that incident, nor would I. David Nugent was always lovely to me. So were Fred Winter and Fulke Walwyn. They were the most genuine people you could meet and they always treated me with the utmost kindness.

I'd never had what you'd call a depressive personality, but if you're a human being and you get one stress piled on top of you after another, then eventually it gets you down. That spring, after the boys went back to school, I came as close to experiencing real depression as I ever want to get. Night after night I'd sit on my own and watch the small telly in my living room. In those days, at close-down, a little dot would come up on the screen, and then the national anthem would play. I'd sit there all evening till 'God Save the Queen', but I couldn't have told you what I'd watched. I was living in a daze. I probably hadn't fully recovered from my infection. I certainly wasn't eating properly. In the space of a few months I became as thin as a lath.

Towards the end of the season, to make matters worse, my pick-up broke down. It meant I was left without transport, and had to hitch a lift everywhere. I was at my lowest ebb. I just didn't see how I could keep going for another season. My dream of carrying on training seemed in tatters. One day I begged a lift to Wincanton races from Fred Winter. Johnny Francome was driving, and Fred Winter turned round to face me in the back seat. It was as if he could read what was going through my mind. 'What are you going to do, Jenny?' he asked. I shrugged. 'I'm probably going to pack it in and get another job.' He looked at me sternly over the top of his glasses. 'Like what?' 'I dunno,' I said. 'Working in a shoe shop or something.'

I thought he was going to explode. For the next half-hour he gave me the biggest rollocking I have ever had. He went on and on about how I wasn't to give up, how everyone went through rough times and wanted to throw in the towel, but how you just had to hang on until your luck turned. 'If you carry on doing your job right, Jenny,' he promised, 'then in the end your luck will turn. Believe me.'

For the rest of the journey I sat in silence, mulling over his words. In my heart I knew what he was saying could be right. I'd needed a pep talk, and it had come at just the right time. But I had to hang on for a long time before that turning point arrived. For years after Richard left, life was a battle. When you're struggling against the world, everything is such an effort. Sometimes I even had to force myself to tack up and ride out. But once I'd done it I never regretted it. An hour or so on horseback up on the Downs, high above Lambourn, always made me feel better. Riding is the best therapy in the world and being with my horses was the best and only therapy I needed.

Sometimes, though, it was painful therapy. A couple of years earlier, while I'd still been at Hinton Parva, I'd had a fall on the road and damaged my hip. Ever since then riding with short leathers had been uncomfortable, especially in cold weather. Coming back from the gallops I'd have to take my bad leg out of the stirrup and let it hang down till the ache eased off a bit.

In both my previous seasons I'd had twelve winners, but in 1977–78 I managed only six. This was bad news. It meant that new owners weren't encouraged to come to me, plus there wasn't much prize money to help balance my books. Paying off my bank loan was a constant worry. But I had always been resourceful in keeping my cash-flow healthy. One of my owners was a farmer, and when he offered to pay his training bills in hay I gratefully accepted. Somehow Peter Callander heard of this arrangement, and he sent me the following letter.

Dear Jenny,
I think this bartering is an excellent idea and I have
decided to employ the same system. Please accept the

chorus written below for your next month's bill. I will
send a couple of verses to cover the following month.

'Oh my Deario – my dearest deario,
I must say cheerio – to you tonight
Oh my deario – my sweetest deario
I feel so weario – I must go home.'

If you find I have overpaid you with the above please
feel free to put one or two words into the lads' holiday
fund.
Best wishes
Peter

Peter was constantly trying to think of ways of keeping
my spirits up. I think he saw himself as my guardian angel,
steering me through life's difficult patches. When I was out
with Peter and his wife Connie I used to feel like a little girl
being taken out for her first ice-cream. Not that I objected
to being looked after. At that time I needed all the tlc I
could get.

Peter and I decided to enter The Songwriter in the Grand
National for a second time in 1978. The Aintree meeting fell
during the school Easter holidays and, as a treat, I took Paul
and Mark up to Liverpool for the race. Peter and Connie
met us, and as usual were very generous, not only paying for
the boys and me to stay in their hotel, but taking us out to
dinner in a smart restaurant the night before the race. We
were having a lovely time until the sweet trolley came round,
with a big bowl of strawberries on top. I nearly choked when
I saw them. I'd never ever seen strawberries in April and I
thought they must be expensive.

'What would you like, boys?' Peter asked.

I saw Mark's eyes roam the trolley. I wanted to put my
hand over his mouth to stop him speaking, but it was too
late. I'm sure he sensed my anxiety, so he quickly blurted

143

out, 'May I have some strawberries, please?' before I could stop him.

Dear Peter didn't bat an eyelid. Mark seemed totally unaware of my embarrassment, and ate his fill.

The next day The Songwriter rewarded Peter handsomely by skipping round Aintree and finishing eighth to Lucius. Since he hadn't been quite as fit as I would have liked because of training problems, his performance encouraged me. I can do better than this, I thought, and once again I decided to keep trying my luck at Aintree.

One of my horses that season was a gelding called Golden Bob, who was owned by a group of friends. One member of this group, a builder called David Stait, had become friendly with Bryan Smart, and visited the yard quite often. As a result, he was one of the few owners who hadn't just seen my public face but had sometimes seen me at my lowest ebb.

One evening David, Bryan and Bryan's girlfriend Debbie asked me to go with them to a nearby pub for a steak. I said no at first, but they refused to leave the house unless I joined them, so in the end, with rather bad grace, I agreed. I was surprised at how much I enjoyed myself. I actually found myself laughing. It was a noise I hadn't heard for so long, it sounded strange in my ears. For the first time I realized how morose I'd become. We repeated our evening out a few times after that, and David started to drop in at the stables more often.

In the beginning I think he simply felt concerned for me. And because I was grateful for that concern I started to look forward to his visits. David had a wicked sense of humour, similar to my own, and always seemed able to make me laugh. He was also a handy person to have around the house. It was David who mended the cooker door that was hanging off and who finally fixed the window that had blown in the night I had appendicitis. All winter there'd been a board wedged in the space where the glass had come out. When David restored it without charge I was able to take several

144

layers of blankets off my bed. I was terribly grateful, but it was several months before I admitted to myself that my feelings for David had grown into something more than gratitude.

I tried to resist it. The thought of getting involved with someone terrified me. I didn't want to risk being hurt by another man. Once was enough. On top of that, there were Mark's and Paul's feelings to consider. They were coping pretty well, but I didn't know how they'd respond to the idea of a new man in my life. Fortunately, they'd got to know David while our relationship was still at the 'just good friends' stage, and they'd hit it off very well. David has a genuine knack for getting on with children. He became really involved in their world, played cricket and other sports, so it was obvious he wasn't taking an interest in them just for appearances, the way some people did. Mark and Paul seemed to recognize that David was genuine, too, and they became good mates.

It was a tragic event in the summer of 1979, a whole year after our first pub meal, that set the seal on my relationship with David. At that time there were no paddocks at Weathercock House, so when the jumping season ended I used to send my horses to a farm near Basingstoke to spend their summers out at grass. The farm belonged to Alan Davies, who was a friend from my point-to-point days. He was a good stockman, and kept a knowledgeable eye on them. That summer, one of the horses we sent to Alan was Fettimist. He was now nine years old, and ever since we'd sorted out the problem of his temperament, he'd been running well. In my first season on my own he'd won a handicap chase at Wincanton, and had been placed five times. In the 1978–79 season he won two more races. He was one of those horses who was honest rather than brilliant, and always tried his hardest. Whenever things were going badly, and I felt as if I'd never have another winner, Fettimist always managed to pull one out of the bag for me.

145

I hoped he'd keep on racing for at least a couple more seasons.

One evening I had a phone call from Alan Davies to say that Fettimist had gone down with colic. Dave was in the yard at the time and offered to drive me down to Basingstoke. By the time we arrived at Alan's place Fettimist was in a bad way. His belly was tucked up, he was sweating profusely and he was clearly in a lot of pain. The vet was there and had given him an injection to stop the gut spasms, but he wasn't hopeful. Vets didn't often operate on colic in those days, so there wasn't much we could do except pray. I wasn't going to leave Fettimist in that state and we decided to stay the night. Dave parked his car outside the stable and we took it in turns to go in and check on him every half-hour.

At about 4 a.m. I was beginning to feel hopeful. Fettimist had stopped sweating and looked more comfortable. He even picked at his hay. But it was only a temporary respite. By six o'clock he was in agony again. We called the vet out a second time, but there was nothing more he could do. I had no choice. Rather than let the horse carry on suffering we decided to put him down. I was devastated. For the three years he'd been with me I'd ridden Fettimist for nearly all his exercise, and I'd developed a special relationship with him. He had been a difficult sod at first, but in the end, when we'd reached an understanding, I felt I knew what he was thinking before he did and he'd been one of the horses who'd helped dig me out of the mire. Losing him felt like losing a close friend.

To my relief, David understood. He seemed to know that words wouldn't help, but somehow, without saying much, he managed to give me comfort and support by just being there. It was during our sad drive home from Basingstoke to Upper Lambourn that I realized how much I appreciated Dave's quiet presence when things were difficult. By the time we arrived at Weathercock House I'd admitted to myself what most of my family had known for a long time. I loved David. I hadn't been looking for another man in my life, but there didn't seem much point in fighting fate. I might as well accept that David was here to stay.

CHAPTER TEN

STARTING AGAIN

Life at Weathercock House in those early days felt a bit like swimming the Irish Sea against the tide. All day. Every day. Sometimes things would start to go right, and I'd nearly reach the other side, and I'd think, This is it, I've landed. The next moment, a wave would knock me off my feet and I'd be swept right back to where I'd started.

Losing Fettimist was one of a string of disasters in the late seventies and early eighties that tested my stamina. Not long afterwards one of Dorothy Squires' horses, Norwegian Flag, broke his back when he was brought down during a race at Sandown. At around the same time, also at Sandown, my best five-year-old, Roll Of Drums, who'd won three races for me that season, dropped dead from a heart attack. The worst blow of all came when my big handsome horse Lord Gulliver, who'd been running so brilliantly, also collapsed and died, this time on the gallops at Lambourn.

Mandy had been riding him at the time. He'd been working with Burrough Hill Lad round Mandown Bottom, a round gallop with an uphill finish. They were just about to turn the bend to go up the hill to finish off their piece of work when Lord Gulliver, who was probably a length and half behind Burrough Hill Lad, suddenly took off. As he quickened he cannoned into the other horse on his outside. With the force of the collision Mandy seemed to fly off his back. I stood on top of the hill, watching in total horror as Lord Gulliver carried on, hurtled through a fence and crashed to the floor in a lifeless heap. In the same split second I registered that Mandy had not moved a muscle. I let out a gasp and ran down the gallop absolutely flat out, one thought rattling through my head. Please let her be all right, please let her be all right. By the time I reached her she was beginning to stir and was mumbling. 'Where's the horse?' she kept saying. 'Don't worry about the horse – he's gone,' I replied. With that she started crying. She seemed about to get out of control so I had no option but to give her a bollocking. 'It's no use you getting in this state, Mandy. The horse is dead. There's nothing you can do about it,' I said. It was one of the most horrible things I've ever had to do in my life, because I knew exactly how Mandy was feeling. I wanted to lie on the grass and sob with her, but I was in charge and I knew it was my responsibility to stay in control for everybody's sake.

Until that spring Peter Callander had always insured his horses for 'all risk mortality', but a month earlier, when his insurance had come up for renewal, he'd told me, 'I think I'll insure him for accident only because the premium's a lot less. After all, he's hardly likely to drop dead now, is he?' Lord Gulliver had in fact suffered a fatal heart attack, so not only had Peter lost his horse, he also received no insurance money.

Throughout all these tragedies David's love and support helped me to keep going, but, strangely, one of my biggest setbacks in those years happened precisely because we *were* so close. When we'd first started going out together, David's brother, Keith, had a good horse called Canit, which he'd purchased some years earlier as a young horse, in training with me. Canit was a natural jumper, who I'd always felt would skip round the fences at Aintree. I also felt that because of his breeding he wouldn't stay the distance of the Grand National, but I saw him as an ideal candidate for the Topham Trophy. The Topham was the only professional race, apart from the Grand National, to be run over the National course, but because it was only two and three-quarter miles instead of four and a half it required less stamina. I'd already entered Canit for the Topham when, without warning, Keith Stait announced that he was taking the horse away from me and sending him to be trained by Fred Rimell. The reason Keith gave was that he didn't like the way David's relationship with me was developing. Exactly why he didn't like it wasn't clear, but looking back my guess is that he felt I was making use of David, and he didn't believe my feelings for him were genuine.

David was very upset and said that perhaps it would be better if we stopped seeing one another. I told him I didn't take kindly to being bullied or threatened, although losing Canit was a terrible loss.

I hadn't expected love to pay the bills, but I'd never imagined it would cost me so much either. It was a blow I could have done without. Even so, when Fred Rimell rang a few days later to ask about the horse I tried not to let my hurt show. Most people lose horses to other trainers sooner or later, and I knew it was important for my reputation that I behaved professionally. I decided there was no point in letting all the groundwork I'd done to prepare Canit for Aintree go to waste.

'Whatever else you do with him,' I told Fred, 'there's one race that horse should run in.'

'Oh yes, what's that?' said Fred, sounding amused.

'The Topham Trophy,' I said. 'It's made for him.'

When the declarations for the race were later published, I was pleased and flattered to see that Fred Rimell had followed my advice. David and I watched the Topham on the television at home, and we had very mixed feelings when Canit stormed home by five lengths. David just got up from his chair and quietly left the room. I could see how hurt he was too. He didn't reappear for some time. Of course I was pleased for the horse, who deserved to win the race, but the Topham was a prestigious race, worth a lot of money. If I'd still been training Canit it would have been my biggest win ever. It would almost certainly have brought me new owners. But there was no point in crying over spilt milk. I just had to keep my chin up and do the best I could with the horses I had left in my yard.

Around this time I suddenly developed an allergy to horses. It was the latest in a long line of allergies. In recent years I'd become sensitive to every chemical under the sun. Just a whiff of creosote, disinfectant, floor or furniture polish, perfume or similar products was all it took to trigger an attack of wheezing. I hardly dared go into the vet's surgery, because within minutes I'd be struggling for breath. Now, sweating horses joined the list of things that made me feel ill. Riding out brought on fits of sneezing, while brushing or clipping a horse indoors became nearly impossible. If I wanted to do any jobs like that, I had to wear a face mask. I'd never suffered from asthma or chest problems as a child, so it was all a bit of a mystery; and it was not until many years later, after an acute bout of illness, that the doctors discovered the most likely reason for my problems.

As part of the renovation work at Weathercock House, the timbers had been chemically treated to prevent woodworm and other pests. At the time, the danger of inhaling pesticide fumes wasn't known, so I wasn't asked to leave the house and had carried on living and sleeping there while the treatment went on. A few months later, when the timbers were treated again, I received my second dose of pesticide. Within weeks, I suffered my first bouts of asthma. At the time I didn't put two and two together.

The usual treatment for serious asthma in those days was a course of oral steroids. Unfortunately, one of the side effects is considerable weight gain. A couple of years earlier, after having my appendix out, I'd been as thin as a rake. Now, in the space of a couple of months, I went up two dress sizes. I was quite self-conscious about it, but I knew that vanity had to take a back seat if I wanted to get on with my job.

In spite of the setbacks, the number of winners sent out from Weathercock House was increasing. In 1977–78 the total had been six. In 1978–79 it was ten. In 1979–80, sixteen. Then, in the 1980–81 season, I had just the stroke of luck I'd been hoping for, when the Bielby family, who owned several businesses in Shropshire, sent me fourteen horses, doubling the size of my team almost overnight. Robin Platt, my accountant, had always told me I needed twenty-five horses in training to make the business viable, so I felt that at last I was turning the corner.

One of the Bielby string was Roll Of Drums, who was to have a fatal heart attack at Sandown. But I had better fortune with another, a chestnut gelding called Bueche Giorod. When he arrived, Bueche Giorod didn't in fact seem a very exciting prospect. Already nine years of age, he had only ever won two hurdle races and a maiden chase. However, at Weathercock House he improved out of all recognition. Bueche Giorod was a bold, front-running horse who in the space of ten weeks won six steeplechases for me, worth £20,260. His biggest success came at Cheltenham in December 1980, when he won the Massey Ferguson Gold Cup by six lengths. It was far and away the most important race that a horse of mine had ever won. And later that season Bueche Giorod very nearly gave me my first win at the Cheltenham Festival, when he finished a good second in the Mildmay of Flete Chase. The old horse's dramatic improvement since moving to my stable did not go unnoticed, and was well reported in the newspapers. By the end of that season my string of twenty-nine horses had won twenty-eight races between them and earned a total of £52,000 in prize money. According to the annual bible of jump racing, Timeform's *Chasers and Hurdlers,* I'd set a new record for a woman training over jumps. That was news to me, but it was exactly the sort of publicity I needed. At last, I thought, I could feel the shore on the other side. Maybe I was going to make it after all. I was not to know that another wave was about to come crashing down on me.

The Bielby family were now my biggest owners. However, I was becoming increasingly unhappy about the way their horses were being ridden in races. Any instructions or plans we had made before the race seemed to David and myself to be a waste of time. At first I put it down to bad luck, but when it continued to happen I started to wonder. Finally, one day at Nottingham when one of the Bielby horses lost a race, I decided I'd had enough.

'I'm not working my arse off seven days a week to play at these games,' I told Dave angrily on the way home. 'I'm not interested in being taken for a bloody mug.' I knew the time had come for some plain speaking. I was the trainer and part of my job was telling the jockey how to ride the race. If there was a reason for my instructions to be ignored, I felt I should be told why.

The outcome was predictable. The Bielbys took Bueche Giorod away and sent him to be trained by Michael Dickinson. A short while afterwards, they moved all their other horses to different yards. I wasn't the first trainer they'd treated like that, but that wasn't much comfort.

One or two people suggested afterwards that I might have handled the situation differently, and maybe sold my soul a little to keep the peace. But that wasn't the way I saw things. I have always said that you only know if you have principles when it costs you, either financially or emotionally. This was to cost me both ways. I later learned that a member of the Bielby family had been running tipping lines in a racing newspaper and that they were being investigated by the police. Now I was positive I had done the right thing.

As a result of this fiasco, half my income from training fees vanished overnight, and because most of my best horses had been Bielby horses, my chances of winning good prize money dropped too. In effect, in the 1981–82 season, I was right back at the beginning yet again.

Three years earlier, it had been Fred Winter who'd encouraged me to hang on. Now it was Dave's turn. At times, it was only his support that gave me the strength to keep going. In spite of his brother's prediction that our relationship wouldn't last six weeks, Dave and I were closer than ever. In fact we'd recently become engaged, and with Mark and Paul's blessing Dave had moved into Weathercock House. Throughout our relationship we had kept the boys fully involved. We always discussed each turn of events before taking the next step, but we had no immediate plans to get married. I didn't think it would be fair on the boys. My surname, Pitman, was their surname too. If I changed it, I thought Mark and Paul would feel I was divorcing them. They'd been through more than enough already, without my putting them through more turmoil. Anyway, I didn't need a piece of paper to prove that David and I loved and respected one another and, to be perfectly honest, as long as Mark and Paul were happy with the situation, that's all that mattered to us.

When we first got together Dave had been working with his brother as a builder in Worcestershire. He continued to do that for quite a while before deciding to help me full time. Becoming my assistant was quite an undertaking on his part because, although he knew a lot about racing, he knew very little about horses. Our stable routine was a real eye-opener for him. 'Do you know what, Jenny?' he said when he saw me treating injured legs morning, noon and night. 'People are always amazed how fit your horses are when they get to the races. But what amazes me is that they ever get there at all ... '

Dave was a quick learner and he didn't often have to be

shown twice how to do something. I taught him to ride on my old hack, Black Plover, and while he never roadworked, he was soon competent enough to ride quiet horses to and from the gallops. It was a skill I made use of a couple of times, in difficult situations. But on one particular occasion when I'd asked Dave to ride home he put his foot down. 'Next time you want to effing sack somebody, Jenny,' he said, 'would you please wait till they get back to the yard!'

Dave had quickly picked up the basics of stable management, and could help muck out, feed and even put bandages on, but he was still a bit wary if a horse misbehaved. Not long after I lost the Bielby horses his nerve was really put to the test.

When he heard about all my empty boxes, Dad decided that the best way to support me was to send me a horse of his own to train. He rang up to offer me a four-year-old he'd bred who he thought 'might just win a little race'. I'd have been prepared to train a camel at that point, and Dave and I set off in the old horsebox to pick it up from Leicestershire.

We arrived at Enderby to discover that the horse was still out in one of the fields Dad rented. Not only that, but running in the field with it were its mother, that year's foal, her yearling and her two-year-old. None of them had ever been weaned off the mare. Dad also confessed that the four-year-old – his potential racehorse – had never been caught in its life.

Getting into the field was the first problem. The gate was tied up with so many bits of baler twine that Houdini would have found it a challenge. Eventually we got it open and backed the box through the gateway. Dad had decided that the best way to catch the horse was to lead the mare on board the box and hope that the rest of her family would follow. To everyone's amazement his plan worked. Suddenly poor Dave, who three years before had never been near a horse in his life except to lean over the rails at the races, found himself pinned at the back of the box with five horses milling around him. He managed to duck out just as Dad and I whistled the partition across, trapping the four-year-old at the front of the wagon. Quick as a flash we pushed the other four horses back out again and slammed the ramp up.

'Now get going, quick as you can,' Dad told Dave. 'Once you're moving he'll settle down.'

He was being optimistic. As Dave leapt into the driving seat and turned on the ignition we heard a crashing and banging above our heads. Dave looked as if he was going to have a litter of pups at any moment.

'Jen! It's on the Luton!' he yelled. The Luton was the bit of the box above the cab where we carried hay and tack. Because we hadn't dared tie the horse up, he had been able to rear up and get his front legs onto it. The noise was deafening. 'Don't worry,' I smiled, trying to reassure Dave. 'He probably wants to drive. Shove it in gear and let's get on. He'll soon get down.' I knew a horse couldn't possibly travel standing on its two hind legs and thought it best not to tell David that it might try and get all four legs onto the Luton.

Sure enough, by the time we arrived back at Weathercock House, Dad's horse had got all four legs back on the floor. Persuading him out of the box was the next problem. The poor animal had only ever set foot on grass, so when he stepped on the ramp and heard the sound of his own feet he froze with fear. By now it was dark and I think Dave was beginning to have serious misgivings about ever getting himself involved with me and my horses. In the end we backed the horsebox up to a corner stable, and with three of us heaving with all our might we managed to manhandle the horse down the ramp and into its loose-box.

Worse was to come. The next day the horse refused to eat. At first I put it down to the stress of the journey, but after twenty-four hours, when he was still ignoring every titbit I offered him, I started to get worried. I rang my father. 'Dad,

I can't get this horse to eat,' I said. 'What've you been feeding him? I need to get him some.'

'Ah,' said Dad. 'That could be a bit difficult.'

It turned out that Dad had come to an arrangement with a local bakery, who supplied him with biscuit waste. It was no wonder this horse found oats boring. He was used to jam tarts, individual apple pies and Swiss rolls! In the end I decided to indulge him before he starved himself to death. I drove back up to Leicester and picked up two half-hundredweight bags of bakery waste. That evening we all watched in relief and disbelief as Dad's horse ate his first square meal in two days. In the week that followed, bit by bit I diluted his biscuit and mix with oats and cubes, until I'd weaned him on to normal feeds.

Dad named the horse All Being Well, which was a catch-phrase of his. Once he'd started eating and had stopped being frightened of the noise the straw made when he walked round his box, All Being Well started to behave like a normal horse. We broke him in and eventually got him to the races, but he never did win that 'little race' Dad dreamed of, and in the end he went off to the sales to be sold as a hunter.

Another way I tried to increase my numbers was by visiting the bloodstock sales at Ballsbridge in Ireland. I was looking for unbroken three- or four-year-olds, which I'd heard could be bought cheaply in Ireland. I reasoned that if I started off with a horse that nobody else had raced, then it should have a better chance of staying sound than some of the invalids people usually sent me. My experience at the sales was very limited, which meant I was a sitting target for Irish blarney. I ended up with a very good-looking animal who, according to the man selling him, moved so well at home that he was sure to 'greet the judge' the first time he ran. When we got him home his new owner named him Queen's Ride, as he looked like he would be more at home strolling down the Mall. I hoped for better things.

When Queen's Ride had been broken in I showed him

proudly to Mandy and asked her to put her leg over the horse and give him a work-out. She came back ten minutes later with a gloomy face.

'I hope this horse stays,' she said.

'Why?' I asked, puzzled.

She shook her head. ''Cos it can't bloody well gallop!' she replied.

Thankfully she was wrong, and eventually Queen's Ride learned to gallop well enough to win three hurdle races for me, but those wins were quite a while off. The season after the Bielbys took their horses away was disastrous. Twelve months earlier I'd been the leading woman National Hunt trainer. In 1981–82 I had only eight winners. I was seriously worried. At the time I kept a reporter's notebook to record my income and outgoings. My maths wasn't anything special, but even I could see that the figures did not balance. In 1982 I visited my accountant and waved my little notepad under his nose. 'It doesn't add up, Robin,' I told him. He looked at my figures and agreed, but said, 'Well, Jenny, I think you ought to give it a few months longer.'

I struggled on obediently, but nothing seemed to improve. I didn't have enough horses and I wasn't winning enough races. I started to think seriously again about giving up training. I didn't *want* to give up – I was still passionate about my job. But at the end of the day I had to be realistic. To be a professional racehorse trainer you needed enough horses to pay the bills, and I simply didn't have them. I couldn't ignore that fact, especially given the number of obligations I had. Not only was there the mortgage and bank loan to pay off, but half the boys' school fees as well, and that was before I'd even started on the routine bills for feed-stuffs and wages.

By now I'd slithered so far down the slippery slope that my only hope of surviving was to find a star – a horse the public would fall in love with – who would earn me big prize money and bring me the sort of publicity I needed to attract new owners. Realistically, my chances of finding a star in a stable down to fifteen horses was remote, but there was no harm in dreaming. And in my dreams there was one horse in my stables at Weathercock House who just fitted the bill.

Five years earlier, in the summer of my first year at Weathercock House, a man called Jeremy Norman, who'd been introduced to me by Tony Stratton-Smith, had asked me to go with him to a yard at Bampton, twenty miles from Lambourn, to take a look at an unnamed two-year-old he was thinking of buying. When we first saw the horse he was carrying so much condition he wouldn't have looked out of place in the show ring, but I'd liked the look of him and had advised Jeremy to buy him. He was just the stamp of horse that Dad had always tried to breed – a big strong chestnut gelding with a white face and a bold, kind eye. His pedigree appealed to me, too. He was by Harwell, a good National Hunt sire who'd won seven hurdle races, out of a well-bred Irish mare.

By the time he was sent to us as a three-year-old, Jeremy's new horse had filled out so much that the horsebox ramp literally groaned as he came down it. It was hard to believe he was a thoroughbred. He reminded me of the picture I'd seen of a carthorse on the Heinz Ploughman's Pickle jars. Since buying the horse, Jeremy Norman had sold a half-share in him to a cousin from the Channel Islands called Alan Burrough. The Burrough family decided to name him after the lighthouse on Jersey. Weatherbys duly approved the name, and early in 1979 my Ploughman's Pickle horse had been rechristened Corbiere, commonly known in the yard as Corky.

Even though I liked Corbiere a lot as a youngster, I didn't get too carried away, or start having silly dreams about what he might do at that stage. I'd been training long enough by then to know that however good looking a horse was, and however perfectly it moved, if it hadn't got guts and courage then it wouldn't win races. However, it soon became obvious that Corbiere had more guts and courage than any horse I'd ever trained. The first time he showed it to me was on the Lambourn gallops one horrible winter morning when there were hailstones pelting across the Downs. Most of my string were doing what horses usually do in that sort of weather, turning their heads away from the wind and sleet and going up the hill sideways, like crabs, to protect their faces. But Corbiere was different. He galloped up the hill like a tank, straight into all that dreadful weather.

That was the first time I realized that Corbiere was an extraordinary horse. From then on everything he did confirmed it. Ordinary horses didn't behave like he did. All he wanted to do was please you. If you'd set him to gallop from Lambourn to Scotland he would have kept on galloping until he collapsed. He never, ever questioned what you asked him to do. He was so genuine you had to protect him from himself to prevent him working too hard.

He also showed his courage to the public the first time he ran. I'd decided to introduce him to racing in a 'bumper', or National Hunt flat race, which had just been introduced in England, at Nottingham. I didn't feel Corbiere was ready at four to run over hurdles and I had no great expectations of him, because he was still immature and hadn't shown much of a turn of foot at home. But I hadn't taken the weather into account.

That day the ground was so deep that horses were sinking nearly up to their fetlocks. On top of that, it was raining so hard you could hardly see your hand in front of your face. Twenty seconds after the race started the runners were just grey blobs on the far side of the course, and even through my binoculars I couldn't pick out any of the colours. Somehow the commentator managed to identify a few of them, and, to my total amazement, he announced that Corbiere was making the running. As soon as I focused on the horse at the front of the field, thundering along the course like an armoured vehicle, I knew he was right – that could only be Corbiere. To both his owner's and his trainer's delight he romped home well ahead of the rest of the field. Nobody in the yard had a penny on him that day, but they never made the same mistake again.

Corbiere's second race, also a bumper, was a little disappointing, but the ground at Chepstow was much quicker. In his third and final bumper at Warwick he was back to his best and I felt he ought to have won. At one point he was fifteen lengths clear, but his jockey, Paddy O'Brien, spent so much time looking over his shoulder for dangers that I thought he'd crick his neck. Unfortunately he was looking the wrong way. He didn't see Oliver Sherwood riding Esparto for Fred Winter coming up on his other side until it was too late, and Esparto caught him just before the line. It was no disgrace. Esparto was a good horse. In fact, his owner, George Ward, was so impressed by Corbiere's showing that day that he offered the Burroughs £20,000 for the horse there and then in the unsaddling enclosure. I held my breath. To my relief Alan Burrough explained firmly that they had promised their half-share in Corbiere to their son Brian, as a twenty-first birthday present, so the horse would never be for sale. If it hadn't been for Brian, Corbiere's story might have turned out very differently.

In his second season the plan was to send Corbiere hurdling. But after his summer holidays out at grass he was absolutely gross, and I had to be very careful not to put too much strain on his legs when he came back into training. I had a small bare paddock at Weathercock House which I called Alcatraz and I turned Corky out there to get rid of his grass belly before I started to do anything too strenuous with him. There followed two months' roadwork.

After he had lost quite a lot of his excess weight we schooled him over hurdles and he was a natural – very accurate and careful in his jumping. For his first outing of the season I again took him to Nottingham, this time for a two-mile hurdle race. It wasn't far enough for him, but he was only young and still a bit burly, and finished a respectable seventh. It was obvious to me that he needed a real test of stamina, so that season I gradually increased the distance of his races. It took three more attempts before he won his first hurdle race – a three-mile novice handicap at Kempton Park. Some people felt he was a bit lucky that day, because at the last flight the horse upsides him, a dark brown imposing horse called Burrough Hill Lad, took a crashing fall, leaving Corbiere in the lead. But lucky or not, a win was a win.

He ran in three more races that season, all in very good company, and though he didn't win any of them he finished in the money each time. His third place in the Philip Cornes Saddle of Gold Hurdle Final brought him a lot of compliments in the press. However, for me his best effort was his last one, when he came sixth in the Waterford Crystal Stayers Hurdle at the Cheltenham Festival.

By the time he was six Corbiere was ready to begin racing over fences. He took to it enthusiastically, as I'd always guessed he would. He won at the first attempt at Leicester, and scored twice more before rounding off the season by finishing second to Lesley Ann in the Sun Alliance Chase at Cheltenham. The Sun Alliance was the most important race of the year for staying novice chasers, so it was a great achievement. Behind him that day were Wayward Lad, Pilot Officer, Easter Eel and Captain John, all highly regarded young horses. By the time I sent him off down to Alan Davies' farm at Basingstoke for his summer holidays I was already looking forward to the next season.

Dad used to say, 'Don't count your chickens . . .' and he was right. In Corbiere's next race, six months later, he fell for the first time in his career. Not because he jumped badly but because of a patch of slippery ground on the landing side of the third fence from home. His front feet slid as he touched down and he crashed heavily to the ground. That was bad enough, but in struggling to get up he struck into

162

himself and bruised a tendon. The injury was nothing much – it could have gone either way – but fate wasn't on my side. When I schooled him at home a week or two later he came back with a bit of heat in the leg and my dreams for the season collapsed. There was nothing for it but to give him twelve months off. It wasn't an easy decision to make, especially that year when the Bielby horses had gone and Corbiere was far and away the best horse I had in the yard – at the end of the 1981–82 season *Chasers and Hurdlers'* verdict on him was that he was 'one of the best long-distance novices of his year' – but I had no real choice. If I'd run him and he'd broken down, I'd never have forgiven myself. I knew I had to think of the horse and his whole career, not just the next few months.

After talking it over with the vets we decided to line-fire him, a treatment which creates scar tissue to strengthen the tendons. These days it's a controversial practice, but I'd often seen it used during my years at Hinton Parva and to my mind it was a tried and tested method which carried less risk than the split-tendon operations and carbon-fibre implants that were becoming fashionable at that time.

After three months of box rest and being led out daily in hand, Corbiere was sent back to Alan Davies at Basingstoke. He was a regular resident there now, but he wasn't one of their most popular paying guests. In fact, Alan was always complaining about him. Since the first day he'd arrived there, Corky had been what Alan called 'a cantankerous old sod' and had taken to chasing Alan out of the field whenever he ventured in. On top of that, Corbiere used to find it amusing to round up the cattle which were grazed with the horses. He'd spend all day herding them round and round the field. 'Chasing the arses off them,' Alan grumbled.

One day in the summer of 1982, while Corbiere was still recuperating, Alan telephoned me. 'Jenny, you know that bloody chestnut horse of yours? The one with the white face?'

I braced myself. 'Why? What's he done now, Alan?'

'You're not going to believe this,' Alan said. 'I put a mare in the field next to him today. There's two rows of fencing between those fields as big as bloody motorway fencing, and he's just jumped the first railing, bounced through the middle bit and straight out over the next railing to reach the filly.'

I sighed, imagining another bill. 'All right, what's the damage?'

Alan chuckled. 'Nothing. He never touched a rail. Jumped them as clean as a whistle. I'm telling you, Jenny, that horse'll win the bloody Grand National one day!'

CHAPTER ELEVEN

CORBIERE

Ever since 1977, when I'd first run The Songwriter in the Grand National, the race had been drawing me back like a magnet, and every year since then, except one, I'd entered a horse at Aintree. So far, Lady Luck hadn't smiled on me. In 1979, after The Songwriter's second attempt, I ran an eight-year-old gelding called Artistic Prince, who'd gone well for most of two circuits only to fall four fences from home. In 1980 Lord Gulliver, whom I'd seen as my best chance yet, had a setback in training just a few weeks before the big race, so didn't run. The following year he'd made it to Aintree but had fallen at the thirteenth fence. Even so he got up and completed the course riderless, jumping every fence like a stag, and leading the field for most of the way. In 1982 Artistic Prince had run again, but he'd got no further than the first fence. My other runner that year, a quirky old character called Monty Python, had been going well until he was hampered by a loose horse at Becher's second time round and decided enough was enough.

In short, my record to date wasn't exactly impressive, but I hadn't given up my dream of winning the Grand National.

Not long after Corbiere came back into training in the late summer of 1982 I made up my mind to enter him for the

1983 race. Admittedly he would be eight years old, but I had always considered him an ideal National type – he was tough, jumped for fun and stayed all day. If I waited another year there might not even *be* a Grand National. The course had been put up for sale, and unless the Jockey Club raised enough funds to buy it, developers were planning to build on it. That year – 1983 – could be our last chance ever of winning the race.

As usual, in spite of Alan Davies' efforts to ration his grazing, Corbiere had become gross during the summer. Getting him lean and fit enough to run was always going to be a major problem. In fact, keeping the weight off once he was in training could be a problem too. Corbiere wasn't a horse you'd want to give too many easy days at home. Fortunately, he could cope mentally with plenty of work. Not all horses could – some of them you had to train like butterflies – but Corky had a solid character. Even when he was fit his cruising speed was never very high, so on the gallops I'd always work him with something a bit faster than he was so he'd have to stretch himself, though not to the point of disappointing him. That applied to all my horses. I'd never let them work away from each other, because it was discouraging for the horse that was left behind. It was only common sense. If somebody beat you easily at squash several times, you wouldn't want to play them too regularly. We always work horses with similar ability together and with their riders carrying about the same weight.

Corbiere took his training well following his twelve-month lay-off. In the mornings, on the way back from the gallops, he'd buck so high that Gary Curran, his lad, used to reckon he could see the Severn Bridge. Often he would buck the whole way home. I wouldn't ever let Gary correct him for it, because he wasn't being wayward, it was just his way of showing his well-being.

My plan was to start him off over hurdles. It was something I often did with horses coming back after fitness problems. When they've been off the racetrack for a long period of time, however much work they've done at home, they're bound to get leg-weary in their first race. When that happens in a hurdle race it's not quite so risky as in a chase. If they're tired and make a mistake at a fence they can fall, but in a hurdle race you can look after them better because they're not jumping so high and the hurdles can be knocked down. I booked an up-and-coming young jockey called Ben de Haan for Corbiere's comeback race. Ben was Fred Winter's second jockey that year, and I admired his riding a lot. He was a real horseman, which not all jockeys are. I told Ben that Corbiere would be a bit rusty and to let him run the best race he could without picking up his stick. It wasn't a matter of cheating. It was a matter of doing my job, which was to get the horse back on the racetrack, for him to enjoy the race and above all for them to finish safe and sound.

Following two hurdle races – in which he ran well, finishing in mid-field – I brought him back over fences at the beginning of November, at Sandown. He came third to Leney Dual and Colonel Christy, who were both respectable chasers. Ben was impressed enough to echo Alan Davies. 'This horse'll win you the Grand National,' he said as he dismounted. That confirmed my own thoughts and revitalized my hopes and dreams.

Three weeks later I ran Corky again, this time in the Hennessy Cognac Gold Cup, which is a big handicap chase run over three and a quarter miles at Newbury. Ideally, he needed even further than that, but really long-distance chases were few and far between, so, if I wanted to see how he ran in the very best company, I had to compromise. In the circumstances, I was delighted with his fifth place behind Bregawn. The way he was running on at the end convinced me that he'd find the four and a half miles of the Grand National no problem. Unfortunately, Alan Burrough (who by now had bought up Jeremy Norman's half-share in

Corbiere) saw the performance in a different light, and talked of entering him for the Cheltenham Gold Cup. Personally I'd never really felt, watching Corbiere, that he was a Gold Cup horse. They always go a serious clip in the Gold Cup, and then quicken off that pace. Corbiere didn't have quite enough speed to do that. His talent lay in his jumping, his courage and his stamina, rather than his speed. He was an out-and-out stayer – the sort of horse who, unless he was going flat out from start to finish, wasn't going fast enough.

My worry wasn't just that Corbiere would be beaten in the Gold Cup. I was more afraid that such a testing race, three weeks before the Grand National, would take the shine off him. History showed that very few horses who'd run a good race in the Gold Cup came out again, some three weeks later, and ran as well at Aintree. At that time, before the fences were adapted, the National course was a lot more demanding than it is these days, and it took a lot more jumping. I've always felt that horses have to be spot on for the National, both mentally and physically.

I'd never believed in overruling owners. They paid the bills and the horses belonged to them. All I could do was discuss the matter and advise. To my relief, Alan and Brian decided to take my advice, and agreed to enter Corky in the Ritz Club Trophy Chase at Cheltenham instead of the Gold Cup. Both races were at the Festival meeting, and both were run over a similar distance, but the Ritz, being a handicap, was likely to be less competitive, and would keep Corbiere fit so that I could then leave him on 'simmer' until Aintree.

Even the best laid plans go astray. At Worcester, in December, it seemed for a moment that we'd have to forget about both Cheltenham and Aintree. After starting favourite in a three-and-a-half-mile chase Corbiere ran very disappointingly, finishing a thoroughly tired seventh. I don't expect animals to be machines, and I'd seen horses run inexplicably badly before. But Corbiere wasn't the sort of horse who would jack it in. For him to run as poorly as that I knew there had to be something physically wrong. I was right. Blood tests showed that Corky was anaemic, a condition that fortunately was treatable. We gave him an iron supplement and some multi-vitamin injections, and soon his blood count was back to normal and he was once again bucking.

His next big test, three weeks later, was the Welsh National at Chepstow. My instructions to Ben were simple: 'I don't care what happens today so long as you're not too hard on him.' Quite early in the race a mistake at the eighth fence cost him ground and for a moment I feared that he might drop out of contention again, just as he had done at Worcester. But this time he managed to stay in touch until his stamina began to come into play. The race conditions at Chepstow were ideal for Corbiere – three and three-quarter miles in deep, clinging mud – and my heart began to pound as I saw him close on the leaders turning for home with five fences still left to jump.

Slowly, agonizingly, he was beginning to reel in Pilot Officer all the way up that seemingly never-ending finishing straight. At the final fence, nothing else was in sight although Pilot Officer was still just in front. On the flat Corbiere battled bravely into the lead. Pilot Officer tried to rally, but Corbiere would not be denied and held on resolutely by a head.

The merit of this gritty performance can be gauged by the fact that the previous year's runaway winner, Peaty Sandy, finished a weary third, twenty lengths behind Corbiere. Winning the Welsh National was a landmark for me, and it was doubly sweet after the near miss I had experienced with Gylippus back in 1976. I was also hugely encouraged by the knowledge that Rag Trade, the horse who won on that occasion, had gone on to triumph at Aintree.

Early in the new year the weather turned bitterly cold, and the Lambourn gallops froze so hard that it was impossible to work horses on them. It meant that Corky's preparation, as well as that of my two other Grand National entries, Artistic Prince and Monty Python, was in danger of being interrupted. My solution was to take them in the horsebox to Burnham-on-Sea, fifty miles away in Somerset, and canter them along the sand. Working on the beach was a tried and tested preparation for the Grand National – in fact it was well documented that Red Rum had been prepared for all three of his wins on the Southport sands. If it was good enough for him it was good enough for Corky.

Twice a week, throughout the freezing conditions, Steve Fox, my travelling head lad, drove the horsebox down to Burnham, while Dave and I followed in my Datsun Cherry. Often it was so cold that as soon as the tide went back the wet sand would freeze instantly. Even some of the seagulls were frozen solid in the water's edge. I'd tell the lads to canter the horses just in the edge of the water, where it was about four or five inches deep. As they cantered I'd drive alongside them in my Datsun on the hard sand, setting the pace. One day I was concentrating so much on the horses and my speedometer that I drove onto some mudflats, and my wheels started spinning. Before I knew what was happening, my car had sunk up to its axles. Luckily, when they saw what was happening, the lads rode back and two of them held the horses while the others pushed my car out of the mud. They found it very amusing and of course I had to contend with all the usual jokes about women drivers.

I never allowed my horses to do more than twenty miles an hour on the beach, because even at the edge of the water the sand was quite firm. The beach was only a mile and a half long, so to do enough work they'd have to canter one way, turn round and canter back. When they'd finished I'd step out of the car, have a look at them and send one or two back for another little canter if I thought they needed it. After that I'd let them have a play in the sea and splash around up to their bellies, which they absolutely loved. To finish off we'd bring them back up to the dunes, where the sand was dry, soft and deep, take their tack off and let them dig holes and have a roll. Corbiere's favourite pastime at Basingstoke had been digging holes in Alan's fields, and he enjoyed this bit best of all. He'd paw at the sand like a circus horse, and kick it as high as a house. After a week or two he started anticipating the sand play, and if we weren't careful he'd try and get down to roll before he'd even cantered. The minute we arrived at the beach and took him out of the box to saddle him up, his knees would start to buckle. He was like a mischievous kid. All the horses loved the beach, but the benefit was especially obvious with Corbiere.

Not everyone appreciated Corky's exuberance. Often, if our farrier Derek King called to shoe him when we were riding out, he would spend half an hour just trying to catch him in his box. He could be a cantankerous old sod. He wasn't so bad around me, but that was because he was a bit of a cupboard lover. At night, when I did my last stable check, he'd whinny for his titbit, but once he'd emptied my pockets he'd turn his back on me as if to say, 'Right, I've got what I wanted. You can clear off now.'

Two weeks later, it was the Cheltenham Festival. Bregawn, who'd beaten us in the Hennessy, won the Gold Cup easily, making me certain that we'd been right not to run Corbiere in the race. In the Ritz Club Handicap Corky ran well, finishing second in a big field, though he had a harder race than I'd have liked. Fortunately, the timing of Easter that year meant that he had a week longer than usual to recover before the Grand National. A few days before Aintree Corbiere was bouncing. I've never had him in better nick, I thought to myself.

I had a strange feeling during that final week. Not exactly confidence, more like being in the hands of fate. More importantly, of fate being on my side. With only a few days to go, the heavens opened and the going at Aintree turned soft. Corbiere could act on any sort of ground, but as his stamina was bottomless the soft ground would also give him a big advantage. 'I want the boys and Mum and Dad to go this year,' I told Dave. 'I think this is going to be the best chance I'll ever have of winning the National.' I tried not to get too carried away. After all, this wasn't an ordinary race. There were thirty huge fences to be jumped, not to mention hazards like loose horses to be avoided. But I couldn't stop my confidence bubbling to the surface. When Mr Atrib, one of my owners, rang to ask after his own horse, and said, 'How is Corbiere? What chance has he got on Saturday?' I threw caution to the winds. 'If it was any other race than the Grand National, I'd say he would be a certainty,' I said. It was the only time I let my guard slip, but my vibes must have been going out to other people because when Alan Burrough came to see Corbiere a few days before the race he said casually, 'Oh, Jenny, we've got two coachloads going to Aintree from our business in London. We've put the champagne on the coach for them to celebrate after the race.' My blood ran cold and I started to backpedal rapidly. 'If this horse gets brought down at the first,' I said to Dave, 'you'll see me heading for the car park.' Why, oh why, I thought, did I let my mouth take control of my brain?

At the beginning of the week there were forty-two intended runners, though by the Friday the heavy rain had led to the top weight Ashley House being withdrawn. Among Corbiere's rivals were the 1982 Grand National winner Grittar (who was a strong favourite), Greasepaint (a good Irish horse who'd won the Kim Muir Chase at the Cheltenham Festival), and four horses who'd been placed in previous Grand Nationals, Delmoss, Spartan Missile, Royal Mail and Three To One. Corbiere was very much the novice of the party, as well as being one of the youngest horses.

Though Corbiere wasn't my only runner in the Grand National that year, realistically the chances of the other two were slimmer. Artistic Prince was now twelve years old and hadn't completed the course in his previous National, while

Monty Python was an erratic performer. Not surprisingly, they started at longer odds. In contrast, after his win in the Welsh National, the bookies seemed to view Corbiere's prospects favourably. By the off he was fifth favourite, at 13–1. That win at Chepstow had also persuaded the handicapper to lumber him with 11st 4lb, which I thought was plenty for such a young horse.

Dave, the boys, Mandy and I travelled up to Liverpool on the Friday before the race and booked into the Sunnyville boarding house. We always stayed in boarding houses in those days. Even if I had been able to afford hotels, I thought boarding houses were better value for money, and more adaptable for people like us, who wanted breakfast or supper at odd hours. On Friday afternoon we were invited to the box of Artistic Prince's owner, Robert Stigwood, by his manager Rod Gunner. It was a very good place to watch from, and the box was, as expected, packed with racing people. Among them was the young trainer who, three weeks before, had saddled the first five home in the Cheltenham Gold Cup. It was a magnificent achievement, and Michael Dickinson's adrenaline was obviously still flowing at a great rate of knots. As the afternoon wore on he started giving me a bit of stick, then a bit more, and eventually declared, 'I've always had a soft spot for you, Mrs P.'

'Oh yes?' I said, feeling my hackles rise.

'Yes, I've got the same soft spot for my mother.' He smirked. 'It's a bog in Ireland.'

One thing that makes me see red is people being disrespectful to or about their parents. I decided it was time to put his leg through his collar. 'You ought to watch what you say, Michael,' I replied angrily. 'If it hadn't been for your parents, where do you think you'd be today?'

He looked at me rather sheepishly and replied, 'Probably training half a dozen selling platers in a back yard somewhere.'

'Yes, you probably would,' I said, 'so don't you forget it.'

My own mum and dad were staying in Birkenshaw, near Bradford, where my brother Joe now lived with his wife Diane. They were both well into their sixties, and I was a bit worried about how they'd cope with the crowds. Fortunately Rod Gunner, who'd heard of my concerns, kindly invited me to bring them up to the box the next day, so that was one less thing for me to worry about.

On the Saturday morning I got up to find the sun shining from a blue sky. It was a long-standing tradition for the jockeys to ride the horses out on the course early on Grand National morning (Fred Winter used to say that this custom originated so that the trainers could check that the jockeys were sober). I gave my horses a walk, trot and a short canter up the straight, nothing too strenuous, but I felt it did them good to stretch their legs. Then they would go back to their stables for a light breakfast and to relax before the race. Afterwards, following another tradition, our owners and jockeys walked the course with me. At each fence we stopped and I spent a few moments with each jockey talking about the approach and how they'd tackle it. I followed the same route as Fred Winter had done when I walked the course with him, and tried to remember his advice. Two of my jockeys, Colin Brown and Paddy O'Brien, had ridden the course before, but this would be Ben de Haan's first National. He hung back from the others, ignoring the chatter and joking, focusing his mind. The fences were as daunting as ever. Just looking at them made me glad I was not riding in the race.

Afterwards we returned to the guesthouse and hung around, killing time, until Mum and Dad arrived in the late morning. On reaching Aintree I took them up to the Stigwoods' box, where a buffet lunch had been laid on. There was a lovely lady serving behind the table and an hour or so later, when it was time to get my horses ready, I asked her quietly, 'Could you look after my mum and dad while I'm gone, please.' Then I turned to Mum. 'Now, whatever happens,' I said, 'don't go worrying yourself. If something goes wrong I'll deal with it. You just stay here and enjoy yourselves.' Poor Mum looked as white as a ghost. She had obviously sensed my nervous state. I left her and Dad with Joe and the boys, while Dave, Mandy and I went off to tack up the horses.

This is always the time when my nerves try getting the better of me. Every trainer recognizes that there's an element of risk to the jockeys and the horses in any race. You train them and teach them to jump, so the risk is as minimal as you can possibly make it, but it exists, and there's no point in pretending it doesn't. Racehorses have a hell of a good life, but knowing that doesn't make these few minutes before a big race any easier.

When you have more than one runner in the National, it's not an easy job to get everything done at the right time, particularly if your jockeys are riding in the preceding race. But finally all three horses were ready and all three jockeys were on board. As they left the parade ring Dave and I went back to Mr Stigwood's box to watch the race with my family. Most of them had been to Aintree with me before, but today, as they gathered around, I sensed something different in the air. Not expectation – my family had seen too much jump racing to have expectations – but a real sense of hope. All my folks knew what I thought of Corbiere, and every single one of them appreciated how much this race meant to me. To win it would be the best present I could ever give them by way of a thank you for their support. To lose would mean they would be disappointed for me again.

Suddenly I wanted to be on my own. Dave seemed to sense that and without saying a word he walked out onto the balcony in front of the box. I joined him for a while, then went back inside to watch the race on television. The parade down the course seemed to take for ever. By now I wasn't feeling at all well. Despite my keenness on Aintree it had always been a love–hate relationship, and this was the time when the hate surfaced. At that moment I could quite easily have run out onto the course and said, 'I don't want them to run,' but the knowledge that that wouldn't go down too well with the owners held me back! Then, as always, the moment passed.

The runners were finally called into line and a big roar went up from the crowd.

And then they were off. All I wanted then was to watch the race in complete silence. I shut off all the sound around me and concentrated on the screen. Corbiere was right up with Delmoss on the inside where I'd told Ben to take him. Out of trouble, and up with the pace. There was no point in sitting at the back when you're one-paced like Corbiere. My other two were also where we'd planned, Artistic Prince on the inside, behind Corbiere, Monty further towards the outside. I registered them, but my heart was with Corbiere. In my mind I was talking to his jockey. Mind this! Go on a bit! Go on a bit! Exactly the same as if I was alongside him. All the way round the first circuit, Corbiere was up in the first three or four and jumping well. In fact he was jumping *brilliantly*. He'd flown Becher's and was well out of harm's way when two horses fell. At the Chair, the biggest fence on the course, more horses departed. The horse in front of Monty Python slammed on his brakes and Monty had no choice but to do the same. Unaware of the happenings behind them, Ben and Corbiere were galloping on. Corky was jumping so boldly, his big ears pricked. By the time they started on the second circuit half of the forty-one starters had dropped out of the race. At the twentieth fence Artistic Prince went too, balked by a loose horse. Delmoss started to drop back now, and as they reached Valentine's second time round, Corbiere was sharing the lead with an outsider, Hallo Dandy. Beside me my brother Joe started getting excited. 'Cor, he's going really well, Jen! He's gonna win, Jen.' My whole body felt like a rubberband stretched to its maximum. 'Shut up, Joe. Shut *up,* Joe!' I said almost hysterically.

Joe shut up for a minute or two, and we watched them come back across the Melling Road for the final time. Corbiere was still going really well but I was looking anxiously at the others behind him, trying to see how much petrol was in their tanks. Hallo Dandy didn't look to me as if he'd last as long as Corbiere, but maybe that was wishful thinking. The two horses took the next three fences together, both of them jumping cleanly. Then, two from home, Hallo Dandy started to drop away, and, on my right, Mandy burst into tears. That started me off, and by the time Corbiere was going to the last and flying it, I was screaming at the top of my voice. But there was still that long run-in to come, and all at once I understood what people meant by déjà vu. I was having flashbacks of Red Rum getting up and collaring Crisp in this race, ten years before. Pictures of that finish kept flashing into my head and blurring the real scene. Then, as they raced up the straight, I saw Greasepaint, the Irish horse, closing on Corbiere and I prayed that history wasn't going to repeat itself. I could hardly bear to watch, but I couldn't turn away either. I stared at the screen in despair, then as Greasepaint reached Corbiere's quarters something amazing happened. Corbiere surged. He didn't quicken. He simply surged. His final strides were a last, desperate gasp. Nothing to do with speed or ability but everything to do with courage. I knew then he wasn't going to be caught. He was never ever going to let that horse past and he reached the line three-quarters of a length in front. Corbiere had won the Grand National.

All hell broke loose. Everybody in the box was crying and shouting – the Burroughs, Mandy, Joe, Mark and Paul. As we hugged each other the glass doors that led to the balcony flew open and Dave came bursting in. He threw his arms around me and kissed me. 'God, you've done it!' he said. 'You've done it, Jen!'

177

Until then it hadn't occurred to me that I had anything to do with it. It was just my most wonderful horse winning the Grand National. But hearing Dave's words, the reality hit me. 'Yeah,' I thought, 'we bloody well have.'

Dave and I ran down the rattling iron steps at the end of the stand and pushed through the crowds heading for the winners' enclosure. By the time we reached it my legs were like jelly. Suddenly everything seemed out of my control. Microphones were shoved in front of my face and I was pulled and pushed from all directions. The fact that the Grand National's future had been threatened, together with the realization that I'd just become the first woman in history to train the winner, meant that the press were scrambling to get to me. David Coleman from the BBC was the first one to collar me. Answering his questions was an uncanny experience. I felt as if it wasn't me he was interviewing. I was up in the air, looking down on everything that was going on in the unsaddling enclosure. In the past, when I'd heard people say that things like that had happened to them, that they'd been on cloud nine riding on a magic carpet, I'd thought what a load of tripe. But it really did happen – it was the strangest experience. A bit unnerving at the time, I must say.

After David Coleman had finished his interviews, two policemen were assigned to escort me through the crowds to the next interview, and the next and the next. All I wanted to do now was to have a cup of tea with my folks and share this moment with them, but my wishes didn't come into it. All of a sudden I'd become public property. All around me people were saying, Jenny, don't forget to do this, don't forget to do that.

'Please just hang on a minute and let me have a fag,' I begged one of the policemen.

He shook his head. 'No, you haven't got time. There's a radio interview to do in two minutes.' As we passed the ladies', I dug my heels in. 'I'm sorry, I've just got to go in there.' I nodded towards the ladies'. Inside, all the women standing in line watched in amazement as I fell against the wall, lit a fag, had half a dozen desperate puffs, put it out, then went outside again. As I rejoined the policemen I felt drained. I desperately wanted to go back up to the Stigwoods' box and shut the door.

Instead I was hustled into a tiny room packed full of reporters and placed behind some trestle tables. People were firing questions left, right and centre, and I felt totally bewildered. Suddenly, in the chaos, I heard a voice I recognized. 'Jenny! Jenny!' I looked up and saw Richard, my ex-husband, standing on a chair at the back of the room. He asked me some question I don't even remember now. I was so taken aback that it took me a second or two to reply. I regained my composure, found my voice and hoped no-one had noticed, then answered him. I knew then that the door had closed on that chapter of my life with Richard.

At long last the interviews were over and I was allowed to return to the Stigwood box. It was immediately apparent that the lady I'd asked to look after Dad had done her job a bit too well. I'd never seen my dad drunk before. Mum told me that at one stage during the afternoon, full of Dutch courage, he'd even tackled Michael Dickinson, saying, 'Now then, me boy, what was that you were saying about our Jenny yesterday?' It wasn't like Dad at all, but nothing was normal that day.

The Burrough family were more reserved about showing their emotions than the Harveys, but they were just as overjoyed. After we'd packed Dad off home with Mum and Joe, the Burroughs very kindly took Mandy, Dave, me and the two boys out to dinner in Southport to celebrate. It was past midnight before we set off back to Lambourn.

I remember that journey home as if it was yesterday. I drove and Dave sat next to me in the front with Mandy and the two boys squashed into the back. After ten minutes they were all sound asleep, but I'd never felt more wide awake in my life. I've never taken drugs, but I imagined this was what it must feel like. On the way home I had to stop for petrol. The others didn't even wake up when I went into the garage to pay. The young man behind the till looked up at me and a big smile split his face. 'I think I've seen you somewhere before today, haven't I?' he queried. I'd seldom been recognized before by anyone outside the tightknit world of racing. It was my first inkling that winning the Grand National might change my life.

Back in the car I thought back over the events of the day and relived them again and again, relishing every moment. I'd fulfilled a dream. The fact that I was the first woman to do it did matter, but it wasn't the most important thing. What mattered most was the joy on the faces of the people close to me. As I drove along the deserted motorway I thought about the people who'd supported me through the bad times, people like Lord Cadogan, Tony Stratton-Smith and Peter Callander. 'Well, I hope that's given a bit back to you all,' I thought. I had a little smile to myself about a few others who wouldn't be so pleased. I thought about my family. About Granddad Pitman, who'd died just a few years before, and who'd always been so kind to me. I knew he'd be looking down with a smile on his face today. I thought about my mum, who'd always encouraged me in whatever I'd done, however mad my ideas may have sounded to others. Most of all, I thought about my dad, who'd taught me so much of what I knew about horses. That day, for the first time I could remember, I'd seen Dad moved to tears. Proud wasn't a word Dad ever used. It wasn't a word he rated. But I think he'd come as close to being proud of me that day as he'd ever come in his life, and that meant a lot.

It was three o'clock in the morning when we arrived home. The house was heaving with flowers. My sister Jacquie had stayed up, and when I walked in she put her arms around me and burst into tears. We watched the race on video one more time and then Dave and I went to bed. Dave slept, but I lay on top of the bed. I felt strange, not excited any more, but something else. I struggled to put a name to it. Then it came to me. I felt comfortable, peaceful and content. It had been a long time since I had felt that way.

CHAPTER TWELVE

IN THE LIMELIGHT

In the seven years I'd been training horses at Weathercock House it had never crossed my mind that one day I would become well known. That hadn't been the point of the exercise. I'd just been doing the only job I knew, in order to keep a roof over our heads. So it came as quite a shock to find myself on the television news and to see my name splashed across the front pages of national newspapers. Because its future was threatened, the Grand National was bigger news than usual. And the fact that the race had been won by a woman trainer was a gift as far as the media were concerned. For the next month or so hardly a day went by without someone phoning to ask for an in-depth interview with me. I was asked to appear on television programmes, to talk not just about my horses but about my house and the contents of my wardrobe. It was a jolt to my system. I wasn't prepared for celebrity status. I certainly wasn't prepared for seeing people nudge each other and stare as I walked down the street in Newbury. One day I was in Marks & Spencer buying some underwear when I heard someone giggling behind me. I looked round and saw a woman and her teenage daughter tittering away. Eventually they came over. 'Are you Jenny Pitman?'

'Afraid so,' I replied.

The girl laughed, 'My dad said you were, but I didn't believe him.' She waved to a man who was standing at the other end of the lingerie department, looking towards me and smiling. I felt most embarrassed, with my basket half full of underclothes, none of which missed their notice. Dave thought it was hilarious. 'I can just imagine their conversation down the pub tonight,' he said. 'They'll be saying "And do you know what colour knickers she wears?"' At that we both burst out laughing and I realized it was something I was going to have to get used to.

What I found harder to deal with, however, was the way some people's attitudes changed when they found out who I was. Like the day I went into Swindon to buy some tiles for my shower. I hadn't changed out of my work clothes and the bloke in the shop was ignoring me. When I asked for his advice he was so rude and offhand I'd have walked out there and then except for the fact that I liked the tiles. When I'd chosen the ones I wanted I gave him my name to fill in the invoice, and all of a sudden this man couldn't do enough for me. 'Oh, if you go and fetch your car, Mrs Pitman, I'll stack these in the boot for you,' he said. I found it seriously irritating. To me, people are what they are, irrespective of what their name is or how they dress or speak. It was even more amusing when I pulled up outside the shop in our scruffy van, which we used for all sorts of jobs and so the back was full of hay baler twine, bits of hay and empty paper feed sacks. When I opened the back door and saw his horrified expression I had a struggle to keep a straight face.

I do look a bit of a ragbag when I'm dressed for work – I usually go round the yard dressed in jeans and a sweater with holes in it – so the one place people tended not to recognize me was at home. When people drove up in their cars they would start talking to me as if I was the person who cleaned out the drains. 'Is Mrs Pitman about?' they'd ask.

'You're speaking to her,' I'd say.

'Oh, I didn't recognize you,' someone stammered once. 'You looked so nice on TV!'

Some of the things that happened after Corbiere's Grand National win were quite daunting – like being asked to speak at the Women of the Year luncheon at the Savoy Hotel. I'd never done any public speaking before – and I've done very little since as I find it such an ordeal – and I found I was expected to follow speakers who were well versed in the task, but there was a sense of magic in the room, which was packed full of the country's famous and successful women.

Like the other four speakers, I had been asked to talk to the assembled guests for four and a half minutes on the subject of 'my best friend'. I didn't have to think twice about what or who that was. One speaker's subject was her address book, another's her make-up bag, but I chose to speak about my dad, telling them about my childhood and about his support through hard times. I described his skill in judging horses, my childhood and finished off by telling them about his tears when I won the Grand National. I felt it was well received. People had laughed and applauded, but I was still very relieved when my time was up.

In 1984 I received another honour, but this time I wasn't given any warning. Or rather, I was misled about what the occasion was. One day Dave told me that we had been invited by Max Kingsley to a party at the Sportsman's Club in London. When I'd been married to Richard, Max had always made me welcome at events like the Champion Jockeys' Dinner held at the Sportsman's Club. At some of those functions jockeys' wives can feel about as important as an umbrella on a sunny day, but Max was always charming to the ladies, so I didn't think it odd that I'd been invited to his party. I'd just had a book published – called *Glorious Uncertainty* – and as I was going to London anyway to do a radio programme with John Dunn it would all fit in rather nicely. As we had some time to kill I said to

David that I'd like to go to buy a new dress for the evening. I tried on several different ones and I suppose I should have smelt a rat, as David was showing unusual patience for a man in a woman's dress department. I was due to be taken by a car provided by the publishers to be photographed at a theatre, something I had protested about, but had been strongly overruled, and was duly transported to the Theatre Royal. There I was met by a man who had a camera hanging around his neck, and as we walked up the stairs I heard a voice singing. 'Is that Dot Squires?' I asked, 'Yes, it is,' said the photographer. 'She's rehearsing. Would you like to say hello?' We approached the double doors, which the photographer pushed open. As I stepped inside I could see Dot singing with the band in the spotlight and then vaguely in the dimmed light I could see my solicitor, the vet, and one or two other familiar faces. Oh, I thought, this must be a surprise party, but the next second, from behind a screen on my left, out popped Eamon Andrews. 'Jenny Pitman,' he said, 'this is your life.' I had been led like a lamb to the slaughter. I was caught. Thinking back, there had been the odd strange phonecall with David disappearing for an hour or two at a time; and there'd been other clues too. Dave and Mandy had both been taking more notice than usual about the fact that my hair could do with a cut and style and when we'd arrived at the theatre David had even asked me if I wanted to go and put some lipstick on!

I was whisked away to the BBC studios, where I sat in a daze as people from my past were produced. First there was my family, then Miss Adkins, my primary school teacher. Tony Stratton-Smith, Michael Dunkley, an amateur rider, John Joe Howlett, my Irish horse adviser, and many other treasured friends. They even managed to find Geoffrey Dodd, my oldest childhood 'blood-brother', who was guilty of introducing me to cigarettes. They also persuaded Florence Nagle – who'd fought for women to be allowed to hold training licences – to appear. It was such a thrill meeting her. But perhaps the most moving moment of all came when they showed a film of Major Champneys, now in his eighties and housebound. I was extremely touched by the nice things people said about me. The only let-down of the evening was when I discovered that the famous red book they present you with afterwards doesn't contain the story of your life at all, but just a selection of photographs from the show!

But of course, it was Corbiere who was the real celebrity. Straight after the National, we were asked if we'd let him raise funds for the 'Save the Grand National' appeal. Soon Corky was attending social functions such as boxing matches, which were usually stag nights around the country. I'd always wondered what went on at stag nights, and I had to win the Grand National to find out! It was during a stag night in Bradford that Corbiere first discovered how to play to the gallery. The function was at a big hotel and I started the proceedings by saying a few words and auctioning a replica of Corbiere's National sash (these used to raise anything from £600 to £1,200). After the auction came Corbiere's big moment. He had to walk into the hotel down a very steep concrete slope, which was a bit of a worry. As he appeared at the top of the slope the lights were dimmed. I held my breath until he had reached the bottom safely, and they switched the spotlight on him. I swear Corbiere knew he was the star of the show. He blinked, looked around at all the men sitting there in their penguin suits, then slowly he stretched his neck up like an emu, and showed all his teeth. They loved it. There was a boxing match afterwards, but Corbiere was the hit of the night. People jostled to have their photographs taken with him at £50 a time. The Burroughs used to pay Corky's travel expenses and I paid my own, so between us I like to think that we did our bit to help save the National.

We attended hospices, garden fêtes and agricultural shows; we opened shops; and Corbiere loved every minute. I wouldn't have dared let one lad take him on his own, because being guest of honour did on occasion go to Corbiere's head. After his first taste of showbiz in Bradford he used to come on stage like a rock star, rearing and leaping around as if to say, 'Look at me!' If people applauded he'd be even worse. Two lads had to lead him round to stop him getting seriously out of hand. It wasn't wickedness, just pure showing off. But once he became lit up you wouldn't dare let anyone touch him. If we attended an event I would ask people not to clap him before he appeared. The magic when somebody from a hospice or hospital stroked Corky was wonderful. Something passed between that person and the horse that is impossible to describe. You couldn't see it but you could certainly feel it. I have noticed it since with visitors to the yard. If the people are not well, most horses will stand quietly while they are being touched. It's very humbling.

One day that summer Corbiere was asked to appear at the Leicestershire County Show at Braunstone Park. He stayed at my uncle's farm outside Leicester the night before, and in the morning, before he left, we dressed him over and plaited him up so that he looked absolutely magnificent. Unfortunately, by the time we got to the showground, it was pouring with rain. The stable waiting for him was a temporary wooden box with no proper floor, so that he just stood on the grass with a bale of straw spread over it.

He wasn't due to parade till halfway through the afternoon, so his two lads and I decided to go off for a cup of tea and a hotdog in one of the tents. The whole time we sat there we could hear the rain hammering down on the canvas, and by the time we came out, an hour or so later, just before Corky was due to parade, there were lakes of water all over the showground. We got back to Corbiere's 'stable' to find disaster. While we'd been away water had flooded under the edge of his box and Corky obviously thought he was back at the seaside. He'd pawed up the straw, dug a hole in the soil, and then, when it was nice and full of water, he'd laid down and rolled in it. Our immaculate, shining horse was plastered with wet mud from head to tail. We stared at him in horror while he smiled and blinked back at us through his muddy eyelashes, looking like a hippopotamus who'd just had a nice wallow.

'You old bastard,' I said angrily, but he couldn't care less.

We had thirty minutes to clean him off before he was due in the ring. In a panic we ran back to the hotdog stands and begged for some warm water. Then we desperately started to wash him down. In the end we managed to get him reasonably clean, but he didn't bear much resemblance to the beautifully groomed superstar we'd set off with that morning.

My life altered quite a lot the year that Corbiere won the Grand National, and not just because of that famous victory. One of the most important changes around that time was that I gave up riding. Ever since I'd started training I'd been breaking and riding the young horses myself. It was my friend Eric Wheeler who made me realize that perhaps that wasn't very sensible. He arrived at the yard one day just as I was riding away a youngster. The horse was playing up a bit and Eric shook his head at me. 'What on earth are you doing on that?' he asked.

Until then I'd never given it a thought. I liked riding the young horses. It meant I finished them the way I wanted them, instead of inheriting somebody else's problems.

'What's going to happen if you get bust up, Jenny? Who's going to run the yard then?' Eric asked. It had never occurred to me, but as soon as he said it, I knew he was right. You never go out thinking you're going to have a fall, but however careful you are they do still happen now and then. So I decided to take Eric's advice and let someone else back the young horses.

Changes were happening in my family life, too. Mark was no longer a little boy. In 1983 he was seventeen and a student at Wycliffe College. That summer he left school after passing six O-levels. I'd tried to get him to stay on to take his

A-levels, or at least to follow what I saw as a sensible career, but I'd been fighting a lost cause. I'd first suspected it a couple of years earlier when we'd all gone to the races at Newton Abbot. While Dave drove us back in the car I started giving Mark a bit of a career talk. 'Why don't you think about going into the army?' I said. 'There are lots of opportunities. You can train to do all sorts of things and you could still ride as an amateur.' A slightly desperate voice came back at me from the rear seat of the car. 'But I want to ride, Mum. All I have ever wanted to be is a jockey.'

That was just what I didn't want to hear. If anyone knew about the realities of race-riding it was me. I'd seen enough broken bones and bust-up faces in my time. I looked round at him, because the tone of his voice had changed, and I saw he had tears in his eyes. Though I was not at all happy about it, I knew then what Mark would do and I felt it would be very wrong of me to try to change his mind.

At the age of fourteen Mark had ridden Artistic Prince for me in the Newmarket Town Plate, an amateur flat race. He finished seventh, and the look on his face as he was led in said it all. He was like a greyhound who'd just seen a rabbit. I still felt he should take his O-levels, though, so that he would have something to fall back on. He was due to sit them in June 1983. At Aintree that spring he'd been telling John Joe Howlett, a very good friend of ours from Ireland, how he was going to leave school that summer. 'Mark,' I interrupted, 'do you realize that if you don't get your maths and English O-levels you're going to have to go back to school and take them again?'

Mark's face fell and Jonjo laughed. 'Bejasus, Mark, you don't want to worry about your O-levels. It won't matter how many of them duck eggs you've got when you jump the last at Cheltenham. They won't do you any good.' I glared at him in anger.

'Thank you very much, Jonjo,' I said. I could have throttled him.

Mark passed his English – as well as five other subjects – but we did a deal over his maths, which he'd failed badly. We agreed that if he had private maths lessons in the evenings while he worked for David Nicholson and re-sat his O-level maths in the autumn, he could leave Wycliffe College that summer. Mark grasped the chance like a drowning man seizing a lifebelt. He duly passed his maths O-level.

In July 1983, Mark joined David Nicholson's yard as a pupil-assistant. He'd already had his first ride under National Hunt Rules the previous November, on Monty Python for me in a hurdle race at Folkestone. Monty was a horse who could make you feel like a king or a clown, depending on his mood. He never ran the same race twice. Sometimes he'd set off in front and make the running. Other times you'd have a job to get him to take much part. But at least he was a safe jumper. Mark had finished eighth of sixteen that day – not bad for a first attempt.

I gave him several more rides after he joined David Nicholson and soon learned that I needed to shut down on my personal feelings when Mark was riding for me. At the races ours had to be a strictly professional relationship, and, hardest of all, I had to stop being his mother. There were two reasons for this: one was to stop the other jockeys giving him stick, the other was so that I could cope. I was well aware of the risks, but I couldn't allow myself to think about them.

Other trainers started to give Mark rides in amateur races, and he also had a few rides in point-to-points. However, in his second season with David Nicholson, following talks with his dad, Mark decided that he wanted to turn professional. I was not at all happy about him taking the plunge so soon, and we had a bit of a disagreement about it. There was no doubt in my mind that he could have been champion amateur. On top of that, he would make contacts with farmers and point-to-point folk that would be helpful later on when he was looking for rides as a professional. For Mark, though, riding as an amateur had one big drawback

– he would not be paid. He and Paul were very different in that respect. Mark had always lived for the moment, while Paul was more of a long-term planner. When they were small, if I'd given them both a pound to go to the fair Mark would have spent his in the first ten minutes, while Paul would come home with seventy-five pence still in his pocket. Now they were in their teens, Paul wanted to be an accountant, while Mark wanted to take up the very risky occupation of being a National Hunt jockey.

Mark and I are so alike. Recently a service engineer was changing some of my equipment without okaying it first with me, so I pulled him up short and asked him to first give me a price for the changes he was about to make. When we had agreed the price and the job was completed I was duly signing his cheque when he suddenly said, 'I get the same from that lad of yours.' Not knowing what he was talking about I asked him to explain. 'The knock-back, he does just the same,' he replied. I felt a big smile inside me and said, 'You know what, mate, that is music to my ears.' He looked at me, puzzled. 'Because he used to be such a prat with his money,' I said. As the engineer left quietly I wondered if we would see him again.

Mark wasn't the only one worried about his finances. Money was still causing me headaches. I'd used my percentage of the Grand National prize money to buy a small strip of land from my next-door neighbour, who was none other than Major Champneys, on which I'd built eleven more stables. I'd been sure that with all the publicity which followed the National people would send me more horses, but it didn't quite work out that way. Six months later I still only had twenty-two horses in training, and part of my new stable block remained empty for the whole of the next season. In fact not one new owner came to me after Corbiere's Grand National win. I couldn't understand it. It wasn't just me who found it frustrating – it depressed the staff too. Bryan Smart had recently moved on to work for

Fred Winter, and I now had a new head lad called Martin James. More than once 'Jesse' complained, 'It drives me mad that owners aren't flocking to the door after all the winners we've had.'

It took a while for the penny to drop. The truth was that most people believed Corbiere's win to be a fluke, the sort of thing that could happen to any trainer who got lucky. It was obviously going to take more than one good horse to convince people that I could train racehorses. But I was in a Catch 22 situation. Unless I was sent more horses I was unlikely to find another superstar. Only a small percentage of horses become champions, and lightning doesn't usually strike twice in the same place – or so people say. Happily, in my case, they were wrong.

The horse who was to save the day for me was already in my yard. He had arrived at Weathercock House unexpectedly, in 1981. That summer, my mum had telephoned, saying, 'When are you coming up to see us again, Jenny? We've a friend who'd like you to take a look at a horse of his and tell him what you think.'

I didn't hold my breath. In those days people quite often asked my opinion about their horses. Sometimes they wanted to know whether to buy. Sometimes they were thinking of selling. It did not necessarily mean they wanted me to train it. 'What sort of horse is it?' I asked Mum.

'I don't know much about it, me duck, except it's one he's bred himself,' she said. 'I think it might have had some sort of injury. It's called Burrough Hill Lad.'

The name rang a bell. Then I remembered why. Burrough Hill Lad was the horse who had fallen at the last hurdle when Corbiere had won at Kempton as a novice in January 1980. It had been an X-certificate fall, with the horse landing vertically on his head. He'd not moved for at least five minutes – in fact there'd been a big cheer from the crowd when he got up on his feet. A few weeks later I'd seen his trainer, Jimmy Harris, at Nottingham, and asked him how his horse was.

Jimmy had replied gloomily, 'Not good at all, Jenny. He's done something to his neck and he can't pick his head up more than two feet from the ground.'

I'd suggested he take the horse to Ronnie Longford, a talented equine chiropractor, and the next time I saw Jimmy he told me he'd followed my advice. 'I can't believe the difference in the horse,' he said. 'He'll be running again in a couple of weeks.' I'd been pleased that Ronnie's treatment had worked, but had not followed Burrough Hill Lad's career since then.

Soon after Mum's phonecall, Dave and I drove up to Leicester, and Mum and Dad took us along to see the horse. Burrough Hill Lad belonged at that time to a man called Stan Riley, who turned out to be a brother of Albert Riley, the man who had allowed us to use his stable for our point-to-pointer Dan Archer. When we arrived, the horse was turned out in a field surrounded by an old barbed-wire fence. Stan Riley caught Burrough Hill Lad and led him over to us. He was a big, dark brown gelding, only five years old, and Stan told us that he'd already won four hurdle races. The first thing I noticed about the horse was that he stood terribly straight in front. His foreleg came straight down from his shoulder joint and straight up from his fetlock joint – if you'd dropped a plumbline down it could not have been straighter. Conformation like that puts more strain on the legs, and in Burrough Hill Lad's case that strain was already showing. Stan Riley told me his legs had been treated with a series of injections before he'd been turned out for the summer.

The horse's forelegs were obviously going to need lots of tlc and he also had a nasty scar on the pastern of his off-hind leg. 'He did that as a youngster,' Stan explained. 'He caught it in some barbed wire.'

Unfortunately the wound hadn't been stitched, and as a result the whole area was very sensitive. When Stan trotted the horse away from me I saw that he moved very wide behind, and his movement was not quite square. He was obviously trying to keep the injured hind leg away from the other one to avoid knocking it. That in turn was putting even more strain on his forelegs, making him move with an unbalanced action. Clearly Burrough Hill Lad had problems, but he had one saving grace, which I saw when Stan trotted him back past us. When you looked at his movement from the side rather than from behind, he was the most unbelievable athlete. He trotted with a very straight action, and covered an enormous amount of ground with each stride.

'What's the verdict, then?' Stan asked. I told him what I thought – that he was a nice stamp of horse, an exceptional mover, but that if he was in training his legs would be a cause for concern. I went back off to Enderby with Mum and Dad and thought no more about it. Three or four months later I had a phonecall from Stan Riley. 'I've been doing some roadwork with this horse of mine,' he said. 'He's about ready to start cantering now. Would you like to train him for me?'

I was taken aback. When I'd gone to see him Stan hadn't given me the slightest indication that he wanted me to train the horse. Naturally, I was pleased to have any addition to my numbers, though when Burrough Hill Lad arrived and I saw his legs again I had a few misgivings. 'You're going to be no easy task, are you, mate?' I thought.

My first instinct was to try to boot up the injured hind leg to protect it so that he would not swing his other leg so wide trying to avoid it. But however I booted or bandaged it, I couldn't really protect it because the injury was in such an awkward place. Every boot I tried rubbed the scar, which would then become sore and make him go even wider with his other leg. I spent sleepless nights trying to think of a way round it. And his legs were not the only problem. His jumping left a lot to be desired. Not even his biggest fan would describe Burrough Hill Lad as a natural jumper, and certainly Colin Brown, the jockey who was schooling him at the time, was far from being his biggest fan. It was no wonder: one of the first times we tried to school him over fences, he buried Colin. The horse galloped into the open ditch and hit it hard. There was a crunch and a crack as he broke the back rail of the fence – it looked as if a tank had gone through it. Colin picked himself up from the grass. 'Are you all right?' I asked. 'My shoulder hurts a bit,' came the reply. 'Well, just hop up on him and do it again, only miss out the falling bit,' I said. I must say, Colin did look a bit taken aback.

Burrough Hill Lad's problem was that he'd never bother to change his stride. He had such a great big long stride that if he was going into a fence and he was wrong he wouldn't even try to shorten it. If he met it right, he was brilliant. If not, he didn't give a stuff: he would just leave a bloody great hole in it. 'That horse drives me nuts,' I said to Fred Winter one day after we'd watched yet another demolition job. The guv'nor started laughing. He thought Burrough Hill Lad was hilarious. 'I used to ride an old horse like that,' he said. 'It could jump brilliantly, and then it would crunch one, and I swear it used to look round at me and say, "Are you still there, Fred?"'

I decided that there were two possible explanations for Burrough Hill Lad's clumsiness. The first was his laidback temperament. Perhaps he simply couldn't be bothered to make the effort of sorting himself out because it was too much trouble. The second explanation, which was more likely, was that he was not very bright. That is not to insult the horse, who was the loveliest character you could imagine, but people differ in intelligence, so why shouldn't horses? Perhaps, I thought, Burrough Hill Lad was just a slow learner. If so, the only answer was to take him right back to basics and start again.

The horse had no problem getting the height of his fences. It was the way he approached them that was wrong. To re-educate him, and to get him to change his technique, I put him back through kindergarten. First of all I placed a single pole on the ground, then a few more, and made him trot over them. Then I sent him over a row of telegraph poles about two feet high. Some days he'd trot over them and he'd be fine, and I'd think, thank God, I've got through to you. The next day he'd stand on the poles and just trip over them. He was unbelievably frustrating, but I was not going to throw in the towel.

Whatever it took, as long as it took, I was determined to teach Burrough Hill Lad to jump. Over the years I'd had a lot of practice at this. If a horse had a problem I'd stick at it all day and all night if necessary. I would very rarely fall out with a horse because that would mean I'd failed. No horse, I reasoned, could keep jumping as badly as Burrough Hill Lad. If I went over the basics with him enough times I knew he would have to improve. His jumping might always be dodgy, but we all knew he could gallop.

Burrough Hill Lad had shown me his ability very early on. When I'd first started to work him with another horse around Mandown Bottom I used to say to his rider, 'Jump off here and just quicken up with that other horse for the last mile.' In the beginning when I looked at the way Burrough Hill Lad was galloping, I'd be saying, 'Go on a bit, go on a bit,' because from his action it didn't look as if he was going fast enough. Then I'd look at the horse behind him and see that he was off the bridle and struggling to keep up. And these were not ordinary horses I was working him with either. 'This is no good,' I thought. 'If I'm not careful he's going to end up destroying them.' I had nothing in the yard that could match strides with him. In the end I used to get him to do the first part of his work on his own, then jump another horse, like Bueche Giorod, in with him for the last few furlongs.

In his first season at Weathercock House Burrough Hill Lad ran quite a few times, and towards the end, to my relief, his jumping started to come together. Altogether, in 1981–82, he won three novice chases, two at Newton Abbot on soft ground, and one at Aintree. In October of the next season, Philip Tuck rode him in a chase at Stratford, which he won impressively. A week later Philip rode him again, this time at Ascot, where he won by twenty-five lengths. I decided that the time had come to move up a class. At this stage, all his wins had been in reasonably modest company, so some eyebrows were raised when in November 1982 I entered him in the Edward Hanmer Memorial Chase at Haydock, a race which always attracted a high-class field. That year Silver Buck, the winner of the 1982 Cheltenham Gold Cup, was also entered. Silver Buck's trainer was Michael Dickinson, with whom I'd had one or two gentle 'antler-clashes' (not least at the National) over the years. One paper suggested, 'Michael is less worried about Jenny's horse than he is frightened of the trainer.' Though I think somebody made that up, as it turned out Michael would soon realize that he would have to respect my horse as well!

Burrough Hill Lad ran brilliantly and finished second, only two and a half lengths behind Silver Buck. I was really pleased with him. His jumping was still not perfect – indeed, he made a number of mistakes, but he survived them. Not only that, but he comprehensively beat one Cheltenham Gold Cup winner, Master Smudge, and was only narrowly pipped by another. As we were driving home from Haydock that afternoon I said, 'Do you know what, Dave? I think Burrough Hill Lad could be a Gold Cup horse.' His jaw dropped. He was obviously remembering Burrough Hill Lad tripping over the telegraph poles in our paddock.

My fears about Burrough Hill Lad's legs had been justified. He had a 'show', a slight thickening of one of his tendons. It was nothing major but I knew that if I kept going with him it could turn into something much more significant. There was no way I wanted that to happen. His performance against Silver Buck at Haydock had convinced me that if I could keep him sound I had a very, very good horse on my hands.

There was nothing for it but to give him a year on the sidelines to allow the injury sufficient time to heal. Line-firing had worked well on Corbiere, so I decided to give Burrough Hill Lad's legs the same treatment. Some owners might have argued that since the horse was still sound treatment was unnecessary, but Stan Riley never questioned my training decisions. After the horse was fired he returned to Stan's farm to be turned out while his legs rested and recovered. It was a frustrating time, to say the least, although Corbiere's efforts that year helped make up for the disappointment. In fact, I was able to enjoy Corbiere's achievements even more, knowing I had another good prospect waiting in the wings.

The authors of *Chasers and Hurdlers* had this to say about Burrough Hill Lad in 1983: 'If his jumping improves, and he can carry on where he left off, he will make some of the top chasers look to their laurels on his return.'

It was almost as if they had a crystal ball.

CHAPTER THIRTEEN

BURROUGH HILL LAD

Stan Riley was always on an economy drive. He expected his wife, Kath, to knit his colours, because he thought the professionally made ones were far too expensive, and he always liked to do his horse's roadwork himself as it saved him a few weeks' training fees. That worried me, because although Burrough Hill Lad was a Christian when he first came up from grass, when he became fitter he could be exceedingly naughty. The year after he'd been fired those fears were realized. Stan rang up one morning, in the autumn of 1983, sounding very shaken.

'I think you'd better have this horse back, Jenny,' he said.

'Why, what's up, Stan?' I asked.

'He's just been upside down on a railway embankment,' Stan replied. 'I was nearly run over by a train!'

To our relief, Burrough Hill Lad came back to finish his roadwork at Weathercock House. By now he'd become a real favourite in the yard, not just because he was such a good racehorse but because of his funny habits. When he came in after work he would plunge his head into his water bucket right up to his eyes instead of sipping water like most horses. He looked a bit like a hippopotamus, then he'd blow down his nostrils so the water exploded over the edge of the bucket and soaked you if you didn't watch out. But what was important was that he still had his ability. Before his lay-off his jumping had become a lot more reliable, and though occasionally he'd have a lapse and get it wrong it did not happen nearly so often.

I was determined to raise my sights with him that season, so in the autumn I entered him in the Welsh National, which in 1983 was to be run at Chepstow on 27 December. When the weights came out in the racing calendar several weeks ahead I nearly fell off my chair. The handicapper had given him only 9st 12lb. It was like Father Christmas arriving early. I was convinced there was no way the horse could be beaten at that weight. I don't bet, but if I'd been a gambler I'd have mortgaged Weathercock House and lumped it all on him there and then.

As a preparatory race for the Welsh National I followed the same path I'd taken with Corbiere after his year off, and ran Burrough Hill Lad over hurdles at Nottingham. I'd entered Queen's Ride in the same race, and Mark was to ride him, so I found it a pretty nerve-racking afternoon, but the result was satisfactory all round. Mark rode his first winner under Rules, while just behind them Phil Tuck and Burrough Hill Lad finished a respectable third. The next twenty-four hours, I knew, would be crucial. If Burrough Hill Lad's legs stayed as good as they had been in the run-up to that race I felt I would have an excellent chance of keeping him sound. Fortunately they did.

With the Welsh National a couple of weeks away, Stan Riley told me he wanted Johnny Francome to ride Burrough Hill Lad, as he felt John was simply the best jockey around at the time. I also felt he would get on well with the horse. Because John had been a showjumper he was very good at seeing a stride, which was essential with this horse. Even so, I felt it necessary for John to get a feel for him before the big race, so on the Sunday morning before the race I telephoned him. 'I need you to school my horse before the National, John.'

He immediately started making excuses. 'No, no, no, I can't do it Monday 'cos I've got to do this, and I can't do it Tuesday 'cos I've got to do that, and I can't do it Wednesday—'

I interrupted him. 'John, you've got two effing choices. Either you school it or you don't ride it.'

There was a pause. 'Well, if you put it like that, Jen . . . I'll do it now.'

Dave and I went out, there and then, to tack up the horse, while John put his joddies on. We met him up on the gallops half an hour later. It was quite unusual to school on a Sunday morning, but I had no intention of letting tradition stand in the way.

'Right, Johnny,' I said. 'Just pop him over those three fences.'

John cocked his leg over Burrough Hill Lad and the pair of them went up the schooling ground like poetry in motion. One, two, three. It was beautiful to watch. They gelled immediately. Francome had such skill, of that there was no doubt. But I also knew what the horse could be like. 'I tell you what,' I said when John rode back to us. 'Just pop him up again, will you?'

'No, no, no. You can over-school them, Jen.'

'John, take him up there once more,' I insisted. 'This horse can miss. And when he makes a mistake you'll be sat on your Castlemaine Four X looking up at him unless you know what to expect.'

John looked exceedingly grumpy. 'Oh, all right, then.'

He swung round and set off, sitting like a bag of 'taties because he didn't really want to do it. He jumped the first fence brilliantly, cleared the second fence just as well, went into the third, which was the ditch, and, bang . . . he went up in the air, full jerks, like Desperate Dan, then crashed back

201

down again. He must have given his manhood a rare old milling on the pommel of the saddle, but to be fair to him he came back laughing his head off.

'I'm glad I did that, Jen,' he said. 'I know him now.'

It had rained practically non-stop during the week of the Welsh National. Not only was the going heavy but the weights had gone up. Burrough Hill Lad now had 10st 6lb to carry through the mud, on top of which John was putting up 3lb overweight. But I still thought the horse was well in at the weights, and I was not alone. When the betting opened Burrough Hill Lad had been 33–1, but on the big day he started favourite at 100–30. Most of the price had probably been taken by Dougie Shaw, who I was to learn was his greatest fan. Burrough Hill Lad was such a funny old horse. He was so laid back that he looked half asleep most of the time. That day at Chepstow he walked round the parade ring like Freddie Starr's stuffed dog. He could have been on wheels too. If you didn't know him you'd have thought there was something wrong with him. But the minute the jockeys came into the paddock his ears pricked and he did a little bounce and jig-jog, and I could see he meant business.

Afterwards John told us that from the time the starter dropped his flag the horse had given him such a good feel that he was confident all the way. The horse jumped brilliantly and travelled with perfect ease. As he'd gone round the bottom bend the final time on the run towards home, John found himself upsides Graham McCourt and Paul Barton. Paul was riding the second favourite and was having a right old ding-dong with Graham. Apparently John shouted across at them, 'What's your problem? As soon as I see daylight neither of you is going to win, so stop effing arguing.' And he was right. Burrough Hill Lad went on to win very impressively from Royal Judgement and Lucky Vane. I'd now won the Welsh National two years running with two different horses. As John rode him into the winners' enclosure I had only one question for him: 'Do you think he could be good enough to run in the Gold Cup?'

John frowned. 'I dunno, but I suppose you could enter him. It's very soft ground here today.' But I knew from Burrough Hill Lad's work at home that any ground apart from firm suited him. That was enough for me. The Cheltenham Gold Cup is the pinnacle of jump racing, the championship race for top-class staying chasers. John seemed a bit lukewarm about it, but I felt sure that Burrough Hill Lad was good enough to at least take his chance. He'd annihilated some of my best horses on the gallops at home, his jumping had improved and he was as fit and sound as he had ever been. I felt he had to be entered.

His next race was the Anthony Mildmay, Peter Cazalet Memorial Chase at Sandown on 7 January 1984. Once again Burrough Hill Lad lived up to my faith in him. In spite of carrying a penalty for his win, and six pounds overweight, he was again ridden by John Francome and won easily from Lucky Vane. It was a very different kind of race from the Welsh National, which had been a long, hard slog. This time the pace was faster, and he had to quicken to get his head in front, rather than just outstay the field. He did it well, going to the front three fences from home and increasing his lead with each remaining jump. Even more encouraging, his jumping was as near perfect as I'd ever seen it.

In February John Francome again rode him at Sandown in the Gainsborough Chase. This time he was less confident than I was. 'D'you think this horse'll win today?' he asked as I got ready to leg him up.

'Yes,' I replied.

'I don't know,' he said. 'That horse of Dickinson's, Silver Buck, is a good horse, and the ground's a lot better now than it was at Chepstow.'

'Don't you worry about the ground. The ground'll make no difference to this horse. I think he's a better horse on better ground anyway,' I said.

That is what was so extraordinary about Burrough Hill

Lad. When the going was heavy, as it had been at Chepstow and at Newton Abbot two seasons before, he had floated along the top of the ground as if it was good going. But on a sounder surface he was just as good, if not better. He was simply amazing.

He jumped well again in the Gainsborough, and was never off the bridle. This time John was as impressed as I was. So much so that after the race he told the press it would take a very good horse to beat him at Cheltenham. Burrough Hill Lad had one more race before the Gold Cup, at Wincanton, where Bregawn, his only serious rival, refused at the fourteenth fence. After that, Burrough Hill Lad virtually had a school round rather than a race, and finished two fences in front of the other two runners.

As the big day drew close I started to suffer from a bad case of nerves. By now John Francome and I were not the only people who thought Burrough Hill Lad had a good chance in the Gold Cup, and at the beginning of March he was second favourite. I found the pressure of training a well-backed horse in such a big race quite stressful, especially as he was not the only fancied horse we had at home. Only two weeks after the Gold Cup Corbiere was due to run again in the Grand National, and he'd already been backed down to favourite. I began to have sleepless nights, which were not helped when I took another runner to Windsor one day shortly before the Cheltenham Festival. As I walked through the entrance gate a crowd of pressmen pounced on me.

'What's all this about, then?' I asked.

'We were hoping you could tell us something about the rumours regarding Burrough Hill Lad,' a reporter said.

My blood ran cold. 'What rumours?' My first thought was that something must have happened to him since I'd left home.

'We hear the horse has been breaking blood vessels.'

'That's a load of cobblers,' I replied.

The horse had come back in from exercise earlier that morning before I left for Windsor and I'd checked him over, as I always did. There had been nothing wrong with him at all.

'Well, we've heard it from a reliable source,' the reporter insisted.

'You can write what you effing like,' I said. 'It won't stop him winning the Gold Cup.'

It was the 'reliable source' statement that had annoyed me. I had had the same phrase levelled at me during my marriage break-up, and other unhelpful phrases like, 'One of your friends said'. I used to think 'Friends, they don't tell tales.' Of course, when we returned home there was nothing wrong with the horse. There never had been, but the scare did panic me. A lot of money had been piling onto Burrough Hill Lad for the Gold Cup, and where money is concerned you often see the worst side of people. I decided to install security beams around the stables, which would sound an alarm if they were broken by an intruder moving about. It turned out not to be such a good idea, because it went off every single night. Time after time Dave leapt out of bed as the noise of the alarms woke half the village of Upper Lambourn. There was never anyone there, nor any sign that the horses had been disturbed. In the end Dave refused to get up when it went off. So I did, and discovered the culprit. One of our horses, Artistic Prince, had a heat lamp in his box, and every night the yard cat used to sleep curled up on his back, basking under the lamp. When the cat woke up and decided to go off hunting mice, he'd jump out over the box door. Theoretically, it was not possible for small animals to trigger the alarm, but the night I saw the cat he leapt so fast through both beams that he managed to trigger them. When I went back to bed and told Dave he was not amused.

We soon sorted that problem out, but dealing with the rumours about Burrough Hill Lad was less easy. The story about him breaking a blood vessel was repeated in the newspapers, and even good friends rang up to ask if it was true. I told them, as I'd told the press, that it wasn't. As far as I was concerned the horse had as good a chance of winning the Gold Cup as any other horse in the race. We were not a certainty, by any means; I had learned from my earlier days that there are very few certainties, particularly in the Gold Cup, but I was sure that Burrough Hill Lad had never been in better nick. At that time Terry Biddlecombe was working for Central TV and was making a feature for them about Burrough Hill Lad. A week before the Gold Cup I invited him to bring his crew up to the gallops. After Burrough Hill Lad had worked I called Terry over.

'Here, stick that camera up his nose,' I told him. 'Then I can prove to the whole bloody world that he's not bursting blood vessels!'

With all these worries, I could hardly believe it when Stan Riley came up with a new money-saving scheme. He'd decided that travelling Burrough Hill Lad to the races by horsebox was costing him too much money, and he was going to buy a horse-trailer. His plan was to drive down to Weathercock House the day before the races, spend the night there, then put the horse in the trailer the next morning and tow it to Cheltenham behind his dormobile. For once words failed me. Just as well, really. Dave has always been much more diplomatic than I am and is known for putting pins back into hand grenades. After quietly pointing out that Burrough Hill Lad had earned several thousand pounds already for Stan that year, he said, 'If this horse is as good as we think he is, Stan, then we'd better get a chauffeur-driven Rolls-Royce to take him to the races, never mind a trailer!' No more was heard of that particular plan.

But I had a more serious problem to deal with than Stan's penny-pinching schemes. John Francome had been claimed to ride Brown Chamberlin, Fred Winter's entry in the race, and was unable to ride my horse. After some thought, we decided to book Phil Tuck instead. Philip had ridden

Burrough Hill Lad for both his previous trainers, as well as for me, and had won on him several times, so he knew the horse well. While he might not be the greatest stylist you'd ever seen, there was no doubt Philip was a bloody good jockey. In addition, he was quick on the uptake. If you went through a race with him beforehand and discussed how you wanted a horse ridden, then that's what would happen.

Dave, Philip and I sat down the night before the Gold Cup and watched tapes of other races and the other runners while we made our plan. One thing we'd learned about Burrough Hill Lad was that he always had a flat spot in the middle of his races. He'd be off the bridle for half a furlong and if you didn't know him you'd think he was getting to the bottom of his petrol supply. Then all of a sudden his turbo would kick in and he'd be away again. I reminded Philip of that. Then we planned our tactics, which involved taking advantage of John Francome!

Unlike Burrough Hill Lad, Brown Chamberlin had run at Cheltenham several times before and had in fact won the Sun Alliance Chase there in 1982. When we'd been watching videos of his Cheltenham races we'd noticed that Brown Chamberlin always ran wide right-handed off the bottom bend, so we planned to turn that knowledge to our advantage.

'I think Brown Chamberlin will make the running,' I told Philip, 'but I want you to sit in mid-division for the first circuit, move up on the second circuit and if you can track Brown Chamberlin down the hill, when he runs wide, you'll be able to nip up the inside. Take it up going to the last and keep going.' Plan A was made.

It is not often that a race works out exactly as you expect, but if ever there was a copy-book performance it was Burrough Hill Lad's run in the 1984 Cheltenham Gold Cup. There were twelve runners on the day, with Wayward Lad the 6–4 favourite, Burrough Hill Lad at 7–2 and Brown Chamberlin at 5–1. I was a complete bag of nerves before the race, and, for once, not just for the horse. If Burrough Hill Lad didn't win, I knew the press would shred me. They'd assume the rumours about broken blood vessels were true, no matter what I'd said.

As we'd expected, Brown Chamberlin moved straight into the lead, setting a good strong gallop. Burrough Hill Lad had settled nicely in the group following him, moving and jumping well. But the favourite, Wayward Lad, wasn't. He hit the second ditch so hard his jockey Robert Earnshaw did well to stay on board, and he carried on making errors as the race went on. Bregawn, who'd won the race the year before, never looked like getting seriously involved. He was running in blinkers and seemed to be sulking. Along the back straight John Francome began to turn up the pace and the field became more strung out. Behind Brown Chamberlin there were now just four horses in with a chance – the outsider Scot Lane, Drumlargan, Canny Danny and Burrough Hill Lad. Things were going according to the script. Each move Philip made on that horse was like turning a page of an instruction manual. Coming down the hill he tucked Burrough Hill Lad in behind Brown Chamberlin, with Drumlargan close behind him. At the third last any one of them could have won it, but when Brown Chamberlin and Burrough Hill Lad started to leave Drumlargan behind, it was clear that the race was between the two of them. Coming round the final bend Brown Chamberlin started to drift wide, as predicted, giving Philip enough room to nip up inside with Burrough Hill Lad. At the last he jumped into the lead and, with Philip riding him like a man possessed, he ran on brilliantly to win by three lengths.

I had watched the race from the stand, with Dave and my mum and dad. Paul – who'd been given the day off from Wycliffe College – watched from the BBC tower with his dad. By the time the horses passed the post Mum and Dad were literally having to hold me up. To have won the two greatest races in jumping inside twelve months was a complete fairytale. Fairytales had always seemed to happen to other people, not me, I thought later.

My legs had gone to jelly and I had a job walking down from the stand. It sounds ridiculous, I know, but at one stage I was so overcome I thought I was going to collapse. The agony and the ecstasy. As we walked towards the crowded winners' enclosure, however, I managed to pull myself together. The Queen Mother was presenting the trophy, and I most certainly had no intention of collapsing on the floor in front of her. The last time I'd met the Queen Mother was when we'd been invited to Windsor after the Grand Military Gold Cup. But today, meeting her in public with the Cheltenham crowd cheering, I found the whole occasion overwhelming. The only thing I remember clearly is her smiling during the presentation and inviting me to the royal box.

Naturally I was delighted to accept the invitation, but as I was beginning to come down to earth I knew that Burrough Hill Lad's delicate legs would need bandaging first. I also knew that if I didn't see to him straight away I'd have no horse left to train the next day. 'Thank you very much, ma'am,' I answered, 'but would you mind if I do the horse's legs first?' Her Majesty seemed fine about it, but one or two other people near by looked a little taken aback.

Edward Gillespie, who is now the managing director of Cheltenham racecourse but who was very much a junior at that time, was sent along to chaperone me. David and I went up to the dope-box where Burrough Hill Lad had been taken for his routine test, and waited while his lad finished washing him down. I took off my coat and hung it up – I thought I'd better keep it clean – and then washed the horse's legs spotlessly clean and put his bandages on. As I finished and turned to reach for my coat I saw Edward Gillespie watching me with his mouth half open.

'What's up with you, then, Edward?' I asked.

He shook his head. 'I can't believe what I've just seen.'

What's he on about, I thought. He looked so shocked you'd think I'd just stripped off and stood there stark naked. I thought no more about it and put on my coat and headed off with Edward for the royal box. As I walked through the entrance the attendant at the door stepped forward.

'Excuse me, madam. May I take your coat?'

I started to unbutton it then froze as I remembered with horror what I was wearing underneath, and wondered whether that was what had shocked Edward. The trouble was that I'd never been good about dressing up. Deciding what I wore to the races always came a very poor second to the horses' clothing. Usually I wore white crew-necked jumpers, because they were easy. I had a collection of them, but one seemed particularly lucky and I'd put it on that morning. Unfortunately it was quite well worn and it had recently had a bit of an accident on the ironing board, so there was a great big hole as big as an orange at the bottom in the front.

As I quickly refastened my coat I said, 'N-n-no. It's all right, thank you. I can't stop very long.' I was extremely relieved that he did not insist.

I made my escape as quickly as I could. They must have thought I was the strangest person they'd ever had in that lovely warm box, clutching my coat around me as if I had pneumonia. Thinking about it, I'm sure if the Queen Mother *had* seen my lucky sweater she wouldn't have minded at all.

Afterwards I had a chat with Stan and Kath Riley, who were naturally overjoyed, and then rejoined Dave and my mum and dad, who were going to spend the night with us. On the journey home Dad sat in the front of the car with Dave. Dad was unusually quiet, so quiet in fact, that I felt a bit worried about him. Usually after the races he'd be talking about who he'd bumped into and what he thought of other people's horses, but today he said nothing, nothing at all.

I leaned forward. 'What's up, Dad? You're a bit quiet. Are you all right?'

'Yes, I'm fine, me duck,' he said. Then after a pause he added quietly, 'I just can't quite believe it, that's all.'

None of us could believe it. Back home everyone, all the staff, including some neighbours and friends, crowded into the living room at Weathercock House to watch a video of the race. 'Are you coming out for a meal?' someone asked.

'I'm sorry, I can't,' I replied because I felt totally and utterly exhausted. So we ended up ringing up the local fish and chip shop to order twenty-nine portions of fish and chicken and chips. It was a brilliant night. After Corbiere's Grand National I'd been really wide awake, but now I just couldn't wait to go to bed. It was well before midnight when my head hit the pillow. It had been ages since I'd slept so soundly.

There were some unexpected sequels to the Gold Cup. Though I hadn't bet a penny on Burrough Hill Lad, several of our friends and acquaintances had. One of these lucky punters was a young man of about thirty, who we'd met on the gallops the season before. It had been a freezing cold day and he'd been standing by the side of the shavings when Dave and I had pulled up near by. We started talking to him and found he was from Haydock but was staying with a cousin near Marlborough and had come up to watch the horses on the gallops because racing was his passion. He was freezing cold and shivering like a leaf.

'I'll tell you what,' I said. 'Come back to the yard and have a cup of tea and you can have a look round if you like.'

His eyes lit up. You'd think I'd offered him tea at the Ritz. 'Oh, that'd be great,' he said. 'I'd love to see Burrough Hill Lad.' It turned out 'The Lad' was his favourite racehorse, even though he'd not yet set the world alight.

Back in the yard I introduced the pair of them, he patted the horse, and went away happy as Larry.

We didn't see the young man again until a week or so after the Gold Cup, when he appeared in the yard with his fiancée.

The pair of them were beaming from ear to ear. The story he told us was hard to believe. It seemed they'd been saving up to get married, but the housing market was booming at that time and whenever they'd saved enough money for a deposit, house prices went up again, so they were beginning to despair. After meeting Burrough Hill Lad the season before, this chap had followed him whenever he ran, and all through the year he'd been backing him for the Gold Cup. When the horse's odds suddenly drifted from 2–1 to 4–1, he said to his fiancée, 'I'm going to back Jenny's horse again.'

She wasn't keen. 'There's rumours about him,' she'd said.

'Well, if Jenny says it's all right, as far as I'm concerned it's all right,' he said, and he put all the money they'd saved for their house deposit on the horse. If Burrough Hill Lad had lost, I guess the engagement would have been off. As a result, they ended up with enough money to buy the whole house!

The Shaw family from Yorkshire pulled off an even bigger coup. Jim Shaw was a pig farmer and a friend of my brother Joe. He and his son Dougie had visited the yard several times and made friends with Burrough Hill Lad. Dougie, who was a young man in his thirties, was Burrough Hill Lad's biggest fan. The Shaws never let on much about their betting activities, but I did know that they'd backed him at 33–1 to win the Welsh National. However, it wasn't until Dougie came to visit us a couple of weeks after the Gold Cup that we heard the final chapter of the story.

'Eee, we've had a right do,' Dougie beamed.

'Oh yes?' I said. 'What have you been up to, then?'

'Well, you know we backed Burrough Hill Lad to win at Chepstow?'

'Yes.'

'Well, we didn't collect it. We let the f— ing lot ride on the Gold Cup!'

The Shaws had won a total of £97,000. They'd placed the bet with a northern bookmaker, and when they went to the betting shop to collect they asked for cash. It took the bookie three weeks to pay them out, and when they got their last wad of notes he threw it at them across the betting shop and told them never to darken his door again – or words to that effect! If I'd known about either of the two bets before the race I might have needed psychiatric care!

The events before and during the Festival had left me feeling a bit drained, and I felt in need of a summer break, but the season wasn't over yet. A few weeks after the Gold Cup I found myself on another emotional rollercoaster as I watched Corbiere run in the Grand National for the second time.

The handicapper had been very harsh with him in 1984. Even though he'd not won a race for twelve months he'd been given top weight of 12st, 10lb more than in 1983. For some reason, good horses like Ashley House, which had been giving weight to Corbiere all season, were set to carry *less* weight than he was in the Grand National. It was obvious to me that he was being handicapped because of the name of the race. It struck me as being deeply unfair, and I said so, loudly and in public, quite a few times. If that didn't go down too well with the establishment then too bad. I felt the horse had been treated harshly.

Brian Burrough's dad rang up the day the weights were published. 'What difference will it make?' he wanted to know.

'The difference between winning and losing,' I told him.

I was right. But it didn't stop him trying. He absolutely ran his heart out and he very nearly did it. His jumping was every bit as clean as it had been the year before. He lay seventh or eighth nearly all the way round until the last half-mile of the race, when he made up a dozen lengths. After the Elbow, he was gaining on the two leaders with every stride and in the end the winner, Hallo Dandy, carrying twenty-six pounds less, beat Corbiere by only five and a half lengths. In second place, one pound better off than in 1983, was Greasepaint.

213

Afterwards, Jesse James and I returned to the box to wash Corbiere down. Jesse had recently left the yard to work for the Atomic Energy Authority at Harwell, but he loved Corky as much as I did and had come back specially for the day. Corky had tried so hard, and it broke my heart to look at him. I had to go round the other side of the horse to wash him off, because I was crying my eyes out. When I caught sight of Jesse I realized I need not have bothered because he was crying too. Some people say it's a fault to fall in love with your horses, but I couldn't do my job if I didn't love them. You can't live and work with a horse like Corbiere for as long as we'd done and not care deeply about him. But to be third in the Grand National was no disgrace. Corky was bloody fantastic.

CHAPTER FOURTEEN

THE TURNING TIDE

There is no doubt that the National Hunt season of 1983–84 turned the tide for me as a trainer. After Burrough Hill Lad's Gold Cup win, total strangers started to ring me up, asking me to train their horses, and by the following season every single one of my boxes was occupied. Between them, Corbiere and Burrough Hill Lad had finally convinced people that my early success in the Grand National had not just been luck. But though the expression on my bank manager's face was definitely beginning to thaw, I still had a long way to go before I would be home and dry.

Burrough Hill Lad took all the credit for one set of new owners. The Shaw family decided to spend some of the bookmakers' money they'd received for their successful bet on a horse of their own, a bay gelding called Fame The Spur. I'm not sure why, but David Shaw, Dougie's brother, always managed to call him Frame The Sperm. Another couple who contacted me in the summer of 1984 were Robert and Elizabeth Hitchins. They were keen racing people who'd originally lived in Cheltenham but had moved to Guernsey. When they came to visit us Mrs Hitchins said: 'Do you know why we asked you to buy us a horse?' I felt myself begin to preen a little. 'Well,' she continued, 'I've always liked people who wear red hats, and when we saw you on television being interviewed you were wearing a red hat!' My ego was quickly deflated.

Well, I thought, that must be the most obscure way of being chosen as a racehorse trainer; but Mr and Mrs Hitchins became two very loyal and supportive owners. The comment about my hat was actually quite significant. Mrs Hitchins was a lovely lady, very elegant, feminine and kind. But she also had a strong character and could make her point without ever raising her voice, which is something I myself have never quite mastered. She was also very particular and felt strongly about colour, which she believed affected people's moods and reflected their character. During the early days as an owner she changed her racing colours eighteen times before we had them made, and she would regularly send us swatches of colour and other material to match up with makers' fabrics. She eventually settled on red and grey as her new colours, but soon afterwards, when she arrived at Warwick races and I had legged the jockey up on her horse, she decided the grey in the jacket clashed with the grey coat of her horse, Mamora Bay, so we had to organize new colours before the horse ran again. After that Mr and Mrs Hitchins' horses ran in blue and orange diamonds, which have now become very well known on the racetracks.

Mrs Hitchins had always had a soft spot for the colour grey. In 1984, when we were looking for her first horse, she was very keen that it should be a grey. The bloodstock agent Johnny Harrington took Dad, David and me round most of Ireland in search of the right animal. For two and a half days we looked at every grey horse that every Irish farmer could pull out of a field for us. Some were like pit ponies and some like Shires. Finally, to our relief, we found a four-year-old that really looked the business. We were about to shake hands on the deal when Dad decided to look in its mouth to check that it really was a four-year-old, and lo and behold, it had no front teeth at all! The farmer had declined to tell us that they'd all been knocked out. The horse actually looked very well, but I did not dare buy an animal that might have trouble eating, so we came back without him. However, another visit to Ireland on Mr and Mrs Hitchins' behalf a few years later was much more successful. The horse I found on that occasion wasn't grey, but a bay. I knew the colour wasn't right but he was such a nice horse, he was already named, and he'd raced with a lot of promise. In the years that followed, Toby Tobias proved to be more than worth waiting for.

Other new owners who came to us at that time included several showbusiness personalities, like the comedian Freddie Starr and the singer Errol Brown. Errol had a share in a brown gelding called Gainsay, who was to win five races for us, including the Ritz Club Chase at Cheltenham in 1987 and the Sporting Life Weekender Handicap Chase at Aintree.

Several horses were also sent to me by Terry Ramsden. He was one of the most flamboyant personalities in racing and had a reputation for extravagant gambling. People were never indifferent to Terry. It seemed they either loved him or hated him. He had a lot of horses with different trainers, and when he sent some to me several people told me to be careful. They told me that some owners who liked to bet looked for inside information from trainers. I certainly have no idea what happened with other trainers but I can say, with my hand on my heart, that the whole time he was with me, Terry Ramsden never, ever, asked me about anybody else's horse.

The first time I met him, we were up at Aintree in 1986 with a horse he owned called I Bin Zaidoon, which had come to us from Flat racing and which we were running in a novice hurdle. I Bin Zaidoon was a lovely little horse, a cheeky, playful character. Just as the horse entered the parade ring the sun came out and cast a shadow across the path under one of the trees, and every time I Bin Zaidoon came to this shadow he struck out at it with a front leg. I saw Terry Ramsden approaching and, being aware of his reputation, I started to feel a bit on edge. I hope we get on, I thought, and I hope this horse runs well . . . We shook hands and I pointed across the paddock. 'There's your horse over there,' I said, and just at that second I Bin Zaidoon reached the shadow, struck out at it again but misjudged the situation and fell onto his knees.

'Jesus Christ!' I gasped. 'That's a good start,' as the horse quietly jumped back to his feet. I decided the best thing to do was to turn it into a joke. Graham McCourt was to ride him, and as he walked up to us I said, 'I hope he jumps better than that on the track, Graham. That looked like he couldn't jump his own shadow.' Terry laughed, not looking the least bit worried, and I knew then we'd get on. Luckily, I Bin Zaidoon's concentration improved when the race started, and won nicely. Later, when another of the horses he'd sent me, Stearsby, won the same afternoon, Terry was delighted and asked us up to his box for a drink. That day I happened to be wearing my little gold horse brooch, studded with tiny diamond chips. I'd fallen in love with this brooch in a jeweller's window many years earlier and had saved up for ages, putting a bit away each week. While we were chatting in his box I saw Terry having a good look at this brooch. 'Do you collect those?' he asked me suddenly.

Collect them? I thought. Christ, it took me about four years to save enough money to buy this one! 'Well, you know . . .' I managed, but before I could finish my sentence Terry responded, 'Oh, good, I've got one that I'd like you to have. I'll send somebody to fetch it.'

I saw him again the following day, but the brooch was not mentioned and I assumed he'd forgotten about it. But on the final day of the Grand National meeting Terry suddenly marched up to me as the runners were circling in the paddock for the big race. I was talking to the owners of

Corbiere, when Terry stepped forward, said, 'Here you are,' and slipped a box into my hand. I put it into my handbag and went to watch Corbiere, who fell at the fourth fence, much to my dismay. Fortunately, both he and his jockey Ben de Haan escaped unscathed.

It was much later that I discovered that Terry's box contained a beautiful gold and diamond brooch. Nine months later, in December 1986, Stearsby was to win my third Welsh National, so I felt I had returned Terry's kind and generous deed.

Some new owners were quite different from Terry Ramsden. I came across Gary Johnson when I was looking for a van for my dad and rang a telephone number in the *Thames Valley Auto Trader* newspaper. The bloke who answered started giving me the usual story – 'Oh, I haven't got that van any more, but I've got one similar . . .' when suddenly he said, 'Don't I know you? Your voice sounds familiar.'

'No,' I said, because I had the distinct impression that if I told him who I was the van would cost me another few quid.

'What's your surname?' he asked.

'Stait,' I lied.

'No, it isn't,' he said. 'Your name's Jenny Pitman. I've heard you speaking on the telly.' The game was up and I had to admit it.

'I've always wanted to meet you,' he continued. 'I've got a racehorse myself actually. Guess what it's called, bearing in mind what I do for a living.'

'I give up,' I said.

'Vantastic!' he said.

Terrific! I thought.

I never did buy a van from Gary Johnson, but soon afterwards he came to see me and asked me if I would train Vantastic for him. The horse belonged to him, his brother Libby and their father Fred. When he brought Vantastic to see me he turned out to be a light-framed horse, who was also a rig, which meant he had only one testicle. This was bad news, because rigs are difficult to train and are generally a bit of a nuisance as they can also be rather colty. Vantastic didn't have much ability, but I figured he'd be capable of winning a selling race. Over the next year I did my best to persuade the Johnsons to sell him and spend their training fees on a horse with more potential, but for a long time my arguments fell on deaf ears.

In the past most of my horses had come to me second-hand, and I'd got used to making the best of what I was given to train. Fortunately, this was no longer my only option. Some of my new owners wanted me to go to the sales and buy young horses for them. It was a dream come true. Though in the past I had sometimes bought horses at the sales, now I had a freer hand to look for my own raw material, and had a bit more money to spend. Even so, it was quite daunting to be putting my own judgement on the line. Finding a potential star amongst horses that haven't even been broken in is a lot harder than spotting one that has run already and has had its form exposed. However, I felt I had the best tutor in the world to help me – my dad, and, what's more, I never lost that feeling.

In those early days I always took Dad along to the sales with me when I was buying youngsters. When the thought of spending thousands of pounds of someone else's money made me jittery, Dad used to help keep my nerves steady. To him, a horse was a horse and it was there to do a job – it didn't matter to him if it cost £100 or £100,000. What he always looked for, regardless of the price tag, was quality. A horse could have the best pedigree in the world and be the best-turned-out horse in the sale, but if its conformation, movement and temperament didn't measure up he would not be interested. Gradually, because we both generally liked the same horses, my own confidence developed.

The sort of horses I liked were inclined to be 'butty' (com-pact), with a well-balanced movement. If possible, they had to have something else, too, which I found much harder to put into words. Sometimes, when people ask me why I'd bought a particular horse, all I can say is that it has magic. You can't see it, you can't touch it, but you can feel it.

As well as being a good judge, Dad was experienced in bidding at the sales. He'd been buying cows at auction before I was born, so he knew all about dealing and the sharp practices that went on, and he gave me the benefit of that experience as well. The very first time we went to a young-stock sale in Ireland we had found a horse we both liked. According to Dad, it was 'the only horse worth a light in the sale'. Unfortunately I made the mistake of not keeping my cards close enough to my chest. When the horse came into the ring the bidding was fast and furious, and it soon reached a price close to my limit. To my dismay, a couple of people were still bidding against me. I was just about to make another bid, when Dad tugged my sleeve. 'Stop, Jenny. They're running you!' he said. Somehow he'd realized that the other bidders weren't genuine but were friends of the vendor and were running up the price because they knew I was interested. I quickly shook my head at the auctioneer, and the horse was knocked down to an Irishman standing on the other side of the ring. I was quite upset at losing it, and wasn't totally convinced Dad had been right. But half an hour later, as we were looking at another horse, the vendor came up to me looking sheepish.

'What are you doing here, then, Jenny?'

'Well, I'm looking to see if there's anything else I can buy,' I said.

He stroked his chin. 'Would you still like that horse of mine?'

'I did like him,' I said. 'But I thought he was sold.'

He hesitated. 'Ah, well now, not exactly. I tell you what. You can have him for your last bid. Will that do you?'

I was not at all pleased and I decided that now it was my turn, so we renegotiated and, having knocked several hundred pounds off the price, I bought the horse. The experience taught me a valuable lesson. If you took a liking to a horse at the sales you didn't go round telling people you liked it.

I generally preferred to go to Ireland to buy my youngstock, because there was a much bigger choice there. In Ireland you can see five hundred jumpers at the Derby sale. I would still buy young homebred horses, but they're just not around in England in the quantity, or quality, to give me the choice I am looking for. Looking at five hundred horses in two days is very hard work. You're on your feet all day long, from early morning to half past ten or eleven at night, and you really do have to stick at it to get value for money. When you come home you feel as if you've run in the London marathon two days running. But it's worth it.

Not that the Irish sales were perfect. In those days a lot of the horses were not nearly as well polished and presented as they would be at an English sale. Though the horses produced by the dealer and professional studs would be in their Sunday best, some of the others, who'd been brought in by the farmers who bred them, would be in what you might call their work clothes. But seeing animals not dressed up had never bothered Dad, and it didn't concern me either. When I looked at a horse I had to try to decide what it could grow into. What would it be like in a year's time? Could I improve it? Spotting the potential in young horses was a serious challenge if they were to become my shop window, and not every ugly duckling was going to turn into a swan.

On one of our first trips to Ballsbridge sales we'd come across one such duckling. Mark had come with us and was shadowing his granddad, keen to pick up knowledge. Going round the sales with Dad was a bit of an endurance test because he wanted to look at every single horse in the catalogue. Not just look at it, either, but get it out of its box and have a conversation about it. I had a different approach. If I went into a box and saw that a horse was obviously not going to do I'd say thank you and walk out again. On this day I'd got a few boxes ahead of my dad and Mark when I suddenly heard roars of laughter. I went back to find them. 'Here, don't laugh at people's horses, Mark,' I told him. 'They'll find it offensive.'

'I wasn't laughing at the horse, Mother,' Mark said. 'I was laughing at something Granddad said.' He told me my dad had asked to see this horse out of its box, and when it came out it was nearly eighteen hands high, with a great big head and long hairy legs. Mark had looked at his catalogue and said, 'What kind of horse is this, then, Granddad?' meaning was it a hurdler or chaser. Dad had whispered in his ear, 'Cart, me boy,' and Mark had cracked up.

As well as my new young horses, I still had my old faithfuls. At the start of the 1984–85 season Burrough Hill Lad seemed as good as ever. He was still only eight years old, which, if you forgot about his dodgy 'wheels', meant he was in his prime. The obvious next step for a horse of his class would be the King George VI Chase on Boxing Day. With that at the back of my mind I decided to run him in the Hennessy Gold Cup at Newbury on 24 November, a race of over three and a quarter miles.

At the request of Stan Riley, John Francome was back on Burrough Hill Lad that day. Racing is a tough, competitive business, and things were apt to change when John became available. Stan was not a wealthy man and we were racing for big money at Newbury. I respected his decision and thought it was the right one, although it was tough on Phil Tuck.

No-one could argue with the quality of Burrough Hill Lad's triumph that day, which confirmed his status as the best staying chaser in training. What's more, he did it under top weight of twelve stone. In the long history of the Hennessy at that point only the peerless Arkle had won it carrying more weight than Burrough Hill Lad. This time he made only one serious mistake, seven fences from home. It was bad enough to have caused some horses to fall, but it barely interrupted Burrough Hill Lad's relentless progress. He led for the first time approaching the second last, quickly sprinted clear and won in the manner of a true champion. Canny Danny, who was receiving a stone and a half in weight, plugged on to take second place, four lengths behind the winner, with Gaye Chance fully twenty lengths further back in third. John Francome was almost purring with delight when he returned, and has always described that race as the finest performance of Burrough Hill Lad's career.

I now had to make up my mind whether to run him in the King George VI Chase at Kempton on Boxing Day at level weights, or tackle the Welsh National again, where he would undoubtedly have top weight of twelve stone. I was worried about running him at Kempton; it was the track where, five years earlier, he had been injured in that terrible fall over hurdles. In addition, the conditions of the King George did not really favour us. Kempton is a fast three miles on a flat course, and I wasn't convinced he'd be quick enough in a high-class race. So far, Burrough Hill Lad had performed best on galloping tracks like Cheltenham and Newbury, and over distances in excess of three miles. For the past two years the King George had been won by Wayward Lad, who *was* suited by the conditions, and I knew he was almost certain to try for the hat-trick. Although we'd beaten Wayward Lad in the Gold Cup, I wasn't at all certain we'd be able to confirm that form at Kempton. The more I thought about it, the more I wondered whether it might be more sensible to have another go at the Welsh National, which was to be run on 22 December.

To help me decide which route to take, I planned to run Burrough Hill Lad on 8 December in the Charlie Hall Memorial Pattern Chase at Wetherby. It was Wayward Lad's local course, and I knew he would be entered in the same race. Wetherby is quite a tight track, though not as flat as Kempton, but I felt that if we couldn't beat Wayward

Lad in the Charlie Hall then we wouldn't beat him in the King George, in which case I would run Burrough Hill Lad in the Welsh National again. Few people thought we had a chance against Wayward Lad at either Wetherby or Kempton, and in fact the racing journalist Michael Seely went so far as to ring me up on the Tuesday before the race, saying, 'Jenny, you're mad to take on Wayward Lad at Wetherby. Everybody's talking about it and you can't possibly beat him.' I was furious. I already had enough on my mind without the press having their 'five pence worth'.

'How many winners have you trained, Michael?' I asked.

'Well, well none actually, Jenny . . .' he replied.

'Well, sod off, and don't try to tell me how to train my horses,' I replied angrily.

Afterwards, when I'd calmed down, I felt guilty. I'd known Michael for many years and I realized he was only trying to protect me and loved him for it.

My mum hadn't been at all well, so Dave and I decided to go up to Leicestershire and stay the Friday night before the race at my parents' house. Mark was to ride a horse called Nader for me in the first race, and the plan was for him to drive up on the Saturday morning and meet us at Grandma's at nine o'clock, then we'd all drive on to Wetherby together.

On Saturday morning, nine o'clock came and went and there was no sign of Mark. He was never late, and by twenty past I was hopping up and down with worry. At twenty-five past the phone rang. It was Mandy, ringing from my office. 'Jenny, Mark's been involved in a car accident. He's in Warwick Hospital.'

My heart stood still. 'What's happened? Is he all right?'

'They think he's broken his arm. But apart from that he's okay.'

By now it was twenty-five to ten, and since it would take us a good two hours to get to Wetherby there was nothing for it but to accept what I'd been told, jump in the car and set off up the M1. When we arrived at the racecourse I booked a substitute jockey to ride Nader and found a phone to ring the police. I was worried about Mark's belongings. If he'd been taken off to hospital in an ambulance I was afraid his car could have been left anywhere, and I didn't want people removing his saddlery from it. Eventually I got through to the policeman dealing with the accident.

'No, the car's safe in a garage,' he told me. 'They took it away as soon as we got him out of it.'

'Got him out of it?' I echoed.

'Yes, didn't they tell you? He was trapped in the car and it took over an hour to cut him out.'

I'd been imagining a minor shunt. Suddenly it was a complete nightmare.

It was a freezing cold day and Mum was still far from well. I'd refused to take her racing because I felt she should be at home in the warm, but she'd talked Stan Riley into taking her. I decided not to tell her this latest news and desperately tried to stay calm while we had a cup of tea before the race. This was impossible, as I was now imagining all sorts of horrors. As we sat there in the owners' and trainers' bar, the Yorkshire trainers Mick and Peter Easterby came over to us.

'Now, then, Jenny,' said Mick. 'What are you doing, coming up here to take on Wayward Lad? He's a bloody ten pound better 'oss at Wetherby than anywhere else. You've no chance of beating 'im. No bloody chance.' And with that he walked off. Great, I thought. I need that like I need a hole in the head. I was also asked to do a television interview with Wayward Lad's trainer, Mrs Dickinson. How I got through that I'll never know.

As I saddled up Burrough Hill Lad, it took everything I could muster to keep going and do my job. All I wanted to do was leave the tack on the ground and go to Warwick Hospital. Fourteen years later, pretty much all I can remember about the race is that Burrough Hill Lad won it by ten lengths. Beating Wayward Lad like that should have made me as pleased as Punch, particularly after all the things people had said, but my mind was elsewhere. I didn't want to be at Wetherby. I wanted to be with my son.

When we stopped at Enderby to drop Mum off I rang the hospital, hoping to hear that Mark had been discharged.

'I'm afraid Mark will be staying with us for quite some time, Mrs Pitman,' the sister in charge told me.

'Why? What's the problem?' I thought his arm must be very badly broken if they needed to keep him in.

'Nothing to worry about,' she said. 'He's coming round. He can hear you now if you shout.'

'What do you mean "if you shout"? Is he unconscious?'

'Yes. Didn't you know?'

That was the final straw. I broke down completely. My eldest sister Jacquie was dispatched with Dave to keep an eye on me during the journey to Warwick Hospital. When we arrived we hurried to Mark's room to find an even worse scene than I could have imagined. Mark lay deathly still in the bed. His head was massive, his face swollen like a football and unrecognizable. Worse, when I said his name he made a horrible groaning noise like someone who had brain damage. I stood there looking at him in disbelief and the next thing – crash, bang wallop – everything went black. I opened my eyes to find myself in a small recovery room. I'd fainted.

Fortunately Mark's injuries were not nearly as severe as they appeared to be. I'm told the swelling in his head was mainly due to his hanging upside down for so long. He was discharged from hospital a few days later. It was several days before we pieced together what had happened. Nobody had seen Mark leave the road. His car had been found by a couple driving in the same direction who'd come over the brow of a hill when their car skidded on black ice. As they recovered, they saw something steaming in the field ahead of them. They pulled over and ran to find Mark's car upside down, with the engine roaring its head off, the accelerator jammed down and the doors jammed. Mark probably owed his life to two big men who appeared on the scene, wrenched open a door and switched off the engine. Apparently at the time all Mark kept mumbling was, 'I've got to get to the races . . . I've got to get to the races,' so the rescuers thought he might be a bookmaker!

The day after the accident, when Dave and I went up to the garage at Stowe to recover Mark's tack, we found his car under a tarpaulin. The roof was absolutely flat, his saddles were torn and cut, and all bar a few of his dozens of cassette tapes were smashed to smithereens. The accident cost Mark several weeks of riding but I was only grateful that it hadn't cost him a whole lot more. There is no doubt in my mind that he was lucky to be alive.

It was obvious following Burrough Hill Lad's performance at Wetherby that the King George VI Chase at Kempton had to be our target. By Boxing Day the field had shrunk to three, but it was still set to be an exciting contest because those three horses were the country's top staying chasers: Wayward Lad, Burrough Hill Lad and Combs Ditch. Most people thought the battle would be between Wayward Lad and Burrough Hill Lad, but I wasn't so sure. We'd booked John Francome to ride our horse again, and, beforehand, I warned him, 'Don't rule out Combs Ditch, because he's a better horse than people think and this small field will suit him.'

With only three runners, the King George was always going to be a tactical race, and, as I'd expected, it unfolded in a completely different way from the Hennessy. Nobody wanted to make the running, so, as I had feared, the pace was not strong. By the time they came to the twelfth, Burrough Hill Lad and Wayward Lad were still matching strides, with Combs Ditch tucked in just behind them. At that point, any one of them could have won it. They took the fourth from home in line abreast. Then, suddenly, we could see Wayward Lad receive a couple of slaps from his jockey and it was obvious he had run his race. Coming to the third last, Burrough Hill Lad and Combs Ditch had left him behind and from then on they had the race between them. At this point, Burrough Hill Lad was starting to jump a bit left-handed, which is sometimes the sign of a tired horse, while Combs Ditch was still going extremely well. At the last fence, while Combs Ditch's jockey urged him on, John sat quite still for three or four strides, which I felt cost Burrough Hill Lad valuable ground. By the time they landed over the fence he was now a couple of lengths behind Combs Ditch. John drove Burrough Hill Lad out to make up the ground, Combs Ditch battled back, and it was nip and tuck all the way to the line. They flashed past the post locked together in the tightest possible finish and I feared the worst. I was so relieved when the announcement came over the PA system that Burrough Hill Lad had won.

It had been an extremely nerve-racking race, and I wasn't too happy with the way Johnny had ridden the horse at the last fence, where he'd lost ground. My face must have told its own story, because as Johnny rode into the winners' enclosure he said, 'What's up with you?'

'Nothing,' I said. 'Why?'

'Yes, there is.' John gave me one of his cheeky grins. 'Go on. What's up?'

'All right, what were you playing at?'

Still smiling, John explained that he'd had to sit still at the last fence because Burrough Hill Lad hadn't been quite right as he approached it, and if he'd really caught hold of him at that point there would have been no sort of stride there at all. Nobody saw a stride better than John, and since the end result had been that he'd won the race there wasn't a lot more to say!

After the race, as I was surrounded by journalists and well-wishers, I turned around to see an elderly lady peering in my direction. It was the Queen Mother. She was smiling and nodding in recognition. I stepped forward to receive my trophy and was invited up again to the royal box for a drink.

I was also asked if I had anyone with me that I'd like to take along. Dave was at Wolverhampton, where we had other runners that day, but I knew two people who would love an invitation.

'I've got my mum and my dad with me, ma'am,' I said.

The Queen Mother obviously remembered my routine at Cheltenham and excused me as she invited my parents to join her in the royal box. I was touched by her kindness and surprised that she had remembered so much about my horse. Unfortunately, by the time I got back to the royal box the Queen Mother was just leaving, but my mum was over the moon. 'Oh, we've had a lovely time, me duck,' she said. 'The Queen Mum was stood talking to your dad the longest time.'

I was really pleased for my parents. If anyone deserved to share in the perks of my success it was them. Winning the King George was special, but seeing Mum and Dad so happy was best of all.

CHAPTER FIFTEEN

THE MID-EIGHTIES

My family continued to play an important role at Weathercock House, and indeed over the next few years the support they gave me was to increase. In 1986 Paul, who'd been head boy at Wycliffe College in his last year there and had passed three A-levels in addition to his AO-level and ten other O-levels, left school and started training to be an accountant. Although he was a very good rider, he'd never considered following the rest of the family into racing. In Paul's opinion we were all barmy. 'Anybody who works the hours you do for the returns you get wants certifying,' he has told me more than once.

The same year that Paul left school my sister Mandy, who for the past six years had been acting as my secretary, married Mike Bowlby, a successful young jockey who was riding for us and for Nicky Henderson. Mark had left David Nicholson's to spend some time working for Martin Pipe and had now returned home to become stable jockey for me at Weathercock House. It was something I'd been looking forward to. I knew that riding for his mother wouldn't be easy for Mark in the weighing room, but I felt that it would be rewarding not only for me but also for our owners, especially when it came to getting feedback about how horses performed in their races. Mark and I thought so much alike about the horses and how they should be ridden. Often when I was watching him through my binoculars, I'd be thinking, 'Go on, Mark . . . Go on a bit, Mark,' or 'Steady up a bit,' and no sooner had I thought what he should be doing next than he'd be doing it.

My brother Richard was by now running his own thriving meat business, and between us we were able to help our parents buy a bungalow so that they didn't have to climb stairs any more. By now Mum and Dad both had health problems. A couple of years after Burrough Hill Lad's King George, Dad had a bad stroke, which took him a long time to get over. Sadly it ended his trips to the Irish sales, which he had always enjoyed. Soon afterwards Mum, who hadn't been well for some time, was diagnosed as having an enlarged heart. Typically, she refused to take it easy. Even when I persuaded her to come for a 'rest' at Weathercock House I couldn't get her to sit still for five minutes. All she wanted to do was move the furniture and dust the corners of the room or do the ironing. She'd always been a great one for charity work, selling poppies or sitting on committees. Even when her own health got bad she never stopped looking out for others to help and support. She used to remind me of a great big hen, always sheltering someone under her wings. As far as I'm concerned, Mum was one of the unsung heroes of this world – but even that didn't stop her driving me nuts sometimes.

One day she rang up to tell me she was helping out with a party of disabled people on a trip to Brighton and wanted to bring them to look round the yard on the way back to Leicester. The thought of her spending a week pushing wheelchairs around Brighton when she should have been in one herself made me want to throttle her, but I knew nothing I could say would stop her. We were very busy with the horses and the visit slipped my mind until one lunchtime, when Mum poked her head round the kitchen door.

'Well, we've arrived,' she said. 'Which horses are you going to show us?'

Oh, bloody hell, I thought. I'd been looking forward to watching the racing on TV that afternoon and I wasn't feeling very charitable at all. I followed Mum out to the yard to find about twenty people unloading themselves from the coach with their frames and crutches. Those who were mobile enough followed a couple of the lads to have a look around the yard. The others sat in their wheelchairs outside while we made tea, sandwiches and squash for them. An hour or so later, as they were getting back on the bus, I spotted a woman hobbling on her frame towards the stables. I'd noticed her about twenty minutes earlier but I'd been too preoccupied to help her. In all that time she'd only managed to move about fifty yards. 'Come on, Margaret,' Mum said. 'We're all getting back on the bus now.'

Margaret looked as if she was going to cry. 'Oh, Mrs Harvey, please wait a bit longer. I want to see Corbiere.'

I knew there was no way she'd manage to get to Corbiere's stable on her own, so I told Gary, his lad, to go and fetch him to us. To my amazement Corbiere stood quite still next to Margaret while she stroked and patted him. That did it. The next thing, everyone else was climbing back off the bus, just throwing their walking sticks and frames on the ground around him and patting the horse too. Before I could warn them not to, some of them had actually caught hold of his rugs and were keeping themselves upright by hanging onto them. It was complete chaos. I held my breath, waiting for him to explode, but he didn't. Corbiere stood there like a seaside donkey and let them play with him. I watched in total amazement. It was a wonderful and sobering experience.

When they finally reloaded and the coach pulled out of the yard, all those people were smiling as if they'd been given the crown jewels. I felt ashamed of myself for caring about missing the racing on TV. You're a disgrace, I thought. Those people have got so little; just look how happy this has made them. That day proved to me that my mother had got her priorities right. If you're not very careful you can surround yourself with material things and still have nothing.

Not long after that visit we were asked to help raise money for a scanner appeal for the Princess Margaret Hospital in Swindon. I had been told that the nearest scanner to Lambourn was in Oxford, which meant that anybody with any kind of serious injury had to travel nearly forty-five minutes to get a proper assessment. Where serious head injuries were involved, that was far too long. Having been in racing all my life and seen several bad injuries, I felt it was our duty to help as much as possible, so I arranged to have an open day at Weathercock House. Most of the big stables around Lambourn opened their gates once a year on Good Friday to allow people to look around. In 1987, with all our stables full, I felt we had enough horses to hold an open day ourselves. So, with the help of my family, friends, neighbours and owners, the scene was set.

Mum was in her element. For weeks beforehand she was at her cooker, boiling and baking for a produce stall. Somehow she managed to spend hardly any money in the process. She'd always been thrifty, and from my brother Richard's days running a butcher's stall in Leicester market she'd been on good terms with the other stallholders there. Because it was for a good cause, she went in at the end of market day and begged them for their unsold fruit and vegetables to make her pickles and jams, and they were happy to oblige. Richard is a wicked prankster, and while Mum was boiling all this stuff up to make her produce, he got one of his mates to ring up and pretend that he was from the Environmental Health department.

'We believe you're making products to sell, Mrs Harvey,' this bloke said in a posh voice. 'Are you aware that you need a licence for this type of operation?'

Mum was horrified. 'No! Do I?' she replied.

'Yes, I'm afraid you do. We'll have to come round and inspect your premises to see if they meet current hygiene requirements.' He strung her along for quite a while before he confessed. She nearly murdered Richard for that, and so did I!

By the time the open day arrived we had enough jars of marmalade, chutney, pickled red cabbage and pickled shallots (Mum considered pickled onions very second-rate) to stock two big trestle tables. Hundreds of people turned up, and between Mum's pickles and visitors' donations, we ended up with £12,000. A short while before, a gunman had run riot in the nearby town of Hungerford, so with the hospital's agreement we gave £2,000 to that town's appeal and the rest to the scanner fund.

In 1984, after his brilliant wins in the Gold Cup, the Hennessy and the King George VI Chase, Burrough Hill Lad had been voted the National Hunt Horse of the Year. I'd half thought about running him in the 1985 Grand National, but the handicapper's giving him 12st 4lb to carry at Aintree put paid to that idea, and we returned to our original plan, which was to run in the Cheltenham Gold Cup again. Unfortunately, that had to go by the board too when he cut the inside of his knee with his teeth! When Burrough Hill Lad was at his strongest and fittest he used to carry his head very low on the gallops and sometimes his knees would collide with his head. The damage on this occasion was a nasty deep cut which was enough to put him out of action for some time.

The following season we had some special protective knee boots made, which did the trick, and in November, Burrough Hill Lad won the Rehearsal Chase at Chepstow, followed in February by the Gainsborough Chase at Sandown which he won by ten lengths. It was his third Gainsborough in a row. Everything seemed set for us to have another crack at the Gold Cup, but eight days before the 1986 Cheltenham Festival he developed a bit of heat in his

235

leg, and we had to withdraw him for a second year running.

Over the next two seasons, training Burrough Hill Lad became a nightmare of frustrations. If it wasn't his front legs, it was his injured off hind. Actually the word frustrated doesn't come close: it was soul-destroying rather than frustrating to have such a brilliant horse and not be able to race him. In 1986–87 we had to miss the whole season with him, and we weren't able to get him ready to run again until Wincanton, in February 1988, when with Richard Rowe on board he ran an absolute blinder. As he came to the third last he was still travelling very easily, and it was obvious he hadn't lost any of his ability. Before the end of the race, his first for two years, he began to tire, but I felt certain that next time out we'd see the old Burrough Hill Lad again. Sadly, there never was a next time. Three weeks later we took him for a racecourse workout at Newbury, and as he pulled up I could see he was slightly sore, so I knew the time had come to call it a day. I was sad but I was also relieved.

There was no doubt in my mind that, considering the many problems Burrough Hill Lad had, we had been blessed to win the races with him that we did. He'd won seventeen of his twenty-seven outings over fences, among them all of the country's top chases including the Welsh National, the Cheltenham Gold Cup, the Hennessy Gold Cup and the King George VI Chase. He'd won first-prize money of £195,609, more than any other horse in history except Dawn Run and Wayward Lad. And everything he'd achieved had been done on just one completely sound leg. He was, in a word, magnificent.

Stan Riley had by now got a bit fed up with having this champion racehorse who couldn't race. When I told him we could no longer patch up Burrough Hill Lad to race, he didn't argue. Nevertheless, a few days later he rang, saying he wanted to come and see me. Mandy had taken the call.

'You know what Stan's coming down for, don't you?' she asked me disapprovingly. I nodded. 'Well you can't afford to buy that horse. So don't you even go thinking about it,' she cautioned. As Mandy was my book-keeper I had no doubt she was right.

When Stan arrived he sat down in the living room.

'Well, what are you going to do with him, then, Stan?' I asked.

'I think I'm going to sell him, Jenny,' he said. 'Someone'll have him for point-to-pointing.'

I stared at him, thinking angrily, I'm going to kill him in a minute.

But he knew, and I knew, that he was playing a game with me. At the time he owed me about two months' training fees. I couldn't bear this bargaining over the horse, so I said, 'I'll tell you what, Stan. How about if you don't pay me and I keep the horse?'

Stan smiled slowly. 'All right, Jenny. That's what we'll do, then,' he replied before getting up and wandering out to the yard. I waited at the door, thinking he'd go to see Burrough Hill Lad for a private cheerio, but he simply got into his car and drove off. I slowly walked over to the old horse's box. Burrough Hill Lad was standing half asleep, facing the back wall. I went in and put my arm around his neck. He stood there lapping it up, the way he always did. 'Well, nobody else is going to make any decisions about you now but me, mate,' I told him. I felt so content. A little sad, too, but happy.

Suddenly I heard footsteps coming across the yard. They stopped outside the door and even though my back was turned I could feel somebody watching me.

'You've bought that horse, haven't you?' said Mandy's accusing voice. I didn't answer.

'I told you that you couldn't afford it,' she said.

'Mandy,' I replied, 'there are some things in life more important than money and this is one of them.'

She didn't speak and a few moments later she walked off. That was the end of it. Nothing more was ever said.

The question was, what did we do with him next? Total

retirement wouldn't have been fair on a horse who loved his work as much as Burrough Hill Lad did. He was still only eleven, and anyway I don't think racehorses are suited to being chucked out in a field. They're used to five-star hotel treatment and they've not been bred to tolerate total outdoor life. While his legs would no longer stand up to racing, they were strong enough for other work. I decided to look out for a knowledgeable home to loan him to, and eventually I found one. After a short stay with Kay Birchenough, whom he 'jumped off' out hunting one day, breaking her wrist, he went to Yorkshire, to Charlie Ward-Aldam, a Master of Foxhounds. Today, as I write, he is still going strong at the grand age of twenty-two, and until recently still followed hounds once a week at a sedate pace. He is looked after by the most marvellous girl groom, Jane Hindemarsh, who worships the ground he walks on, and Burrough Hill Lad loves her to bits. Every year she plaits him up and turns him out like a show horse for the annual parade of champions at Cheltenham, Doncaster and other horse venues. After all these years it's surprising how many people lovingly remember him and crowd round just to touch him.

Perhaps, on second thoughts, it's not so surprising that he was such a superstar. John Francome called him the best chaser he'd ever ridden. When the time comes he'll return home to Weathercock House, where there will always be a special place reserved for him.

Corbiere did not have the same problems with unsoundness as Burrough Hill Lad, and he continued racing with all his heart for another two seasons. In 1985 he ran in the Grand National for a third time and once again finished a very brave third, this time to Last Suspect. The following year he won the George Coney Chase at Warwick, before going again for the National. The weather at Aintree in 1986 was dreadful. There had been a blizzard and the snow didn't completely thaw off the track until late in the morning. The grass was also quite long, which made the going slippery. As Corbiere prepared to launch himself at the fourth fence, his hind feet seemed not to take a proper hold, and as he started to rise in front his hind feet carried on travelling, which meant he lost his impulsion, couldn't get high enough and took quite a nasty fall. My heart was in my mouth before he was caught and brought back to the stables for me to check him over. Thankfully, both he and Ben de Haan were unhurt.

Following his early departure at Aintree we decided to go up to Ayr for the Scottish Grand National a couple of weeks later. The reception we were given from the Scottish crowd was unbelievable. They turned up that day with Polos, barley sugars and even toffee apples for him. I was so pleased we had made the journey, as was Corbiere. He was in tremendous form that day. Twenty-four runners set out and Corbiere looked like leading them all home once he galloped into the lead approaching the third last fence. As he jumped the second last in front, the crowd began cheering as though he had already won. For a moment I thought that he would hold on, but then Hardy Lad, a 28–1 outsider, came out of the pack and caught him at the last fence. Corbiere rallied bravely and kept on well to the line to take second place behind Hardy Lad. It was a tremendous run by the old boy in the twilight of his career.

I'd already decided that 1987 would be Corbiere's last attempt at the Grand National. The thought of retirement had been at the back of my mind for a while, but I'd put it off because the horse seemed as well as ever. On 20 December 1986 he finished fourth to Stearsby in the Welsh National. That was a fantastic race for me, as my three runners finished first, second and fourth. Seeing that Corbiere was in such good heart, we all agreed he should have one last crack at the Aintree race. Plenty of twelve-year-olds had won the Grand National. As it turned out, I was to regret the decision. When I walked into the saddling box to tack him up for the race, Corky looked at me in a way he never had before. He had a strange, worried look in his eyes. I knew he was trying to tell me that he didn't really want to do it. Over the years there've been a few times at the races when I wanted to jack the job in and walk off, and this was one of them. But what could I do? It was obvious he wasn't ill. I couldn't go to the stewards and say, 'I'm sorry, sir, I don't want my horse to run today. He looks frightened.' They'd think I needed locking up. I would have to keep my feelings to myself.

I finished tacking him up, thinking, 'I don't want to do this. If anything happens to this horse today I'll never forgive myself.' As I legged Ben de Haan up into the saddle I said, 'Just look after him today, Ben. If he's not liking it, pull him up.' I made a vow then that this would be his last race. The horse was telling me he'd had enough and I was going to listen to him.

The next twenty minutes seemed some of the longest in my life, but my prayers were answered. During the race Corky jumped well and eventually finished twelfth, just behind Smith's Man, who was my other runner that year. Actually, when the chips are down you don't give a damn where your horses finish as long as they are safe.

The Burroughs and I loved Corbiere too much to want anything to happen to him, and we brought him home to an honourable retirement. The next season, as well as going out for the occasional day's hunting, which he loved, he started acting as the Weathercock House schoolmaster, showing young horses and jockeys the ropes. Nobody, human or horse, could have had a better teacher, and in the process he gave us such joy and a lot of laughs. On one occasion the old horse taught our claiming jockey, Wayne O'Callaghan, a lesson he'll never forget. We were coming back from the gallops past the schooling fences when I said to Corbiere's rider, 'Get off a minute, so Wayne can have a pop over these.' Wayne climbed aboard and set off to face the line of fences. He couldn't have had his brain in gear that morning because he turned Corbiere in really short and wouldn't have been more than ten yards away when he started revving him up. The result was that Corky slammed his brakes on hard and refused, and Wayne was chucked up round his ears.

Fred Winter and Oliver Sherwood happened to be watching, and they looked at each other in total amazement as the Grand National winner refused to jump the small schooling fence. 'That was your sodding fault for turning him in too short!' I shouted at Wayne. 'Now take him back, do it again and get it right this time.'

Wayne rode back to do it again, but by now Corbiere was so wound up that his tail was going round in circles like a windmill. He decided to take the decisions out of Wayne's hands and as he turned this time he took off as if he had high-octane fuel inside him. You could almost hear him laughing: 'Well, you've been a prat. Now I'll show you what I can do.' He galloped up the line of fences absolutely flat out like a rocket, never checking once, taking off outside the wings at each one. The three of us stood there laughing our heads off as the old horse educated this young jockey.

Among the horses Corbiere helped school over jumps were four youngsters I'd bought in Ireland as unbroken three-year-olds in the autumn of 1986: Garrison Savannah, Royal Athlete, Esha Ness and Willsford. The chances of buying one star at a horse sale are pretty slim and the odds against buying four in one season must be enormous. But 1986 was a vintage year for me. Between them, over the next ten years, these four horses were to win me a number of big races and provide some dramatic moments.

Of the four, the horse who for me became the biggest star of all was the one I nearly didn't buy. The story of Garrison Savannah began towards the end of the Derby sale, at Ballsbridge in Ireland. I had already filled my orders but was looking again at the tail-enders, just in case I'd missed something. I was watching a horse walk up in the passageway in the barn when I noticed two farmers. The older one was holding a big brown horse on an old head-collar with a bit of rope. That's a bloody nice horse, I thought. Instantly it struck me how like Corbiere he looked. Apart from his colour and the shape of his face, the rest of him was very similar: his body, the way he held himself. In fact, I'm sure if you'd made a mould of Corbiere this horse would have fitted it almost perfectly.

I kept my eye on him while I finished examining the other horse I'd already got out of its stable, then I ambled around the brown horse to reassure myself that he was as nice as I'd first thought. According to the catalogue, he was by Random Shot, a stallion some people considered to be a bit soft, which meant he might be a bit cheaper and I might be able to afford him. A young horse of his quality by a more fashionable sire could have fetched around £20,000 at the time, but I hoped I might get this one for much less. His sire didn't bother me. If a horse looks tough and is out of a good mare, I've never been too worried about its sire.

Following discussions with Dave, we went off to bid for him. My face was becoming known at Ballsbridge and I felt that if people saw me bidding someone might try and 'run' me. David made a couple of bids, but the horse was led out unsold, as he hadn't reached his reserve. I nipped round and waited by the horse's stable, and when the old man came back round the corner I said to him, 'How much do you want for your horse?'

'Six thousand,' came the reply.

'Oh, go on with you!' I said. 'He's not worth that. I'll give you four.' I didn't dare offer more because I didn't have a customer for him, and I didn't think Lloyds Bank would take kindly to having another horse thrust upon them, even though we all knew about their black one! But the farmers wouldn't wear it. They were sticking at £6,000, no matter what, so we came home without the horse. I felt really empty leaving him behind. I couldn't explain why – it was just a gut feeling I had. The horse had a magic about him which I could neither describe nor forget.

I spent the entire ferry crossing home moaning to Dave, 'I should have bought that horse. I know I should have bought that horse.' All day Saturday and Sunday, back at Weathercock House, I was still cross with myself. In the end Dave sighed, 'Will you bloody well stop going on about that horse? If you want it ring up Willie O'Rourke and find out where it went, and buy it.'

'Right,' I said. 'I will.' So there and then I rang up Willie, one of the directors of the sales company, and he told me that as far as he knew the horse was still unsold. I asked him to see if he could get me the horse for £5,000. In the end I paid £5,600 for him. I couldn't afford it, and we didn't really need another horse, but I just had to have him.

When he arrived and strode out of the horsebox at Weathercock House a few days later I knew I'd done the right thing. He was everything I liked in a young racehorse, powerfully made yet still with a lot of quality, but I knew I would have to find an owner other than Lloyds Bank. My first idea was to offer him to the Johnson family, but Freddie, Libby and Gary decided they weren't quite ready to give up hope on Vantastic. Then, a week after the new horse arrived, I had a telephone call from three businessmen who were thinking of buying a racehorse. Malcolm Burdock, Roger Voysey and John Davies duly paid us a visit. It turned out they owned a company called Autofour Engineering in Cheltenham, and their greatest ambition was to have a runner at their local course, where they were all members. 'Just to take part would mean everything to us,' said Roger. 'We don't necessarily expect to win.'

They wanted to know what I had for sale, so I told them about my new brown horse, who was still unnamed. 'What's he like?' they asked. 'Like Corbiere, with a different-coloured coat,' I told them, and that was enough. I don't

243

charge my owners commission, so for £6,000 (which included the travelling costs) the horse became theirs. A few weeks later he was named Garrison Savannah, after the racecourse they'd visited while on holiday in Barbados. From that day onwards he was known in the yard as Gary.

His first run was in a National Hunt flat race at Kempton on 28 February 1987, where he was ridden by John Smith, one of my claiming jockeys. I'd also entered one of Terry Ramsden's horses in the race, Saddlers Night. That horse started at 8–1, partly, I expect, because Terry had backed him. In contrast, Garrison Savannah, who hadn't shown as much speed at home, was 25–1 in the betting. The weather was so wet that by the end of the day the horses were floundering through the mud. Saddlers Night had looked likely to win, but who should come thundering up the straight from the back of the field but Garrison Savannah? He pipped Terry Ramsden's horse on the line by three-quarters of a length. I was taken aback because Gary certainly wasn't a fast horse, but what he'd shown me that day was a first glimpse of his courage. When Royal Athlete, one of my other young Irish horses, also ran for the first time in the second division of the bumper that same afternoon and finished a promising third, I felt pretty pleased with my shopping trip to Ballsbridge sales.

I always look at young horses as kids going through school. First there's nursery school, then junior school, then senior school. At four years old they're still very much like babies, so I don't push any of them too hard before they're ready both physically and mentally for the next step. They've got their whole careers in front of them and I'm thinking three or four years ahead, not just the next season. You'll often see young footballers or tennis players who are quite brilliant in their early teens finished before they're twenty because they've burnt out from being under too much pressure too soon. Horses aren't that different. I want my horses to be at their peak and ready to compete in the big races when they're seven, eight or nine years old, and to do that I need to look after their minds as well as their bodies. They need to continue enjoying what they're doing; as my dad would say, 'You must leave a bit of petrol in the tank.'

All of which explains why Gary ran only once more that season, when he finished fourth in another bumper at Newbury. We waited until he was into his fifth year before we started teaching him to jump proper hurdles. The idea of leaving the ground wasn't totally alien to him. All our horses are introduced to jumping as part of being broken in as three- or four-year-olds. Personally I think the term 'breaking' is unfortunate. It sounds to me as if you're destroying something and that's the last thing I want to do. I like to leave their character intact when I educate them, but I do think it's important that they receive a proper education. Starting horses off, schooling them and teaching them to jump are all lessons that are going to stay with them the rest of their lives, so you can't afford to make a poor job of it.

I ask my young horses to step over telegraph poles while they're still trotting in circles on the lunge, even before they've had anyone on their backs. When they're trotting over them easily I'll get them to break into a very slow canter. Some horses are naturals even at that stage, and buck for fun when they land over the other side, loving every minute of it. Some of them can be a bit gormless, like Burrough Hill Lad was, and take a lot longer to get it right.

Gary had always been one of the naturals, so it was no surprise, when the time came to introduce him to the proper jumps in the summer of 1987, that he got the idea quickly. I always try to teach my horses to jump hurdles cleanly. The margin between disaster and success is quite narrow in jump racing and I try to widen that margin a little bit. I also like to teach my horses to be clever, to look and think what they are doing, to check their own stride if they need to, and to show the hurdle some respect. I reason that if a horse is taught to jump cleanly then he won't be rattling the top bars of the hurdles and knocking his knees and shins about.

Gary learned his lessons well. In November of the 1987–88 season he won his first novice hurdle race, over two and a half miles at Worcester. Two weeks later Mark rode him at Bangor, where he came third. He had a couple more placed runs before he picked up an injury and had to finish the season early, but I was more than happy with what I'd seen of his performances. I'd never expected him to set the world alight as a hurdler. He had always looked like a chaser and was built like a chaser, so hurdling was always going to be just a stepping stone along the way. Luckily the injury was nothing too serious, and I was confident he'd be ready to run again by the start of the following season.

Meanwhile, we had another patient in the yard, who was causing me a great deal of worry. Corbiere had been having troubles with his circulation, and this had affected his feet. For a couple of weeks he'd been quite poorly and the vet had been coming in every day, working with the farrier to treat him. At one stage I'd been very concerned about him, but I thought the problem was now under control. He'd just started to call out to me again when I'd been going round the yard at evening stables, looking for his Polo mints the way he used to, giving me plenty of cupboard love until they were finished. That's it, he's going to be all right now, I'd thought happily. Then, suddenly one Saturday morning, he was a bit off-colour again, so I rang the vet and farrier to ask them to come and see him. I had a runner at Chepstow that day and unfortunately had to leave for the races before they arrived.

When Dave and I reached the racecourse I was told there was a phonecall for me. I took it in the secretary's office. It was the vet, Bill Eaton Evans. 'Jenny, Derek and I are not happy about Corbiere,' he said. 'I'd like your permission to put him to sleep.' I was knocked sideways. I really thought we had had the problem beat. For a moment I couldn't think straight. I just wanted to say no, no, no. But then I came to my senses. Nobody understood his job better than Bill, and I knew his main concern would be to see that the horse would not suffer. I was so upset I could hardly get the words out.

'If that's what you feel has got to be done, then you'll have to do it, Bill,' I said. 'But I don't want him there when I get home. I couldn't bear to see him.' I put the phone down and started to sob. I thought I'd never stop. It was a long time before I dared go outside. Dr Allen, the Jockey Club doctor, was standing near the weighing room. 'Jenny,' he said, 'your eyes are red. Is your allergy bothering you today?'

I nodded. 'Yeah, I'm not too good today, Doc.' I just wanted to go home. I didn't, of course. We stayed for the race, and somehow I even managed to do an interview with Julian Wilson for the BBC. I don't know how I got through it. We drove back to Lambourn to face the awful sight of Corky's empty stable. The moment I saw it I realized I'd made a dreadful mistake in telling them to take him away. I knew I would always regret not having him buried at Weathercock House, where he belonged.

One of the worst telephone calls I've ever had to make was to Brian Burrough that day. I explained to him that we had no alternative but to put Corbiere to sleep. For many weeks afterwards there was such a sense of gloom in the yard. Something very special was now missing.

Ten years on, I still miss him. He was a very good friend to me. And what hurts terribly is the fact that I never had the chance to say goodbye.

CHAPTER SIXTEEN

GARRISON SAVANNAH

In the 1988–89 season Garrison Savannah had a couple more runs over hurdles, and in December Mark rode him to victory in the three-mile Coral Golden Hurdle at Cheltenham. Mark completed a treble for me that afternoon on Cool Sun and Hawthorn Hill Lad, which made it his best day at Cheltenham to date. I was really pleased for him. He deserved a bit of a boost. One or two journalists had been giving Mark an unnecessarily hard time, criticizing his riding and implying that if I hadn't been his mother he wouldn't be riding these horses. Plenty of jockeys rode for their fathers and the press made no big deal out of it, but apparently, for some reason, riding for your mother was different. The press liked to paint Mark as a mummy's boy, which was not only hurtful but insulting to us both. I trained horses for a living, and if Mark wasn't good enough for our job he wouldn't have been doing it. I certainly didn't favour him. In fact I was probably harder on him than I was on other jockeys, because I wanted him to be the best he could possibly be and because we both needed to push ourselves to the limit.

Soon after Gary's Cheltenham win, we discovered that he had a slight stress fracture of his cannon bone, which sidelined him for the rest of the season. It healed well, however, and by the following autumn he was ready for Mark to start schooling him over the bigger fences. Steeplechase fences are wide and solid, and a good deal higher than hurdles. Not all horses make the change from hurdling to chasing easily, but Gary took to it straight away. He knew what to do the very first time Mark took him up the line of schooling fences, and jumped like a stag. Mark cantered back towards me grinning from ear to ear. 'This horse is effing brilliant,' he said. 'He'll win the Sun Alliance at Cheltenham.'

The Sun Alliance Chase is, in effect, the juniors' Gold Cup, so it was an ambitious statement, to say the least. Cheltenham is such a testing course that if you send young horses there before they're ready it can over-face them. But Mark was a pretty good judge. The feedback he gave me on the horses was not often wrong, so I allowed myself a secret smile.

In December it was Mandy's husband, Mike Bowlby, who rode Garrison Savannah in his first chase, at Haydock. It's a tough course for a novice first time out, but he jumped well and finished third to Highfrith. Considering he hadn't run for twelve months, this was most encouraging, and from that point he never stopped improving. Three outings later, with Mark in the saddle, he annihilated the field in a nineteen-runner novice chase at Wincanton, winning by twenty-five lengths. In his next race he was only just beaten by a good young horse called Party Politics, trained by my neighbour, Nick Gaselee. We decided that that was good enough form to have a crack at the Sun Alliance Chase.

I had also entered another of my novices, Royal Athlete, in the same race. He had been running so well that he was the favourite. For Mark, deciding which horse to ride was a real dilemma, and in the end what swayed it was the fact that Royal Athlete was a bit of a tricky customer. If you rode him quietly and got him settled he was really sensible, but he could become totally unreasonable and start pulling like a train. The final choice was Mark's, but I guess my views had helped persuade him to pick Royal Athlete. So Ben de Haan was booked to ride Garrison Savannah.

Unfortunately, on the big day as the field turned down the hill Royal Athlete switched on his 'silly head'. He was pulling very hard and not concentrating, and consequently capsized. In contrast, Garrison Savannah jumped brilliantly throughout. Although Ben had to keep him up to his work when the pace quickened on the second circuit, he stayed on well, took the lead at the last fence and won by five lengths. It was a great thrill to add another big race to our list, but for me the best part was seeing Mark pick himself up off the ground and run to the last fence, where he stood screaming and shouting support and encouragement to Gary and Ben.

Garrison Savannah's owners, Roger, Malcolm and John, went absolutely crackers. All they had ever dreamed of was having a runner at Cheltenham, and now they had won the top novice chase of the Cheltenham Festival. Before we saddled our next runner, David and I managed a quick drink in their box. It was like walking into a riot and it was obvious that the celebrations were set to go on all night.

On the Thursday Mark almost gained compensation for Royal Athlete's fall when he rode Toby Tobias for Mr and Mrs Hitchins in the Gold Cup. Almost, but not quite. Toby was in a good position throughout the race, and going to the last fence he held a slender lead, but following a duel of epic proportions he was just beaten on the run-in by Norton's Coin, a 100–1 outsider. Desert Orchid, who had started the odds-on favourite, was third. It was terribly disappointing for us all to come so close to winning the Gold Cup but, on reflection, not a total surprise. Toby was a lovely-natured horse – you could have left a baby in his box and he wouldn't have hurt it – and that was his problem really. He had enough class to win that Gold Cup, but when it came down to it he was too much of a gentleman and probably less of a street fighter than some I know!

Nevertheless, it had been a pretty good Cheltenham for the Pitman family and our owners, and a good season all round. The best yet. Between them, our horses had won ninety-three races and over half a million pounds in prize money.

I held a very strong hand for the 1990–91 season. My three stars, Garrison Savannah, Toby Tobias and Royal Athlete, were now among the highest-rated steeplechasers in the country. After Cheltenham, Toby and 'Alfie' (the yard's nickname for Royal Athlete) had redeemed their reputations by winning two big chases at Aintree. Toby won the Martell Cup and Alfie took the Mumm Club Novice Chase at the Grand National meeting, so I felt that they all stood a good chance in the 1991 Gold Cup.

Dad's comment on Royal Athlete, the first time we'd seen him at the Ballsbridge sales, had always stuck in my mind. 'There ain't a lot of him, but what's there is all quality.' That summed Alfie up to a tee. He was quite a lightly built horse in comparison to some of my others, but he had a good staying pedigree and was certainly the fastest of the three on the gallops. His big weakness was his tendency to be a bit headstrong, and as we all know that can be difficult to control in animals and in humans!

Toby Tobias was the kindest horse in the yard, and not nearly as macho as the other two. I always felt that if they'd been humans, Royal Athlete and Garrison Savannah would have been rugby players, and Toby would have been happy doing ballet. Though he'd put effort into a race there was a question mark over his toughness, which is an essential ingredient for any athlete to be a champion. His form had improved considerably since he'd come to us, but it had not been plain sailing. He was quite a difficult horse to keep happy, because he didn't like to do too much work. If I'd asked him to gallop as far as my other long-distance horses, when I stood in his box at evening stables he would totally ignore me and stare at the wall. He was like a man who after

251

a tiff would sulk and not speak to you for three or four days. Even so, I've always found that I can understand my horses more easily than I can people of the same ilk.

Gary, on the other hand, was more like me in temperament: while things might get pretty hot at the time, that would be the end of it. Although he was not the fastest horse in the world, he was an aggressive competitor and always wanted to get his head in front. If I was judging them on speed alone, I'd have said that Royal Athlete and Toby Tobias probably had a better chance than Gary. But courage and stamina count for a lot in the Gold Cup, and Gary liked the course – he'd already won twice at Cheltenham – so he certainly was not a no-hoper, as some of the press were suggesting. One racing writer poured scorn on his Sun Alliance win, saying that because there had been only nine runners, and Royal Athlete had fallen, the race had been easier to win than usual. Someone else wrote that though Gary was a good handicapper he was not in the same league as Royal Athlete. These public comparisons made me feel uneasy. It was like setting Steve Cram against Seb Coe. To me, Gary was like Cram, thickset and powerful. Royal Athlete, on the other hand, was more like Coe, a smaller, sleek machine. As it turned out, we never did find out which one would come out on top in the Gold Cup. Both Royal Athlete and Toby Tobias had leg problems which prevented them running that season, and by December 1990 all our hopes rested on Garrison Savannah.

I had never managed to kick my allergies and winter weather had compounded the problem. Despite the steroids and antibiotics I took to treat them, I still used to pick up every chest infection going. Oral antibiotics never completely cleared them up, so I sometimes had to go to the Ridgeway Hospital in Swindon or the Brompton Hospital in London for a course of intravenous antibiotics. On the day of Gary's first run of the season at Haydock I found myself hitched up to an IV bag at the Brompton, fretting because the payphone would not let me dial the 0898 race-line number to listen to the race commentary. Eventually, Dave rang me to say that Gary had run a blinder and had finished second to Celtic Shot, but that was the end of the good news. Gary had been so fresh and well that he'd apparently set off at a rapid rate of knots and 'rooted' one of the early fences. As he walked back to his stable it was obvious he was lame in his shoulder.

'Try not to worry,' Dave said. 'The vet doesn't think anything's broken, but he's probably pulled a muscle.'

It was as if someone had fired a rocket straight through my yard. Two months before, I'd had three Gold Cup prospects. Now it looked as if I had none, and Dave was telling me not to worry! For the next few days I was not a good patient. All I wanted was to go home. There was nothing I could do that the vets weren't already doing, and I knew that if I failed to finish my own course of treatment I'd soon be back in hospital. Even so, I was still desperate to see Gary for myself. Would he be all right for Cheltenham or was it pointless even thinking about it?

The answer, when I was finally allowed home four days later, was not clear-cut. Gary was not actually lame, but nor was he completely sound. It was as if his shoulder had gone a bit rusty. When he was at his best Gary had a wonderful walk. He didn't just put his foot out and down, he extended it an extra quarter of an inch, and *then* put it down. His near fore was still doing that, but his off fore had lost its edge. It was hardly noticeable, but I knew my horse and I knew there was a problem.

What was even more worrying was that when you took his rugs off there was a small damp patch on his off fore shoulder, which meant that there was extra heat there. The heat, I knew, was a sign of the injury. Sometimes a hairline stress fracture can cause symptoms like Gary's, but the vets felt it was more likely that he had injured his shoulder ligaments. They suggested box rest, which we gave him, but it

253

made little difference. By the middle of January the horse had been standing in his box for six weeks and was still not sound. There were only eight weeks to go before the Gold Cup and I was 'off the wall'.

In desperation I rang our vet, Alan Walker. 'Alan, what are we going to do about this horse?'

'Well, you've had everybody to see him, Jenny. You know that.'

'I know, but there has to be something else we can try.'

There was a long pause. 'Well,' Alan said at last, 'there's a vet I've heard of who does homeopathic treatments and acupuncture. I don't know much about him, but it might be worth a try.'

'That's all I need!' I exploded. 'An effing witchdoctor.' I would never have spoken to Alan like that before, but the pressure of having every one of my Gold Cup horses off games had really affected me.

But after I hung up I thought to myself, That was a bit unnecessary, he was only trying to help. I pondered on Alan's idea all evening, and by bedtime I was thinking, What have you got to lose? First thing next morning I rang Alan's surgery. 'Alan, I'm sorry about last night. I was out of order,' I said.

'Oh, we all get like that at times,' said Alan quietly.

'What was the name of that bloke who does acupuncture?'

'A fellow called Chris Day. I'll get you his number.'

I rang Chris Day immediately and asked him if he would come over to Weathercock House to see my horse. By the time he arrived all the staff had heard about this magician who was coming to treat Garrison Savannah, and most of them found a reason to hang around the yard to see the fun. To my relief, when Chris stepped out of his car with his assistant he looked quite normal. We led Gary out of his box and walked him down the yard while I explained the problem. I showed Chris the sweaty patch on Gary's shoulder, which was about the size of the palm of my hand.

I'd never seen acupuncture done on a horse before, so I was quite worried when Chris started sticking big needles into Gary's shoulder and elsewhere. Gary was the sort of horse who could get very cross indeed if something hurt him, but to my surprise he just stood there. I admit he looked a bit puzzled and perhaps a bit pissed off while Chris did his treatment, but that was Gary's normal behaviour when any vet arrived to treat him.

Chris left the needles in for a few minutes and, while we waited for the magic to work, he told me he would give Gary some homeopathic pills as well. Oh yeah, I thought, because quite frankly I was still highly sceptical. The most amazing thing was that when Chris took the needles out and Gary walked back up the yard, he did seem to be moving more easily. He was like a stiff gate that had been oiled. I wasn't going to make a fool of myself and say anything – I was well aware that when you wanted something badly your mind could play tricks on you – but after Chris and everybody else had left the yard I went back and put a headcollar on Gary, and walked him a couple of strides up and down the yard. I ain't imagining it, I thought. Back in the house I told Dave what I'd seen.

'Funny you should say that,' Dave said. 'I thought he walked easier as well.' That coming from David, who is very sceptical about such things, was very reassuring.

After Chris Day had been treating the horse for a few days, everyone could see a difference. Chris himself seemed pleased with Gary's progress. He was still not out of the woods, but we were on the right road. Yet time was running out fast. After all that time in his box Gary was far from fit. I asked Chris how he wanted me to restart training him.

He shrugged. 'I don't know anything about training horses. You're going to have to train him as you find him, but don't go giving him too much work too soon.'

That was just common sense. What I wanted was a programme to follow. But all Chris would say was, 'It's up

255

to you.' For the next six weeks Chris and I worked as a team. 'Right, Chris,' I'd say. 'What I'd like to try tomorrow is a little trot or canter.' Usually he'd say, 'Give it a go and see what happens.' The road to recovery wasn't smooth. Some days we'd make good progress and some days we'd take several steps backwards. Each time we had a setback I felt like chucking in the towel. It would have been the easy option, because what we were trying to do, in less than eight weeks, was basically an impossibility. There came a point when I really did not *want* Gary to run in the Gold Cup, but something kept me going, something kept pushing me. It's hard to put it into words, but it actually felt as if something or somebody was steering me, telling me what to do.

I'd never trained a horse that way before, and nor have I trained one like it since. It was a bit like winding up an antique watch with a dodgy spring which might break at any moment. I felt that little and often would put less strain on him, so I exercised him twice daily rather than once. In the morning he'd go out on his own, walk and trot, followed by a slow canter round Mandown Bottom. In the afternoon he'd do the same again. From the day he hurt himself at Haydock till the day of the Gold Cup, three months later, he never worked with another horse. I didn't dare let him near the rest of the string in case he got lit up and started doing too much. He had such a competitive nature that if another horse had worked alongside him he'd have tried to beat it and that, I felt, could put paid to our efforts.

Under normal circumstances so close to the race I would have done some sprint work to improve his wind but as I didn't want to gallop him too sharply I took him instead to Oliver Sherwood's equine swimming pool once or twice a week and gave him a few circuits in the water to make him blow hard. Because he wasn't galloping, the only way I could gauge his fitness was from the shape of him. When his rugs were stripped off at night, I'd look at him and picture the way his body had been when he was at his best, and think, I need a bit of belly off here. I need a bit more weight up there. Then I'd canter him a bit longer, or give him an extra turn in the swimming pool, until his shape pleased my eye. In an ideal world I would have given him a run before Cheltenham, but in the circumstances I decided not to.

A couple of weeks before the Festival the Autofour lads asked me what his chances of running in the Gold Cup were. 'The long and short of it is, if you see him walking round the pre-parade ring you can take it he'll run,' I told them. At least Mark wouldn't pick the wrong horse this time!

Then, the weekend before the Gold Cup, came a bombshell. As Gary pulled out in the morning, he showed a slight hint of lameness. I was devastated. I came into the house, kicked the back door and sat down at the table with my head in my hands. 'Well, that's it,' I said. 'He ain't going anywhere.' Then I felt this gentle push again. 'You can't quit now. You've got another four days.' By now I didn't want to carry on. I was so disappointed, but I knew that somehow I had to.

Chris Day was abroad, giving a lecture, but before he'd left he'd taught me how to stimulate the acupuncture points myself with a laser machine, 'just in case'. I had asked Chris to mark the exact areas with a permanent marker pen, which had made Gary look like an Appaloosa, but now proved invaluable. That day I gave him two sessions with our cold-laser machine. The next morning, when he walked out of his box, the difference was clearly visible. I'm happy with that, I thought.

On the Monday preceding the Gold Cup the Autofour lads came over early to Weathercock House to watch their horse canter, and stayed for breakfast. Mum and Dad had come down for Cheltenham, and after breakfast Roger, Malcolm and John sat in the dining room chatting to Dad while I went to the office to make the declarations and entries. It was only after the race that I found out what Dad had been up to.

'Who do you think will win the Gold Cup, Mr Harvey?' Roger had asked.

'Well, I don't know, m'boy.'

'What about Celtic Shot?'

'No, I won't have him. He ain't got good enough hocks to win around Cheltenham over fences.'

They went through the rest of the fourteen entries and, one by one, my dad dismissed them.

'What about this one?'

'No, I don't like that.'

'Well, what about Dessie?'

'No, he's had his chance. He's a bit long in the tooth now.'

'What about The Fellow?'

'Ah well now, he might be the fly in the ointment. I don't know much about him. He's the French hoss ain't he?'

So then John said, 'Who *do* you think will win it, then?'

Dad smiled. 'Well, I don't want to build your hopes up . . .'

If I'd known I'd have squeezed his liver and lights out, but on the strength of Dad's summing up the lads went tootling off and had a serious bet on their horse.

It was only on the morning before the race that I finally decided to run Garrison Savannah. Right up until the last moment I'd been so doubtful of his making it to Cheltenham that I hadn't wanted to tempt fate. Mark and I had not even discussed the race, or watched videos of the other runners as we normally did. When I eventually said we were going, it caused another problem, because my mother announced she was going too. In recent months Mum's heart condition had worsened. She had been in hospital a couple of times and I did not welcome the thought of her having a tricky turn at the races. But in the past twenty years Mum had only ever missed one Festival meeting, and if her grandson was going to ride her daughter's horse in the Gold Cup, there was no telling her she could not go, I reasoned, so I decided to keep my fears to myself.

By Thursday morning I knew that Garrison Savannah

was very well in himself. He looked special. You can sense a horse's well-being just as you can with your own kids. Mentally, he was at boiling point. Nonetheless, as we left Weathercock House I still did not feel really confident. I just hoped I was doing the right thing.

When we reached the races we parked Mum with my two brothers in a marquee near the pre-parade ring. A very nice lady served them coffee and promised them lunch in half an hour, so that was one worry out of the way. As we came out of the marquee I saw Mark walking in through the gate with his girlfriend. He looked in a foul mood. 'What's up with him?' I asked Lesley as he went off to the weighing room. She said she didn't know but that Mark had hardly spoken a word for the whole journey. That's handy, I thought. I already had my mother and my horse to worry about. Now I had Mark in a bad mood too. I guessed at the problem. There'd been some unflattering comments about Mark in the newspapers that week which, I thought, might have got to him. He was also still disappointed about losing the Gold Cup on Toby Tobias, and I knew that he felt he had something to prove to himself.

His frame of mind didn't bother me too much, though, because Mark was single-minded when it came to big races and often became a bit aggressive. He and Garrison Savannah made a good pair. Mark always rode well when he was in a bad mood. The lads in the yard knew this, and on big race days they'd sometimes aggravate him on purpose, like a matador infuriating a bull with his cape.

Everybody was unusually quiet while we were tacking up the horse. I was praying desperately that I wasn't making a mistake. If he came back lame I knew that I'd hate myself. I never ran my horses if I did not think they were a hundred per cent, so this was the biggest risk I'd ever taken. We walked over to the paddock with Gary's owners and their wives. A few minutes later Mark joined us. As the bell rang for the jockeys to mount I put my arm round Mark's

259

shoulder and walked with him across the paddock to Garrison Savannah. At this point I'd still not given him any riding instructions.

'What do you want me to do on this horse, then?' he asked.

'There's no point in coming here if you're not going to be positive,' I said. 'Ride him like you rode Toby Tobias last year. Only don't get beat this time.'

As I legged him up I thought, What a cow! In my heart I didn't believe that Garrison Savannah would be able to produce as much as Toby Tobias had done. If he finished in one piece I'd be more than happy. If he finished in the first six I'd be delighted. But letting Mark detect my doubts would give him negative vibes too. I felt awful about it, because it was not something I'd ever done with my boys before.

The Autofour lads came over as I watched the horse leave the paddock. 'What do you think, then, Jen?' asked Roger.

'To be perfectly honest,' I said, 'I haven't a clue where the horse is fitness-wise, because I've never had to train a horse like this before. But one thing I do know: in his mind he's ready to take on the world.'

I walked up to the owners' and trainers' stand on my own to watch the race. The stand was so full and we were wedged in so tight I had a job getting my binoculars up to my eyes. As the tapes went up there was a roar from the crowd that I felt right through my body. They'd jumped off and were over the first few fences before I started to breathe properly again. Thank God for that, I thought, when I saw Gary was all right and travelling well. As they completed the first circuit and came past the stand I was thinking rapidly and quietly talking to myself: I'm dead happy with the position you're in, mate, it's been a good race so far, but there's still an awful long way to go. They jumped the water, then the next fence. As the pace of the race increased, each jockey was jostling to get in a good position at the top of the hill. Just as they entered the bend things began to get a bit rough, and Gary lost a few places. He's getting to the bottom of his tank, I thought. That's it, I said to myself.

As they reached the top of the hill the leader Celtic Shot made a mistake and another horse jumped to the front with a spectacular leap. That horse was Garrison Savannah. Where have you come from? I thought. My binoculars were shaking. Shit, I thought. He's still going well. It was too soon to be in front really, but there was no point in taking a pull at this stage and giving the ground away. Don't lose your cool, Mark, I thought. Sit still.

Mark looked across to the horse on his inside. Then, as if he'd heard my thoughts, he sat there quietly, accepting the situation. As they started to run down the hill I scanned the field with my binoculars, looking at the horses behind him and thinking, That's going well, that's not. That ain't going as well as some might think . . . then I saw the French horse, The Fellow, and my heart sank. He was travelling really easily, but he still had an awful lot of ground to make up. As they came off the bottom bend the picture of the race started to change dramatically. One moment I was looking at Gary and thinking, You're still going well enough, mate. The next, out of the corner of my eye, I saw The Fellow start to make his run. As he did, the others tried to go with him and you could see the petrol gauges on some of them start to register empty. But Gary still seemed to have a bit more fuel left. Where he was getting it from I just don't know, but as they raced to the last he still seemed full of running. Just for a moment, a few strides out, he seemed to falter, but then he quickened again and I thought I must have imagined it. As they came to the last fence Mark asked Gary for an almighty effort, and he stood off outside the wings and absolutely flew it. It was a spectacular leap, which brought a great roar from the crowd, who were now going wild. I wasn't shouting out loud myself, but inside my whole body was screaming and urging Gary and Mark on.

Then, as I watched, I saw Gary's petrol needle give a couple of flickers and at the same moment Peter O'Sullevan's voice came blasting out from somewhere: '. . . The Fellow's finishing strongly, he's making ground on Garrison Savannah . . . The Fellow's beginning to get up . . . The Fellow's getting up!'

Suddenly all around me life seemed to run in slow motion. I was looking at The Fellow. Looking at Mark. Looking at the winning post. Thinking, Is Gary going fast enough? How much fuel has he got left? The Fellow was staying on so powerfully. If he continued his late surge then Mark was going to be beaten again. As they flashed past the winning post, neck and neck, both horses had given their all. Peter O'Sullevan's voice was still ringing in my ears. 'The Fellow's going to get up. He's getting up. The Fellow is beginning to get up.' I was shattered. It was as if I was not just watching this race, I was reliving Norton's Coin beating Toby Tobias. Reliving The Dikler beating Pendil, reliving Red Rum catching Crisp. The nightmares are about to return, I thought.

If we had not been packed so tightly in that stand I would have collapsed. I was in shock. I could hear myself making a funny noise, like crying, but the tears stubbornly refused to come. I could hear one voice saying, 'It's all right, you've won,' but another, in my mind, was saying, 'What are you going to do now? He's got beaten again and it's your fault.' People were coming up to me, shouting, 'He's won it, Jenny. He's got it!' But I could hear other voices muttering, 'Well, I think The Fellow's got it.' In the background, Peter O'Sullevan's voice was still going round and round in my head, like a tumble-dryer full of washing.

Then, as I stood there transfixed, something wonderful happened. As the horses pulled up, Mark turned Gary round, rode over to Adam Kondrat, who was riding the French horse, put out his hand, and they shook hands. I was immensely proud of him, whatever the result. The fact that he didn't know if he'd won or lost but could still show genuine sportsmanship meant the world to me.

I put my head down and started pushing my way through the crowd. I was having another conversation with myself now. If you didn't train the horse you wouldn't be putting him through this . . . This will destroy him . . . He's still only a young chap and he's your son. Then, as I headed for the unsaddling enclosure, I heard the announcement over the PA. 'First, number six . . .' The crowd's roar drowned out the rest. Garrison Savannah had won! I should have burst with joy, but somehow I couldn't. I felt drained. The Autofour lads came rushing into the parade ring ready to greet their champion. They were already riding on the magic carpet.

I walked alongside Mark, Garrison Savannah and his owners to the winners' enclosure. Mark's face was bursting with joy as he thanked the well-wishers. His face said everything. To see the relief pouring out of him made me realize just what he'd been through during all those years of self-doubt and public criticism. He looked up at the BBC commentary box and gave his dad a clenched-fist salute. I knew that meant he'd put the record straight for the Pitman family. He wanted Richard to share and appreciate that, too, and I'm sure he did.

I might not have been feeling joyful yet, but I felt so very proud. Mark had given the horse the ride of his life, a ride to remember. He had not lost his cool when Gary flew the fence at the top of the hill, he'd nursed him through the tricky patch when he'd lost his position, and had also shown great courage to ask him for a big leap at the last fence, even when he felt the fuel needle on the horse wavering. I don't honestly think many jockeys would have won on Gary that day; the two of them have always been so alike. I looked round at the cameras clicking and the reporters with their notebooks out. There, I thought. He's done it. Put that in your pipe and smoke it, as my mother might say.

As Mark dismounted I gave him a quick hug. 'Okay?'

'Yeah, I'm fine,' he said. I could tell he was having a job keeping the lid on his emotions. Beside me, Paul and Mandy and David weren't even trying; there were tears rolling down their cheeks. But for some reason my lid was bolted down like a hatch on a submarine. I wanted to open it and let a bit of light in, but it wouldn't. I was on auto-pilot. I'd put myself through such torture that day that my emotions seemed to be frozen solid. I still could not register that we'd won the Gold Cup for a second time. All I wanted was to deal with my horse and go and see my mother.

Mark walked off to weigh in, and came back for the presentation by the Queen Mother. She was as lovely as ever. 'You must be very proud,' she smiled as she shook my hand.

'Yes, I am, ma'am,' I said. 'I'm proud of both of them.'

As I watched Mark go up for his award, the lid began to loosen a little. I thought, 'I wonder what Mum's doing, I hope she's all right.' I wanted to get back as soon as possible to share the moment with her.

As Mark came back, carrying his trophy, he asked, 'Do you still want me to ride that horse in the last?'

He was booked to ride Run To Form in the County Hurdle.

'Why are you asking?' I said.

''Cos I've got to go back in the sweatbox if you do.'

I hesitated. Run To Form had a light weight to carry and Mark was struggling to do it. If any other jockey had won the Gold Cup for me and asked me to let him off his next ride I'd have said yes. But Mark was my son. I felt I couldn't be seen to be doing him any favours whatsoever. I didn't want to give the press the chance to write 'Mummy lets her boy off riding in the County Hurdle.'

'Then get back in the sauna, Mark,' I said. 'I need you to ride it.'

Our triumph was about to turn into disaster.

CHAPTER SEVENTEEN

TRIUMPH AND DISASTER

There were two more races to be run before the County
Hurdle, so while Mark sweated in the sauna I had time to
go and see my mother. As Mandy, Joe and I started to walk
towards the marquee, deep in thought, I was trying to understand what had just happened. Suddenly out of my mouth
came the words, 'Isn't it bloody marvellous? It's like a
swan-song for the old lady, isn't it?' I hadn't meant to speak
the words and I suppose it wasn't until that moment that
any of us wanted to admit to ourselves just how ill Mum was.
Once I'd put it into words it was like a dam bursting and
Mandy and I started to cry. By the time we reached the
marquee we were crying so uncontrollably that we had to
find another table to sit at in the hope that Mother wouldn't
see us. Everyone was asking, 'What are you crying for?' but
of course we couldn't explain for fear of spoiling everyone
else's day. I just sat there bent double, with Mandy opposite
me, both of us sobbing our hearts out, while Joe tried to
shield us from the public gaze.

After a while my brother Richard came over. 'Jenny, that
was bloody fantastic,' he said. 'You should have been in the
marquee. The old girl had her hands over her eyes looking
through her fingers and kept saying, "I can't watch. I can't

265

watch. Tell me what's happening. What's he doing now?"'

With that graphic description Mandy and I started to laugh. It was sad that Mother hadn't been able to get to the winners' enclosure to share that moment with us, but at least she'd seen it on TV. She really had wanted to be at the races, and she was there. The smile on her face told me that all the months of anguish with Garrison Savannah had been worth it.

It wasn't long before I had to leave to saddle Run To Form for the County Hurdle. Mark came into the paddock looking a bit gaunt after his sauna. He was quite tall and chunky for a jockey, and had a struggle to do less than 10st 7lb. Run To Form's owners, the Heyfleet Partnership, were still bubbling about the Gold Cup, but the Gold Cup was behind us. We now had to focus on the job in hand.

Run To Form had suffered a couple of setbacks in the past twelve months and I'd felt that a run over hurdles at Cheltenham would benefit him. The horse was in good nick, and although the County Hurdle is a competitive race, I still expected him to run well. When the starting tape rose, Mark set off two-thirds of the way down the field. The race was over two miles, just one circuit of the course, so they travel pretty fast nearly all the way. As they ran down the hill towards the second last hurdle Mark started to close on the leaders. Through my binoculars I saw Run To Form make a mistake and peck as he landed. Then, because the runners were all so tightly packed, another horse collided with his backside. That was it. Down he went. Mark was pitchforked right in the middle of the field and several horses galloped over him. As they ran on to the final hurdle Run To Form struggled to his feet and cantered off, but Mark had not moved. Several minutes later, with the race over, he was still on the ground with the St John Ambulance men attending him. The stand was emptying all around me now, but I stayed rooted to the spot. It did not look good. Normally if a jockey is in a bit of pain he'll writhe around and at least move something. Mark had not moved a muscle. Suddenly I recognized Run To Form's lad and Steve Fox, my travelling head lad, running along, trying to catch the horse. But I knew I had to get across the course to Mark. I knew if he had not got up by now things must be pretty serious. I fought my way through the crowds and once I reached the course and found my path clear I started running. While I was running, questions kept whizzing round my head: Why did you do this to him? Why did you make him ride that horse? This should have been the best day of his life. Now look what's happened.

I was soon heaving, but it didn't stop me. Suddenly I heard footsteps running along behind me and I turned slightly to see my brother Joe. Together we carried on running across the course until we reached the hurdle where he'd fallen. Mark was surrounded by people. His legs had been tied together, he was trussed up like a turkey and there was an oxygen mask over his face, so it was quite obvious that he wasn't just winded. The ambulancemen were talking quietly to Mark and ignoring us. I stood alongside Joe where Mark could see me. I wanted to say, 'I'm here for you, Mark,' but I felt it better not to speak. Dr O'Donnell was there already, and after he'd examined Mark one of the ambulancemen fetched a scoop stretcher out of the ambulance. 'We're going to put this underneath you,' he told Mark. 'When we do, I want you to take a good gulp from the mask.'

Mark turned his head slightly, looked at Joe and gestured with his head towards me. Joe put his arm round my shoulders, turned me around, and walked me away, but not far enough. I could hear Mark's painful cries as they lifted him onto the stretcher. Once Joe told me Mark was safely in the ambulance we climbed into the back to be with him. The ambulanceman knelt on the floor and tried to hold Mark steady while the ambulance very slowly made its way back to the weighing room, which has a treatment room attached to it. Seeing Mark lying there helplessly, with his legs tied together, the thought came to me that he might be totally paralysed. I forced it out of my mind. The ambulance stopped briefly outside the weighing room and I overheard Dr O'Donnell and the ambulancemen discussing whether to transfer Mark to a road ambulance for the journey to Cheltenham hospital, but they decided against it. That confirmed my thoughts that it must be pretty serious.

There were a lot of press men outside the treatment room, but for once nobody asked me any questions. Perhaps the look on my face told them it was not a good time. I climbed into the front of the ambulance next to the driver, and a moment later we were heading for the racecourse exit. Racing had finished, so there were thousands of people and cars swarming everywhere. I was wondering how on earth we were going to get through the crowds and traffic when a police motorcyclist suddenly appeared in front of us with his lights and siren on. The crowds parted in front of him like the Red Sea, so we followed the motorcycle down the wrong side of the road, the wrong way round every roundabout, and within a very short time we were at the hospital. I walked alongside Mark's stretcher as he was wheeled into casualty. 'You all right, mate?' I asked him, a silly question, I know, but I needed to say something.

'I don't know what's wrong,' Mark answered, 'but it's pretty painful.' I was asked to wait outside the cubicle while the doctors examined him, and a few minutes later I was joined by David and by Dr O'Donnell, who went to speak to the consultant. When he returned he said, 'Jenny, they think Mark has a fractured pelvis.'

'What does that mean?' I asked. 'Is he going to be all right?'

'We won't know how bad it is until he's been X-rayed,' he replied.

While Mark was down in X-ray, Dr O'Donnell, his wife,

David and I were sitting in a side-room, when through the window I saw two men walking down the corridor, one with a big press camera. 'I don't believe it, I just don't believe this,' I said. I went to the door and watched them walk along the casualty ward, peeping behind the curtains. 'Can I help you?' I called.

'Oh, we were looking for Mark Pitman,' one of them stammered.

'I can see that,' I said. 'I think your behaviour's disgusting. Can't you see how distressing this is for us without you behaving like this?'

'We don't want to upset anybody, Jenny.'

'Good. I tell you what. Leave us alone while we find out what the problem is. If Mark is all right you can come back tomorrow and take all the pictures you want.'

'Okay, fine,' they agreed and walked towards the door.

Ten minutes later Dr O'Donnell popped out for a cup of tea and came back to say that the newsmen were still hanging about near the X-ray room. This time I was not so polite to them, and they decided to scarper.

The X-rays confirmed that Mark's pelvis was fractured but, fortunately, it was not as bad as they'd feared. The consultant told us the bone wasn't displaced, which meant the healing should be straightforward.

'How long will it take?' Mark asked him.

I knew straight away what was going through his mind.

'Listen,' I told him, 'it'll be a long time after the Grand National before you're fit, so don't even think about it.'

Mark totally ignored me. 'How long?' he said again.

'Four weeks if you're lucky,' the consultant said. 'If the pieces move it will be longer, maybe six weeks.'

Mark looked at me. 'How long is it till Aintree?'

'You're mental,' I said. 'I just don't want to hear this, Mark.'

'How many days?' he persisted. 'What's the date?'

'Mark, it's April sixth,' I said. 'That's three weeks and two days away. You heard what the doctor said. You can forget all about the Grand National.'

After Mark had been settled as comfortably as was possible under the circumstances Dave and I left, promising to be back the next day. Neither of us said much during the journey back to Lambourn. I felt stunned as I kept thinking how much worse it might have been, wondering how Mark would have coped if he had been paralysed. How *I* would have coped. Was I right to put my family and friends through this? I asked myself. When disasters happened the ripples spread far and wide. Mark and I were not the only ones affected. Dave had gone through the mill today, as had Paul, Mum, Dad and Mark's girlfriend . . . Dave tried to cheer me up by reminding me of Mark's lunacy in wanting to ride in the Grand National. We decided he was completely bloody barmy, but if Mark wanted to ride at all after a fall like that we still had a lot to be grateful for.

Garrison Savannah came out of Cheltenham an awful lot better than his jockey. The day after the Gold Cup, when I pulled him out of his box, he trotted up like somebody who had enjoyed a good game of squash. A little bit stiff, but no more than you would expect of any horse who had completed a long hard race. His only injury was a tiny over-reach where his hind hoof had clipped the heel of a front one.

Emotionally, I was pretty raw, so I wasn't up to thinking too far ahead. I hadn't forgotten about the Grand National, but that morning I was simply relieved to see Gary pull out in such good order. I'd already rung the hospital to be told that Mark had been in a bit of discomfort but was generally fine. We drove to the hospital after morning stables, and arrived at the same time as Garrison Savannah's owners. They'd brought the Gold Cup with them and a bottle of champagne, though they didn't look in need of any topping up! They tried to make us laugh, telling us how they'd struck a big on-course bet and had won a small fortune. After the racing they'd got legless and they'd been throwing the money around their box like confetti, until a security man had come in and told them to be more careful. He'd fetched a black binliner, collected all the money up and put it away in a safe for them to collect the next morning when they'd sobered up! Meeting the Autofour lads did us good, as I hadn't been in a jovial mood. I had a trauma hangover, which was very different from the kind from which they were suffering.

We found Mark in unbelievably good spirits. All he wanted to talk about was the Gold Cup. Of course, we hadn't had a chance to discuss his win. 'Something really funny happened when Gary walked out onto the course,' he told us. 'I swear to you, the moment his feet touched the grass he seemed to grow three inches. He just sort of grew and swelled up.'

'Go on with you,' I said. I thought Mark must have had too much gas. With hindsight, I'm not so cynical. Some inexplicable things happened that day, and maybe Mark had experienced one of them.

Mark was still going on about riding in the National. I listened to him but I definitely didn't want to hear what he said. The part of me that was Mark's mother was saying, 'I don't want you to do this any more. I can't bear it.' But the professional trainer in me was smiling and saying, 'That's my boy . . .'

Several days after the accident Mark was discharged from hospital, though in a wheelchair. Straight away he made an appointment with John Skull, a local physiotherapist who specialized in helping injured jockeys back into action. After Mark had spent two or three treatment sessions with John, I had a quiet word with him. 'Talk sense to him. Tell him it's madness to think of riding in the National,' I begged him.

John smiled. 'Well, actually, Jenny, you know, it's not that mad. I think he might just be all right. He might just make it if he doesn't have any setbacks,' he replied.

'John, for Christ's sake, don't do this to me,' I said. 'I thought you were a friend of mine!'

In the days after the Gold Cup we had a lot of lovely telephone calls and letters congratulating us. One I treasured came from Major Dick Hern, whom I'd always had the greatest respect for as a trainer. He'd written it by hand, which, considering he is paralysed, must have been very difficult for him. 'What a wonderful achievement,' he wrote, 'and what a brave young man Mark is, to ask his horse to jump the last the way he did.' It meant so much to me that he had taken the trouble to write, and his comments meant a lot to Mark as well.

Although I did not envisage Mark riding in the National, Garrison Savannah's participation in the race was now becoming a distinct possibility. He'd come out of the Gold Cup really well, with no trace of his old shoulder problem. My biggest worry was that after such a hard race he might pick up the cough that was going around by mixing with all the horses at the racecourse. Horses are susceptible to infection, so we decided to give Gary a precautionary course of antibiotics to help him ward off any bugs. It would also help his over-reach injury to heal. He was to have a five-day course of injections starting a few days after Cheltenham. Alan Walker gave him a jab in the rump on Thursday, and I gave him his second on the Friday. On the Saturday we were racing, so I asked my assistant to inject the third dose into Gary's rump that evening.

On Sunday, at evening stables, I thought Gary had an odd look on his face. I thought, What's up with you, old lad, then? I noticed that Gary's chest was very swollen, and when I felt it, there was a large hard hot lump there.

I was distraught. 'What on earth's happened to this effing horse? He looks like Samantha Fox!' I exploded.

I saw an anxious look pass between the assistant and the head lad. It turned out that instead of injecting the horse in the rump the assistant had injected him in the breast. When he received my frantic telephone message Alan Walker came straight over from Warwickshire. Gary walked out of his box with his forelegs splayed out and it was obvious that he was in considerable pain. At Alan's suggestion we treated him with alternate hot and cold compresses to try and soften the lump. It meant holding hot towels on his breast for five minutes, followed by towels soaked in cold water. Gary wasn't happy about it. Normally you could do what you wanted with him with a few packets of Polos as a bribe, but when we put those towels on his chest you could see anger burning in his eyes. Whenever they turned that deep crimson colour you knew to watch out because he would usually clear everyone out of the stable.

After the compresses had softened the swelling we had to try and disperse it by walking him. I thought, This is unbelievable. We'd just spent eight weeks on one treadmill with him, and now we were back on another. That night we were out with him till nine o'clock, bathing, walking, bathing, walking. In the middle of the night we led him out again, because I knew that if I left him standing overnight the swelling would build up and become a great deal worse. By Monday evening it was a bit better, so I decided he was ready for something a little more strenuous. For the next three nights I made the assistant and the head lad responsible for the problem climb out of bed, turn the car headlights onto the paddock near the house and they had to trot Gary round on the end of a lunge-line for twenty minutes a night.

To say a huge spanner had been thrown in the works was an understatement. If we wanted him to run in the Grand National it was vital I kept Gary on the move. Although he'd been fit enough to win the Gold Cup, he would not remain so without some work. For four solid days we slaved nonstop with him until the swelling was gone. With only eight days to go till the Grand National, he was back on course, but I still wasn't sure about running him.

It had been fifty-seven years since a horse had won the

Cheltenham Gold Cup and the Grand National in the same year. Only a handful of horses had ever tried the double and only one, Golden Miller, had succeeded, in 1934. The reason so few had attempted it was simple. The two races are completely different. The Cheltenham Gold Cup is a three-and-a-quarter-mile chase run at level weights, while the Grand National is a four-and-a-half-mile handicap with a weight range of two stone. To win the Gold Cup a horse needs a high cruising speed and a good turn of foot at the finish, while the National requires a horse to be an out-and-out stayer. Although Gary had won the Gold Cup I had always thought of him as a National horse. In normal circumstances I'd have had no doubts at all about running him at Aintree. What I could not forget was that in 1979 Alverton, the last horse to try to win both races, had been killed jumping Becher's. The press didn't forget it either. They were completely divided about whether we should go for the race. At the end of the day, however, Garrison Savannah belonged to the Autofour lads. It was my job to prepare him, and the choice about whether to run or not was theirs. It helped that the fences at Aintree had been modified since 1979 and were not so daunting.

It was just over a week before the race when we finally decided to let Gary run in the National. Because of his chest problem I had had to rearrange his training and had not been able to give him a really strong gallop, which I would have done under normal circumstances. Mark had not even been back on a horse since his fall at Cheltenham, but if Gary ran he was determined to be on board. In the end I thought, right, I'll fix you.

'Wonder Man runs in the Welsh Champion Hurdle on Monday, Mark. You'd better ride him,' I said. I had bought Wonder Man as a three-year-old, and I thought he had a good chance of winning the race.

'Why?' asked Mark.

'Because if you can't ride Wonder Man in a two-mile

274

Burrough Hill Lad leads Wayward Lad on his way to victory in the King George VI Chase, Kempton Park, 1984. *George Selwyn*

The Queen Mother presents me with a carriage clock for winning the King George VI Chase. My red hat is the one that inspired Mr and Mrs Hitchins to become owners with me. The horse brooch is the one much admired by Terry Ramsden. *Trevor Jones*

With the trophy presented to mark my third Welsh National win with Stearsby in December 1986. Burrough Hill Lad won in 1983, preceded by Corbiere in 1982. *George Selwyn*

With Garrison Savannah and Mark on Lambourn Downs. *Gerry Cranham*

This is how close it was! Mark looks across as Gary clinches the Gold Cup from The Fellow and Adam Kondrat, March 1991.
Racecourse Technical Services

A very proud moment. Paul, David, Mark and I with Gary and the Autofour lads in the winner's enclosure at Cheltenham. *Gerry Cranham*

With my mum and dad, summer 1991. *Gerry Cranham*

Esha Ness and John White lead The Committee and Norman Williamson upsides Romany King and Adrian Maguire over the last in 'the National that never was', April 1993. *Gerry Cranham*

What a line-up! Our Grand National hopes for 1995. *Left to right:* Superior Finish, Royal Athlete, Garrison Savannah, Esha Ness, Do Be Brief, Lusty Light, with Mark, myself and the lads at Weathercock House. *Author's collection*

Jason Titley salutes the Aintree crowd as Royal Athlete wins a second Grand National for me in 1995. *Chris Cole/Allsport*

Willsford jumps the last to land the 1995 Scottish Grand National under Rodney Farrant. *Alec Russell*

A full hand! Mudahim and Jason Titley edge out Amble Speedy and Francis Woods in the Irish Grand National, Fairyhouse, April 1997. *Caroline Norris*

David and I sign the register after our wedding, July 1997.
Scope Features

Receiving my OBE at Buckingham Palace with Paul, David and Mark, March 1998.
Charles Green

A rare moment of relaxation with Paul and Mark at Weathercock House. Luckily, we've always shared the same wicked sense of humour!
David Shopland

Princeful wins the Stayers' Hurdle under Rodney Farrant, Cheltenham Festival, March 1998.
Gerry Cranham

Princeful with one of my most loyal owners, Mr Hitchins, in the winner's enclosure at Cheltenham.
Gerry Cranham

The press went into overdrive when I announced my retirement at the 1999 Cheltenham Festival!

LEGEND JENNY SAYS FAREWELL IN TEARS

Nation's favourite trainer bows out to cheers

Jenny Pitman rides into the Cheltenham sunset

Pitman reins in her racing career

Mrs P. hands the reins over to her son

Farewell to the Cuddly One

Pitman hands over the reins

I was very touched when Patrick Martell presented me with a special gift on behalf of the National sponsors at the 1999 Martell Grand National.
Gerry Cranham

hurdle at Chepstow you are not going to be fit to ride Garrison Savannah four and a half miles over fences at Aintree.'

Mark nodded. 'Right, then, I'll ride him,' he declared defiantly.

I had hoped that by backing Mark into a corner it might focus his mind on the stupidity of what he planned to do. But my plan misfired. On the Saturday before the National, Mark came to ride out with the first lot of horses. He persuaded one of the lads to leg him up out of my sight and then set off for the gallops with the others. Over an hour later, when he came back, I could see he was uncomfortable, but neither of us said anything. The next day he rode out again, and this time he confessed afterwards that he ached a bit.

'Well, best not ride that horse tomorrow, then,' I said. 'Not only that, best forget about the Grand National.'

'No, no, no,' Mark said. 'I'll be fine. I'm only a bit stiff. I'm perfectly capable of riding,' he insisted.

You're lying to me, I thought. But all right, prove it. I also knew that Mark would have to be passed fit to ride by the Jockey Club doctor, and I was convinced that it just would not be possible. But I also knew that while he may have told me fibs about other things I had never known him to be untruthful about his job.

On the morning of the Welsh Champion Hurdle Mark rode out, then drove straight over to see Chris Day for some acupuncture and homeopathic pills. I guess his reasoning was that if it had worked for Gary in the past it might work for the jockey too.

A few hours later we were in the paddock at Chepstow. As we walked across to Wonder Man Mark said quietly, 'When you leg me up on this horse, make sure you chuck me well up in the air.'

'Why?'

'I don't want to have to stretch my leg too far across him,' he said.

275

Mark, you're sodding nuts, I thought.

I felt that Wonder Man had a good chance of winning his race but I was a bit nervous about his jumping because he took his hurdles dangerously fast; in fact I used to school him over fences to make him have a bit more respect for them. As I expected, he jumped cleanly and beautifully in the early part of the race, but by the time they started running down to the last two flights he was going so fast he was whipping the tops off the hurdles. As I watched, my heart was in my mouth. He flew the last and won easily.

'Are you all right?' I asked Mark as he came up the chute to the unsaddling enclosure.

He nodded. 'When I get off, just stand close to me.' I knew what that meant. His legs were tired because of the injury and because he hadn't race-ridden for three weeks, and I reasoned by the look on his face that he was in some pain. As Mark raised his leg to dismount I put my arm around him. In the newspaper photograph the next day this appeared to be a loving gesture, but my arm was actually there to help hold him up.

Right, you've learned your lesson now, I thought. Let's scrub the Grand National. I was already planning who would ride Gary on Saturday instead of Mark – probably Ben de Haan, since he had won the Sun Alliance on him. We had a lot of horses running at the Liverpool meeting and Ben was already booked to ride a couple for me, so it shouldn't be a problem. I intended to tell Mark my plan the next morning, but on the Tuesday when he came in to work, before I could open my mouth, he said, 'Oh, about Liverpool . . .'

'What about Liverpool?'

'I want to be careful what I ride in the races before the National. I'll ride the hurdlers.'

At that point I gave up. My only consolation was knowing that Mark would not pull the wool over my eyes. If he thought he'd let the horse or me down, he would not ride. If he felt he was up to the job then I had to support him. For the Thursday I picked what I thought were two safe rides for him: Esha Ness, who was a very sound jumper in the novice chase, and Smith's Cracker in the three-mile novice hurdle. Things started well when Esha Ness finished second, and just over an hour later I legged Mark up on the other horse. Smith's Cracker was a good hurdler who belonged to Arthur Smith, one of my very first owners. He had already won the Saddle of Gold final at Newbury that season, so was well fancied. I watched the race from a hospitality box with Mr and Mrs Hitchins. At the second last hurdle Smith's Cracker was upsides another horse and looked likely to win when he clipped the top of the hurdle, somersaulted and crashed to the ground. Mark lay still beside the horse.

All I wanted to do was run down the course to them, but I held back. People must not think I was unable to cope. Jockeys fell regularly. They did not all have their mothers hurtling down the course to pick them up. As I looked down the course through my binoculars I realized that Smith's Cracker was motionless. I knew he was dead. Now I no longer had a decision to make. I didn't care what people might say, I started running down the course. Someone was running behind me and I took a quick look over my shoulder and saw a man with a bag over his shoulder. As I looked, he started to take a camera out of his bag. I pulled up. 'Don't you dare,' I said. 'How dare you even think about it . . .' The man slowed down. By the time he reached me he had stopped altogether. I stood there giving him full throttle. Without saying a word, he put his camera back in the bag and walked back up the course.

Amazingly, while all this was going on Mark had got to his feet and was waving the ambulancemen away. He looked deathly white and was obviously very distressed about Smith's Cracker. You didn't need this, did you? I thought. We walked back up the course together. Mark looked dreadful. I thought there was no way he was going to be riding in the National. Much later, when he'd been examined by the racecourse doctor and had gone back to the weighing room, I went to see him.

'How are you?' I asked him.

'A bit sore.' He looked me in the eye. 'But I'll be all right by Saturday . . .'

Most days I love what I do. Most days there is not a person in the world I'd change places with. But two days later, as I counted down the hours before the Grand National, I was not enjoying it at all. I didn't want to be at the races. I didn't want my horse to run. Most of all I didn't want my son to ride in it. I'd completely lost my bottle.

A couple of hours before the big race Aintree is like an oven warming up to cooking temperature. People are swarming in and out of the bars and marquees and there's such a buzz of anticipation in the air it's hard to hear yourself speak. But that day I didn't feel a part of it, I didn't want to be a part of it. I always get butterflies when I have a runner, particularly in the Grand National – you'd have to be made of stone not to feel apprehensive – but at that moment it felt more like broken glass than butterflies in my stomach. I was seriously rattled, so much so that I found Dr Allen, the Jockey Club doctor, and told him how I felt. He gave me some mild tranquillizers. That morning's newspapers had hardly helped my state of mind. Some of the press obviously thought I was crackers to run Garrison Savannah and even more crackers to allow Mark to ride him. At that moment I felt they could be right. Maybe what I was trying to do was impossible.

Usually at Aintree I can put on a brave face for the media, answering questions and generally doing my bit, but that day I hid away in a little marquee with Dave, trying to avoid people. I didn't want to be interviewed, I didn't want to sign autographs. I just wanted to go home. In the corner of the marquee was a television perched on a bracket, showing

Garrison Savannah's position as joint second favourite. Normally I don't worry at all about the betting. Whether my horses are 4–6 or 20–1 doesn't make me care any more or less about them, but knowing that Gary was so strongly fancied was a pressure I could have done without. I knew it would make the press focus on him even more, and they would be watching for every little error by either the horse or Mark.

'If something goes wrong today they're going to go for me,' I told Dave. 'They'll put me through the shredder and spit me out in pieces.'

In addition to Garrison Savannah I also ran Abba Lad, Golden Freeze and Team Challenge, so there was a lot of work in tacking up all four horses. The crowds were so thick we had to push our way to the saddling boxes. As usual Gary was feeling full of himself, stamping his feet, fidgeting, and that familiar deep crimson was showing at the back of his eyes. Secretly I still wished I could have given him that last bit of work, but all I could do now was pray that what we had done was enough. After twenty or so frantic minutes all four horses were saddled and ready to parade, and there was only time for a quick word with each owner. Mr and Mrs Hitchins had two runners, Team Challenge and Golden Freeze, and they were naturally nervous. The Autofour lads were quieter than I'd ever known them. In the paddock I legged Ben de Haan, Dean Gallagher and my brother-in-law Mike Bowlby onto their horses and wished them luck. Their riding plans had already been made when I'd walked the course with them that morning. When it came to Mark's turn I legged him up and as he slid his foot into the stirrup I squeezed his leg through his boot.

'Have a good ride, mate.'

He gave me a quick smile, and for a split second it was as if we shared the same skin.

As Garrison Savannah's lad led him round the parade ring with the thirty-nine other runners my mind was in turmoil about Mark's decision to ride in the race. A moment later the horses left the paddock and it was too late to stop him, even if I'd wanted to.

I wasn't at all good company by now, so I left Dave with the owners and made my way to the lady jockeys' changing room to watch the race on the television. The field was already circling at the start. As the starter called them into line I said a silent prayer. 'Please, God.'

As the flag came down Mark and Gary set off down the inside as we'd planned, where the fences are bigger but where there is usually more room. Good jumpers like Gary who keep to the inside are more likely to keep out of trouble. As usual the runners charged to the first fence at a serious rate of knots and I held my breath until I saw Gary and my other three land safely. By the second, they were beginning to settle down a bit. They took that safely too. Golden Freeze, who was big and bold and liked to dominate, was leading the field. The third fence is big, with a ditch in front of it. They were still going pretty fast as they reached it, but Gary found a good stride at it, and landed athletically. All four were over safely. By now the field was sorting itself out. They'd begun to settle into a more sensible pace and I could see that Gary was galloping in a lovely relaxed rhythm. I thought, That looks good. I was starting to feel a lot happier inside. Horse and rider looked comfortable together.

Over the next few fences Golden Freeze was still making the running and Mark had settled Gary not far behind the leaders. As they came towards Becher's Brook for the first time I prayed for another good stride. You cannot afford to get it wrong at Becher's, especially on the inside where the drop is steepest. They didn't. Mark would be happy with that, I thought. I imagined how he must be feeling, knowing his horse was on song and feeling at one with him. Watching the pair of them reminded me of the advert where a ball-bearing is running through oil. It was so smooth, so easy.

They were totally in unison, each one confident in what the other was doing.

By the start of the second circuit the broken glass inside me had been replaced by a warm glow, not because I thought Mark and Gary would win but because I'd started to enjoy the race, the way an artist appreciates a fine painting. I kept hearing myself saying, 'Lovely, lovely,' each time they put a fence behind them. I took my eyes off them for a moment to watch my other runners and saw Team Challenge make a mistake at the eighteenth fence. He recovered, but it had disappointed him and he refused at the next. Then a roar from the crowd drew me back to the leaders. Mark and Gary were steadily making up ground, and at the twenty-third they moved past Golden Freeze into the lead. Ridden with aggressive confidence and jumping with a thrilling blend of boldness and accuracy, Garrison Savannah, wearing vivid blue blinkers, was being called the winner from a long way out. He took a clear advantage once more with another soaring leap at the second last fence and led by six lengths, perhaps more, landing over the final fence. One of the lady jockeys grabbed me by the arm and started shouting. 'Mark's going to do it! He's going to win!' And I thought, 'Oh God, yes. He is!'

But I wasn't shouting. Something was holding me back. I wanted them to jump the last safely. They jumped it well, and as they landed I felt the most incredible relief. I didn't even care about the winning post any more. I'd been to Aintree for a great many years, and I knew the race wasn't over yet, but for me it was. Both of them were going to come home safe and sound in one piece. Anything that happened now wasn't too important. They'd proved themselves. The decision to run the horse wasn't wrong. The decision to let Mark ride him wasn't wrong. Their guts and courage had prevailed.

Then, suddenly, as they reached the Elbow, I saw Gary's legs falter. Behind me I heard somebody shouting, 'Come on, Nigel!' Another horse full of running was thundering up the straight behind him. It was Seagram. Mark saw him too. He sensed that Gary had given his all and he knew better than to hit a beaten horse. That missed piece of work was taking its toll. He was beginning to tire noticeably now. As they passed the elbow Mark and Gary were still in front, but only just. Then as the winning post beckoned Seagram drew upsides. A moment later Seagram surged past Garrison Savannah like a fresh horse and galloped on to win by five lengths. It was all over.

As I pushed my way through the crowds to the unsaddling enclosure total strangers patted me on the back and offered their sympathy. They were like mourners at a funeral and must have imagined I was heartbroken. But I wasn't upset, I was grinning like an idiot. I must have looked completely mad. But for me, winning was not that important that day. My horse and my son had given their all and they had come home safe. That was all that mattered. Of course it would have been truly wonderful to have won as well. They had proved the doubters wrong, and for me that was enough. There was always next year!

CHAPTER EIGHTEEN

HITTING THE HEADLINES

If this had been written as a novel people would think it was too far-fetched. You couldn't train a horse the way I'd had to train Garrison Savannah and get him to perform the way he did by winning the Cheltenham Gold Cup and finishing second in the Grand National. A jockey couldn't fracture his pelvis, then, three weeks later, ride round Aintree and nearly win the Grand National. It couldn't happen. But it did. There are some things in life I have always felt that you cannot explain rationally.

Looking back, I think it's possible that Gary's performances that year didn't have much to do with my training ability. When I'd been trying to get the horse over his health and fitness problems I'd always had a strong sense of something or somebody pushing and guiding me towards the next step. There were times when I really hadn't wanted to carry on, but I felt I had to continue. Something I couldn't explain forced me to persevere. It was only four months after the Gold Cup, when my mother died in her sleep, that I felt I knew why. I believe it all happened for her. Someone or something other than me had taken a hand in these events. After all those years of looking after other people, and putting herself last, Mum deserved a reward, and I felt that seeing her grandson and daughter win the Cheltenham Gold Cup together had been that reward. It's the only way I can explain it.

Somehow or other, because your parents have always been there, you never really believe they will die. I suppose you kid yourself that they will cheat the system. Mum's death was a shattering blow. For forty-four years she'd been there for me and others, rarely interfering but always ready to help. Too late, I realized I'd never really let her know how much I appreciated her. Like a lot of kids I always thought I'd get around to telling her one day. The only way I could start to cope with losing her was by writing her a long letter, telling her how much she had meant to me. When I went to see her in the chapel of rest I carefully placed it in her hand, but I dearly wished I had told her. The months after Mum died were very tough. I had a business to run and I couldn't be seen to be letting my personal life interfere with it, but I struggled to keep a brave face. I found it difficult to share my feelings with my family because I knew they were hurting too. Anyway, in the past they had usually come to me with their troubles, and I felt as if I was expected to be the strong one. Fortunately the horses were good listeners. If it hadn't been for them I don't know how I'd have got through those early days. I'd wait until the evening when no-one was about and go and sit in the paddock on a bale of straw, smoke a cigarette and quietly mull things over. I was doing just that when the four horses in the paddock walked over to me. As I put up my hand to stroke one of them one of the others snapped at him. 'Oh, sod off if you're going to be like that,' I said loudly, because I didn't want any hassle. As I stood up and walked slowly back towards the gate I could hear their footsteps behind me, and when I glanced round I saw all four horses following me across the paddock with their heads bent low down by their knees, nose to tail, like elephants in the dusk. They couldn't have said sorry more plainly if they'd spoken out loud. I felt a little light inside me, and a brief smile across my face. It was the first time that had happened for many weeks.

There was a time when I felt every journalist had to find a different label to describe my perceived image as a tough cookie. In addition to the usual adjectives – 'formidable', 'fearsome', 'cantankerous' – I've been called 'daunting', 'the Iron Lady' and, once, a 'virago'. 'What the bloody hell is a virago?' I asked Alan Walker. 'A cantankerous old cow,' he replied. 'Pretty accurate, then,' I said and we burst out laughing.

My public image causes great amusement in my family. It also creates quite a bit of confusion whenever magazine writers come to interview me. They seem to expect to find a right old battleaxe and often express surprise that I'm quite different from what they've been led to believe. I don't claim to be made in the same mould as Mother Teresa, though, and freely admit that I'm quite formidable at times and can reach boiling point rather rapidly. Before I go to the races I head straight for the cloakroom and put on my coat, which I envisage as my armour plating. In part this goes back to the early days when I started on my own in this business and discovered that many people deal with women as if they are complete morons.

Florence Nagle bravely opened the door for us in 1966, when she fought a fierce legal battle against the Jockey Club. Although she and other females had been training success-fully for many years the Club stubbornly refused to grant them licences. They were forced to adopt the shameful subterfuge of using male nominees to hold their licences. Mrs Nagle sought a judicial ruling that she should not be refused a licence on the grounds of her sex. Eventually the court of appeal ruled that the Jockey Club's policy was arbi-trary and entirely out of touch with the state of society in Great Britain at that time. Facing certain defeat, the Jockey Club capitulated. But the fact that we had to wait until 1966 for a woman to hold a trainer's licence for the first time underlines the prejudice we have faced in racing – and still do, though to a lesser degree these days. I feel it shows in other ways, too. When people see a male trainer with tears in his eyes after one of his horses is injured at the races they immediately feel sympathy. If I were to cry in a similar circumstance, I decided, they'd be more likely to suggest that I couldn't cope, so I try not to cry in public, even when I am dealing with a tragic situation, however much I feel the hurt inside.

It was just like that when Mark broke his pelvis at Cheltenham, shortly after winning the Gold Cup on Garrison Savannah. I looked and felt dreadful but I didn't cry until I was in a more private place, later that evening.

The pressures of training can be extremely hard, though the horses are not always the problem, by any means. There are so many other demands – travelling to the races nearly every day, working seven days a week and bank holidays and weekends, the ever-increasing paperwork, which I have always hated, and the press. The press and I have enjoyed a love–hate relationship for quite a few years. One of our first 'antler clashes' was when they spread rumours about Burrough Hill Lad breaking blood vessels. Since then, every time there has been a whiff of controversy about either me or one of my horses, some newspaper or other has pounced on it. At times there were far juicier stories doing the rounds than any of mine have ever been, but these were ignored. Maybe this was because they felt a woman made an easier target, especially after the stories in the press that I was a 'formidable character' with a 'fearsome reputation' – and these just for starters! Actually, it did come in handy at times; people usually approached me with caution, and we haven't had anyone wanting to tarmac our drive for years!

If doing your job properly and expecting a square deal from people is being tough and formidable, then I *am* tough and formidable. I had had to learn the hard way, and I was not about to be taken for a ride. But I have always tried to be straight, fair and honest with people and to treat them as I would expect to be treated myself. However, for reasons best known to themselves, some sections of the press liked to paint me if I was a dragon with smoke and flames coming out of my nostrils all the time. So as far as they were concerned, an incident at Ayr racecourse in 1990 involving the jockey Jamie Osborne was heaven-sent.

Trouble had been brewing between Jamie and me for some time. In the Mumm Club Chase at Aintree a couple of weeks earlier Mark had been riding Royal Athlete and Jamie had been riding Arctic Call for his guv'nor Oliver Sherwood. After jumping the last fence on the far side of the course, Jamie's horse had run very wide round the bottom bend. Mark was on Jamie's inside all the time and had followed the line of the rail properly. Jamie then changed direction and came back into the fence at an acute angle, cutting Mark off as they approached the next fence. Mark's horse had been squeezed up so tight that the bunch of birch, which is always tied to the inside of the fence, whipped back as he and Royal Athlete hit it. At the end of the race Royal Athlete won by half a length from Arctic Call, but his run might easily have ended at that fence. I went to the weighing room and told 'Ossie' that racing was dangerous enough without him being a 'prat' and if that was the best he could do he ought to get some wing mirrors.

A fortnight later I ran my good young hurdler, Run To Form, in a novice hurdle race at Ayr during the Scottish National meeting. Seamus O'Neill was riding him as Mark was on my main hope, Do Be Brief, who finished second. I was watching the race through my binoculars, feeling happy with the way things were going, when suddenly, as they started into the bend at the top end of the racetrack, I saw the white plastic running rail fly up in the air and a horse crash through it. It was Run To Form. Seamus managed to stay on board but the horse was obviously shaken, and they coasted home in mid-field. By the time I reached the unsaddling area Seamus had disappeared and Run To Form was being led around by his lad. He was in a real state, trembling with fright, and had a very nasty cut with scratches and white paint all down his side where he'd hit the railing. I was livid and went off to track down Seamus. I found him coming out of the changing rooms. 'What went on there?' I asked.

'F—ing Osborne!' he said.

'What did he do?'

Seamus shook his head. 'I shouted to him, "I'm on your inner, Jamie!" And he shouted "F— off," then slapped me straight through the rails. I've reported him to the stewards.'

I next tackled Oliver Sherwood. 'Oliver, it's about time you got hold of that lad and squared him up.'

Oliver shrugged. 'I've tried, Jenny, believe me, I've tried.'

'Well, you either want to clip him around the ears or give him some sodding wing mirrors,' I said. I was furious. To me, Oliver didn't seem as concerned as I felt he should have been about his young jockey's behaviour.

I eventually went to find Mark to ask if he'd seen what had happened, but was told he'd been called to see the stewards. I found him waiting outside the stewards' room with Jamie Osborne and Seamus O'Neill. Jamie was sitting bare-footed on a table, dangling his legs and looking a real smart alec.

'Why don't you f—ing grow up, Osborne?' I said. 'I told you at Aintree, this job's dangerous enough without you being an arsehole.' I turned to Seamus and said, 'You shouldn't be reporting him to the stewards either. You should be sorting this out between yourselves in the changing room, like they did in the old days.' With that I turned and walked away.

I'd gone about six paces when Osborne said in a high-pitched, mocking voice, 'Yes, Mrs Pitman.'

That made me see red. I turned round, walked straight back to him and drew my hand back to slap his face. The blow was just about to land when the stewards' room door opened and out popped a steward. It was too late to stop. Even if I'd wanted to I couldn't. 'Whack!' went the sound (a bit like a midwife slapping a new-born baby's bum) as my hand struck Jamie's face. I turned and walked off. But I knew I was going to get called back. The next announcement to come over the loudspeakers was that the stewards wanted to see Mrs Pitman. Once inside the stewards' room the chairman put his first question to the steward who'd seen the slap.

'What did you witness when you went out through this door?'

'I saw Mrs Pitman's hand going up to Jamie Osborne's face,' he answered.

'Was it in a friendly manner?'

I nearly choked. Jamie had a bright-red hand-print on the side of his face, which told its own story. Then they turned to Mark and Seamus and asked them in turn what they'd seen. I looked at them and silently pleaded, 'Don't lie for me, boys, please don't lie.' I had tried several times to interrupt to say I did smack Jamie's face. I know I shouldn't have done it, but I had. I was told to be quiet and speak when I was spoken to, which was not easy when I was so full of passion and anger and trying to defend what I loved – my horses. Eventually they turned to me.

'What happened, Mrs Pitman?'

'You know what happened,' I said.

'Just answer the questions as we ask them, please.'

It turned out that the stewards weren't interested in hearing about the Aintree incident or what had led up to my slapping Jamie Osborne. They only wanted to know one thing: 'Did you slap Osborne?'

'Yes,' I freely admitted.

They fined me £200 for bringing racing into disrepute. The words were far more hurtful to me than the fine, because I had never in my life wanted to bring racing into disrepute. I felt incredibly angry with Jamie Osborne, who was walking away with his halo still intact when he knew perfectly well what had happened. I personally felt that he was guilty of reckless riding and should have been fined. It took a long time for us to bury the hatchet. I'm not excusing what I did. I was out of order. But racing has enough risks, even when jockeys behave themselves. Over the years there have been some terrible accidents – jockeys paralysed and also killed, as well as horses. There has to be a code of conduct to keep the risks to a minimum.

Jamie Osborne has since grown up a lot and has ridden for me many times. But I felt Run To Form was never the same horse again. He had the potential to be a very good hurdler but afterwards, if other horses squeezed him up, he panicked. It was almost exactly a year later, in a tightly packed field at Cheltenham when horses were crowding him, that Run To Form fell and put Mark in hospital with a fractured pelvis.

Naturally the newspapers made a feast out of my slapping Jamie. They loved it. By the time it was printed the slap had become a punch and I was portrayed as the Frank Bruno of the racing world. It didn't make my relationship with them any easier, and in 1992 it became even more strained, after what became known throughout racing as the Golden Freeze Affair.

Golden Freeze was originally owned by Asil Nadir, who had six horses in training with me. In the early nineties, before his financial affairs came to grief, Asil Nadir had asked me to try and find clients to buy his horses. On my recommendation, Mr and Mrs Hitchins had bought Golden Freeze and Don Valentino. Golden Freeze had won some decent races and I'd always considered him a good horse, but he was extremely eccentric. He had two gears: slow and running away. One day when he had one of his 'silly heads' on, he hurtled round Mandown gallop like he was a motorbike on the wall of death, until he had exhausted himself. When he pulled up his eyes were so wild and bloodshot you'd think he had been smoking marijuana. We tried all sorts of different bridles and bits to stop him running away, but nothing really worked. When we put him in a citation bridle, which would cure most runaways, he just jacked it in altogether, stood stock still and refused to walk onto the gallops.

He could be an eccentric horse at home, too. He was more trusting with women than with men, but you only had to walk into his box with a brightly coloured coat on and he'd look at you suspiciously, with his eyes sticking out of his head like golfballs. We'd bought him in Ireland as a 'made' horse, from Ted Walsh, who had broken him in. Ted eventually told me a story that might explain why Golden Freeze was so nervous and highly strung. One day Ted had ridden him out wearing a full-length wax coat, which he hadn't fastened up properly. Golden Freeze had taken fright at this coat flapping in the wind and rain and had bolted with Ted for about five miles. The more the coat flapped the faster he ran. Whether that experience was at the root of his problems I couldn't be sure, but he was certainly a horse you had to use psychology with to get the best out of him. At the races we usually got special permission to go down to the start early or late to try to keep him as calm as possible, because if other horses galloped past him he would try to take off. During a race we found the best way to handle him was to let him go out and make the running, then try and settle him. The trouble was, once he'd settled you had to try not to let him be headed. If that happened he was liable to down tools completely. Mandy's husband Mike got on very well with the horse and had ridden him in most of his races.

In 1992 Mr and Mrs Hitchins' best horse, Toby Tobias, was entered in the Gold Cup, but we'd had a few niggly problems with him and there was a possibility that he might have to miss the race for the second year running. Since they come from Cheltenham Mr and Mrs Hitchins always liked to have a runner in a big race there. Golden Freeze had been entered in the Cathcart and the Mildmay of Flete Chase, as well as in the Gold Cup.

'What sort of chance do you think Golden Freeze would have in the Gold Cup?' Mr Hitchins asked me.

As it happened, that year there were question marks against a lot of the Gold Cup entries, not least Martin Pipe's horse Carvill's Hill, who was the red-hot favourite. Although Carvill's Hill had won the Rehearsal Chase, the Welsh National and the Irish Hennessy Gold Cup, many professionals voiced doubts about him, and I shared these. His jumping was always suspect and the Cheltenham track and fences were a lot stiffer than those at Chepstow or Leopardstown. I'd also been given some interesting information about the horse. Someone, whom I had no reason to doubt, had told me that all wasn't well with him. I know about rumours in racing – I'd been the subject of some of them myself – but I thought that if Carvill's Hill did have problems it would leave the Gold Cup even wider open.

'I think Golden Freeze would have to be lucky to win,' I told Mr Hitchins. 'But he could easily run into a place, and if Carvill's Hill doesn't run, I could even see him finishing in the first four, and there's prize money down to sixth place.'

'Well, I'd sooner run in the Gold Cup than the Mildmay of Flete if you think he's got a chance,' said Mr Hitchins, so the decision was made.

During Cheltenham week we were invited up to the box of some other owners of ours, Peter and Michael Mines. We were sitting chatting when on the television in the corner I noticed Julian Wilson interviewing Peter Scudamore, Carvill's Hill's jockey, so I went over and listened to the interview. They were talking about the big race and it occurred to me that I couldn't ever remember a jockey booked to ride the favourite in the Gold Cup so downbeat about his chances.

That evening Mike Bowlby and Mark came over to

Weathercock House and, as usual before a big race, we sat and watched videos of all the runners, noting how they ran their races, so we could decide how our horse would best be ridden. I told Mike about the interview I'd seen that afternoon. 'I don't know what, if anything, is going on with Carvill's Hill, but I just have a gut feeling that something's wrong. Either that or there's something wrong with Scudamore, because I saw him being interviewed today and he looked licked. Anyway, whatever you do, don't go down his inside. He told Julian Wilson he always takes Carvill's Hill down the inner because he tends to jump left-handed' – something we already knew –'and if he jumps into you he'll turn you over because he's bloody massive.' Golden Freeze was a big horse but nowhere near as powerful as Carvill's Hill.

I told Mike that in an ideal situation I wanted Golden Freeze to make the running. However, we knew that Carvill's Hill liked to make the running too, so we guessed he would try and take us on. 'You'll have to watch your step,' I said. 'You don't want to get your horse so wound up that he pisses off with you. If you find he's getting too strong you'll have to do your best to ease him back. Otherwise he's only going to get two miles and fall in a heap.'

After saddling up my Gold Cup horses I watched the race with Jeremy Hitchins on a lower step of the owners' and trainers' stand. Through my binoculars I noticed Carvill's Hill lined up in the middle of the field. I thought, What's going on here, then? I turned to Jeremy and said, 'Why do you think Carvill's Hill's lined up in the middle of the field? Perhaps they're going to hold him up and try to settle him in. That'll suit Golden Freeze if they do.'

As the tapes rose, both Golden Freeze and Carvill's Hill shot to the front of the field like rockets. Because of the width between them I was hopeful that Mike would still be able to settle his horse. However, as I watched, Peter Scudamore cut diagonally across the track and made a beeline for the inside – and for Golden Freeze. I watched in total dismay as Carvill's Hill got closer and closer to Golden Freeze. There would soon be no running rail on the inside because they were at a point where two tracks joined each other, and as they ran across the open space Carvill's Hill was leaning and intimidating Golden Freeze further and further off the true line of the track, into no-man's land. For Christ's sake, I said to myself. The running rail leading up to the first fence was coming up fast, and it was obvious that if he kept on the same line Golden Freeze was going to hit it. In the nick of time, and with Golden Freeze leaning back onto the other horse, Mike just managed to steer his mount the right side of the rail. But his troubles were not over. A man with a bright yellow fluorescent jacket was standing right by the wing of the fence. I could see Golden Freeze staring and hanging away from him – it was just the sort of thing to make Golden Freeze's eyes pop out of his head. Watching all this unfold, with my heart in my mouth, I was thinking, This is a sodding nightmare.

Somehow, Golden Freeze flew the first and now I knew he would try and bolt, and that it would take all Mike could muster to hang on to him. Carvill's Hill, however, had made a complete hash of the fence, and had lost a lot of ground. Mike tried to settle his horse, who was by now trying to run away, and pulled him back. We also knew he might try to run off the course on the bend. However, Carvill's Hill came up on his outside again and he was off again, the pair of them going like shit off a shovel. It continued like that for most of the first circuit, with Golden Freeze trying his best to bolt and Michael trying to settle him, Carvill's Hill taking him on again and Golden Freeze speeding up once more. First one was in front, then the other. I knew it was a complete disaster and had certainly put paid to Golden Freeze's chances.

Behind them Toby Tobias and the rest of the field seemed oblivious to their antics. Toby was travelling well, but for most of the time I was too concerned about Golden Freeze to appreciate it. By the second circuit, as I'd feared, Golden Freeze had burned himself out and dropped out of the race. Carvill's Hill, too, seemed to have nothing much left in his tank and ended up finishing fifth behind Cool Ground. Toby Tobias ran on bravely to finish fourth, but even that didn't bring us the pleasure it should have done, as he struck into himself landing over the last and seriously damaged his tendon.

I was dealing with Toby's injury when I heard the bell go to announce a stewards' inquiry. 'What's that about?' I asked.

'Oh, they've asked Martin Pipe to go in and explain the running of Carvill's Hill,' somebody said.

I never dreamed the problem would involve one of my horses, unless it was to do with Carvill's Hill trying to squeeze Golden Freeze out at the first. But gradually, as reporters crowded around us, I realized that the race I'd been watching and the race the press had seen were very different indeed. Apparently, the story doing the rounds was that I had run Golden Freeze as a spoiler (a term coined by Julian Wilson as he commentated on the race). Judging by their questions, most of the reporters seemed to believe that my only intention in running Golden Freeze had been to take on Carvill's Hill and make him jump badly. They were talking as though my horse had not run in the race on his merits, because he wasn't good enough, which was nonsense. He might have started at long odds, but several horses had won the Gold Cup at long odds before then. Two years earlier Norton's Coin had won it at 100–1. However, the press can also wear blinkers when it suits them.

They even had a swipe at Mr Hitchins, who was infuriated by the way they dismissed his horse as a no-hoper and sarcastically replied, 'We played Carvill's Hill like a violin.' The press chose to latch onto his words as proof that we'd been trying to make Carvill's Hill fall. To this day I have a copy of a betting slip Mr Hitchins gave me, which was proof of the bets he had had on Golden Freeze leading up to the Gold Cup.

Over the next week the controversy grew. It was like a snowball that was rolling down from the top of a hill, growing bigger and bigger as it went. There were articles and letters in the newspapers, some accusing me of being unsportsmanlike, some defending me. I had lots of letters of support and only two others. I just couldn't believe what was happening. Then Peter Scudamore put a spin on the ball when he said in a statement that Mike Bowlby had called to him during the race, 'I'm sorry. It's not me. I'm riding to my orders. I hope you win anyway.' Jockeys often call out to each other while they are racing. There was no reason for Mike to say such a thing, and I found this very hard to believe. A few days later, when I was travelling with Mike to Newbury races, I turned the car radio off. 'Right, Mike,' I said. 'There's only you and me in this car, so I want to ask you a question. Whatever you answer, I promise I won't mention it again. Did you say to Peter Scudamore that you were sorry, that you didn't want to do this?'

'No. Most definitely not,' Mike said. 'I can assure you. You've got more on your mind when you're riding Golden Freeze in a race than having polite conversation with the jockey next to you!'

That was enough for me. By now I was sick to death of the whole business. My name and my reputation were being dragged through the mud. I consulted a solicitor. 'Why don't you ring the Jockey Club and ask them to hold an inquiry?' he said. 'If they say no, insist they hold one. That way it'll all come out in the open.' 'Right,' I said. 'I bloody well will.'

I spoke to David Pipe at the Jockey Club. 'As I see it, you've got two choices,' I said. 'Either you've got to say that you've inquired into this business and you've found nothing amiss, or you have to have an inquiry.'

'We're not planning to hold an inquiry into the matter, Mrs Pitman,' replied Pipe.

The next day I was travelling to the races when I received a telephone call from my office. A fax had arrived from the Jockey Club announcing that an inquiry *was* after all to be held into the running of Golden Freeze in the Gold Cup. After what David Pipe had said I was surprised, but also pleased that I'd be able to give my side of the story at last. I wasn't the least bit worried that I was going to be found guilty of misconduct, but I was angry because I felt the media had poured gallons of petrol on something that should not have even been a fire. It struck me that some people were talking through their pockets. If it had been any other horse out in front with Golden Freeze in the Gold Cup nothing would have been said. But ever since Carvill's Hill had won the Welsh Grand National he'd been built up by the media, culminating in the BBC's extended and over-hyped feature on him at the start of Cheltenham. In short, he had become the media's darling. Before the race Julian Wilson had been talking about him as if he had winged heels. They had all been expecting a fairytale end to their story, and possibly fuller wallets. When that didn't happen they had to find someone to blame. That someone, it seemed, was to be me.

As far as the press was concerned, the crucial thing was Scudamore's claim that Mike Bowlby had apologized. For them that clinched it. Somehow I had to convince the stewards that it wasn't true. A few days before the inquiry I was talking it over with Jesse, who was as livid as me about the whole thing.

'Wait a minute,' he said suddenly. 'It was so bloody windy that day I don't think they could have had a conversation as Scudamore suggests.'

'What do you mean?'

'Well, when Esha Ness fell in the race before the Gold Cup I went up to catch him with his lad because he was galloping about at the top end of the course. It was so windy up there that when you opened your mouth you couldn't get any words out. The wind blew them straight back down your throat. I was trying to shout to his lad to cut Esha Ness off, and I couldn't get the words out.'

I suddenly remembered that earlier on Gold Cup day Dave and I had been in a box waiting for some people who were due to arrive at the course by helicopter. We'd been watching them coming in to land, and the strong wind had been tossing them about like kites.

I rang the airfield at Staverton, from where a lot of the helicopters flew in. 'Could you tell me the wind speeds immediately before and after the Cheltenham Gold Cup on the twelfth of March, please?' I enquired.

Their records showed that the wind had been gusting up to thirty-five miles an hour. For me there was no possibility that the jockeys on two horses galloping around thirty miles an hour plus the wind speed could have had a conversation in winds like that. I watched videos of the Gold Cup again and again, trying to see if either jockey turned his head towards the other as if he was saying something. It was clear to me that neither of them did. I contacted my solicitor, Peter McCormick, again and he came down to see me. When I showed him the tapes he agreed to represent me, but only if I guaranteed to let him do the talking! To my annoyance, the date of the case, when it was announced, clashed with a sale in Ireland, but Peter McCormick would not hear of a postponement. 'You are going to the Jockey Club that day,' he told me. 'Not only that, but you're going to be wearing a sodding straitjacket and your mouth's going to be taped up.'

On the day Peter McCormick did his job well. Though he didn't know all the racing terminology, he didn't need telling twice. He gave them the evidence about the wind speeds, then he pointed out to the stewards that there might have been other reasons for the flop of Carvill's Hill. He reminded them that the horse's previous trainer had always said he had doubts about the horse, and that the horse was renowned for having back problems. David and I had had a fearful row because I would not call on the evidence of the person who'd told us previously Carvill's Hill had been having training problems. To do that I would have had to name the person who had told me, and there was no way I was going to get him sacked to save my own skin.

After Peter McCormick spoke, the stewards interviewed me. One of them asked me a question that I obviously didn't answer to his satisfaction. He pulled out a copy of the *Sun* newspaper from under his desk. 'It says in here, Mrs Pitman . . .' he began.

'Well, if it says it in the *Sun*, then it must be right, mustn't it?' I replied angrily. Peter McCormick shot me a warning look, but I was simmering. After they'd interviewed Mike Bowlby and me, they called in Peter Scudamore and played tapes of the race, first at normal speed, then in slow motion.

'Now, Mr Scudamore, could you point out where you had this conversation with Michael Bowlby?' he was asked.

At no stage could he tell the stewards where that conversation was supposed to have taken place, even though they played the tapes at least three times in slow motion.

Finally Peter McCormick asked, 'When you were interviewed by Julian Wilson before the race, you said you always went down the inside on Carvill's Hill. Why did you line up towards the outside? Was it your intention to cut off Golden Freeze going to the first?'

To my amazement, Peter Scudamore said yes.

'And why did Carvill's Hill not win the race when he was favourite?'

'Because he broke down. He had leg trouble,' said Peter, then added quickly, 'but we didn't know that at the time.'

That was it. I was exonerated of any misconduct, as was Michael Bowlby. In the end I felt sorry for Peter Scudamore, although earlier I have to admit I could quite easily have pushed him under a London bus.

Even then the press couldn't accept defeat gracefully. They sneered that it had taken the Jockey Club an awfully long time to hear the case, implying that the stewards had been arguing over the decision. Actually what had taken such a long time was running the tapes over and over in slow motion to give Peter Scudamore a chance to back up his allegations.

The hurt over the way the press had treated me went deep. I'd been in racing all my life and the thought that people who knew me could possibly believe I would deliberately set out to injure a horse was unthinkable. I did, in fact, find it necessary to issue a writ for slander to one of the men from the media. It wouldn't have taken much at that point to stop me talking to them altogether, and not long afterwards that's exactly what I did. I'd had enough of their spiteful, vindictive attitude.

I had seen the split coming for a while. One of my owners, Bill Robins, had recently suggested a scheme which I didn't like one bit. Over the years I'd bought and trained some very good horses for the Robinses, such as Wonder Man, who won the Welsh Champion Hurdle, Mighty Mogul, who won the Crown Paints Hurdle at Chepstow and was favourite for the Champion Hurdle, and Baydon Star, a top-class novice chaser. I spoke to David and Mark about Bill's idea and they both felt, as I did, that it wasn't something I ought to get involved in. Three weeks later, when Bill Robins asked me if I'd thought about his proposition, I told him I couldn't do it. We all knew what the price of my refusal would be and, true enough, shortly afterwards his horses were moved. Some joined Stan Mellor, some moved to Andy Turnell and some were sent to David Nicholson.

The press pricked up their ears when the Robinses left me, sensing scandal. Some very hurtful articles were written, implying that I'd not been training their horses properly and listing horses who had shown improved form after they had gone to David Nicholson. The fact that these were young horses that we had nursed along and whose form could only have improved anyway seemed to go over their heads. I felt more upset for Mark than I did for myself, because he in particular put a lot of work into those horses and it was a bigger loss to him. But we still believed we had made the right decision.

It was not in my interests to get involved in another slanging match in the newspapers, so I didn't say a word in public about what had really happened. But the way the reporters had treated me this time was the final straw. Half the time they didn't even bother to ask me for my side of a story and when they did ask they nearly always managed to misquote me or take words out of context and twist the whole meaning of what I said. Some of them worked to the old Fleet Street motto, 'Don't let the truth spoil a good story.'

The old school knew there was very good reason for my silence and we retained a mutual respect for one another. As I saw it, there was one solution: keep quiet. If I said nothing at all they couldn't misquote me. I didn't make a public announcement that I wasn't going to speak to the press, I just stopped answering questions after races. Word spread, and for the rest of that season, whenever I had a winner, the reporters crowded round me as if it were Cheltenham to see if I was going to say anything. I didn't. I'd talk to the jockey, talk to the owners, deal with the horse, then walk off and leave the owners to talk to the press. It was a surprise to several of my owners that some of the statements they made to journalists were taken completely out of context. In the past, when I'd complained, 'I never said anything like that,' I'm sure they had not always believed me. Now they found out for themselves what it was like.

My press boycott lasted for several months. I was sorry that a few journalists whom I'd known and trusted for a long time had to get the same treatment, but I wasn't prepared to be selective, as information tends to be shared in the press room.

Eventually, the following season, I came to a compromise. I would give interviews but I would tape-record them all myself. That way, if there was any dispute, I could call on my own evidence. It is a system that works well. I find journalists are more careful now in what they write. They say, 'You don't mind if I record this, do you?' and I say, 'No, and you won't mind if I do as well, will you?'

CHAPTER NINETEEN

THE RACE THAT NEVER WAS

My long-running love affair with the Grand National has, at times, stretched my emotions to breaking point, one moment taking me to unbelievable heights, the next to the depths of despair. But nothing I had experienced at Aintree over the years prepared me for the dramatic events that led to the 1993 race being declared void after a monumental cock-up.

That year I had three runners: Royal Athlete, Esha Ness and what I considered my best hope, Garrison Savannah. I felt he had a great chance of putting the record straight after his defeat two years earlier. In my heart of hearts I really did believe that he would make amends this time, because I felt he was in the best nick he could possibly be in.

But from the moment I set foot on the course early on the Saturday morning to watch my horses stretch their legs I felt a quietness about myself that I could not explain. Normally you cannot fail to be swept up by the pre-race buzz, but this was not happening; for some reason my usual feelings of excitement and anticipation were not there. I could not explain it then and I cannot now.

I remember saying to Dave, 'Something ain't right here.' He put it down to my being wound up about the race and was chatting away as usual. That year I had invited our friend Dr Rick Reddan from America to join us at Aintree. He is a brilliant vet and had looked after Gary's feet in the past. As I walked onto the course before racing I found myself spilling out my fears to him. I told him I had this terrible feeling that something was wrong and it would not go away. Afterwards I set off to check our horses with a fine-tooth comb, and also the tack they would be wearing in the National, but I could find nothing wrong with either. The next couple of hours passed in a bit of a blur before it was time to leg up the jockeys and watch the horses being led out onto the course. The nagging doubts at the back of my mind had resurfaced, and I wondered if the animal rights protesters might try to disrupt the race.

I set off to join the Autofour lads in the owners' and trainers' marquee while Dave stayed out on the course. We seemed to wait an age for the race to start and all the time it was becoming hotter and hotter in the marquee. At first we couldn't understand the reasons for the delay. We later learned that the confusion was indeed being caused by a protest at the first fence by animal rights campaigners as the field of runners was being called into line by the starter, Keith Brown, who was in charge of his final Grand National.

The start was initially delayed by eight or nine minutes while the protesters were bundled away from the racecourse by police and securitymen. But when the field did eventually set off a false start was immediately declared because the antiquated starting tape had become caught around some of the runners. In these days of modern communications you might suppose that a sophisticated system was in place to halt the race quickly after a false start, but it wasn't.

Once Keith Brown decided it was a false start he waved a flag and the recall man, Ken Evans, who was standing a furlong down the course, responded by waving his red flag frantically as thirty-nine horses charged towards him. This time the system worked, but another seemingly endless delay followed while the field pulled up, turned round and cantered back to the starting area. By now my temperature, and many others', felt close to boiling point. I could not bear what was happening and was confused by the further delays and the ensuing mayhem as the field milled round impatiently waiting to set off again. By this time the horses and I'm sure some of the jockeys were a great deal more anxious than normal.

When Keith Brown let them go for the second time there was another false start. The starting tape had only partially risen and yet again some horses and their riders had become entangled in it. But this time, crucially, it was alleged that Mr Evans did not wave his red flag vigorously enough to alert the jockeys to another false start. Thousands of people at the course and millions of television viewers around the world watched in total disbelief as the majority of runners galloped off while nine others remained forlornly at the start.

By this stage I was in shock. There was pandemonium in the marquee. Everyone was shouting, some people convinced that the race would be stopped while others argued that the runners should be allowed to continue. Sitting in the middle of all this mayhem in the marquee I felt as if I were suffocating in an endless nightmare. I did not know how my horses were doing and was in no state to watch. I could not stand it a minute longer. At that point I experienced all the symptoms of a kettle that had boiled over.

I thought, I can't take any more, I'm off, and pushed my way through the crowd, emerged into the fresh air and set off in the vague direction of the weighing room. While I was doing this I missed the sight of officials trying to stop the race after a circuit by putting out cones on the approach to the Chair and calling out to the jockeys to pull up. It was here that Mark pulled up Garrison Savannah, but in the confusion several other jockeys and their horses continued on to the second circuit, including John White on Esha Ness.

Once I reached the weighing room I found the clerk of the scales and his assistant sitting disconsolately behind the scales. 'For Christ's sake, what the f— is going on?' I said in despair.

'We don't know any more than you, Mrs P. Why don't you ask the stewards?' he replied.

Like a complete idiot I duly knocked on the door of the stewards' room, even though I must have known that they would not be in there. As I turned round I just caught sight of the television in the jockeys' changing room and saw Esha Ness cross the finishing line in the lead. But I knew of course that the result would not stand. With that I broke down sobbing. John Buckingham, famously the winning jockey in the 1967 National on the 100–1 shot Foinavon and now a valet, put his arm around me, led me to a nearby chair and found me a glass of water. I sat there for a long time in a state of total shock and disbelief.

People were angry in the immediate aftermath of the race. We all knew that the race and result would be declared void, even though it took some time for the official announcement to be made. The worst sight of that day was the forlorn figure of Patrick Bancroft, the owner of Esha Ness, arriving ashen-faced in the weighing room. It was like looking at a dead man, as if there was no-one inside his body. For years Patrick had dreamed of having a runner in the Grand National. Now he had seen his horse jump round in spectacular style as he recorded the second fastest time in the history of the race. But a famous triumph had been cruelly snatched from Patrick's grasp. It was such a shattering blow and it broke his heart. I knew that nothing we could say would ever make it up to him.

Seeing Patrick in such a dreadful state finished me off. At that point I felt that I could no longer continue as a trainer and I immediately told Mandy I was finished. Eventually I made my way back to the stable yard to see my horses, Esha Ness, whose 50–1 victory would never now be recognized, Garrison Savannah, who had been pulled up after a circuit, and Royal Athlete, who had fallen. Back in the yard with the lads and girls there were many hugs and tears. I realized then that I could not let them down. I had to be strong for them.

When I caught up with John White, Esha Ness's jockey, we spoke briefly about the race but couldn't really make much sense of what had happened. It was only much later when I studied a video of the race that I saw him holding his hand to his face in a gesture of disbelief after he and Esha Ness had passed the winning post. I felt he deserved an Oscar for the moment when he peeped despairingly through his fingers. Certainly, looking at that shot again he obviously already knew that his win would not count, but we have never talked about it at length.

Mark explained that all the jockeys who had continued after the second false start could hear snatches of the race commentary all the way round on the loudspeakers. It was enough to persuade them that the race was on. I could never blame them for continuing, because there was sufficient doubt in their minds. I simply don't know if John realized the truth of his situation on the way round.

For fully forty-five minutes there was widespread speculation that the race would be run again late in the afternoon, but that could never be a serious option. Once the race was declared void bookmakers were required to refund all bets to punters. It proved to be a costly exercise, not only to them but to the country as a whole. The mood around the course in the immediate aftermath was extremely sombre. My son Paul, who had been watching the drama from the stands, told me later there would have been a riot in similar circumstances at any other sporting venture. As it was he saw a large group of racegoers baying as they gathered beneath the scaffolding leading to the stewards' box.

Of course the false starts should never have happened. For there to be such a cock-up in the world's greatest steeplechase because of a faulty catch on a starting gate makes my blood boil. It later emerged in the official report that it was known the previous year that the catch on the start gate was faulty, so it was my understanding that the void National could and should have been prevented. Before all major meetings I check all my tack and replace it with new equipment where necessary. I also insist that my jockeys do the same with their saddles. But Aintree continued using a faulty starting system, with the most disastrous consequences.

An equally disgraceful aspect of the whole shameful affair was the way the blame seemed to shift onto the recall man, Mr Evans, who was accused of not waving his flag properly. I have always believed that if you are the captain and things go wrong you hold up your hands and admit it rather than point the finger at someone else.

I must say I felt distraught the night of the National that never was, and once again I was caught up in the centre of things: everybody wanted to talk to me while I just felt the need to hide away. I declined to go on television after the race finished because I was in no state to conduct an interview, and that evening David, Mandy and my boys protected me from journalists trying to track me down. Later on that night as Dave lay sleeping in our hotel room I wandered along the corridor trying to find Paul's room. I wasn't at all sure which it was and I was so relieved when he answered my knock on his door. Over a cup of tea I poured out all my troubles to him. Earlier in the day I had promised a little boy that if we won I would let him lead my horse into the winners' enclosure. What if he thought I had broken my promise?

At once Paul gave me a lecture. 'Now look, Ma, you can't keep on taking the blame for everything,' he said. He was right, I knew it. Sometimes you have to put the past behind you. Even so, the next day I cried most of the way home. I kept bursting into tears from the time we left Southport until we reached Wantage, a few miles from home. I'd been warned that journalists had been swarming all over the place waiting to hear my views on the void race. The last thing I wanted at that stage was to face them, because I was still in a state of shock, which lasted several more days.

But I knew I couldn't avoid the press, so we stopped at Jesse's house, where I curled my hair, put on some make-up and pulled on my armour-plating before heading home to face them. In the days that followed, they continued to pester me so much that I asked for help from Aintree in dealing with them. Unfortunately it was of little use.

In truth I was devastated by the 1993 Grand National. It had developed into the worst possible nightmare and scarred so many of us. I felt the great race had been tainted, but somehow I knew it would survive.

CHAPTER TWENTY

NINETIES NATIONALS

Racehorses are always prone to pick up infections when they are under stress, and at this particular time I seemed to be in the same boat. Even by the end of the eighties I was going down with regular bouts of bronchitis. One year I was in hospital six times for intravenous antibiotic treatment. Going to the races became a bit like walking through a minefield. If I found myself next to someone with a cough or cold in the weighing room or any of the bars, I'd move away as fast as I could. I did the same if an afflicted owner came to the house. I got some funny looks, and I'm sure people thought I was being antisocial, but I just couldn't afford to be ill. I did my best to keep my problem quiet. I didn't want anyone to know because, as I saw it, the captain of the ship couldn't be seen to be having trouble.

By a stroke of good fortune a visitor to one of our open days, Nick Poole, had been talking to David. Dave had told Nick about my allergies and Nick said he might be able to help by supplying me with a special mask to protect me from dust and chemicals. It turned out that he was an expert in dealing with similar problems in industry. The mask did help, and I wore it whenever I could, but it did not keep out the germs.

One of my worst chest infections coincided with the Racehorse Owners' dinner in London in 1990. I was in Brompton Hospital again that December and I'd not had a very good day. However, both Toby Tobias and Royal Athlete had been nominated for awards, and I knew it would look odd if I was missing – and I did not wish to let Mr and Mrs Hitchins or the Johnsons down. When I explained the situation to Professor Newman-Taylor of the Brompton Hospital, he reluctantly agreed that I could go, provided I came straight back to hospital. 'Get David to bring your things up and you can change here,' he said.

There was no way I was going to do that. I'd have felt a right plonker walking out of the Brompton Hospital in evening clothes. Instead we booked a hotel room and I took a taxi from the hospital and met Dave there. I had a bath, lay on the bed for an hour feeling like death, then dressed and set off for the Hilton Hotel in Park Lane. Throughout the function I sat at the table with Dave, Mark and the owners trying not to let anyone see how ill I was feeling. At one stage it all got too much for me and I went to the ladies' loo and sat in one of the cubicles, trying to compose myself. Luckily, by the time I returned the lights were lowered for the ceremony and, as Royal Athlete's award for outstanding novice chaser was presented, nobody seemed to notice the state of my eyes. By eight o'clock the next morning I was back in the Brompton Hospital, with only Dave, Mark and the Professor any the wiser.

Things finally came to a head one night in the autumn of 1991. I had spent the day clearing the graveyard at Enderby, where we had laid a memorial plaque on the day of my mother's funeral. It had been in a terrible state, looking more like a rubbish tip than a graveyard, and I'd been extremely upset about it, so I had driven to Leicester the next weekend to set about cleaning up the tin cans, dead flowers, old wreaths and paper. Halfway through the afternoon I was drenched not only with sweat but also with rain. Some weeks later I woke in the middle of the night feeling very poorly indeed. I was having serious trouble with my breathing, so much so that I was afraid to go back to sleep for fear of not waking up. I sat propped up in bed for the rest of the night, wheezing away. The first thing next morning, Dave rang the Brompton Hospital and spoke to Kim Harrison, the registrar, who told him to bring me in straight away. All I remember of that journey is thinking that I mustn't peg it, because if I did Dave would crash the car and then both of us would be dead. By the time we got to the hospital I was in quite a bad way. They ran all sorts of tests to find out what was going on, and it seemed I had legionnaires' disease, a serious bacterial illness similar to pneumonia. On returning home, my own local doctor told me that he'd never met anyone with the disease before as sufferers usually died. A very unfunny joke, I thought!

It took me two weeks to turn the corner, and a long time after that to completely get over it. It was around this time that a doctor who knew my history of chest problems suggested that we investigate the environment at Weathercock House. A company was called in to take samples for chemical analysis. To everyone's horror they discovered traces of lindane and dieldrin in an open watertank, which should have had a covering lid, in the roof space. Suddenly everything added up. My asthma dated back to the time just after the timbers were treated with insecticide. Often, when I'd been forced to go to bed ill and had nobody to play Florence Nightingale, I would drink water out of the bathroom tap. I had also cleaned my teeth and swallowed water at the same time. I'd often wondered why I always felt worse when David sent me to bed! Of course, as soon as the pollution was discovered we had the roof space thoroughly decontaminated, but the damage to my immune system had been done. I was told that after a long exposure like that my chances of making a full recovery were no higher than 10 per cent. On the bright side though, the chances of my condition getting worse were apparently also 10 per cent! The most likely scenario was that my health would stay exactly the same, and I would just have to learn to live with my allergies and infections.

Several advisers pointed out at this time that in the circumstances my job wasn't exactly healthy for me. Dave, Mark and Paul took this very seriously and in turn they all tried to persuade me to consider giving up training. Nothing was worth paying for with your life, they reasoned. However, to my relief, Professor Newman-Taylor said that he personally had no strong objection to my carrying on doing the same work, provided I did less of it. Fortunately, Dr Cocker at the Ridgeway Hospital in Swindon, where I was sometimes a patient, agreed. One doctor friend told Dave, 'Jenny's job is much too demanding for her, but on the other hand it's what keeps her going. If she packed it up she'd be dead in six weeks.' That really cheered Dave up no end!

Even so, my spell in hospital gave me time to reflect. The sight of all the young people around me dealing with problems much worse than mine was humbling. There were a number of teenagers in my ward with cystic fibrosis, and to hear those kids talking about heart and lung transplants and debating which of them should or would have a transplant if one became available was amazing. They spoke about living and dying as if they were planning a trip to the supermarket. It certainly put all my troubles into perspective.

I came home from hospital with strict instructions from the Professor to stay in bed and not to leave the house for a week. After a lifetime of being outdoors it was extremely hard to adapt, and I felt a bit down in the dumps. One afternoon as I was lying in bed with the sun shining through the window I quietly waited till around half past two, when I knew everyone would have left the yard and Dave was probably having a nap in the armchair. I put on my dressing gown and crept downstairs. Outside, it was the most lovely autumn afternoon. As I crossed the yard the sun was warm on my back. The horses were asleep with their heads hanging over the doors and I wandered up to the top of the yard, walking from one box to the next chatting to each of them. Straight away, I started to feel a whole lot better.

Suddenly I heard footsteps running so fast it could have been Seb Coe. 'Jenny, Jenny!' I heard him shout. My heart stood still. I felt like a little kid who'd been caught scrumping apples. I knew he was going to start nagging me and I could feel myself cringing. Please don't shout, I thought. Dave came running into the yard and screeched to a halt. 'Jenny, what the hell are you doing? You know you're not meant to be outside.'

'Please don't get on at me, Dave, please don't,' I pleaded. 'Being out here is doing me more good than all the medicine they've got in that hospital.' I don't know what Dave saw when he looked at me, but it must have been an improvement on what he'd been seeing because his face suddenly relaxed and he smiled. 'Come on then,' he said. We spent some time together before we walked back into the house. I'd only been chatting to my horses for ten or fifteen minutes, but I was knackered and went straight back to bed. Dave brought me a cup of tea, and as I sat there sipping it I felt happier than I had for weeks because the question mark hanging over my future had gone. I knew now that I couldn't possibly give up training. I'd always loved horses and I couldn't do without them. That was that. Somehow, I had to find a way round my health problem.

There is nothing like a serious illness for making you stand back and take a good hard look at your life. It took legionnaires' disease to make me realize that I should take better care of myself. My owners had been saying it to me for years, but until now my own health had always come a poor second to the welfare of my horses. If I'd had the flu or didn't feel very well, I'd put it to the back of my mind and carry on working until I ground myself to a halt. I knew it was nonsense. I wouldn't dream of treating my horses the way I treated myself. You'd better get your act together, I told myself.

With around eighty horses in training that was easier said than done. I made myself take naps in the afternoons if I wasn't racing, but that did not bring about a miracle cure, and as my visits to hospital were quite frequent it became clear that I needed to delegate more. The obvious person to help take some of the load off my shoulders was Mark. I never exactly said, 'Please, Mark, will you give up riding,' but I did make it clear to him that I couldn't keep on at the same pace any more, working from six thirty in the morning until ten at night, Saturdays, Sundays, Christmas Day, every day the same, never taking any time off. So, following a family discussion in the autumn of 1993, Mark told me he had decided to give up race-riding and join Dave and me as an assistant trainer. It was a tremendous weight off my shoulders. In my heart I was relieved, not just for me but for Mark himself. He'd had some awful falls over the years and had been giving his body much more punishment than was good for it. He had also been struggling with his weight for quite some time. Every day he'd go in the sweatbox, and when he came out his face would be drawn and his eyes at times like those of a panda, with dark rings around them. If he had a drink and a steak on a Saturday night he'd sit at the breakfast table the next day with half a slice of toast and two-thirds of a cup of coffee while everyone around him ate bacon and eggs. Then, straight afterwards, he'd be back in the sauna. Probably as a result, he was having problems with his stomach. A lot of jockeys end up with ulcers, and it worried me that the same would happen to him.

Having Mark as my assistant worked well. The biggest immediate difference was in the amount of travelling I had to do. We always have a representative at the races when our owners' horses run, and at the height of the season this often required me to drive several hundred miles a week, which I found extremely tiring. Now I had Mark and Dave to attend while I stayed at home and dealt with any problems there. Mark had always got on well with the owners and enjoyed the socializing and PR side of things, while I'd always been best at the 'hands-on' part of training horses, so this suited us both. It also meant that when a horse sustained a cut or a sprain, I could deal with it myself, the way I'd done in the early days, rather than delegate the job to someone else.

In April 1995 we all had a fantastic boost when one of our old favourites, Royal Athlete, won my second Grand National.

Royal Athlete – Alfie – had a bit of a chequered history. He was one of the horses I'd bought at the Ballsbridge sale in 1986, and although he'd always shown great ability he had a long history of leg problems. His first owner had been a keen betting man and after his first season, when he'd run well in a bumper, the owner had asked me to prepare the horse to run early the next summer. I was not at all keen on the plan, because I felt that training a horse like Royal Athlete on artificial surfaces early in the season was taking a serious risk. I told him so but he insisted. Sure enough, one evening we discovered some heat in his foreleg. I then had to tell his owner that I could not carry on as I felt that to do so would only compound the injury. 'Well, sell him, then,' he replied.

Reluctantly I entered Royal Athlete in the Ascot sales. It was then that fate took a hand. The Johnson family had finally sold their little hurdler Vantastic, and Gary rang me up one day to see if I could find them another horse. 'Well, strangely enough, I've got a horse here called Royal Athlete who's going to the sales,' I said.

'Is he nice?' he enquired.

'Yes, he is. The only thing is he has a bit of a problem. He has a bit of a leg,' I said.

'Oh bloody hell, Jen! They usually get a leg *after* we've bought them, not before,' he replied.

'Well, I think he's going to be a nice horse,' I said, 'but you'll have to be patient. He's going to need twelve months off.'

'What will he make at the sales?'

'Between fifteen and seventeen hundred, I'd think – because of his leg,' I suggested.

The Johnsons were car dealers, so Gary knew the score. 'Offer the owner fifteen hundred quid,' he said. 'Tell him he won't have the cost of taking him to the sales.'

Twenty-four hours later the horse was theirs.

When Royal Athlete first came back into training in the 1988–89 season I think his new owners had serious doubts about whether they'd done the right thing. The horse's first run was at Newbury, in a novices' hurdle. It had been nearly two years since he'd seen a racecourse and I warned the Johnsons not to expect too much. I don't cheat with my horses, but at the same time you can't be too hard on them when they're coming back after a long lay-off.

'Don't get excited about your horse today,' I told them. 'I don't want you to worry about where he finishes, because this is probably going to be the most important race of his life.'

I didn't spell it out, but if he were to come back with another leg problem I knew it would probably be the end of his racing career. That day he beat only eight horses home and the Johnsons came walking up to me afterwards with their faces full of gloom. 'Oh dear, what a happy little gang we've got here,' I teased them. 'Listen, the horse has finished sound and that's all that matters.' I personally thought the horse had run a very promising race, considering his lay-off.

I'm not sure that they believed me then but they did by the end of that season, when Royal Athlete had won two novice hurdle races. The following December he started the 1989–90 season with a bang by winning the prestigious Long Walk Hurdle at Ascot. A month later I sent him chasing for the first time at Leicester, where he won easily. A couple of weeks later he won another chase at Newton Abbot. He jumped so well that day that I felt he was ready to tackle the bigger fences at Ascot, so I entered him in the Reynoldstown Novices Chase. It was probably one of the most incredible races I've ever seen. It was such a high-class field, and Royal Athlete was already clear and travelling really well when he hit the fourth last fence with such force that Mark was flung right up his neck (Mark said later that the only thing that stopped him falling off was the horse's ears). He was brought almost to a standstill and must have lost the best part of twenty lengths but, miraculously, Mark picked him up and got him going again, and they won unchallenged by no less than fifteen lengths. It was an amazing performance.

In his next race, at Kempton, he was brought down early on. Then came another fall in the Sun Alliance at Cheltenham – which was won by Garrison Savannah. Two falls in a row can seriously shake a horse's confidence, but Royal Athlete proved he was as tough as old boots by winning the Mumm Club Chase at the Aintree meeting. Two weeks later in April he finished off the season with another win at Ayr. In five months he had run eight times and won every race that he completed – six in all – winning £64,318.60 prize money and a bonus of £10,000 for adding the Mumm Chase at Aintree. It was obvious that we had a very high-class chaser on our hands, and it was heartbreaking when his leg problems returned and he had to have the next two seasons off. Royal Athlete did not race again until December 1992, and although he managed to win only once that season he was a highly creditable third to Jodami in the Cheltenham Gold Cup in March 1993, so we knew he was as good as ever.

Royal Athlete's victory at Cheltenham in November 1993 was his first for almost four years, but two weeks later his career nearly ended for good. He was being ridden by Jamie Osborne in the Hennessy Cognac Gold Cup at Newbury when he made a terrible mistake at the thirteenth fence and nearly demolished it. He had taken off too far away from the fence, and had been unable to make the far side; both his front feet landed in the middle of the birch. This was to cause yet another serious injury, but he still managed to gallop off down to the bottom of the course and by the time he had been caught the skin on his leg had rolled up like a sock. Something had cut through it like a surgeon's knife. I had been at another meeting but I spoke on the mobile phone to David, who told me that you could see every bit of flesh and sinew. In addition, the wound was also covered in earth and had bits of grass stuck to it. The racecourse vet that day was someone called Charlie Schreiber. When I told David I had never heard of him he replied, 'Well, he's very thorough.' Repairing the damage was a task which would have taxed the most experienced of vets; fortunately, Charlie was more than up to the job. The light in the racecourse stables was poor and as they wanted to avoid the bedding from the stable sticking to the wound Charlie had to spend more than an hour outside in the pouring rain cleaning it before he could stitch it. Dave rang me from the racecourse stables to keep me updated and I realized from what he said that the biggest danger was the wound becoming infected.

'Whatever you do, get him to leave me a stitch out at the back of his leg so it can drain,' I told him.

When Royal Athlete came home that evening he had a huge dressing on his leg and looked very sorry for himself. I was dying to take the dressing off, to see for myself what I was going to have to deal with, but I decided it would be best to leave it until the next morning. This was the start of nine months of nursing. Twice a day, I took a sterile bowl of boiled water and cooking salt and gently cleaned around the stitches on Royal Athlete's legs with cotton wool buds. When the wound was dry I applied a dressing of sugar paste (this paste is made for me by one of our owners and it's brilliant for cleaning wounds and promoting healing). The horse was also on a strong course of intravenous antibiotics.

At first I did not dare walk him out of his stable in case the stitches broke down, so for two weeks Alfie remained in his box. At the end of the fortnight the injury was just a little too wet, and I decided I needed to find a way of drying it. I decided to use the portable floodlight, which I held just far enough away to give a slight hint of heat. Every day I moved the light backwards and forwards from one side of his leg to the other, until the wound stopped seeping. A few months later somebody told me they had read an article in a veterinary journal saying that white light was very good for healing. It seemed, quite by chance, that I'd been giving Alfie the benefit of the latest development in medicine!

Throughout this time Charlie Schreiber visited Alfie and I was very impressed with his diligence and knowledge. Although a young chap, he had a general knowledge about horses that was unusual. It was obvious to me that it wasn't just from a textbook. He had a natural instinct with horses and a common sense that you don't always find in newly qualified vets. It was about eighteen months later, when Charlie arrived at the yard with his mother, that I saw where these qualities had come from. Diana Schreiber is one of those people, like my dad, who could look at a horse and tell you instantly what is wrong with it. Instinctive stockmanship is not something you learn from books; you learn it from the older generation, probably your parents, who learned it from their parents . . . In our parents' day you never had passports to tell you how old a horse was or a scope to tell you if a horse had a lung infection. Sadly, young people today don't always value what they can learn from their elders, but Charlie had obviously absorbed his mum's knowledge just as I'd done from Dad.

On 21 January 1995, fourteen months after his fall in the Hennessy, Royal Athlete was finally ready to run again. His comeback race, which I hoped would give him back his confidence, was over hurdles at Haydock. He ran really well, finishing third to a horse called Mudahim. The long-term

320

plan that season was for him to have another crack at the Gold Cup. Freddie, Mr Johnson senior, had always hoped he'd win it, but very sadly he had died the previous year. However, his sons Gary and Libby were still keen for Royal Athlete to run in the race again. With that in mind, we ran him in the Agfa Diamond Chase at Sandown, where he finished sixth. I was finding it difficult to pick another suitable preparatory chase for him, so we ran him next over hurdles at Doncaster, where he finished fifth. With the Gold Cup two weeks away we were bang on target, but then on Gold Cup day, as he was led out of his box, I could see that he was not quite sound behind and the dream was over. Frustratingly, a couple of days later he was completely sound. It was then that we decided to run him in the National.

That year, 1995, I took six horses to Aintree for the Grand National. Three of them were twelve years old, Esha Ness, Garrison Savannah and Royal Athlete, but this did not worry me: Little Polveir and Ben Nevis were both twelve when they won the National, and in 1977 Red Rum, the most famous twelve-year-old of them all, had crossed the line first. My team was completed by Do Be Brief, Lusty Light and Superior Finish. Of my six runners, Royal Athlete was one of the least fancied by the pundits. I suppose you couldn't blame them, as he had been plagued with injuries. He had also been given an unorthodox preparation for the National, with his last race being over hurdles. On the morning of the National, his odds were 50–1. Garrison Savannah and Superior Finish started at shorter odds, but the hot favourite was Master Oats, who had won the Cheltenham Gold Cup three weeks earlier and, like Garrison Savannah four years previously, was trying to complete the double.

Royal Athlete's temperament had not mellowed much over the years: he was still a hard puller and needed quiet, sensitive handling. Before the race I told Jason Titley, his young Irish jockey, to 'ride him as if his reins were threads of cotton'. Jason followed my instructions to the letter and gave the horse a dream ride. They were close behind the leaders throughout the first circuit and took a definite advantage for the first time going out onto the second circuit. Master Oats then came through soon after Becher's to share the pacemaking, but four fences from home Royal Athlete was back in front once more, jumping economically and moving with a steady rhythm that was raising my hopes by the second. The Johnson family were so nervous that they couldn't bear to watch the race. Instead they all sat on the grass by the statue of Red Rum, listening to the commentary. It was only when they heard that Royal Athlete had jumped the last safely that they ran over to the unsaddling enclosure and saw the last few strides on television.

I watched the race from a settee in an owners' and trainers' marquee with Mark and our farrier's wife Nicola. Mark stood next to me, and all through the race we kept glancing across at each other because neither of us could really believe what we were seeing. To see Alfie finally reaping his reward was pure magic. This time, as my horse galloped past the Elbow, I hadn't the slightest worry that anything was going to catch him. Master Oats was tiring in second place as Royal Athlete stormed clear. As he passed the post some of our gang made a rush for the exit of the marquee to greet the horse. As I sprang up from the settee to follow them my legs turned to jelly and I flopped back down again. For a moment Mark looked shocked. He later told me he thought I was dead. It didn't take long for a rumour to go round the racecourse that Jenny Pitman had collapsed, but that was not quite the case. It was just that the enormous sense of relief at winning our second Grand National had been a bit too much after all the blood, sweat and tears we had shed that year.

It was much later, when I was doing an interview for the BBC, that I noticed a familiar silhouette hanging about in the dimly lit room behind the television lights. It was Julian Wilson. We hadn't spoken to each other since the 1992 Gold Cup when he had described Golden Freeze as a 'spoiler', and, to my mind, sparked off the whole controversy. I did think, Now what—? but decided this was the ideal time to let bygones be bygones. After the interview I walked up to him. 'Are we going to pack all this in, then, Julian?' I asked him. For a moment I wondered what he was going to say, but then he smiled, stepped forward, gave me a kiss and, not before time, we buried the hatchet – I think.

I went back to the stables to find that David and the lads had already washed the horses down, bandaged their legs and given them a nice warm, light supper. When Dave had walked in to Alfie, he found the old horse rolling in the shavings as happy as Larry, with not a single nick on him anywhere. Not one scratch. He was so bright you would never have known he had just run in and won the Grand National. It was bizarre. I often reckon that my mum and old Freddie Johnson were sitting on a cloud somewhere looking down on us that day.

That year, 1995, was the year my 'old boys' surprised everybody. A few weeks after the Grand National it was Willsford's turn. We had bought Willy in Ireland as a three-year-old, the same year that we bought Garrison Savannah, Esha Ness and Royal Athlete, and while he'd never been rated as highly as the other three, Willsford had been a good servant over the years, winning the County Hurdle at Cheltenham in 1989 in the most appalling weather. It was the same day that Desert Orchid splashed through the mud to win the Gold Cup. Racing had nearly been called off because of the flooding, and there seemed to be a small lake at the bottom of the course. When they did start, the sky was so black you couldn't see the jockeys' colours, but two hurdles from home as I peered through the gloom I suddenly picked up a horse that had gone well clear of the field. What the hell's that, making a break so early, I thought, and then I saw the rider's elbows sticking out like eagle's wings and knew it was my jockey, Mike Bowlby, because that was his style of riding. He won by six lengths that day, allowing the owners to fill their pockets. A year later Willy also won the Midlands National at Uttoxeter. He had always been a champion in our eyes because he always did his best. He wasn't a big horse, but he was a tremendous character and always took a keen interest in everything that happened in the yard. If a butterfly flew past his box he'd see it. He'd prick his ears, put his head on one side and watch until it had disappeared. And if you ever went into the yard on a sunny afternoon, when all the other horses were standing with their heads hanging sleepily over the doors, Willy would be looking at you, bright as a button, always smiling and ready to say hello. He never seemed to sleep. He was just so nosy that he had to see everything and missed nothing.

For the past two seasons his form had been a bit in and out. I took great exception to the fact that *Chasers and Hurdlers'* 1993–94 edition had given him a squiggle after his rating – which indicated that he was unreliable – and described him as 'moody and not one to trust'. Willy may have had his own way of doing things, but he was certainly not unreliable. I've found that snap judgements on horses and people are all too common. If something is different and doesn't fit a conventional mould people don't trust it, and that's a mistake. In my experience the best horses are nearly all a bit eccentric, a bit different. It's often the case with people too! On 20 March 1993 I had a run-in with a steward at Uttoxeter, who obviously shared Timeform's opinion. On the day in question, Mark and I were called to the stewards' room after the race because they said Willsford was marked by the whip. I explained that Willy was a very tricky horse because he had to be pushed along in his races, and being a thin-skinned horse he marked easily. Because of that I had always advised his jockeys to use a felt-covered whip.

However, on that particular day even that gentler whip had left a mark because Willy had been clipped a couple of days before and so had much shorter hair on his body.

From the looks on their faces I felt the stewards didn't really understand what I was saying. 'The only way I can explain it, sir,' I said, 'is that if you slapped someone's face who was cleanshaven, it would have more effect than on someone who wasn't cleanshaven.' No sooner had the words left my mouth than I realized that one of the stewards had a big red bushy beard. I also realized that his face had turned nearly the same colour as his beard. I could almost hear him thinking, 'You cow!' and I felt myself going the same colour, but then I felt my eyes begin to sparkle at the mischief.

No action was taken, but when we left the room the stipendiary steward took me aside.

'Perhaps we don't want horses like Willsford racing any more, Mrs Pitman,' he said quietly.

'And I'll thank you not to tell me how to train my horses,' I replied. But I knew that that little outburst would mean serious trouble if I did not watch my step.

Two years later Willy answered his critics better than I could ever have done. By now I'd won the Grand National twice, the Welsh National three times and the Midlands National twice, but I'd never won the Scottish National, and it was still one of my greatest ambitions. In 1995, because Royal Athlete had come out of the Grand National so well, I decided to let him run again two weeks later in the big race at Ayr. That season Willsford had bounced back to form, winning four chases including the Tote National at Warwick, followed by the Eider Chase at Newcastle. The Eider is a tough, four-mile race, which Willsford had turned into a procession. That performance convinced me that he should take his chance in the Scottish National.

When my horses are away overnight my biggest worry is to make sure they drink plenty of water, because they can very easily become dehydrated. By tea-time on the eve of the

Scottish National Willy had not drunk as much water as I wanted, so I asked Louise and Lisa, the two girls who had travelled the horses up to Ayr, to take them out onto the racetrack and let them have a pick of grass to get some moisture into them. While we were out on the course four lads in their twenties wandered up. They'd obviously been at the races all day and were a bit the worse for wear. Willy had a wall eye, with a white halo surrounding the iris, and as he was grazing this eye kept opening and closing, opening and closing, until it caught the lads' attention.

'Look at that horse,' one of them said. 'He's giving me the evil eye.'

I couldn't allow anyone to say things like that about Willsford. 'Of course he's not giving you the evil eye,' I said. 'Have you never heard that saying, "tip the wink"? Well that's what he's doing. You watch that eye. He's winking at you. He's tipping you the wink, he's running in the Scottish National tomorrow and he's telling you he's going to win it.' The blokes stared at him, obviously taking it all in.

'What's his name?'

'Willsford,' I said.

As they went staggering off I did think that I had been a bit naughty pulling their leg, although I often wonder if they remembered the tip when they woke next morning.

Five minutes after they'd gone Robert and David Johnson, two members of the partnership that owned Willsford, rolled up. 'What are you doing here?' they asked. I explained that I was letting the horse have a pick of grass because I was a bit worried about his not drinking enough water.

'Can we get him anything?' David asked.

'You could get him some carrots,' I said. 'That'll put moisture into him as well.'

'Carrots? Where are we going to get carrots from at this time of night?'

'Look.' Louise, Willsford's lass, pointed. A furlong and

a half up the course was the back of a Tesco store.

'Right, you go up there and buy me ten or fourteen pounds,' I said.

They set off walking up the course, and after fifty yards or so they turned back. 'Hey, Jenny,' called Robert. 'Does he want broccoli, frozen peas or onions to go with them?'

When we fed Willsford an hour later I put a couple of pounds of carrots on top of his food and gave him a syringe full of electrolytes as well. By morning he'd drunk a bucket and a half of water and I knew I could stop worrying.

The following day he ran the race magnificently, slipping over the fences in his casual seal-like fashion, cruising into the lead four from home and never looking like being headed. He won with his ears pricked and I no longer had to defend my decision to carry on racing him. Shortly afterwards I bumped into the stipendiary steward who'd spoken to me at Uttoxeter. I smiled at him. I didn't feel the need to remind him of his words.

In 1995–96 Willy carried on where he'd left off, winning decent prizes at Cheltenham and at Sandown. He was also placed on three occasions. He seemed as good as ever, but I had to face the fact that he was now thirteen. Deciding what to do with him when he finished racing was a real dilemma, because he wasn't the sort of horse who would take kindly to retirement. Whenever he was turned out in a field he never did very well, because he wouldn't relax. He'd be on the go all day, walking up and down the fences. Because he was still in wonderful condition, we decided to give him two last runs while we considered his future. At the beginning of November 1996 he ran at Sandown. I had horses at two meetings that day, so Mandy saddled him up. He was full of himself on the day – up to his usual tricks. Every time she put the pad on his back and bent down to pick up the saddle he bucked the pad off onto the floor.

The plan was to let him bow out at Cheltenham, where he had enjoyed one of his finest hours. Rodney Farrant was booked to ride him in the Flowers Original Handicap Chase, November, the race he'd won the year before. It is a day I will never forget. What I remember best is seeing Willy going past the stands on the second circuit with his ears pricked, having a great time. As I watched him I felt the sunshine come out inside me and I thought to myself, 'You really are enjoying this, aren't you, old chap?' He galloped round the bend, jumped the sixteenth fence, staggered for a couple of strides and, as Rodney started to pull him up, keeled over and fell dead.

He'd had a heart attack, we were told. Sudden, without warning, he almost certainly knew nothing about it, but it was still a terrible shock to everyone involved with him. Arnie Kaplan, David and Robert Johnson, his owners, were crying their eyes out. Louise, his girl, was also crying, and Dave had disappeared, unable to cope with it at all. It was like being in a swimming pool with everyone drowning, and I had to be the lifebelt. I was desperately sad too, but I felt Willy had always written his own script and I felt he would have wanted to go this way.

That night we had planned to attend the Champion Jockey's dinner and dance in Cheltenham. Willsford had been a special favourite of Dave's, and he wanted to throw in the towel and go home. But the way I saw it, if we returned to Lambourn we were going to have a silent drive home and we'd sit there all night, not talking, depressed and down. That wasn't Willy, because he had always loved life. So I insisted we went to the dance, and though I can't say I enjoyed the evening I still felt comforted that his life had come to a close while he was enjoying it.

I had asked Cheltenham racecourse to arrange for him to be cremated, and when Willsford finally came back home we buried him in the top lawn, close to the graves of my old dogs, and planted a willow tree over him. In the end, Willy had decided his future for us. He knew he belonged at Weathercock House and he wasn't going anywhere else.

CHAPTER TWENTY-ONE

THE GRAND SLAM

By the beginning of 1997 Mark had been my assistant trainer for three years. During that time there'd been some important developments in his life. In June 1995 he had married Natasha, whom he'd met when she came to Weathercock House for a job interview. Although she didn't get the job, she obviously made a big impression on the assistant trainer!

Mark and Natasha had decided to marry in Barbados, and unfortunately Dave and I were unable to be there. I was very disappointed, but I made sure I didn't reflect that feeling to Mark. When their airline tickets arrived at Weathercock House I flicked through them to check the details and noted that they were due to travel on the Saturday before their wedding. Some days later Natasha asked if we would drive them to the airport on the Sunday.

'Are you sure it's Sunday, Tash?' I asked.

'Yes, I know it is,' she replied confidently.

But when we arrived at Heathrow airport an airline representative took one look at Mark's tickets and asked quite casually, 'Is there any reason why you didn't travel yesterday as arranged?' Talk about the balloon going up. At that moment it crossed my mind that the wedding might not take place at all, but happily all was well in the end. The airline staff could not have been more helpful.

On my return home from the airport I decided to check on a horse we'd turned out in our small nursery paddock after gelding him the previous week.

I bent down to look underneath him and then walked round his other side to check he wasn't swollen. As I bent over, he grabbed the top of my right arm in his mouth. Perhaps he'd had a flashback to the operation! He was biting so hard that the pain was excruciating. Eventually he let go. I felt extremely faint and thought I would collapse. I wasn't even sure at that moment that he hadn't pulled my arm off since I had no feeling in it from the shoulder down. I knew I had to escape from the field because if I collapsed he might have another go and finish me off. I held onto my right hand with my left hand. As I made my way towards the gate I kept saying to myself, 'Don't fall down, don't fall down.' I managed to reach the house and telephone for some help. When Mandy arrived and saw my arm she was on the verge of tears. Feeling somewhat weak, I said, 'Don't you start bloody crying, it should be me that's crying.' With that she took complete control and carted me off to the doctor.

He gave me injections and antibiotics, dressed the wound and sent me home with firm instructions to rest. That was all very well, but I had an appointment at the Derby sales in Ireland later in the week and I did not intend to miss it. On my return from the doctor's surgery I removed the dressing he'd put on the wound and replaced it with a mixture of my own sugar paste that had worked so well in the past on Royal Athlete's injuries.

Although I was in great pain, I defied my doctor's orders and on Wednesday flew to Ireland for the sale. The next few days developed into quite an ordeal. Several times at Fairyhouse I felt so awful that I had to go to the ladies' where I filled up the washbasin with cold water and sank my arm into it to ease the pain. The nurse on duty at the sales was a tremendous help, and also sent me to the local hospital in Fairyhouse where they gave me a further injection. I had seen most of the horses over the last few days and as usual made notes about them in my catalogue. We had bought a few horses and had a bit of time to spare, so on day two of the sale David and I sat in the shade of a small tree, where we could still hear the voice of the auctioneer. As the bidding on one horse rose higher and higher I said to Dave, 'What on earth is that making so much money?' I picked up my catalogue to see that I had written 'Yak!' against his name. 'Yak' is my abbreviated term for 'Don't touch it with a bargepole.' Shortly afterwards a connection of the horse walked past on his way from the sales ring.

He paused when he saw me and said, 'Jenny, I hear you've been badly bitten.' 'Not half as badly bitten as the poor sod who's just bought your horse,' I replied cheekily. With that he turned on his heel and fled, but he knew exactly what I meant.

By the time we flew home on the following Saturday I was feeling really ill. I was so hot that Dave took me straight to hospital, where I lay on a bed with a fan blowing cold air on me for forty-eight hours.

The surgeon Mike Foy, who patches up so many jockeys, gave me a serious bollocking for carrying on at the sales in my condition. He was mad with me and pointed out in the most forceful manner that if I did not improve in the next few days I could forget my plans for an immediate holiday. Instead I would be facing surgery. I know I was pretty stupid to go to Ireland, but business is business and I had bought so many good horses at the Derby sale in the past. Luckily my arm responded to treatment and we were able to leave for a short holiday in Sussex, even though I had to attend hospital there for another seven days.

There had been changes in my life, too, not least the fact

that my health had improved. I suspect this was due partly to the fact that I was looking after myself better. I'd discovered Dr Ray Choy, a Chinese herbalist, who was an expert in allergies, and with his help my allergic reaction to horses, perfumes, polishes, air fresheners, traffic fumes, etc. improved dramatically. Also, thanks to encouragement from Paul, I'd started doing some serious exercising.

Paul had by now qualified as an accountant and in 1995 had taken a new position with an international firm; at the end of January 1996 he was due to be posted to Kuala Lumpur. I knew I would miss him terribly, in fact I was heartbroken. We'd always been very close and I had become used to turning to Paul for advice, not only about the business, which he could dispense in a flash, but over any other problems in my life. However, in 1997 when Dave and I went to visit him in Kuala Lumpur, I was reassured to find that he seemed very happy there. He has always been a keen sportsman and he told us that he'd found a local gym and was working out there four times a week. He took a sideways look at me and said, 'Something like that would do you a lot of good, you know, Ma. It's a great stress-buster.' I thought, silly little sod, he can't have a proper job if he wants to exercise afterwards.

Though I'd laughed it off at first, when I thought about it, it didn't seem such a daft idea after all. I couldn't do anything about getting older, but if I was fitter I might be able to stick the work better as the years caught up with me. I didn't want the embarrassment of going to a gym, so I found myself a personal trainer who lived locally. Lee Hogan won me over at our first meeting by declaring that he didn't want failures because it was bad for his business. He really put me through the mill but, several hundred press-ups later, I'd lost over two stones in weight and felt like a new woman. The decision to fight back at the prevailing years and the allergies worked wonders. I had more energy than I'd had for ages.

This was wonderful for me, but from Mark's point of view I guess my transformation wasn't quite such good news. When Mark had started as my assistant trainer it had seemed that my days at the helm were numbered. But plans change and it was clear to both of us that I wasn't going to be ready to pack up training just yet. Mark was already getting itchy feet for more responsibility. He and Natasha had recently had a baby girl, Darcy Rose, and Mark felt the need to spread his wings professionally. He wanted to be his own man, which was perfectly understandable. But even if I'd been ready to retire I wouldn't have asked a young couple with a new baby to take over a yard the size of Weathercock House. It was too demanding. It wasn't just a question of dealing with seventy horses; there was the business side, too. Running a yard the size of ours is more than a job, it's a way of life, and it takes you over each season. Once horses start coming back in from grass in mid-July, David and I never, ever, escape for a break until the end of the season. I felt that Mark and Natasha needed time to get to know each other and their baby before they took on that sort of commitment.

I think in his heart Mark realized that too, so when a smaller yard came up for rent in Upper Lambourn he saw it as a good compromise, and in the summer of 1997 he and Natasha moved into Saxon House Stables, Fulke Walwyn's old training base. I could understand his wanting to branch out on his own, though I wasn't sure it was a very wise decision. Personally, I thought he was doing it the hard way. But it was no harder than the way I did it twenty years earlier, that's for sure. And at least he had a good sound financial prop behind him – a job commentating for the Racing Channel.

The media speculated that there'd been a big bust-up between us, but they were wrong. I love my sons and will always support them whenever and wherever I can. In fact, I provided a lot of Mark's tack and other bits and pieces when he started out, and no-one was more pleased when he had his first winner, Sailin Minstrel, in a National Hunt flat race at Worcester on 9 July 1997. I saw him most mornings on the gallops and it would have been unnatural for my eyes not to quickly scan his horses as they walked past – after all, we were supposed to be rivals! But it was not really a competition between the two of us. I'm very proud of Mark, and I'd have considered myself to be a very poor tutor if my apprentice hadn't learned to do his job well. Of course there had been times when we'd had our horns down at one another – who hasn't? – but I tell both my sons, 'I'll always love you, but sometimes I just don't like you!' We'd been through a lot together as a family and I had no intention of allowing spiteful gossip to get in the way of our special relationship.

One way and another, 1997 was quite a momentous year. In March my name was again splashed over the papers, but this time for the best of reasons. When Willsford had won the Scottish National in 1995, it meant that horses of mine had won all four Nationals held in the United Kingdom. The only National missing was the Irish, which was held at Fairyhouse. I'd had a couple of cracks at it over the years, but so far without much luck. On 20 April 1987 Mark had ridden Errol Brown's horse, Gainsay, in the race. I'd been worried about flying Gainsay to Ireland because he was such a bad traveller. Even in a horsebox he used to panic and try to get down on the floor if he felt too confined. I certainly wouldn't have wanted to be in the same aeroplane as him! Luckily, the pilot who'd flown him to Ireland was wonderful, taxiing down the runway first to make sure the horse wasn't going to freak out, and even ringing from the air to give a progress report.

Gainsay had finished unplaced in the race that year. In the 1993 running Royal Athlete had fallen, and had struck the small carpal bone at the back of his knee. It turned into quite an amusing episode, because I had gone to the weighing room to ask where I could find some ice to apply to the back of Royal Athlete's swollen knee. One of the doormen went off to see what he could do and ten minutes later he struggled back with a black dustbin liner nearly full of icecubes. He'd been up to the racecourse restaurants and cleared them out of every bit of ice they had. I could hardly lift it. He must have thought we wanted to freeze the whole horse! That was typical of the way the Irish treat you. Nothing is too much trouble for them, particularly where horses are concerned. In Ireland the horse comes first. When we are horse-hunting in the depths of the Irish countryside it's quite common for Dave and me to walk into a bar and suddenly find we have a complete stranger sitting at our table saying, 'Bejasus, you're that Jenny Pitman! You bought a horse off a cousin of a cousin of mine six years ago. He was by so and so. Do you remember him?'

Soon after Royal Athlete won the 1995 Grand National I received a call out of the blue from a representative of the Maktoum ruling family of Dubai, whose horses have dominated Flat racing in this country for the last few years. I was excited and extremely delighted to discover that Sheikh Ahmed, the youngest of the four Maktoum brothers, wanted me to train a horse for him over jumps. Apparently he had watched Royal Athlete's success and my subsequent interview with Des Lynam on BBC television.

The horse he sent me was Master Tribe, who had finished fifth in the Irish Two Thousand Guineas in 1993 when he was trained by Con Collins. Although I have trained a number of ex-Flat horses over the years, Master Tribe was different from the jumping-bred stores I tend to buy. He had won his only race over seven furlongs at two and had bags of speed, but before joining me he'd spent some time in Dubai where he'd lost his way a bit.

Master Tribe turned out to be like a teenager who could

not be bothered to get out of bed in the morning. He was not very enthusiastic and after his morning exercise he was ready to go back to bed and fall asleep again. Because he was so lazy at home we decided to ride him up with the pace on his debut over hurdles at Huntingdon in November 1995, but unfortunately his Flat race instincts took over and he pulled so hard that he simply burned himself out. But when ridden with more restraint he won his next two starts in a manner that offered much hope for the future.

The following season, 1996–97, I entered him in the January Ladbroke Hurdle at Leopardstown, Ireland. At first I was a bit worried that he might be given too little weight to carry by the handicapper and he might not get a run, but Mike Dillon of Ladbrokes persuaded me to take the chance and enter him. Mike later told reporters that I had at first rejected his advice but had rung him back the next morning to apologize.

I have always enjoyed running horses in Ireland and the Ladbroke weekend is always great crack, with Mike Dillon organizing a big party for the owners, trainers and jockeys the night before the race. We'd come very close to winning the race in 1990, when Mark was beaten only half a length on Dis Train, so I had an old score to settle.

I was hoping that Master Tribe could make amends and give me my first success in Ireland. Disappointingly for me I was confined to a hospital bed in London and was unable to be there. I felt a great deal worse knowing I would be missing out on all the fun in Dublin, but I'm told my son Mark (who was still with us at this stage) was rather delighted that I'd had to stay behind; he was able to take charge in Ireland and, I'm told, more than made up for my absence at the pre-race party.

David drove up to London to watch the race with me on television in the hospital. We could hardly believe what we were watching. It was thrilling to see Master Tribe travelling so smoothly throughout the race. As they approached the

336

final bend he was still absolutely cruising. The excitement was so intense that my heart began beating loud and fast enough for me to hear and feel it rocking my body. Approaching the last hurdle I was sure Master Tribe would win, and when he began to draw clear on the run-in I was quietly going crackers, urging him on, shouting, crying and trying to do it all without disturbing anyone in the hospital. Suddenly I noticed another horse come flying out of the pack to challenge him and all my restraint was gone. Happily Master Tribe held on bravely in a nerve-racking, mind-blowing photo-finish.

Watching Master Tribe win the Ladbroke Hurdle was the best medicine I could possibly have had and it certainly tasted a lot sweeter than all the pills and potions I was on at the time.

In the late summer of 1996 I received a phonecall asking if I would like to train a little horse called Mudahim. The call came from a man called Salvo Giannini, who told me he'd just bought the ten-year-old horse at Ascot sales and wanted to send him to me. I already knew a little bit about Mudahim, because he'd been trained by Chris Broad in Gloucestershire, who had run him mainly in long-distance hurdle races. I also had good reason to remember the horse, as he had beaten Royal Athlete at Haydock eighteen months earlier. After that race Chris had asked my advice, because Mudahim was a bit worried about jumping fences and he wanted to build up his confidence. I suggested Chris took him hunting and he duly won over fences at Bangor in April 1996. However, Chris had decided to pack up training and had sent Mudahim to Ascot sales.

Because I knew he hadn't been too keen on steeple-chasing, and because he wasn't a big horse, I didn't immediately think of Mudahim as a potential National candidate. But I did note, when I first saw him, that he looked tough and had a good backside on him. I already knew that he operated on soft ground and that he stayed long distances, so I felt that if we could get him jumping his fences fluently, anything was possible.

For the first few weeks after he arrived we took him very quietly over the Downs. He'd already done a certain amount of roadwork, but when horses first come to us, even if they are fit, we don't push them into a full training schedule straight away. We let them settle and become accustomed to different things about the place before we ask them too many questions.

Mudahim was a smashing character, and the more I got to know him the more I liked him. He reminded me of a cat because he had two little white front socks which stuck out straight in front of him like paws when he was jumping. When we first started schooling him over fences it was immediately obvious that he wasn't very confident, so the first step was to get him to like what he was doing. I used Garrison Savannah as his lead horse and we started by schooling him over baby fences, which are the same height as hurdles. Once he was doing that confidently we progressed to the middle-sized fences. Before each session he would start by jumping the baby fences before moving up to the middle-sized ones. When he was schooling happily over the middle fences, we sent him over the big plain fences. And when I was finally satisfied with the way he was taking them, I put him over the open ditch. Everything was taken one careful step at a time.

Garrison Savannah is a brilliant schoolmaster. The lovely thing about Gary is that he always goes into a fence confidently. I'm sure if you put a blindfold on him and took him up that line of schooling fences he could still do it perfectly. To start with I used to send Gary in front of Mudahim, rather than upsides, so Mudahim would follow and get extra courage from him. In the beginning Mudahim used to back off his fences and he was just a little bit windy. But when Gary went and jumped it, you could see him thinking, 'Oh

338

well, if it's all right for him then I can do it.' Gradually his confidence and jumping blossomed.

He ran a couple of very promising races early in the season. At Uttoxeter he was second to Lord Gyllene, who went on to win the Grand National. Later on in February Mudahim had been entered in two races, one at Uttoxeter, the other the Racing Post Chase at Kempton Park. Salvo Giannini was very keen for him to go to Uttoxeter, where he'd run so well the last time. Salvo and I had always got on well. His business was civil engineering, but racing was his passion. Eventually he started a racing club called In Touch Racing, whose members now owned Mudahim. Salvo acted as their spokesperson, and I had quite a job trying to persuade him to let the horse go to Kempton. I explained that I'd been watching racing from the course on TV and the ground had been riding very dead there all season. I knew Mudahim could operate on that ground. I also knew he was an out-and-out stayer. If he could go off in front at a good pace I thought the other runners would have a job to peg him back. I finally convinced Salvo, but the betting public didn't share my confidence. Mudahim started at odds of 14–1.

The Kempton fences can be quite intimidating. 'What I want you to do on this horse today is to get a lead over those first few fences,' I told his jockey, Rodney Farrant. 'When you feel the horse is confident I want you to start turning up the taps. Keep turning them up gradually, and when you come off that bottom bend for the last time I want that tap wide open.'

The race was poetry in motion. Mudahim made a lot of the running, and although he was briefly headed by David Nicholson's horse King Lucifer, going to the last fence, he showed tremendous courage by fighting back all the way to the line, and won by a neck. It was my first success in the Racing Post Chase. When I was interviewed afterwards by Brough Scott on Channel Four TV I was feeling a bit mischievous. 'This is one of the best races for me to have won,' I told him. 'I can't imagine anything more delightful than having a winning percentage from a newspaper and going out and spending it really recklessly.' I smiled, knowing – which the viewers might not – that Brough was also the editorial director of the *Racing Post*!

Two and a half weeks later Mudahim ran at Cheltenham in the National Hunt Handicap Chase run over three miles one furlong. He had been going well at home so I was full of hope, but when I saddled him up he looked different – slightly worried. So I warned the In Touch Club members: 'I just don't feel so good about him today.' He seemed to have lost a little of his sparkle, and indeed he finished sixth, although he was still only beaten eight lengths.

We had entered Mudahim for the Grand National and also for the Irish National, both of which were a couple of weeks away. Salvo was very keen for him to run at Aintree. Originally I'd been keen, too, but having seen his run at Cheltenham I felt it would be a wrong move. There were likely to be the maximum forty runners that year, and because I felt we'd lost a bit of ground with his confidence I didn't think he would put up with the hustle and bustle of it. This time, Salvo took even more persuading. He had his heart set on Aintree. 'Salvo, I can win the Irish National for you this year,' I told him, 'but I can't win the Grand National.' In the end I said, 'Look, Salvo, you stick to digging holes in the road with your bloody JCB and I'll stick to training horses, okay?'

He burst out laughing, said, 'All right, Jen,' and I got my way.

When we brought Mudahim home after Cheltenham we schooled him over the middle-sized fences again to restore his confidence. To me, training a horse like Mudahim – or any horse that needs a bit of understanding – is like playing a game of chess. I'd have to wait for his next move before I could decide what my next move was going to be. If he jumped confidently, then I might send him up over the bigger fences the next time and if he didn't I might take him back a step and go for the smaller ones. Nor did the game end when I was at home, because half of it was always going on in my mind. I'd be sitting watching *Coronation Street* on the TV and my attention would drift back to this game of chess I was playing with Mudahim. I'd be staring at the screen and suddenly I'd think, I know what he needs . . .

By the time we took him to Ireland at the end of March Mudahim was back to his old self and enjoying his jumping. Even so, I wasn't brimming over with confidence, because he'd never flown before and I knew a bad flight might change his whole outlook on life. Fortunately he had a smooth journey, and when we called to see him in the race-course stables he was relaxed but bright.

Dave didn't come to Ireland with me because we had runners at other meetings, and Mark had by now set up on his own, so it was Mandy who accompanied me. The race-course at Fairyhouse was absolutely heaving that day. To get anywhere you had to force your way through the crowds, only to be pushed and shoved all over the place. I don't know what the maximum crowd for safety was supposed to be – but they are quite relaxed about such matters.

Though not overconfident, I felt good about Mudahim. He only had 10st 3lb to carry, and I believed that if he produced anything like his form he could win the race. But he was going to have to jump well, and be at his best. The one thing that did concern me was the fast ground. Mudahim had done most of his winning on soft or heavy ground. However, Mandy and I walked the course beforehand and decided that it was safe for him to race. As we tacked him up before the parade he looked very small against some of the other horses. Jason Titley, who had won the Grand National on Royal Athlete, was booked to ride him. Before I legged him up I warned him to beware of the Irish jockeys, who would not be doing us any favours. Jason might be Irish himself but he was riding an English horse, I reminded him.

That day people kept tapping me on the shoulder and wanting me to sign autographs. On a normal day's racing I didn't mind at all, but because I was under such pressure I decided to watch the race in the privacy of the weighing room. By looking out through the window and peering over the people sitting on the windowsill, I could just see the big television screen on the other side of the racecourse.

When the tapes rose Mudahim dwelt at the start. It meant he was further down the field than I would have liked. I thought, Oh, bloody hell! But once he got going he was soon travelling and jumping well. By the time they set off down the far side of the course on the final circuit he'd made up all the lost ground and was in second or third place. He was going into his fences flat out and at full stretch, picking up at each one and soaring over them with his little white feet stuck right out under his chin. It was tugging at my heartstrings to see him putting in so much effort. If this little bugger gets it wrong, I thought, he's going to be buried in the ground up to his ankles. At the second last he was still going well. Then there were just two horses fighting out the finish, going hell for leather towards the last. The Irish horse Amble Speedy edged in front of him but made a hash of the fence, while Mudahim jumped it well and regained the lead. There is a very long run-in at Fairyhouse, and it gave Amble Speedy the chance to get back upsides again, but Mudahim wouldn't give in. He stuck his head straight out, just like an athlete running for the tape, and they flashed past the post together. A photo-finish was announced.

I made my way outside. Everyone around me was saying we were beaten. I had been at a very bad angle to the winning line for judging the finish, and at first I wasn't so sure, but then Mandy came out of the press room, where she'd been watching the race on television. One look at her face told

342

me what I didn't want to know. I felt disappointed, not because I hadn't won the Irish National but for Mudahim. I was finding it hard to accept that this little horse of mine should be defeated when he'd jumped so well and run his heart out for me. He'd shown such a lot of courage that he deserved to win. As he rode into the enclosure reserved for the runner-up Jason looked gutted, and I tried to console him.

'He's run a great race,' I said. 'You've got nothing to question yourself about.'

It was only when Jason went off to the weighing room that I noticed that Francis Woods hadn't ridden Amble Speedy into the winners' enclosure but had jumped off him outside. You're not so sure, are you? I thought. We've still got a squeak here.

It seemed an eternity before the PA system crackled into life. 'The result of the photograph for first place is . . .'

The crowd went so quiet you could hear a pin drop.

'First, number eight.'

At that stage I'd forgotten what our number was, but I wasn't in doubt for long. All hell broke loose. There was squealing and cheering. People thumped me on the back. Beside me Salvo went berserk. First he went red, then purple and finally blue. He looked as if he was going to explode. All the noise startled Mudahim, who tried to charge off down the parade ring. I held onto his head, yelling at everyone to shut up before the horse hurt himself.

It was a great race to win, and it was especially poignant because, as I told the press over and over again afterwards, Mudahim owed it all to the best trainer in England – Garrison Savannah – for the way he had taught him to jump.

I was deeply touched to receive the Tom Dreaper Silver Salver as the trainer's prize for winning the Irish Grand National. This commemorated the great Irishman who had guided the career of the peerless Arkle with such a sure touch. It was also an honour to meet the Irish prime minister

343

John Bruton, who assisted Richard Brothers of Irish Distillers during the presentations.

When all the presentations and interviews were over I set off with Mandy for the racecourse stables to bandage the horse's legs. We weren't talking because so much was racing around in my mind. Not least thinking that Dave would be pleased and wishing he was here to share it. Suddenly I heard this odd noise. I looked across at Mandy and saw she was crying. 'What's the matter? What are you crying for?' I asked. In her whole life Mandy has hardly ever paid me a compliment – she isn't known for sentiment. But now she looked at me with her lip quivering and said, 'I'm just so proud of you, that's all.'

'Oh, shut up, you silly cow,' I said and gave her a hug. I didn't want her to start me off blubbering as well.

It was then that it finally sank in. I'd won all the Nationals. The Grand Slam. Something that only Martin Pipe had achieved before. And as I reflected on all the struggles and heartaches that had led up to this day I felt satisfied. Not clever, or proud, or anything like that . . . just very satisfied.

I didn't have time to rest on my laurels. Five days later we were at Aintree for the 1997 Grand National. This time I had two runners, Smith's Band and Nahthen Lad. Smith's Band was a nine-year-old bay gelding owned by Arthur Smith that I'd found at the sales in Ireland a few years before. Over the years I'd bought so many horses, but finding him had stuck in my mind. When I'd gone to look at him an old farmer was sitting outside his stable on a bale of straw. But he couldn't lead the horse out for us to see because he didn't have a bridle or a headcollar. So we had to wait for his grandson to come back from lunch before we could have a proper look. I'd laughed to myself, thinking that this was the Garrison Savannah scenario all over again. Although Smith's Band was not nearly as good looking as Garrison Savannah – in fact he'd been such an ugly duckling as a young horse that

Mandy used to call him 'knobbly knees' – he grew into a very useful animal. He was quite eccentric: if you walked into his box when he was feeling fed up he'd stamp his feet at you like a child having a tantrum. But underneath, he was a really nice chap.

My other runner, Nahthen Lad, was Jim Shaw's latest horse. Jim had named him after the Yorkshire way of greeting people, 'Nah then, lad,' but a lot of commentators missed the joke, and pronounced it in all sorts of peculiar ways, which the Shaw family found very amusing. Nahthen Lad had been a bit of a nightmare in his younger days. He used to become really wound up at the races and refuse to let us saddle him. He hurt me quite badly in the saddling boxes one day at Towcester as we were trying to put the tack on him. By the time the jockeys were entering the parade ring that day we still hadn't got a stitch of equipment on him apart from his bridle. We'd had to find ways of farming round the problem because horses like Nahthen Lad would go berserk if you took them on. These days we saddle him in the racecourse stable yard rather than the traditional saddling box, and he's as good as gold.

I thought both my horses had a decent chance in the 1997 Grand National. Nahthen Lad had won the Sun Alliance Chase the previous year while Smith's Band, although he'd suffered a bit of a setback at the end of the previous season, had won three good chases.

I did my regular feature at Aintree for the BBC with Des Lynam. We get on well – he doesn't try to hit you below the belt – and we had our usual banter before the race. Once again the old adrenaline was flowing, but I had it pretty much under control. At around three o'clock I began to get the horses ready. We'd saddled Nahthen Lad, and I was just about to finish putting the tack on Smith's Band when something about the buzz of noise around the parade ring seemed to change. You could sense that there was something not quite right, though you didn't know what it was.

345

Then we heard the first whisper: 'They've found a bomb.'

In a situation like that you don't want to be alarmist so you carry on as normal. Princess Anne, who was there to unveil a bust of Sir Peter O'Sullevan, had just walked past us with her security guards, and I told myself that she wouldn't still be on the course if there was a problem, so I carried on saddling up Smith's Band. We'd just put the paddock sheet on him when I realized the crowds outside the saddling boxes were getting quieter. The next moment voices were shouting: 'Everybody out! Everybody out!' It was the police. They wanted the horses out of the parade ring and back in the stable yard. Everybody obeyed calmly but it still took quite some time before we could get them back to the stable yard. I felt that there was no point in leaving the horses saddled. Even if we were called back to the parade ring the jockeys would have to weigh out again with their saddles because we'd left the secure area. We took off the tack, put the horses' rugs on and sat down for a cup of tea in the stable security man's office. I'd hardly taken a sip when several police and security officials came in and shouted to everyone to leave the stable yard at once.

Obediently we started to head for the yard gates, but then I saw Nahthen Lad looking over his door, bewildered, as if to say 'Please don't go,' and I stopped. Ten minutes ago Nahthen Lad had been like an actor winding himself up to go on stage. Horses get used to the preparations for a race and they know what's coming. Now suddenly everything had changed, and he didn't know what to expect next. He looked confused and anxious. He looked as if he wanted me to go and make a fuss of him. Normally Nahthen Lad was a hardcase. There are very few horses that would deliberately hurt you, but if he flipped Nahthen Lad wouldn't think twice about it. To see him turn suddenly from a big macho bovver-boy into a little child who needed somebody to love him was very upsetting. 'I'm sorry,' I said to a nearby policeman, 'I can't leave my horse.'

'Either you go, madam, or you'll be escorted out,' he told me. I understood that to be a polite way of saying I'd be arrested, and as I didn't fancy appearing on the front of the newspapers in handcuffs I decided to go quietly. We were all hustled out, only to run straight into Des Lynam, who was interviewing some jockeys in the car park. 'Will you do an interview, Jenny?' he asked.

I agreed, though my mind was in a whirl. Because of the trouble at Aintree with the animal rights people over the years I imagined this was something to do with them. It might sound naïve, but because of the strong Irish connection with horseracing, the thought that the IRA might target us or the horses never crossed my mind.

In any case, at that point I didn't really care *who* was responsible. My main feeling was anger, and determination that we must not be intimidated by crackpots. I'd had to abandon my horses, and if they're upset I'm upset. Normally when I'm on the racecourse I have on a suit of invisible armour. But now, with all these emotions welling up inside me, I was overwhelmed, and as I talked to Des the tears started to flow. I wasn't happy about it. I knew some people might see it as a sign of weakness, but they were tears of anger and frustration as much as anything. There was so much confusion, but it wasn't long after that interview that the race was called off. It was only then that I learned the cause of the evacuation was an IRA bomb threat.

Two hours later Dave and I, together with our farriers Gary Pickford, Micky Towell and Martin Price, found ourselves walking towards the centre of Liverpool. The cars parked at the racecourse had all been impounded and the streets were heaving with people all walking in the same direction; every taxi that passed was packed. We had walked probably half a mile when we passed two women standing on the pavement. One of them called after me, 'Jenny Pitman! Jenny Pitman!' and I turned.

'I'm ever so pleased to meet you,' she said. 'Do you want a cup of tea?'

I had never heard more welcoming words. She took us all to her friend's house, where she made us the promised tea and biscuits. It was heaven. She got her husband to ring a cabby they knew, and he met us a few streets away and took us back to our hotel. Fortunately we had booked for that night anyway. Heaven knows where we'd have found a bed otherwise. The whole of Liverpool was packed to the gills.

All sorts of rumours were flying around, and at that stage we weren't certain if the race was going to be re-run on Monday or not. The horses had been moved to Haydock Park racecourse for safety and had been fed, but although we had plenty of corn for them we'd only taken enough hay to last till the Sunday, so we had to send home to Lambourn for some more (we always feed our own hay when we're racing, because quality can vary so much). On Sunday morning we drove over to Haydock to see the horses. It was alarming to find that there was no proper security on the gates, so every Tom, Dick and Harry was going into the stable yard. By that time the Jockey Club had rung all the trainers with runners in the Grand National to ask their opinion about restaging the race. As far as I was concerned it wasn't a decision that needed thinking about. Martell, the sponsor, had always been very good to us. Between this and the void National in 1993 they had now experienced two major disasters in the space of four years. For their sake, if for nobody else's, I felt the race should be run. Fortunately the other trainers felt the same.

On Saturday evening I had given interviews for TV and radio. I felt like a ping-pong ball bouncing from one reporter to another, but I didn't mind because I felt we should be seen to be putting our shoulders to the wheel and supporting racing. I was booked to do an interview with Sky Television outside Aintree racecourse on Sunday morning, but by this time my staff and I had been told, and the press had not, that during Saturday evening there had been a phonecall to Weathercock House from a man with an Irish accent.

'Tell Jenny Pitman to watch her step because we're watching her,' he said.

Dave was really worried about it, but, while I'd have preferred it hadn't happened, I was not going to change my plans. I felt that I couldn't say that I'm going to stand up and be counted and then turn round and say, 'Well, count everybody else but leave me out.'

The next morning I was slightly surprised when David, Gary Pickford, our farrier, and Martin Price, his apprentice, insisted on coming with me to Aintree for the interview. Their excuse was that they wanted to try to reclaim their car from the racecourse following the evacuation the previous day. Gary is built like a bull terrier and his apprentice is a strong lad, too. They were all walking so close to me that I kept bumping into them.

'Will you get out from under my feet, else we're going to have a stewards' inquiry here,' I said. They looked at each other and I suddenly realized what they were doing. 'Here,' I told them, 'if you want to look like proper securitymen you've got to keep looking over your shoulder like this . . .' At that they looked a bit uneasy, but actually I thought it was wonderful of them to try and protect me in such a manner.

On the Monday morning we arrived early for the restaged Grand National. David and I had already walked a mile, but outside the racecourse the queue already stretched for several hundred yards. Fortunately, the security people were looking out for trainers and jockeys, and when they spotted us they took us to another lane, where we were searched and let in. I thought the Monday meeting might be an anticlimax, but there was a big crowd. People were laughing and jolly, and you could feel a real air of support and defiance about the place, which was wonderful.

However, I just wasn't able to gee myself up to the same

extent second time round. That seemed to be true for some of the horses, too. Perhaps they'd already peaked on the Saturday, when they'd been ready to perform and it hadn't happened. By the Monday it was all a bit late. I wasn't worried about my two horses' physical well-being – they had drunk and eaten well – but to me they were a bit like a lettuce that you've had in the fridge for a couple of days; they'd lost their crispness. The only consolation was that all the horses were in the same boat.

In the race Smith's Band was up with the leaders from very early on, and jumping like an absolute stag, which I knew he would do. Nahthen Lad jumped well on the inside but he got a real buffeting, and several times I saw him stopped in his tracks by horses in front of him. When that happens, a horse loses its momentum. In the National it's very important that you keep a good steady rhythm. I felt that had those checks not happened to Nahthen Lad he'd have finished in the first three, rather than ninth as he did, though I was still pleased with him. But there was sadness to come. Smith's Band was up with the leaders and still jumping for fun when he plummeted over the twentieth fence and fell like a stone. I knew instantly that he was dead. I didn't go running down the course to see if he was all right because there was no point. Most people thought he'd broken his neck, but I actually felt, from the way he dropped, that he was dead before he hit the ground. (Afterwards his jockey, Richard Dunwoody, told me he felt the same. He said he'd watched the video of the race again and again – typical of a champion jockey of his calibre – and he was convinced Smith's Band had suffered a heart attack, because he simply never took off properly before the jump.)

I've been in the job a long time and I'm aware that horses die for all sorts of reasons. It is something you have to accept. Even so I felt an awful emptiness inside. I felt that after all he'd been through that weekend Smith's Band didn't deserve to die. After the race I walked slowly up to the

350

stable yard, psyching myself up to ring Arthur Smith, who had been watching the race on TV at home. When I did, Arthur interrupted me before I could get the words out. 'I know he's dead, Jenny,' he said. 'I saw it happen.'

Afterwards, as I helped wash Nahthen Lad down, the course vet came round. 'Jenny, we've picked your horse up. What do you want us to do with him?'

'Is there anywhere you can have him cremated?' I asked. 'I'd like to have him home.' The racecourse authorities granted my wish, and today Smith's Band lies under a Granny Smith apple tree at Weathercock House.

A lot of emotion was spent that weekend. Afterwards I felt just as drained as I had after Garrison Savannah's Grand National, but at least then there had been a happy ending to make up for it. Somehow, whenever there was a drama at Aintree I seemed to have a front-row seat. I had experienced such a mix of emotions at this course with horses like Crisp, Corbiere, Esha Ness, Royal Athlete, and now Smith's Band. I sometimes wondered why I kept going back. But deep down I knew why. Aintree was addictive. However much I hated it, I knew that the following year it would pull me back again. Triumph and disaster, I had to treat these two impostors just the same.

CHAPTER TWENTY-TWO

TWO BIG OCCASIONS

You can always tell when men are mulling something over. Dave had been a bit quiet all day. In the evening as the two of us were sitting watching *Coronation Street* I could see him looking at me out of the corner of his eye. I had the feeling he was about to make a profound statement. What's on his mind? I thought. I didn't have to wait long to find out. Once *Coronation Street* was over, it came tumbling out.

'I love you, waggle-bum. Why don't we get married?'

It wasn't the most romantic proposal in the world, so it took a while for the words to sink in. 'Could you run that by me again, please?' I asked.

He didn't. After an eighteen-year engagement Dave had finally decided it was safe to make the proposal again. Well, bless my soul, I thought. It was the last thing I expected him to say. I felt a little smile on my face, sat quiet for a moment then strung him along for a bit before I said yes.

Once bitten, twice shy, people said. When I'd first been divorced I was certain I would never let someone get so close to me again. In the years that followed, a perspex screen seemed to have come down around my deepest emotions. But then Dave had come onto the scene, giving me friendship and support and making me laugh, until gradually love had forced a way through that screen. Over the years our relationship had worked well for both of us. Whenever one was having a bad time the other had been strong. We'd been mates before we'd been anything else, and we'd stayed mates through the good times and the bad. When I'd needed someone to support and encourage me, or just to put the pin back in the hand grenade, Dave had been there.

He'd been there for the boys, too. He'd never forced himself into Mark's and Paul's lives, but when they were growing up he'd done everything for them that a natural father would, including teaching them to play cricket, snooker and golf. When Mark started riding, Dave ferried him to and from race meetings, and when he'd been injured in races he reacted as any natural parent would. Mark and Paul were both settled in their lives and were hardly going to object to my changing my name now, I thought, so I had no reason to worry about that. Dave and I had devoted our lives to the horses and the boys. Now it was time we did something for ourselves.

We were married at Southampton Register Office on 18 July 1997. Because everything we do is in the eye of the media we were desperate for our wedding to be a private ceremony. It was hard to keep the day a secret, but we managed it. Dotty Channing-Williams, an old friend of mine, booked the register office in her name so that reporters wouldn't get wind of it. The only people we told beforehand of the date were Mr and Mrs Hitchins and Richard, my brother, who was going to be Dave's best man. I broke the news to the rest of my family the day before the wedding.

Choosing my wedding outfit was a bit of a nightmare. At one stage the *Mail on Sunday* magazine offered to help me find something suitable, but we had a difference of opinion after I went up to London to be photographed in different outfits. It was my understanding that the photographs would appear the weekend after the wedding, but when I discovered that the magazine planned to publish them beforehand I sent the clothes back and went to look for another outfit. I told them I did not know any bride, eighteen or eighty, who wants people to know in advance what they are going to wear when they get married!

Three weeks before the wedding I still hadn't found anything. Then one day I spotted an advert in a bride's magazine for a shop called Familytique in Market Bosworth, not far from where my dad lives. A few days later I drove up there and paid a visit with my sister-in-law, Janet, as adviser. It was like walking into an Aladdin's cave filled with clothes for every possible occasion. Within a couple of hours Jenny Mapp and Christine had kitted me out with a beautiful dress-coat, shoes, tights, the lot, as well as clothes for the honeymoon. When I walked out of that shop I felt as if somebody had untied twenty knots from the top of my head. The only thing left to worry about was transport to the ceremony, but that problem was solved when Mr and Mrs Hitchins kindly offered the use of their lovely blue Rolls-Royce.

The ceremony itself went smoothly, except for the fact that I became a bit choked up when it came to saying our vows. Thomas Bowlby, my nephew, was my pageboy, and I asked Laura, my hairdresser's daughter, to be my flowergirl. Afterwards, we held a reception for eighteen of our family and close friends on board the cruise ship *Oriana* which was docked at Southampton. The food and attention the ship's crew gave us were absolutely wonderful. The chef had even sculpted an ice model of a racehorse's head in our honour. At six o'clock that evening I turned to the guests. 'Right,' I said. 'You can all clear off now,' and after they'd disembarked Dave and I set off for a fortnight's cruise round the Mediterranean.

A month later we held a reception for two hundred and fifty guests in a marquee at Weathercock House. It was a special night, and very moving to be told how happy people were for us that evening. Most of our owners came up and said things like 'About time, too,' and 'Why did you take so long?' I told them that it was because men took a lot more training than horses. Now that Dave was housetrained I didn't want to have to go through it all over again with a new one, so I thought I'd better get him tethered!

One evening, soon after the reception, we were sitting down watching TV and I said to Dave, 'Do you feel any different now we're married?' He thought for a moment, probably wondering if it was a trick question. 'Yes, I think I do,' he said. 'Do you?' I thought about it. 'Yes, I do,' I said. 'I feel complete.' 'So do I,' he said.

I'd made up my mind I was going to be Jenny Stait from now on, because I felt that as David's wife it was right. But Barry Thorpe, who gives me business advice, felt that while I should be Jenny Stait for my private life, the business should carry on as Jenny Pitman Racing Ltd. 'In effect, your name is your business logo, Jenny,' he said. 'It would be folly for you to change it.' After much thought I decided to go along with him. After all, there's not much point in paying a business adviser if you don't listen to him! But then again I've never had a problem taking advice from people I have respected and who are good at their own job.

There wasn't much time to sit back and enjoy being a married woman. At the beginning of August the horses started to come into training and we were off again. We had about twenty young horses for the 1997–98 season, and a good 'middle team', but we were short of older horses. The youngsters that Bill Robins had taken away a few years earlier would have been our older horses now, so there was something of a gap there. Because we were focusing on bringing the younger middle team players through, I knew we wouldn't have as many chances as usual to win the big chases. But the runners we did have performed well.

In early December I was due to be presented with the award for my win in the Ladbroke Hurdle at Leopardstown. I was at Heathrow airport, waiting to catch a plane to

Ireland with Mike Dillon of Ladbrokes, when my mobile telephone rang. It was David.

'Can you talk?' he said.

God, something's happened, I thought.

Dave read my mind. 'Don't worry, it's nothing bad.'

I moved closer to the window to get a better signal on the mobile phone. 'What is it?'

'You've had a letter from the prime minister,' Dave said. 'It says your name has been put forward for the New Year's Honours list, but you're not to discuss it.' I felt my legs go weak. I was completely taken aback.

Mike had gone to get some tea and coffee and when he came back he found me sitting down clutching my phone and staring into space. God knows what he must have thought. I was in a total daze.

'Are you all right?' he asked. I said I was and we sat in silence, sipping our tea, while I tried to get my head round the idea. I didn't know what it meant to have your name put forward – whether that meant I was going to get an OBE or whether I was on a shortlist, or what. I found it quite difficult to deal with and I kept drifting off while Mike was talking. All day long he kept asking, 'Are you all right? Are you sure you're all right?' 'Mike, I'm fine, I'm absolutely fine,' I had to keep replying.

I was relieved to get home that night to read the letter for myself. My first thought was how pleased my dad would be. The one thing the letter made clear was that in no circumstances was I to discuss it with anybody. But I felt I just had to tell Dad. He was now eighty-three. If something happened to him and he didn't know about it I would never forgive myself, I thought. I have always phoned my dad every night. We talk about the horses, how they've raced and if there have been any problems. I still appreciate and respect his opinion. It would become very difficult to have these nightly conversations without spilling the beans!

The following week I went racing at Leicester. I had my

jockeys, Rodney Farrant and Dennis Leahy, in the car with me and on the way home I told them, 'I think I'm going to call in and see my dad for a minute.' I left the two jockeys in Dad's sitting room while I took him into the bedroom, telling him I had a letter to show him. He looked really anxious. 'It's all right, don't worry,' I told him. 'I'll go and make a cup of tea while you read this letter.' I went off to the kitchen and when I came back into the bedroom Dad had got his handkerchief out and was wiping his eyes.

'Look, Dad, you're not to tell a soul,' I said, ''cos it ain't going to happen else.'

'Don't worry, I won't say nowt to nobody,' he replied. It was from the way in which he replied that I knew the secret was safe.

In December a lovely young horse of mine called Mentmore Towers broke his shoulder in a fall at the second last hurdle and had to be put down. It was a terrible blow.

Mentmore Towers was a stunningly good horse. He was still only a baby and he had the potential to be anything. The world was his oyster. On top of that, he had the most lovely temperament; he really was a nice chap.

I'd never liked that second last hurdle at Cheltenham. The approach ran downhill and then on the landing side the ground rose slightly, which made it very tricky for a horse to sight at the best of times. Over the years there had been a number of falls there. Now Mentmore Towers had become the latest casualty.

Over the years I've been training, the general public have always been very supportive of me, and their letters have helped me keep going through tough times. If I said I'd had twenty nasty letters in twenty years, that would be the maximum. After this latest tragedy the number of letters of sympathy was quite overwhelming. One in particular did manage to bring a smile to my face. It was from a man saying how sorry he was and what a lovely horse Mentmore Towers had been. He finished off his letter: 'To the Queen of Weathercock House (but tell Dave not to worry because I'm also a queen).' I was so taken aback by the surprise ending that I started laughing for the first time in days.

On 31 December 1997 all the newspapers carried the announcement that I had been awarded an OBE in the New Year's Honours List for services to horseracing. The phone did not stop ringing all day. I had been advised earlier that it would be wise to have a press statement ready, which I did:

It is a great honour to have been awarded the OBE. I had heard a few weeks ago that my name had been put forward and it has been quite difficult to keep it a secret, particularly from my family. Of course my husband, David Stait, knew and I must confess to showing the letter to my dad. I knew he was pleased when he wiped his eyes with his handkerchief.

It is indeed a very proud moment for us all, as I feel I am receiving this award not just for myself but for my family and the people who have helped me over the years. Without their support I would not be in the position I am today.

I was overwhelmed by cards and letters of congratulation. I was particularly touched that the Queen Mother had also taken the trouble to write. The date for the investiture was set for Tuesday 17 March. Deciding what to wear for it was almost as difficult as choosing my wedding outfit. My first thought was to wear a red suit that I'd bought for an interview for Sky Television in December. The interview had been cancelled, so the suit hadn't seen the light of day. After thinking about it, though, I decided a totally red outfit looked too confrontational, so I returned to Familytique in Market Bosworth and bought an oyster-coloured dress and coat. The only trouble was that none of the hats Jenny Mapp showed me were quite right. Four days before I was due at the Palace I still had nothing to wear on my head! Fortunately, Mandy remembered seeing a milliner who had a trade stand at Newbury Show. Equally fortunately, she'd picked up her card. I gave Sally Hindson a ring. On the Thursday evening Mandy and I called to see her at her studio near Abingdon. I fell in love instantly with one of the hats she showed me. The shape really suited me, but the trouble was, it was the wrong colour. I showed her my outfit, which I'd taken with me. 'I realize it's a long shot,' I said, 'but have you got any material to match this that you could use to make a hat in that style?'

'I'll see what I can do,' Sally promised.

Three days later, when I returned home from a lunch at Cheltenham racecourse, I found a message saying, 'Your hat is ready.' Sally had spent all day Saturday and Sunday working on it, and had made the most lovely job. It was a big, face-framing creation of oyster silk, with brown and oyster silk flowers around the crown. Sally, like many others in the past, had rescued me. I so much wanted the hat to be right with the rest of the outfit, and it was perfect.

I was allowed to take three guests with me to the Palace. Paul came back from Kuala Lumpur for the ceremony and he and Mark and Dave accompanied me, all of them wearing morning suits. There was just one problem with the date chosen for the ceremony. It clashed with the opening day of the Cheltenham Festival, where I had runners in the first race. People were very kind when they heard of my predicament. One chap even came up to me at Wincanton and offered me the use of his helicopter to get from the Palace to the races. Sadly, I had to decline. I told him that if I was guaranteed to win the lottery every week for twelve months he would not get me in a helicopter. Again Mr Hitchins came to the rescue by offering to send his private jet to Northolt to pick us up after the ceremony. When another gentleman, George Dawson, volunteered to drive us between the Palace and Northolt, the problem was solved.

The day before the investiture I had a phone call from the controller at the Palace. 'I think I'm going to be in trouble with my boss,' he said. 'You have another important engagement tomorrow, haven't you?' When I confessed that I had, he promised to seat Dave and the boys near some doors, so that we could leave discreetly after I had received my OBE.

I was terribly nervous on the day itself. I wished there was a book to tell you what to do, whether you should wear gloves or not, and so on. As it turned out, I need not have worried. The moment you walk into the Palace you are guided along so smoothly that there is very little chance of any disaster happening. Everyone who greeted us was very friendly. I was shepherded one way while David, Mark and Paul were taken the other. Unfortunately I'm not good at being on my own, even at ordinary functions, never mind somewhere like the Palace, and I started to feel really nervous. It was hardly surprising. A few years earlier I'd have been lucky to get a job grooming horses at the Palace, and now here I was about to have a chat with the Queen! I felt an awful lot better when a man came up and started talking to me. He was David Waplington, a prison governor I'd seen on the Frost programme the previous week. He knew who I was, too. 'You're Jenny Pitman, aren't you?' he said. 'I hardly recognized you. When I see you on the television you always look so, so . . .' He hesitated.

'Shabby?' I suggested. He smiled. 'No, no, no, I wasn't going to say that. But you just look so glamorous today. You weren't like I expected.'

'Oh well, I'm sorry to disappoint you,' I teased, and we had a giggle about it. I was just so relieved he had come up and started chatting and I started to feel a bit better. We were taken through a dress rehearsal and were told by a Palace official that our audience with the Queen would be over when she shook hands. We should then take three steps backwards, bow or curtsey, turn right and leave. I'm a disaster with my left and right because I'm left-handed, so I was only half joking when I asked the man next to me if he had a pen so I could write it on the back of my hand!

One by one people stepped up to collect their awards. By the time there were only three people in front of me, I was like some Flat horse down at the start about to be loaded into the stalls, I felt so wound up and anxious. I suddenly thought, 'Mother, I wish you were here.' A few moments later I felt an unbelievable calmness come over me and as I relaxed I thought, I'm going to enjoy this now.

All I can say to anyone who is awarded such an honour is, Don't spoil it by getting in a flap, because there really is no need to worry. Enjoy the day. It's the experience of a life-time and quite unique. Nothing can compare with it, not even winning the Grand National or the Gold Cup. I shall treasure the memory for the rest of my life.

The plans for the dash to Cheltenham after the ceremony went like clockwork, and I was pleased I'd made the effort to get there because I was greeted with such warmth by everybody at the races. It felt right that I should share the day with them. Although we didn't have a winner that after-noon, two days later I rewarded Mr Hitchins with his first-ever Cheltenham Festival winner when Princeful ran away with the Bonusprint Stayers' Hurdle. For me it was the highlight of the season. The only sadness was that Mrs Hitchins was not there to share it: she had died the previous August. But I couldn't help feeling that she was smiling down on us.

Judging by the nice things they said to me at that time, being awarded the OBE had earned me several Brownie points with the media. But only three weeks after the Cheltenham Festival I found myself at the centre of yet another controversy.

I had only one runner in the 1998 Grand National. A

potential candidate, Mudahim, had been badly struck into at Ascot, and while we hoped he would recover in time for Aintree our efforts proved to be in vain. Our hopes were consequently focused on Nahthen Lad. The weather the week before the race had been appalling, and everyone knew that the ground was going to be pretty soft. Often, at Aintree, they leave maintenance of the course until the Saturday morning of the race, which normally doesn't matter too much, but very wet conditions are a major concern there. As forecast, it had rained all Friday night. 'I hope to Christ somebody's been putting that ground back after the Foxhunters' and the John Hughes Trophy,' I said to Dave as we lay listening to it. With the amount of rain we'd had I knew the course could be waterlogged and difficult to repair.

On the Saturday morning we reached the course at about quarter past seven, and I took Nahthen Lad out to give him a long walk and a light canter. As we were going back to the stables I bumped into Charles Barnett, the clerk of the course, and Major Arkwright, the clerk from Cheltenham.

'Have you had a look at that ground? It's bloody awful,' I said to them. (To be honest I probably said a bit more than that!) Major Arkwright replied, 'Not my job, actually,' which of course it wasn't, but Charles Barnett assured me he'd have a look at it.

After we'd put the horse back in his box and I'd done several media interviews, Dave and I, Rodney Farrant and a few others set off walking the course. Before we'd even got to the first Melling Road crossing it was apparent that under the covering of long grass on the track there were several nasty holes. Before the first fence we came across a small group of workmen with numbers on their backs; some of them, but by no means all, had forks in their hands. The numbers on their backs went up to the fifties, but that was misleading because there were no more than twenty men in total. As we passed them I felt my foot sink into a really deep hole. When I put the toe of my wellington boot in, my foot disappeared well past the heel (the foot of my boot, I later discovered, measures eleven and three-quarter inches).

'Excuse me,' I said to this group of workmen, 'can you fill this hole in?'

'We don't need you telling us what to do,' one of them said. 'We've got enough bosses already.'

I was livid. 'Look,' I said. 'I don't need your grief either. If a horse puts its foot in this hole and breaks its leg it doesn't just go to bed for a few days.'

We walked on, leaving them pottering about with their forks. Normally when we walk the course we try and walk the line I want the jockey to take. But now we changed our tactics and spread out, desperately searching for better ground. It was a nightmare. From the middle to the inside of those fences right the way to the Canal Turn the course was appalling. It looked as if the ground hadn't been put back after the two previous races. In normal going you can 'lift' the bottom of small holes with a fork to level the ground, but with deep holes like this, which had been left to fill with water, the only answer, we felt, was to fill the holes in with a mixture of sand and grit. I could see no sign of anybody doing that. In fact, nor was there any sign of sand or grit.

At Becher's I found the same situation on the landing side. As I was trying to stamp the holes down, the ground was sinking under my feet. I turned to Rodney and said, 'The only thing you can do is go from the middle to the outer all the way round. Don't even contemplate coming down the inside because if you do you're not going to get this far.' I was so distressed that I rang my office and asked them to contact the clerk of the course. Ian Renton, the assistant clerk of the course, rang me on my mobile phone. 'Ian, this ground is a f—ing disgrace,' I told him.

'Jenny, it was far worse than this in nineteen eighty—' he began.

'Look, Ian,' I said. 'Don't bullshit me. I was walking this course when you were still in your cradle. I've supported you and the National through thick and thin over the years and this is not good enough.'

I was now facing a dilemma. I really didn't want to run my horse, but I was in a no-win situation. If I told the Shaws that we should withdraw Nahthen Lad they would be terribly disappointed. On top of that, the press would say, 'Why have you taken your horse out?' I didn't want to say in public, 'Because I think the ground is absolutely diabolical.' I didn't want to cause a furore. In the end, following discussions with the owner, we decided to run Nahthen Lad. I told the Shaws that because of the state of the ground their horse was going to have to go wide, because that was the only safe route to go.

Naturally, I was more nervous than usual when the race started. All I could think about was those horrible holes in the ground. Before the end of the first circuit Nahthen Lad got in rather close to the eleventh fence, came down very steep and unseated Rodney. It's not often I'm relieved to see one of my horses unseat his rider, but I was that day. He'll be all right now, I thought to myself. Nahthen Lad carried on riderless and was leading the field until he jumped the Chair. Then, realizing where he was, he ran out on the bend and headed for the racecourse stables.

I was still angry after the race. In my opinion a dangerous situation had arisen because somebody hadn't done their job properly. I knew the officials had a lot on their plate with security precautions after the IRA bomb threat the previous year, but in my opinion by concentrating on that they had taken their eye off the ball. When you consider the weather forecast, a pensioner with a windowbox could have seen what was likely to happen if the ground was not put back immediately after each race.

I felt I had to write a letter about it, because what I'd seen was wrong and it could have done so much damage to the race. If horses' and their riders' safety wasn't given priority in the Grand National, then those people who wanted it banned would have just the ammunition they needed. I let the dust settle in my own mind for a few days so the letter wouldn't be written in anger, then wrote to Peter Greenall, Lord Daresbury, who was chairman of Aintree racecourse, outlining my concerns. I did not take this action in order to be controversial and destroy the race, I did it because I wanted to save it. I marked the envelope 'Private and Confidential' and did the same with the copies I sent to the National Trainers' Federation and to the Stewards of the Jockey Club.

Two weeks later I was up at Ayr for the Scottish National. I had phoned home on the Saturday evening and was told that the Aintree clerk, Charles Barnett, had telephoned. As he hadn't left a message I thought it couldn't be too important, so I decided to return his call when I reached Lambourn. It never occurred to me that it might be connected with the confidential letter I had written to Lord Daresbury. In fact, it looked as though someone had taken it upon themselves to show either all or part of the letter to a reporter and sections of it were about to appear in the *Daily Telegraph*.

Whether someone leaked the letter to try to discredit me or whether they wanted to cause a furore about the National I really don't know, but the following Monday the *Telegraph* published critical statements reporting that there was nothing wrong with the ground and accusing me of 'squealing after the event'. Some trainers, who I knew hadn't even walked the course that day, joined in the criticism. What was interesting was that nearly everyone who criticized me was directly linked in some way with the Grand National. There is no doubt in my mind that some 'old school tie' pressure was being brought to bear. One man, who had at first told reporters that he was glad Jenny Pitman had said what she did because the ground was appalling, changed his mind the next day and withdrew the statement, saying, 'Oh, I meant the weather was appalling.' The fact that he happened to train for a senior steward of the Jockey Club may not have been unconnected with his change of heart. It was quite clear to me that various people received an excessive amount of whipping to get them in line.

I don't regret writing that letter, because I felt my point needed making. The authorities claimed they'd sent eighty men round to 'lift' the ground after I walked the course that morning, but I maintain to this day that they could not possibly have lifted those deep holes. People have rung me since and told me that they walked the course at half past eleven and twelve o'clock and it was the same then as I described it. One chap said he'd even picked up a discarded horseshoe with the nails still in it lying face upwards on the course.

On the morning of 21 May 1998 I had a very useful and constructive meeting with Charles Barnett and his assistant, Ian Renton. I'm afraid I dropped my horns at them the moment they stepped into my sitting room. There was some plain speaking done, and suffice to say it was agreed that new measures would be taken. In the future racecourse ground staff will attend the racecourse throughout the Thursday and the Friday and not just the Saturday morning of the National. I have also suggested the vetting of all the Grand National runners on the morning of the race (a practice employed in eventing), to reassure the general public that we are doing everything possible to make racing horses as safe as it can be. On that same afternoon I had a meeting with Jockey Club officials Tony Goodhew and Joey Newton. We discussed the same issues and also the possibility of including an extra steeplechase fence just after the start, which will reduce the long run to what is now the first fence and thus reduce the speed of the runners over the first three fences. This should enable them to get into a sensible rhythm earlier in the race.

At the end of May the season ended on an even pleasanter note when three of my old champions – Burrough Hill Lad, Garrison Savannah and Royal Athlete – paraded at the York Racecourse Festival of Racing in a retired racehorse pageant. It featured horses who had gone on to second careers after racing, and all three of them were held up as good examples. Royal Athlete is now doing well in dressage competitions as well as competing at shows in side-saddle classes; Burrough Hill Lad is of course in the twilight of his long hunting career; and Garrison Savannah is still serving as a schoolmaster to the 'babies' at Weathercock House. They have been truly great champions of the turf and have been loved and admired by many people. I feel very privileged to have trained them.

I am so proud that these three horses and others like them have been able to move on to a new life after racing. In my opinion all horses should be well enough educated in the basics to be able to do something else after their racing careers are over, and many of mine have done just that. Sadly, of course, some racehorses, like Willsford, Smith's Band and Mentmore Towers, don't make it to the end of their racing careers. Others, like Toby Tobias, suffer racing injuries which mean – if they have a genuinely caring owner like Mr Hitchins – that an honourable retirement is the only option.

Despite the risks, I believe that most racehorses have a very good life. I'd sooner be a racehorse any day than a pony stuck out in the New Forest or on the moors, full of worms and hungry on a cold winter's day, or living in a foreign country where so many are ill treated. Come to think of it, some days I'd sooner be a racehorse in my yard than a human being. They get five-star hotel treatment, top-quality medical care, the best food money can buy and love and attention that any human being would be pleased to receive. On top of that, they don't have to do VAT returns, tax forms or other endless such nonsense. Compared with the lot of a racehorse trainer, it is not a bad life. And that's the way it should be.

CHAPTER TWENTY-THREE

FACING FACTS

In the summer of 1998 I had some wonderful news when my son Paul married his long-term girlfriend, Sonia. This was followed by some worrying news about my health. For much of the previous year my voice had become increasingly hoarse.

Eventually, in October 1997, I noticed a tiny lump, about the size of a pea, in the middle of my throat. The next morning our vet Charlie Schreiber was at the yard testing some horses, so I asked him to pop into the house and told him about the lump. He had a good look and advised me to see my doctor who said he would arrange an appointment for me with a specialist in Swindon.

That night I rang Professor Newman-Taylor, who had been such a help in the past, and told him that I had a small lump in my throat. He thought it sounded as though it was on my thyroid and asked me to keep him informed.

When I eventually saw the specialist in Swindon, he suggested that I was suffering from a virus and advised me to rest. It was a diagnosis that clearly disturbed Charlie Schreiber. When he next called in I remember he was very quiet at first, and kept looking at the floor. Then he said, 'I don't like to say this kind of thing Mrs P, but I feel you should seek a second opinion.' It so happened I already had an appointment with Professor Newman-Taylor at London's Brompton Hospital in December to discuss a long-standing allergy problem. He said he thought I looked really well but I was still concerned about the lump in my throat and asked him for his opinion. He examined my throat before saying, 'That will not go away,' and immediately made an appointment for me to visit the Royal Marsden Hospital across the road the same day.

At this point I felt that David and I were struggling, trying not to panic. When someone mentions the Royal Marsden you are bound to be a bit scared. Further examination showed that the lump was a small cyst. Some fluid was taken from it before I was asked to return in three months' time.

By the time I returned in March, it seemed to me that the cyst had grown a baby. Once more some fluid was removed and I was asked to come back in a further three months. The constant worry of this problem hanging over us was becoming unbearable. I was also being nagged by my vets to get the lump removed, which didn't help! Eventually, in May I rang the surgeon, Mr Rhys Evans, and explained that I couldn't cope any longer with the strain the uncertainty was causing David. I added that in my experience the best way to deal with the problems I had in my life was to remove them, so could he please remove the cyst.

The operation was carried out on 1 June 1998 and at first Mr Rhys Evans seemed happy with the outcome of the surgery. But on 17 June he rang to say he needed to see me again. The cyst on my thyroid, he explained, had been benign, but I was horrified to hear him add that the attached tissue was abnormal – and you don't need a degree in medicine to know what that means. They had found traces of cancer. If Frank Bruno had punched me I would not have been more winded. I had been feeling light-hearted that morning because I had been working hard at my fitness – and with a great deal of success – but now I felt myself sinking like a stone to the bottom of a very deep pool.

I sat at the desk in my office in a state of shock as Mr Rhys Evans quietly confirmed that a second operation was necessary. I was so angry because I felt my whole body was letting me down. Through the office window I could see David washing the car. I was in tears, and began kicking the bottom of the desk and swearing at my body, wondering just how on earth I would be able to tell him, Mark and Paul. I knew they would be devastated. It was all developing into a terrible nightmare. My body felt like it wanted to explode; I wanted to scream with despair and fear.

I rang Mark, who fortunately was in his office only a mile away, and asked him to come round to see me. He came immediately. When Mark and David walked into the house the look on David's face was heart wrenching, truly dreadful. He kept asking, 'What's happened? What's happened?' I told him about the phone call as clearly as I could, and then he decided to ring Mr Rhys Evans himself.

Despite our fears we decided to continue with our plans to have a few days away and to attend the Derby sale at Fairyhouse before I returned to hospital for my second operation on 30 June. This time they removed the entire thyroid gland. In my case, the very mention of the word cancer was far more terrifying than the treatment I received to cure it. But in the darkest days, my family and friends were there to support me when I needed them most.

At first I didn't want anyone to know about my cancer. At the time I felt I wasn't coping very well. But I guess you wouldn't be human if you were not full of doubts and fears. You start to think that you're going to have a breakdown – and at one point I really thought I would end up in a straight jacket if I didn't pull myself together. But now, looking back, I appreciate that all the strange thoughts and obscure fears that troubled me will have happened to lots of others in the same position. The problem is, you don't want to talk about your feelings to your closest family so an invisible barrier appears.

I was advised to reduce my stress level, but on 14 July it rose dramatically when I received the report from the Jockey Club with the findings of their inquiry into the 1998 Grand National. Despite our earlier meetings, I felt the report was somewhat misleading. On receiving it I telephoned Tony Goodhew at the Jockey Club to ask what I considered to be a vital question.

'Did you ask the people you interviewed for this report if they had actually walked the course on the Saturday morning before the start of the Grand National?' I inquired.

He said he hadn't, but assumed they had done so!

I know for a fact that some of the people associated with the race and who had made statements afterwards had not walked the course, so to compile a report without asking that specific question seemed to be rather like the police taking statements from people in a service station café after an accident on the motorway.

I stand by what I said in my confidential letter to Aintree, which I wrote because I care deeply about horses, their welfare and the sport in general. My intention was not to damage or try to destroy the race – it seemed to me that they were doing that job themselves. I also told Tony Goodhew that I was very annoyed that the most serious issue – which I considered to be the state of the ground before the 1998 Grand National – had not been addressed as clearly and as honestly as it should have been. In my opinion the safety of the horses and jockeys should be paramount.

At least this on-going saga acted as a diversion before I had to go back to the Royal Marsden Hospital at the end of July for the radiotherapy treatment to deal with any lingering traces of the cancer.

I was given leaflets which explained about the procedure for the treatment in the Nuclear Medicine Department and discovered that whatever I took into the room, I would not be allowed to bring out because it could be contaminated. The room was quite comfortable, but no-one was allowed to enter, so it was a bit like being in solitary confinement for four days.

A solid barrier was placed across the door, so when David came to visit he was only able to stand or sit on the far side while we talked across the barrier. There was no question of his reaching out and touching my hand. All my food and drink was also placed on a tray at the barrier. I felt a bit like Oliver in *Oliver Twist*.

My treatment came in the form of a large capsule, which I was required to swallow. By the time it was produced, I was ready to bolt. Frankly, having read the leaflet, I was absolutely terrified and would have disappeared given half a chance.

When Dr Glenn Flux, the senior physicist, came in with the capsule, I put it in my mouth with some misgivings and swallowed it. I now knew that my opportunity to bolt had gone. Once the 3,000 units of radioactive iodine were in my system I was not going to be leaving for four days no matter how scared I felt because I would be radioactive.

My stay at the Marsden proved to be the longest four days and four nights of my life. It was a time when I desperately needed someone, preferably David, to put his arms around me, hug me and say that I would be all right. But that was not possible.

Coping physically with the treatment was not a problem. I did, in fact, sail through it. But emotionally, I was a wreck.

It didn't help that I had bought some magazines from our local newsagents to help me while away the seemingly endless hours on my own. The first one I picked up contained an article by a woman who had beaten cancer, but who had drifted apart from her husband in the process and, ultimately, she lost him. Of course, having read the headlines, I had to read the entire article, even though it was hardly designed to cheer me up.

When I had the energy I worked like mad on the exercise bicycle in my room in a determined attempt to force the iodine through my system at a rate of knots. I knew the sooner it finished its work, the sooner I'd be allowed to leave. Frankly, I could not bear the thought of staying there a second longer than was strictly necessary. The prospect of a fifth day and night would have finished me.

I don't mind admitting that I felt a bit of a 'Jesse' during my stay in hospital. Outside at lunchtime, I could hear children who were patients laughing and joking. But I was feeling *so* sorry for myself. I didn't want to depress myself any further by seeing them from my window. Yet, curiously, for a place where there were so many sick people, there was an air of brightness about the hospital that I found difficult to understand.

It was such a relief when Dave came to take me home on the Friday, 31 July. At that stage I was still not allowed to come into contact with old people and young children. The next morning was a lovely sunny day so I decided to mow the lawns. Dave was horrified at the very suggestion and refused to bring out the mower for me. I persisted despite his protests, and after I'd been mowing for a while, I began to feel as though I was the luckiest person in the world. It was as if I suddenly realized that health is the greatest gift of all.

During my illness and the subsequent treatment that cured it, I had the most unbelievable support from my owners and staff. They all knew about my problems because I felt it was best to be open with them, although news of my operations didn't become public until my book was published much later in the year. You can't buy that sort of loyalty, it's priceless. It means everything to me and I was able to thank them all at my Open Day in September.

I had to go back into hospital for a crucial scan on 27 November, the day before Princeful won at Newbury. I had gone down to the Royal Marsden Hospital earlier in the week to be given what I hoped would be one final, small capsule of radio iodine. I then returned on the Friday for the scan which would determine the success or failure of the previous treatment.

Lying there while it takes place, you begin to dread bad news. What if I needed another operation or yet more treatment? I could hardly contain my nerves. People say you are brave in this type of situation, but quite honestly, you don't have a choice. You have to be brave.

As I had a runner, Line of Conquest, in the fourth race at Newbury that day, the hospital kindly brought forward the time of my appointment so that I could make it back to the racecourse in time to see him run. Again, I was not allowed to mix with people so I remained in the car while Dave disappeared to saddle the horse and talk to the owners.

When the time came for the horse to run I left the car and wandered over to the wire fence that separates the car park from the racecourse and peered through. Just then, Clare Balding, a BBC Television racing presenter, walked up. She looked very puzzled to see me there and quite naturally asked me what on earth I was doing. Feeling a bit like a kid at school who had been caught smoking a cigarette behind the bike shed, I quickly explained!

The next afternoon, 28 November, was Hennessy day at Newbury. I had been advised to stay at home while Princeful made his seasonal debut in the Solaglas Long Distance Hurdle. It felt a bit strange watching the race on television in the sitting room with my head lad, Murty McGrath. I was quite anxious, but the sight of Princeful and Richard Dunwoody jumping the last flight of hurdles and coming through to catch Shooting Light on the flat and win quite easily, was the best possible medicine for me. I experienced a great surge of elation, but then, all of a sudden, I broke down, sobbing uncontrollably.

Poor Murty didn't know what to do with himself and eventually disappeared to make me a cup of tea. That was the last I saw of him for twenty minutes and I remember thinking that that must be a world record time for making a cup of tea!

Thankfully, my son Paul had recently arrived back from Kuala Lumpur with Sonia. On the Sunday morning, as I was cooking breakfast in the kitchen Paul said, 'That was good Ma, Princeful winning yesterday. I bet that made you feel better.'

I replied, 'Yes, I was crying my eyes out. Have you ever been at work and cried with the sheer pleasure of something?'

He was quiet for a moment, then answered, 'Frustration, Ma, but never pleasure.' We all burst out laughing, but later that day when we were on our own, he put his arms around me and hugged me for ages. We didn't have to speak; we both knew how difficult the past few months had been and how much worse it had been because he'd been so far away. I was so glad to have him home. I also knew he wanted me to slow down a bit.

The last few weeks of the year are such a hectic period for jumping trainers, so it was difficult to make an appointment with Dr Clive Harmer who was in charge of my treatment, and who would be able to give me the results of my final scan. As he was away for a week or two, we pencilled in a date close to Christmas. Naturally, I felt I could not wait that long to hear the result. It was on my mind all the time, so eventually I rang the hospital after about ten days, explaining that I needed to know if I would require any more treatment as a contingency plan would need to be made if that was the case.

Officially, they were not allowed to tell me, but unofficially they gave me the wonderful news that I would not need to go back for more treatment. When I eventually saw Dr Harmer on 23 December he confirmed the news. It was to be the best possible Christmas present ever and I can remember his words as if it was yesterday.

'What I can write here, Jenny, is that you are C U R E D', he said. Despite my earlier contact with the hospital I was still very apprehensive until he said those few words. When I came out of the consulting room I felt as if I was walking on air. This sense of elation was short lived, for as I was leaving I met someone I knew who was arriving for treatment. I was immediately overwhelmed by an enormous sense of guilt.

It was a feeling that returned time and again over the next few weeks. Eventually I broke down crying at home one Sunday evening, and when Dave asked what was troubling me I couldn't answer him. He persisted, so I had to explain that I felt so guilty at recovering while others were still suffering.

'If you think I am going to apologize because you are better, then you are very wrong. You cannot keep carrying everyone else's burden as well as your own,' he said with a quiet anger and much feeling.

When I was first told that I had cancer I felt ashamed. I had a great desire to stand in the shower and wash it all away. Following my second operation, my voice was so poor when I came out of hospital that Mark's little girl, Darcy Rose, backed away from me when I invited her to help me feed the fish in our garden. She was so unsure of me. But a few days later, as I sat on the lawn, she ran up behind me, put her head on my back and her arms around my neck. I could have thrown myself on the ground and wept in relief.

I'm sure the worst ordeal was not mine. David was the one who really suffered, yet for a long time we didn't talk about my illness and its implications. The situation had reached the point where there seemed to be a barrier between us. I felt I couldn't tell him what I was thinking because I didn't want to upset him. The tension between us became quite unbearable until one night, when we were lying in bed, I felt that we had to break down the barrier and talk it through.

The biggest part of the problem was that David's father

had died from cancer, yet he had never discussed this with me. Now, although we were both so worried about upsetting each other, we realized that it had to be dealt with. That night it all came tumbling out and we sat on the bed talking for several hours. It was such an enormous relief to be able to hear his fears and to share our problems and when I popped downstairs to make us both a cup of tea it was well past three o'clock. After that, I had the best night's sleep for months.

I had such high hopes for Princeful. The obvious target after his impressive victory at Newbury was the Smurfit Long Walk Hurdle over almost three and a quarter miles at Ascot on 19 December. It turned out to be one of the best races of the National Hunt season.

Tony McCoy tried to steal the race with a typical ride from the front on Deano's Beeno and had beaten off every other horse except Princeful as he turned for home with two hurdles left to jump. Richard Dunwoody had managed to stay in touch on Princeful and started to wear down the leader on the flat. In the most exciting finish imaginable, Princeful stayed on extremely bravely to catch Deano's Beeno in the last few yards. In fact, the first two finished so far clear of the rest you would have needed a telescope to find the third horse!

When you view horses at the sales, the one thing you cannot examine is their courage, but Princeful showed again at Ascot that he had it to spare. His latest success confirmed his position as the outstanding long-distance hurdler in training. He had already won the Stayers' Hurdle at the Cheltenham Festival the previous March, and I suspect most observers believed he would be going back there to defend his crown. So I suppose it was quite a shock at Ascot when I announced that he would switch to fences.

Over hurdles there are always young horses coming along to challenge the best and I felt that in order to protect him and help him to last longer, it was necessary for him to go chasing mid season. My decision was made easier by the knowledge that he had jumped chase fences so well when I schooled him at home. He was very accurate from the start, and not at all extravagant. In fact, he was very much like Corbiere and Garrison Savannah when they had first schooled. He just did it very well without being flash.

I was also conscious that Corbiere, Burrough Hill Lad and Garrison Savannah had all been at their prime and were racing over fences at eight years of age. I felt confident that Princeful would prove to be a great champion, too. He would be eight years of age on 1 January and the idea was to give him a couple of runs for experience before going for the Sun Alliance Chase at the Cheltenham Festival – and ultimately, the Gold Cup in the millennium when he would have been nine. I still feel it was the right thing to do because he was such a natural jumper.

I chose a straightforward race at Doncaster in January for his first novice chase – but it proved to be a disaster. Princeful was jumping well and moving easily in fourth place when a 25–1 outsider, Optimism Reigns, fell alongside him seven fences from the finish. Princeful had jumped the fence perfectly but became entangled with the faller's legs as he landed. Optimism Reigns seemed to roll under him and although Princeful didn't go right down to the ground, at one stage he had both hind legs splayed out behind him! The next moment Richard Dunwoody was lying on the ground with Princeful running loose.

The problem with Princeful is that you would need to run him over with a steamroller to stop him racing, so it was no surprise to me that he continued riderless in the race and jumped all the remaining fences. But as he landed over the second last I could see that he was feeling uncomfortable. Jumping the final fence, it was quite clear that he didn't want to put his hind leg down. Obviously, something was seriously wrong.

After the race he was immediately examined by the racecourse vet before we took him straight from Doncaster to Blackman O'Gorman, the vets at Newbury. Following X-rays, it emerged that he had fractured the pedal bone, a very delicate, heart-shaped bone, in his near hind foot. It was a similar injury that had ended Arkle's career prematurely.

Princeful is owned by Mr Robert Hitchins and it is a measure of his affection for his horses that he has always wanted them to have the best treatment possible. I phoned my old ally, Dr Rick Reddan in America, and he recommended that we call in Dr Jukka Houttu from the Tampere Equine Clinic in Finland to operate on Princeful.

The pooling of knowledge from different parts of the globe, and the sight of vets with their assistants working together as a team during this time, was tremendous. It was a humbling experience to see them working as a unit in an attempt to save Princeful and give him a quality of life in the years to come.

Dr Houttu took over two hours making the most detailed examination of the damage through a series of fine wire grids and X-rays. He then constructed a metal grid around the damaged foot before inserting the screw which would hold together the fractured pieces of bone. I watched through a small window, absolutely fascinated, as he completed his delicate task.

The most dangerous time for a horse undergoing an operation is when he begins to come round because it is at this point that he can thrash around and undo all the skilful work of the surgeons. Princeful was placed in a massive padded recovery box to lessen the chance of hurting himself and at one point I climbed up a ladder so that I could look at him over the high wall. He was sitting on his haunches like a dog begging. As I talked to him he pricked his ears and I felt him smile. He stayed in that position for twenty minutes or so and was later fit enough to be led back to a normal stable. He has been back at Weathercock House for some time now, but we still don't know if he will ever race again. The fall that so nearly ended his life was a freak accident – and it could easily have happened over hurdles. In all the years I have been training, I've never had a horse suffer that type of injury.

Princeful's racing career is still very much in the balance, but there are other lovely young prospects for Mark to inherit, including King of the Castle and Nervous O'Toole. You would not have described King of the Castle as a 'lovely' young horse when I bought him in Ireland at three. He was in his rough, not his Sunday best, which is how I like to buy my horses, and at that stage he was more like a greenhouse without any glass. By that I mean that he had a frame but nothing much else!

When I buy a horse I'm looking at an individual, trying to picture him in two years' time. King of the Castle would not have been the most handsome I'd ever seen, but there was something special about him that I cannot explain. He was quite keen on his debut at Folkestone in March, but Richard Dunwoody gave him such a masterful ride that he won easily without knowing he'd been to the races. In fact, I felt he was so switched off during the race, he would have done more in a routine canter at home.

CHAPTER TWENTY-FOUR

NEW BEGINNINGS

The previous July, when I knew I had to go into hospital for a second operation, I rang my solicitor, Michelle Machin-Jefferies, to arrange a meeting with her at Weathercock House. When she asked why I needed to see her I explained that I wanted to 'put my house in order' in case things didn't work out well for me following my operation. If that was to happen, I didn't want to have to make hasty decisions while I was in a state of emotional distress. I needed everything to be sorted out as I feel there is nothing like a funeral to cause a good war!

We chose a day in late July when I knew David would be playing golf. Before Michelle came she asked me to sort out various documents, including my will, insurance policies and the deeds to Weathercock House. It was a good job she asked as I hadn't a clue where they were kept.

Since the financial year for my business ends on 30 June, I had also arranged at about the same time to meet Barry Thorpe, my financial adviser, and Ray Honeywill, my accountant, to go through the figures. Ray telephoned to say that Barry wanted to call in on his own. He was a bit evasive when I pressed him for a reason. This gave me a slight cause for concern.

When Barry arrived he asked for permission to go right through my financial affairs. When I asked for an explanation he replied, 'Me and Ray feel that you should retire from training.' I was so shocked I wanted to throttle him! We sat for several minutes without speaking. He then continued, saying that both he and Ray felt that I was too hard on myself and if I did agree to retire I would only be bringing forward by two years the plans that we had already discussed at previous meetings.

Both Barry and Ray were obviously concerned that I put myself on a treadmill at the start of each season and remained there until I was on the verge of collapse at the end. They also added that for what I was earning out of it myself, I would not be any worse off if I ceased working, and I might last a bit longer.

I felt annoyed and rather angry that they should think they could make such a decision on my behalf and a little surprised that they should even suggest it to me. Then, as we talked it through further, I felt a bit embarrassed at my initial reaction. The fact that they had the guts to tell me merely confirmed how much they cared for me.

The next day I told David what Barry and Ray had said and emphasized that I had absolutely no intention of following their advice. But events soon took a significant turn. I was already aware that Mark's lease on his yard at Saxon House in Lambourn was due to end in the summer of 1999. Then one evening David came up with an interesting proposal. He suggested that we give Mark the chance to come back to train at Weathercock House. At first, I was so taken aback that I didn't even answer him. I thought, 'Oh no. Not you, too!' I was, of course, really scared at the prospect of not having my lifebelt, the horses, who have kept me afloat throughout the years. They have provided therapy, medication, frustration, immense joy and anguish all in equal measure. But most of all they have been there when I have needed to talk to them – and they have never told any tales!

Over the next few days I began to think about David's proposal and eventually we decided to raise the subject with Mark. We considered splitting the yard, but much would depend on the number of boxes we would each need. At the moment there are seventy-nine, with planning permission for another ten, but I was not convinced that sharing was the answer. I felt it would not have been an ideal situation to have two sets of staff working either side of a fence.

As we discussed various ideas I started to wonder why on earth I was hanging on. In November Mark had warned me that he was selling his house in Great Shefford to raise funds to help him buy a yard when the time came. He also asked if he, Natasha and Darcy Rose, who was just two years old, could move in for a couple of weeks if he was able to organize an early sale. In fact, the deal was done on 7 January and they have been here ever since!

I suppose the idea of retiring grew on me. It was a bit like a seed germinating. Barry and Ray had planted the seed, and then David had encouraged it to grow. Admittedly, I was a bit irritated at first that everyone was trying to write me off, so with dogged determination I gave the seed a little dose of weed killer. But I soon realized from David's statement that he was also paying a price for the job I was doing. It became clear to me that I had to allow the seed to recover and flourish. We both had to slow down a bit.

We had both endured a traumatic time during my diagnosis and treatment. The loss of one of my favourite horses, Jibber the Kibber, in January had also taken its toll. These were all very serious blows. I may have been a bit raw emotionally at the time, but I still don't regret my decision to retire. I was ninth in the Trainers' Table at the time and thought, it's better to be nine from the top than ninth from the bottom.

The next task was putting the house and the yard on the market, though I made it perfectly clear to the estate agent that if Mark could find a way of training from Weathercock House, then that was what he would do. Initially I didn't think it would be possible for him to afford the whole property, but I'm delighted to say that things changed when one of his owners, Malcolm Denmark, offered to help him raise the capital.

I have always loved working and being with my horses. They have been a constant challenge to me, like a different game of chess every day. They had also been a very important part of my life since before I left school, so I knew it was going to be an enormous wrench to give it all up. But once my mind was made up David contacted Philip Arkwright, the Clerk of the Course at Cheltenham, to ask if I could announce my retirement there on the first day of the Festival meeting. Setting up this arrangement on the opening day also ensured that I wouldn't be tempted into a late change of mind if I had a winner. That would have been so wrong.

I decided to make the announcement at Cheltenham because it attracts the biggest crowd of genuine English and Irish National Hunt racing enthusiasts. They are the very best. As you walk into the unsaddling enclosure they let out such a roar as they show their delight, it feels as if the sun has broken out in your body! The warmth and kindness they have shown me has been just wonderful, and I so wanted to thank the people gathered there for all the support they have given me and my family over the years. Although I was well aware that I could have sold the story of my retirement for quite a lot of money, I felt that it would not have been the right thing to do. How can you put a price on people's loyalty?

I woke up at seven o'clock on the morning of 16 March 1999, the first day of Cheltenham, crying my eyes out and at eight-thirty, with my solicitor present, I signed the papers relating to the sale of Weathercock House. Even then Mark was saying, 'You don't have to do this, Mother, you know.' But I knew the die was cast. It was tough, but I decided you have to go sometime and this seemed the most appropriate moment.

By nine o'clock I had just about regained control and I was holding up well at Cheltenham. Until, that is, Mark asked me again if I was all right, just as it was time to go out and announce my retirement in a pre-racing chat with Jonathan Powell, who was conducting interviews for the large crowd gathered around the paddock. One of the newspapers the following day suggested that I had swaggered across to the podium, but of course, that was far from the truth. In reality, it was more a question of trying to get a firm grip on myself so that I didn't duck out at the last moment! By now I was really struggling to remain in control as I waited for my interview. If I could have walked straight out and made my statement, I would probably have coped much better than I did. Instead, my whole body was trembling as I had to wait while various announcements were made.

The moment I stepped onto the stage I knew I was in trouble. Aware of what I was going to say, Jonathan looked as white as a sheet. As soon as I began talking to him, I was totally overcome with emotion so it all came flooding out, a bit like a burst water main. It was as if I was trying to turn down a tap when suddenly it came off in my hand. There was water everywhere!

For several seconds I was unable to continue. The enormity of what I was saying made it so hard. Now I knew there was no turning back. As I faltered, David, noting my distress, moved closer and put his arm around me. After a pause I managed to pull myself together and I was able to say what I had planned. I tried to explain to the thousands who were listening why I had reached my decision. I said, 'It was a tough choice but you cannot go on for ever and there are so many other things I want to do with my life.' The crowd listened with great sympathy and understanding. Once I had unburdened myself I felt totally drained, but as I walked away I was immediately ambushed by press men.

The next day I felt immense relief. Retirement is very final and I am all too aware that there will be further upsetting experiences in the months ahead, particularly when my tack sale is held and when I finally leave Weathercock House. But hopefully, I am a lot more in control since the initial realization that I had to let go of a job that had consumed a major part of my life.

After my announcement at Cheltenham I was amazed to receive letters from people who were so upset by my plans to retire that they did not feel like returning to Cheltenham. I was also taken aback at the reactions of other female trainers. Di Haine, who is a tough cookie, came up to me and said I couldn't go through with it. So did a young girl who was just starting out as a trainer. If it helps to reassure them, I promise I will still stick up for them if they are not getting a square deal!

There was an amusing interlude before Liverpool when I was invited to appear on the popular television quiz show, *A Question of Sport*. Luckily, a car was laid on to take David and me to Manchester and back for the recording, which was great fun. I joined the legendary George Best on John Parrott's team, with Ilie Nastase and Dickie Bird alongside Ally McCoist. George was quite brilliant. He said barely three things but brought the house down each time. Asked to contribute on the What Happened Next? round, he replied, 'I can't even remember what happened last night!'

In fact, there was a lot of cheerful banter between the two teams and I was mightily relieved that I managed to answer all the racing questions correctly. I was quite worried that I might be a total disaster.

I had just one runner, Nahthen Lad, for my final tilt at the Grand National. Looking back through the records I noted that he was to be my thirty-ninth runner in the race, going back all the way to The Songwriter in 1977. Nahthen Lad has always tended to keep a bit of effort back in his races and it concerned me slightly that he had not enjoyed the best of fortune on his previous visits to Aintree. He has also given me a bruise or two over the years, particularly when I have been saddling him up. But I'm not known to back down from confrontations and I have, in fact, had worse 'bites' from gentlemen with two legs. He certainly hasn't been worse than some of them!

I was hoping that on the day Nahthen Lad's arrogance might be directed to the challenge of the race but, as always, I knew I would only be able to relax when he was safely back in his box. I walked the course as usual on the morning of the Grand National and felt the track was in perfect 'nick'. It seems, I thought to myself, our antler clash twelve months earlier had not been in vain.

Before the race the Aintree executives and the National sponsor, Patrick Martell, organized a special presentation to me, during which I was honoured to be made a member of the exclusive Grand National Club, which meant that David and I were given life membership of the course. The presentation was interrupted by my old friend, Des Lynam from the BBC. As many television viewers will know, Des and I always enjoy a laugh and a joke on National day, but this year I went one step further. I told him, 'Everyone says I have to kiss you!' Being a gallant Romeo, he replied, 'Absolutely, no hardship for me.' There was a cheer and a warm round of applause from the crowd but then, not long after, it was back to business – and time to saddle up my last Grand National runner.

For an awful long way it looked as though Nahthen Lad would play a prominent part in the finish. He was with the leaders from the start and led the field going to Becher's for the first time, where he made a bad mistake. Nahthen Lad remained part of the leading group until he began to tire over the last two fences. When he crossed the finishing line in eleventh place I felt a huge surge of relief. My body was totally rigid because I'd been so anxious. But my final afternoon as a trainer at Aintree wasn't quite over.

After all the publicity about Nahthen Lad and the Grand National, I knew I still had my ace to play, King of the Castle, in the final race of the meeting, the National Hunt flat race. He had absolutely blossomed since Folkestone, just like a flower that you needed to be at its absolute best for the Chelsea Show. His skin was like a peach in condition and I was unusually confident. He travelled comfortably throughout the race and went on to win like a really good horse, too. He is exceptionally fast and will improve out of all recognition for a summer at grass, I hope.

I had watched the race in the owners' and trainers' bar. It was lovely, and it certainly put the icing on the cake when I was cheered by my fellow professionals; that meant so much to me. The crowds at Aintree, as usual, gave me a brilliant reception, absolutely unbelievable. I don't usually lead my horses into the unsaddling enclosure but I felt I had to this time. King of the Castle had given me the perfect finish to a very special day.

There were so many details to sort out in the next two months before my final runners, including an urgent search for a new home and the dispiriting experience of organizing the sale of all my saddlery and general stable equipment.

Since the National Hunt season ended on 1 June, my last runners as a trainer turned out to be at Huntingdon, twenty-four hours earlier at the Bank Holiday meeting. I set out with the deliberate intention of enjoying the day, although I must admit I felt like I was hanging over the edge of a cliff from very early in the morning with my fingernails snapping off. I had started to get a bit tearful on the Sunday night and couldn't get to sleep so I decided to take a sleeping pill.

The racecourse executives had invited David and myself to lunch, but my family turned out in such numbers to support me that we decided to have a picnic in the car park. It was brilliant. Dad was there with my brother Richard and his wife Janet, my brother Joe and my nephew Peter Moseley. Mandy and Michael Bowlby brought their sons, Thomas and Jack, and my friends Jenny and Tom Mapp also came along. Mr Hitchins wanted to be there for my final day, too, so he and his son Jeremy flew in to Stansted to join the party. It was quite a gathering, a special family day out. I am totally aware of all the support they have given me over the years and it would not have been right to leave them on their own while we were swanning off in the directors' box.

The jockey Andrew Thornton was to ride my final winner, Scarlet Emperor, who showed a great deal of courage in a very tight finish to the Maiden Hurdle. After that success we were all invited to the directors' box for a drink and, most unusually, I asked for a vodka. Normally I never drink alcohol at the races. God knows how much vodka they poured for me, but I felt a whole lot better afterwards!

A posse of press men and television cameras seemed to follow me most of the afternoon. That, and the requests for my autograph all added to the tension. But there were lighter moments, like when I was asked to shake the hand of the former Premier, John Major, for the waiting cameras. I suggested that I could do better than that as we had met before at a private party he had given eighteen months earlier. He played his part by putting his arm around me and giving me a hug and a kiss. I have always felt that John Major is a very genuine, warm person. Perhaps his downfall was that he was too nice and too honest.

On race days I am always apprehensive until the racing is over. This day was no exception.

Majiiro, my final runner in the National Hunt flat race, injured himself so badly three furlongs from home that he had to be put down. It was a completely freak accident which left him with a dislocated fetlock joint. The racecourse vet was quickly on the scene to attend to Majiiro and immediately administered painkillers. But when I reached the racecourse stables it was clear that there was no way of saving the horse's life. I had to make the decision along with the vet to have Majiiro put to sleep. It was the last thing you ever want to happen. It was extremely upsetting, but I knew that nothing more could have been done for him.

I woke up on Tuesday morning feeling the terrible emptiness you experience when you have lost one of your mates.

The forthcoming sale of all my tack the following week was something I had been dreading. A few days before Huntingdon I made the mistake of posing in the tack room for a photograph for the *Racing Post* who were putting together a feature article on my last day as a trainer. I will never go back into that room again. Being there brought back too many memories. Everything is laid out immaculately, the bridles in special rows, all the different types of bits, leather rollers and leather lead reins, each with the name *Pitman* inscribed in brass, the initialled paddock sheets. My mind drifted back to days gone by as I remembered the achievements. Grand Nationals – Gold Cups – so many memories.

The auctioneers, Dreweatt Neate, have asked me to be present on the day of the sale, but to be honest, I will only be around first thing in the morning. Before they ring the bell to start proceedings I will be off and nothing will persuade me to return until it is all over. I know I could not bear to be there a moment longer. It might seem strange, but there are things in that sale that mean far more to me than some of the personal possessions in our house.

At times I felt numb at the prospect of leaving Weathercock House after all these years. David and I have both found it immensely difficult. I know that when I walk out of the door for the final time I will need to bandage my wounds for a week or two to allow them to heal. My family call me Horsey Spice, but I think I'll be more like Scary Spice! I do realize that in two years' time it would have been more like major surgery to leave. The way things have turned out, I'm able to get by with micro surgery – but it certainly hasn't been a piece of cake.

They say that moving house is akin to any big disaster in your life, and I'm feeling that way right now. To wind up the business that has been your entire life has taken a toll on both me and David. Searching for the right place to live, and buying it with the usual problems of people changing their minds at the last minute, plus the demands of others, has merely added to our torment.

For the last twenty-five years, training at Weathercock House has been a bit like living in the middle of one the busiest roundabouts in the country. In all those years I have lived as close to my horses as is humanly possible, and once the decision to move was made, I was determined that, in fairness to my family, I wouldn't move too far from Lambourn. Our new home is a converted barn set in two acres, about twenty-five minutes drive away. Anyway, if I had to go to a new doctor he would need three weeks off just to read my medical notes!

My hope is that by taking a step sideways, David and I can help and support Mark and Natasha, and my sister Mandy Bowlby, who is also a trainer, by coming in for a day or two – or at weekends when they are away – just as my parents used to help me. It is not our wish to interfere. Mark has such lovely horses to look forward to, with the cream of his own crop and the cream of mine. They certainly make a formidable youth team. Perhaps Paul and Sonia will have a millennium baby and we will be grandparents for a second time!

Living in our new home we should be close enough to be of assistance to them, when asked, but not so close that it will be a great temptation to pop in all the time. I anticipate my role as being like a horse's grandmother. I can come in to stroke them and spoil them, and then I can walk away, but I certainly won't love them any the less.

As you may have gathered by now, my life would be very empty without horses. I can think of no better description of them than the words below:

'The Horse'
Anon

*Where in this wide world can a man find nobility
    without pride,
Friendship without envy, beauty without vanity?
Here; where grace is laced with muscle, and strength
    by gentleness confined.
He serves without servility; he has fought without
    enmity.
There is nothing so powerful, nothing less violent;
    there is
Nothing so quick, nothing more patient.
England's past has been borne on his back.
All our history is his industry.
We are his heirs, he is our inheritance.*

TRAINING RECORD:
NATIONAL HUNT

Season	Wins	Win Prize Money
1974–75	1	£408
1975–76	12	£8,646
1976–77	12	£13,884
1977–78	6	£4,886
1978–79	10	£11,967
1979–80	16	£19,200
1980–81	28	£52,744
1981–82	8	£16,180
1982–83	20	£97,926
1983–84	18	£110,646
1984–85	41	£128,873
1985–86	46	£98,953
1986–87	39	£130,102
1987–88	45	£91,359
1988–89	62	£153,161
1989–90	93	£395,275
1990–91	43	£276,272
1991–92	50	£203,570
1992–93	36	£117,194
1993–94	26	£93,396
1994–95	36	£340,158
1995–96	49	£327,021
1996–97	17	£81,743
1997–98	36	£177,118
1998–99	47	£234,467

Also: Ireland 2

MAJOR RACES WON

Cheltenham Gold Cup

| 1984 | Burrough Hill Lad | P. Tuck | 100–30 |
| 1991 | Garrison Savannah | M. Pitman | 16–1 |

King George VI Chase

| 1984 | Burrough Hill Lad | J. Francome | 1–2 |

Grand National

| 1983 | Corbiere | B. de Haan | 13–1 |
| 1995 | Royal Athlete | J. Titley | 40–1 |

Welsh Grand National

1982	Corbiere	B. de Haan	12–1
1983	Burrough Hill Lad	J. Francome	100–30
1986	Stearsby	G. Bradley	8–1

Irish Grand National

| 1997 | Mudahim | J. Titley | 13–2 |

Scottish Grand National

| 1995 | Willsford | R. Farrant | 16–1 |

Hennessy Cognac Gold Cup

| 1984 | Burrough Hill Lad | J. Francome | 100–30 |

INDEX

Basingstoke, 145–6, 162, 163, 171
Baydon Star, 300
Ben Nevis, 321
Bengough, Colonel Piers, 105, 106
Bentley, Paul, 84, 86, 87, 91
Best, George, 387
Betty, 31, 40–1, 42
Bewick, Major Verly, 74, 81
Biddlecombe, Terry, 62–3, 64, 206
Bielby family, 152, 153, 154, 155, 158, 163
Birchenough, Kay, 238
Bird, Dickie, 387
Biretta, 101–3, 104, 111
Bishop's Cleeve, 43, 45–8, 59, 115
Black Plover, 155
Blessed Sacrament Church, Leicester, 68
Bonidon, 106–7, 108, 109
Bonusprint Stayers' Hurdle, 361, 378
Bowlby, Jack, *nephew*, 390
Bowlby, Mandy, *sister*: birth, 34; childhood, 1, 4, 34, 44, 47, 75, 87; racing, 34; trainer, 34; JP's bridesmaid, 68–9; Parva Stud, 78, 109; Ian Balding, 117; Lord Gulliver, 148–9; Queen's Ride, 157–8; Grand National (1983), 173, 175, 177, 179; *This Is Your Life*, 185; Mark's car accident, 225; marriage, 231; Burrough Hill Lad, 236–7; Gold Cup (1991), 264, 265; Grand National (1993), 307; Willsford, 327; JP's

injury, 330; Ireland, 341, 342, 344; Smith's Band, 345, support for JP, 390
support from JP, 392
Bowlby, Mike, *brother-in-law*: marriage, 231; Garrison Savannah, 249; Grand National (1991), 279; Golden Freeze, 291, 292–9; Willsford, 323–4; support for JP, 390
Bowlby, Thomas, *nephew*, 354, 390
Bradford, 186, 187
Brand, The, 26
Branford, Ally, 111
Braunstone Park, 187
Breeders' Cup Mile (USA, 1994), 50
Bregawn, 167, 171, 204, 208
Brighton, 139
Brightwell, Peter, 31, 42
Broad, Chris, 337
Brompton Hospital, London, 252, 311, 312, 370
Brooksby Grange, 28, 30–44, 48
Brooksby Hall Farm Institute, 22
Brothers, Richard, 344
Brown, Colin, 174, 194–5
Brown, Errol, 217, 334
Brown, Keith, 304, 305
Brown Chamberlin, 206–8
Bruno, Frank, 290, 370
Bruton, John, 344
Buckingham, John, 306
Bueche Giorod, 152, 153, 196
Burdock, Malcolm, 243–4, 250, 257–8, 260, 263, 271, 274, 304
Burnham-on-Sea, 170
Burrough, Alan and Brian, 159,

400

161, 167–8, 172, 177, 179, 186, 213, 240, 247

Burrough Hill Lad, ix, 148, 199–214, 379; Kempton (1980), 162, 192–3; novice chases (1981–2), 196–7; Edward Hanmer (1982), 197; character, 199, 245; Welsh Grand National (1983), 200, 202; Gold Cup (1984), 203, 204–12; rumours about, 204–5, 286; Hennessy Gold Cup (1984), 223–4; Charlie Hall Memorial (1984), 224, 226; King George VI (1985), 228–9, 232; Rehearsal Chase (1986), 235; Gainsborough (1986), 235; injuries, 236; York Festival, 367

Cadogan, Lord, 81, 88, 91, 92, 93, 96, 97, 105, 106, 180
Callander, Connie, 143
Callander, Peter, 126, 127, 133, 142–3, 149, 180
Canit, 149–51
Canny Danny, 208, 224
Captain John, 162
Carvill's Hill, 292–9
Cathcart, 292
Celtic Shot, 253, 258, 261
Champion Jockeys' dinner, 184
Champneys, Major, 57–8, 59–76, 79, 84, 191
Channing-Williams, Dotty, 353
Charisma Records, 101
Charlie Hall Memorial Pattern Chase (1984), 224–5, 226, 228
Chasers and Hurdlers

(Timeform), 153, 163, 198, 324

Cheltenham, *see* Bonusprint Stayers' Hurdle; Cathcart; Coral Golden Hurdle; County Hurdle; Flowers Original Handicap Chase; Gold Cup; Kim Muir Chase; Mildmay of Flete Chase; National Hunt Handicap Chase; Ritz Club Trophy Chase; Sun Alliance Chase; Waterford Crystal Stayers' Hurdle

Chepstow, *see* Crown Paints Hurdle; Rehearsal Chase; Welsh Champion Hurdle; Welsh Grand National

Chichester, Patrick, Lord Belfast, 98–9
Choy, Dr Ray, 332
Christie, Tony, 126
Christine, 354
Church Farm Stables, 58, 59–76
Cleeve Hill, 51
Clouded Lamp, 50–2
Cocker, Dr, 313
Coleman, David, 178
Colonel Christy, 167
Combs Ditch, 228–9
Cook, Paul, 47–8, 52, 53–4, 119
Cool Ground, 295
Cool Sun, 248
Coral Golden Hurdle (1988), 248
Corbiere, ix, 165–81, 379; character, ix, 159–60, 163–4, 171, 233; Flat races, 160–2; Kempton (1980), 162, 192; line-firing, 163, 198; Sun Alliance (1982),

401

87–8, 323; hospitality, 8, 75; workload, 9–12; voluntary work, 10–11, 232–3; intelligence, 16; money management, 24–5; first meets George, 26; horse shows, 26; health problems, 34, 225, 226, 232, 258; *Archers*, 35; ambitions, 44; grandchildren, 75, 88; JP's marriage breakdown, 116–17; Grand National (1983), 172, 174, 179, 180; Burrough Hill Lad, 192–3; Gold Cup (1984), 210; Queen Mother, 230; scanner appeal, 234–5; Gold Cup (1991), 257–9, 264, 265–6, 270; death, 283–4, 311

Harvey, Percy, *uncle*, 20, 36–7, 187

Harvey, Richard, *brother*, 1, 4, 22, 232, 234–5, 259, 265–6, 353, 390

Harwell, 159

Hawthorn Hill Lad, 248

Haydock Park, 197, 211, 249, 252, 256, 320, 337, 348

health problems, JP's: allergies, 151, 252, 310; appendicitis, 132, 135; childhood accident, 19–20; horse-bite, 330; postnatal depression, 75; throat, 369–75, 376–7

Henderson, Nicky, 97, 231

Hennessy Cognac Gold Cup:
(1982), 167, 171
(1984), 223–4, 235, 236
(1993), 318–19, 320–1
(1998), 375

Hern, Major Dick, 272

Heyfleet Partnership, 266

Heythrop, 97, 109

High Tide, 96

Highfrith, 249

Hills, Barry, 83

Hilton Hotel, London, 311

Hindemarsh, Jane, 238

Hindson, Sally, 359

Hinton Parva, 77–95, 118–19, 121, 142, 163; *see also* Parva Stud

Hitchins, Jeremy, 293, 390

Hitchins, Robert and Elizabeth, 215–17, 250, 277, 279, 290–2, 295, 311, 353, 354, 359, 361, 367, 380, 290

Hoby, 1, 4, 10, 14, 16, 17, 28, 35, 68

Hogan, Lee, 332

Honeywill, Ray, 382–3, 384

Hooley, Josie, 45–9, 50, 51, 52, 57

Horse and Hound, 90

Houttu, Dr Jukka, 380

Howlett, John Joe, 185, 189

Hungerford, 235

Hunter-Chasers and Point-to-Pointers (Sale and Mackenzie), 98

hunting, 17–19, 36–9, 91

Huntingdon, 336, 389–91

I Bin Zaidoon, 217–18

Imperial Cup, 63

In Touch Racing, 339

Indian Spice, 63

Irish Distillers, 344

Irish Grand National:
(1987), 334
(1993), 334–5
(1997), 340, 341, 342–3

Irish Hennessy Gold Cup, 292

410

413